NINETEENTH CENTURY RELIGIOUS THOUGHT IN THE WEST

NINETEENTH CENTURY RELIGIOUS THOUGHT IN THE WEST

NINETEENTH CENTURY RELIGIOUS THOUGHT IN THE WEST

VOLUME I

Edited by
NINIAN SMART, JOHN CLAYTON
STEVEN KATZ *and* PATRICK SHERRY

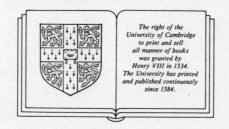

The right of the
University of Cambridge
to print and sell
all manner of books
was granted by
Henry VIII in 1534.
The University has printed
and published continuously
since 1584.

CAMBRIDGE UNIVERSITY PRESS

Cambridge
New York   New Rochelle
Melbourne   Sydney

Published by the Press Syndicate of the University of Cambridge
The Pitt Building, Trumpington Street, Cambridge CB2 1RP
32 East 57th Street, New York, NY 10022, USA
10 Stamford Road, Oakleigh, Melbourne 3166, Australia

First published 1985
First paperback edition 1988

Printed in Great Britain at the University Press, Cambridge

Library of Congress catalogue card number: 84-14207

British Library cataloguing in publication data
Nineteenth century religious thought in the West.
Vol. 1
1. Theology – 19th century
I. Smart, Ninian
209.182′1 BT28

ISBN 0 521 22831 X hard covers (vol. 1)
ISBN 0 521 22832 8 hard covers (vol. 2)
ISBN 0 521 30114 9 hard covers (vol. 3)
ISBN 0 521 32764 4 hard covers (set of three)

ISBN 0 521 35964 3 paperback (vol. 1)
ISBN 0 521 35965 1 paperback (vol. 2)
ISBN 0 521 35966 X paperback (vol. 3)
ISBN 0 521 35967 8 paperback (set of three)

SE

CONTENTS

VOLUME I

EDITORIAL INTRODUCTION

On both sides of the Atlantic and on both sides of the Channel, there has been in recent years a renewed interest in nineteenth-century religious thought. Reasons for this by now widespread revival of interest need not be rehearsed. It is perhaps sufficient to recall that several issues which dominated discussion in the decades following the European Enlightenment remain central in contemporary debate within the academic study of religion and within the theological community, whether Protestant or Roman Catholic or Jewish. In order to make this point, one need only call to mind such recently debated issues as hermeneutics and tradition, faith and history, projectionist and other reductionist accounts of religion, the limits of historical relativism and the nature of rationality, the possibility of a purely 'scientific' study of religion and the legitimacy of theological studies within the university, as well as such religiously intramural concerns as the place of myth in christology or the nature of Jewishness. Each of these problems was either initially raised or significantly recast during the nineteenth century.

Whilst taking care not to underestimate the distance between their world and our own, one must nonetheless allow that greater understanding of these and other contemporary issues can often be gained by attending to those thinkers who in the main have determined the direction of modern religious thought in the West. Theirs was a revolutionary time when the older theistic world-view, already under attack since the Renaissance and throughout the Enlightenment, gave way to a new, more variegated, more complex circumstance for religious thought. Under the pressure first of Kant's radical break with traditional metaphysics and of his attempt to develop a theology centred in morality, followed by Schleiermacher's efforts to generate theology from reflection on the religious self-consciousness alone, and then by Hegel's response in the direction of an absolute Idealism centred in the world-historical process whereby spirit becomes conscious of itself as

I

spirit, the nineteenth century in the West became a laboratory of fresh ideas and new hermeneutical techniques in religious thought. Whether one sees these developments as monuments to human genius or regards them with Karl Barth as perverse deviations from the theologian's proper task, there is no denying the extent to which even contemporary religious thought bears the mark of their influence. Whatever may obtain elsewhere, twentieth-century religious thought is very much the child of the nineteenth.

The nineteenth century tells no single story; nor can it be done justice by a single story teller. Its more successful narrators in recent years have almost without exception confined themselves to a single religious or national tradition, such as French Catholicism; or to a single school or movement, such as Romanticism; or to a single issue, such as historicism. Even though no single story is told in the religious thought of the nineteenth century, the individual story-lines do intertwine in various ways, such that none in isolation tells the whole story. Successful wider-ranging studies there most surely have been, but it would be unreasonable nonetheless to expect a single scholar to give an adequate account of the main developments in Protestant, Roman Catholic and Jewish religious thought, together with the leading options available within the philosophy of religion and the emergence of the various branches of the academic study of religion. In order for such an account to be convincing, a team of scholars would almost certainly be required.

Twenty-nine scholars from five countries have collaborated in an attempt to trace in three volumes the course taken in the nineteenth century by religious thought and its critique in the West. The volumes are not intended to be an anthology of articles merely summarizing historical and exegetical details; they are intended, rather, to engage the thinkers covered in a rigorous manner in order to see what they said and why they said it, and also to explore what is of lasting value in their work. It is hoped that contributions to *Nineteenth Century Religious Thought in the West* will be found sufficiently clear to be of use to students of religion, theology and cognate subjects, but also to have enough depth to be of more than introductory value. The short bibliographical essays appended to each contribution give guidance to further reading, with especial attention having been given to texts and studies in English. Whilst every effort has been made to make the subject matter accessible to the interested reader, no attempt has been made artificially to 'simplify' the thought of those men who have both stimulated and challenged the best minds of their own and successive generations.

A glance at the contents of the three volumes will show that the range of topics covered is wide and varied. We have aimed throughout to strike a reasonable balance in respect to the main national groups, religious communities, and academic disciplines which contributed significantly to Western religious thought and its critique in the nineteenth century. Many of the contributions deal with the work of important individual figures, such as Coleridge or Strauss, focusing critically on particular aspects of their work whilst at the same time developing wider generalizations about their significance for the subject, their influence and their place in the period as a whole. Other articles, including those dealing with the criticism of the Jewish and Christian scriptures, survey key developments within an important area of study; or trace the emergence of largely new areas of study, such as the anthropological, sociological or comparative study of religion. Some contributions, including those having to do with science and religion or with British Agnosticism, may bring into focus an issue widely disputed in the nineteenth century; whilst others, such as those concerning the Roman Catholic Tübingen school and the British Idealists, isolate for special attention certain influential movements of thought which cannot easily be identified with a single leading figure.

Whatever the precise scope of the chapter, contributors have in every case sought to direct attention towards the most important critical and conceptual issues raised in the period. Except where demanded by the subject, such as in the case of the American Transcendentalists or of Nietzsche, biographical and other background information has been kept to a minimum. Authors have also been asked to pin-point wherever possible the relevance of the figure or topic or movement to twentieth-century religious thought.

Within even three volumes of moderate size, it has not been possible to cover all important aspects of nineteenth-century religious thought. Each author has had to write within strict word limits, the exact length having been varied from topic to topic, so that he has not always been able to say all that he might like to have said about his assigned subject. The editors have likewise been limited in respect to the number of topics which could be realistically covered. For instance, it soon became clear that it would not be possible, as one might have liked, also to survey developments in non-Western religious thought. Readers who wish to learn more about the likes of Rāmakrishna and Vivekānanda will have to turn elsewhere for help. Even restricting ourselves just to Western religious thought, the selection of subject-matter still proved difficult in view of the many competing claims. No attempt has been made to cover major doctrinal and ecclesiastical developments. Some names which one would certainly expect to find mentioned in any history of, say, specifically Roman Catholic or Protestant theology have also had to be overlooked in an effort to give a more balanced survey of nineteenth-century religious thought. It has been necessary to deal less directly than hoped with non-intellectual factors – whether social, economic or political – which conditioned the course of religious (and other) thought in the nineteenth century. A social history of religious thought would be a worthwhile project, but a nonetheless separate exercise from that which has been undertaken here. Where appropriate, however, as in the case of the Catholic Tübingen School and of British Agnosticism, contributors have sometimes called the readers' attention to such factors. The editors, in addition, have taken care to ensure coverage of those thinkers – such as Marx, Durkheim, Weber and Troeltsch – who have made our own century aware of the social and economic constraints on religious thought and its history.

In making their final choice of topics, the editors were guided by the following criteria: (i) the intrinsic merit of the writer's or the movement's contribution to Western religious thought or its critique; (ii) the appearance of the individual's or group's major work having been after the ascendancy of Kant's critical philosophy and before the outbreak of the First World War; (iii) the influence and continuing importance of the writer or movement in the twentieth century; (iv) the relevance of the individual or group to the growth of the study of religion as an academic discipline.

The authors of the twenty-seven chapters which make up this three-volume symposium have their own individual tales to tell about the course of Western religious thought in the nineteenth century. Their stories are so many and so varied that it would be hardly feasible to summarize them here. Since the contributors will want to speak for themselves, to anticipate what they each have to say would also serve no useful purpose. Even so, their separate story-lines do overlap and intertwine in various ways. The authors themselves have drawn attention where appropriate to some links between their own and other contributions. The editors want in addition to identify certain key issues which throughout the nineteenth century attracted the interests of its best minds. We would single out the following three clusters of issues as having been determinative: (i) the limits of reason and the nature of rationality; (ii) the idea of 'true humanity' and the question of human nature; (iii) the problems of history and the effects of 'historicism'. These three themes, themselves closely interconnected, constitute together the century's *Leitmotiv* of which all other themes are merely variations.

Reason and rationality

Immanuel Kant, strictly speaking, does not belong to the nineteenth century. Having died in 1804 only months before his eightieth birthday,

Kant belongs more properly to the eighteenth century and to its world of thought, so that a general introduction to his philosophy would be out of place in a survey of nineteenth-century religious thought. His influence of the century following his death was nonetheless determinative, with the result that some account of his significance is required. Kant helped shape the period's religious thought in two main ways. On the one hand, his critical philosophy – challenging as it did many of the fundamental assumptions of traditional theology and metaphysics – can be seen in retrospect to have set the agenda for the whole of the nineteenth century, as well as for much of the twentieth. On the other hand, Kant's own attempt to find a new and firmer foundation for religion by grounding it in moral self-consciousness or 'practical reason' pointed a way forward which belongs more genuinely to the nineteenth than to the eighteenth century. The chapter on Kant concentrates, therefore, on issues relating to the relationship in his thought between religion and morality.

Although a general introduction to Kant's critical philosophy does not come within our brief, it must be clear to all that the lasting effects of his so-called 'Copernican revolution' in philosophy echo loudly in most of the individual contributions to these volumes. Kant's relentless effort to chart the bounds of sense has been perceived by many to have undermined not only school metaphysics, but also any philosophical theology done in the style of Descartes or of Leibniz and Wolff. Reaction to the Kantian critique of rational theology has varied greatly within the main religious traditions of the West. It was not uncommon for Protestant theologians to welcome Kant's demolition of any possible edifice erected upon natural theology. Whilst rejecting vehemently his insistence on ethical autonomy, some Protestant theologians early in the century saw in Kant's critique of metaphysics a means of strengthening their own appeal to the authority of biblical revelation as the only secure foundation for theological reflection (a foundation which seemed increasingly less secure as the century wore on). By the time of Ritschl and his school, however, Kant was widely proclaimed as 'the philosopher of Protestantism' for his emphasis upon ethics as well as for his critique of metaphysics. Although the leading Jewish philosopher of the Enlightenment era, Moses Mendelssohn, conceded late in life that his own religious philosophy had been undercut by Kant, Hermann Cohen felt able by the beginning of the twentieth century to use Kant as the basis for a Jewish philosophy of religion. Roman Catholic theologians, despite a short flirtation with Kantianism early in the nineteenth century, tended to move with the times either toward the transcendentalism of Fichte or toward the more outright Romanticism of Schelling. Many, and not only amongst

5

Roman Catholics, thought that Romanticism – with its repudiation of dualism and its promise of immediacy – offered a certain way round the most difficult epistemological problems raised for religious thought by Kant's *Critique of Pure Reason.* Schleiermacher in Germany, Coleridge in England, and Emerson in America are just some of the spokesmen for this new sensibility which made Romanticism one of the last great international movements of thought in the modern period. More or less independently of these, John Henry Newman stigmatized the previous century, the great age of 'evidences', as 'a time when love was cold': even if the proofs for God's existence were valid, Newman reckoned, they would give us no more than was available to Socrates and would tell us nothing of the love, justice, mercy and faithfulness of God. Within the French- and English-speaking worlds especially, the great scientific advances of the century sharpened the original Kantian critique of metaphysics: in the natural sciences, it seemed, there was a sure method of reaching truth and resolving disagreements – not to mention their practical fruitfulness; but metaphysics, it could be argued, was a battleground of useless theories, in which little agreement and no practical gains had been achieved after two thousand years of speculation. It was this general methodological consideration which, perhaps, underlay the view that there was a conflict between science and religion, as much as any particular disputes about geology, evolution and Genesis. The notion of 'truth' as practical efficacy gave rise within philosophy, including the philosophy of religion, to the Pragmatism of William James.

The limits of reason and the nature of rationality were tested even more radically in the nineteenth century. Marx's claim that the dominant ideas of a society are the ideas of its dominant classes, the French ethnographers' discovery of the 'social fact' of *l'âme collective* and interest in *la mentalité primitive*, and the growing concern in Germany about the relativizing consequences of *Historismus* gave enormous impetus in the latter part of the nineteenth century to a recognition of the social determinants of human reason and rationality. An indication of the extent to which the period's confidence in reason had been shaken by the Kantian critique is suggested additionally by the skeptical and voluntaristic tendencies of such thinkers as Schopenhauer, Kierkegaard and Nietzsche.

However much metaphysics had suffered at the hands of its critics, some of the century's liveliest minds continued to profess its virtues and to practise its craft. 'To understand Kant is to transcend Kant', they proclaimed. It is no slight to the likes of Bradley in England and Royce in America to acknowledge, as one must, that Hegel's philosophical synthesis was the most sustained and the most impressive attempt to transcend the limits imposed on human understanding by Kant. Hegel's influence, like Kant's, varied widely within and without the three main Western religious traditions. Within Roman Catholic theology, it would seem that Hegel was perceived as a greater threat to Christian belief than had been Kant: no Roman Catholic theologian of significance in the nineteenth century was in fact tempted by the Hegelian alternative. Elsewhere, however, Hegel's influence was keenly felt. In addition to his more orthodox pupils of the 'right' and their opponents amongst the Young Hegelians of the 'left', the master's influence permeated progressive Protestant thought through Tübingen professor F. C. Baur and Reform Judaism through Frankfurt Rabbi Samuel Hirsch. The persistence of transcendent metaphysics in (and beyond) the nineteenth century – whether on the Continent, in Britain, or in America – is as noteworthy as is the widespread suspicion of its claims. By the end of the century, however, the call was away from the uncharted depths of speculative metaphysics and 'back to Kant'.

Humanity and human nature

Several not always commensurable trends in nineteenth-century thought led to changes in the doctrine of man. Three areas of change had special importance for religious thought: the precise relationship between the mental process of 'thinking', 'willing' and 'feeling' was much disputed; the assumption that human nature is fixed was increasingly questioned; and the concept of 'humanity', rooted in Enlightenment soil, came to be cultivated in numerous hybrid forms. In addition, and following largely from these three trends, the individual 'sciences of man' came of age in the course of the nineteenth century. Concern about religion was not infrequently a key factor in all these developments.

Reaction against what many had come to believe was the Enlightenment's inflated confidence in reason and unwarranted vaunting of the intellect led in some cases to a new emphasis upon the will and in others, the affect. Either move clearly had implications for the locus of religion in human experience and its role in the formation of human character.

The relationship of morality and religion preoccupied many nineteenth-century writers. Poets and novelists, no less than theologians and philosophers, were much concerned with 'the voice of conscience', a voice which called many to reject and others to accept the claims of religion. An ethical critique of especially the Christian religion featured centrally not only in the writings of Nietzsche, but also in those of such 'left-wing' British agnostics as T. H. Huxley and Leslie Stephen.[1] Others, most notably Newman and

7

Kant, sought to replace the by then discredited traditional arguments for God's existence with some type of moral argument. Whatever differences may exist in detail, they both attempted to do so by distinguishing sharply between that knowledge available to sense experience and that yielded in obedience to moral experience. The voice of conscience, Newman reckoned, has its own absolute authority which can not be shaken by evidence of the senses alone. Although he would have been perplexed by Newman's assent to ecclesiastical authority and astonished by Newman's confidence that conscience establishes the traditional doctrines of Catholic Christianity, Kant himself has through the years both perplexed and astonished many with his own argument that it is necessary to postulate the existence of God, the freedom of the will, and the immortality of the individual soul in order to make sense of the categorical imperative given in moral experience. Both Kant and Newman, however, left their mark on religious ethics. Newman's influence was not decisively felt until the twentieth century, when his significance was belatedly acknowledged. He may nonetheless have influenced individuals such as Tyrrell, for whom conscience was a central ethical notion. Kant's influence on nineteenth-century religious ethics can be seen within Protestant Liberalism, especially in its Ritschlian form, and in the writings of the critical idealists, whose resurgence in the latter part of the century is reported both in the chapter on British Idealism and in that on Jewish thought. Hermann Cohen, adapting characteristically Kantian arguments, attempted to show that the sense of duty which originates in man is identical with the law given by God, so that it is as free moral agent that man takes upon himself the 'yoke of the commandments'. During the period under discussion, many others asserted the primacy of the will, not the least of whom were Schopenhauer (who claimed to be the only true Kantian) and Nietzsche (whose philosophy owes more to Schopenhauer than to Kant). The role of the will in matters religious was stressed also by such diverse figures as Kierkegaard and William James, for both of whom religious belief is grounded in an act of will, rather than in an act of thought.

This revolt against the rule of thought took also another form. The influence of Romanticism on religious sensibility shows itself in part through the rediscovery of feeling as a religiously significant dimension of human nature. Coleridge, for instance, maintained that profound thought was capable of being attained only by one capable of profound feeling. It is the heart, not the head, which was regarded by Coleridge as the centre of faith: the substitution of speculative systems of dogma for that centre, whereby 'religion became a science of shadows under the name of theology', was reckoned to be 'the true and first apostasy'. Coleridge's sharp distinction between the heart of faith and its second-order expression in doctrine and theology closely allied his independently determined stance with that of Friedrich Schleiermacher, who was arguably the greatest theologian of the nineteenth century, if not of the entire modern age. More precisely than any other religious writer of his time Schleiermacher mapped out the place of religion in the structure of human consciousness and its role in the cultivation of human capacities. The centre of religion conceived as a human capacity is 'neither a knowing nor a doing but a determination of feeling or of immediate self-consciousness'. In this appeal to immediacy the nineteenth century found one of its decisive expressions and, for at least a while, its most effective answer to the strictures on religious thought imposed by Kant's *Critique of Pure Reason*.

Schleiermacher was not alone in making such an appeal. Again and again through the course of the nineteenth century thinkers and writers as diverse as Newman, Wordsworth, Arnold, Huxley, William James and Baron von Hügel appealed to an immediately present religious awareness which cannot be vitiated by philosophical critique or by ordinary experience of the way things go in the world. The primacy ascribed to immediate self-consciousness has the effect of relegating 'thinking' or 'knowing' to a second-order activity without independent authority, the sole object of which is as cogently as possible to reflect on the primary datum of immediate experience. Debate and disagreement – whether theological or philosophical – can never touch the 'self-identical essence of piety'. This type of dualism allowed for the continuation of critical reconsideration of theological norms under the impact of modern science as well as the literary and historical criticism of sacred scriptures and tradition, whilst seeming to insulate the very 'essence' of religion from all such modes of attack. For this reason Feuerbach felt justified in regarding 'feeling' as the last refuge of theology. Like Schleiermacher, one of the two giants who had drawn him to the University of Berlin, Feuerbach asserted the primacy of feeling in matters religious. He pushed 'feeling' in a different and more radical direction, however, with the result that 'the feeling of utter dependence' was transposed into 'the utter dependence of feeling'. Thus, 'the beginning, middle and end of religion' was regarded by Feuerbach as man himself.

This humanization of religion, of which Feuerbach is but one example, was a decisive turn in nineteenth-century thought. From different grounds and various motives the 'religion of humanity' became a widespread idea in the nineteenth century. One thinks not only of Feuerbach in Franconia, but Comte in France and Spencer in England. However important their differences in detail, a common denominator can be identified: the object of religion is humankind, not positive knowledge of a supersensible entity called 'God'. Humanity alone is thought to be worthy of the worship once given the gods. Religion, conceived anthropologically rather than theologically, is regarded by them all as a permanent element in the society of man, the cement which bonds us all together. Without religion, human beings are less than fully human.

No consensus obtained in the nineteenth century as to the role of religion in the attainment of 'true humanity'. Religion was seen by some as a constituent feature of human nature, the cultivation of which was necessary for realizing one's full potential as a human being. Even here the options were as diverse as Schleiermacher and Comte. Religion was regarded by others, including Marx, as an accidental feature of only certain social conditions, the existence of which would cease when the social conditions which generated it were themselves changed. Although religion was still regarded by many as having a useful, if somewhat conservative, role to play in human social life, it also came to be regarded by an increasing number during the nineteenth century as an instance, if not a cause, of self-alienation and as an inhibitor of man's achieving 'true humanity'. In any case, 'humanity' was regarded as a goal, as well as the name of a species.

Some leading thinkers no doubt continued to hold, as had the majority of their intellectual forebears, that human nature is universal and invariable. Others, however, were increasingly attracted to the idea, itself rooted in the Enlightenment, that man is his own creation, that human nature is not fixed but malleable. Different motives were at work here. Some writers emphasized the uniqueness of the individual person (Kierkegaard, Dostoyevsky), whilst others stressed the overriding importance of the species (Feuerbach) or of the *Volk* (Hegel, following Herder) or of society (Marx) in the determination of human nature. 'Progress', 'development' and 'evolution' were words with no small effect upon how human nature came to be regarded in the nineteenth century under the impact of the historicizing of thought and of the more or less independent Darwinian revolution. Some writers in the period painted a basically optimistic picture of human nature and its perfectability through education, whilst a few began to probe the darker depths of the human spirit where, as Schelling warned, 'the demons dwell'. Dostoyevsky sought 'to find the man in man', but did not always like what he found. The disturbing implications of Darwin's theories no doubt also contributed to the sense of unease experienced by many in the latter third of the century.

Whatever differences may be noted in respect to specific points, concern about human nature is a principal theme running right the way through the nineteenth century. This concern exhibits itself at a number of levels, not the least significant of which is the development of the several sciences of man. The dictum 'La vraie science et la vraie étude de l'homme, c'est l'homme' was never taken more seriously than in the nineteenth century. The emergence of scientific anthropology, sociology and psychology in this period had decisive influence on the study and interpretation of religion. Moreover, concern about the nature and function of religion in human life was no minor impulse in the development of the sciences of man. Many of the early classics within anthropology, sociology and psychology deal specifically with the question of religion. In addition, a more specialized attempt to deal with religious phenomena produced in the course of the nineteenth century considerable advances in the anthropological (Tylor, Frazer), sociological (Weber, Troeltsch) and psychological (James) study of religion. In line with the advances in philology, the comparative study of religion (Müller) also began to flourish as a scientific discipline. Even theology became in a new sense 'scientific', and there developed within Jewish thought a school known as the 'science of Judaism'. Amongst the factors instrumental in these latter developments was the 'breakthrough of historical thinking', as it has been called.[2]

History and historicism

The historicizing of human consciousness has been acclaimed by more than one interpreter as the decisively new element in modern Western thought. The idea of history cut with a double edge in the nineteenth century. It seemed to substantiate both the confidence of those who thought that historical science enables us with certainty to reconstruct the past *wie es eigentlich gewesen* and the worst fears of those who had become skeptical about our ever being in a position to have certain knowledge of the distant past. This double-edged character of 'history' had especially interesting consequences for religious thought and its development in the nineteenth century. Each side of the sword of history was used both in the defence and in the attack on the cause of religion.

Speculative philosophies of history had been superabundant in the eighteenth century and humankind's drive to 'make sense' of its plight by finding purposive direction in the order of events was much older still. The Enlightenment's philosophies of history in fact have been explained as secularized versions of older theological doctrines of divine providence. The collapse of the religion of reason under the weight of its critique by Hume and Kant, together with the closely parallel rise of Romanticism, contributed to the intensity of interest in history late in the eighteenth century. One thinks of Lessing, Rousseau and Herder, but also of Kant himself, whose own philosophy of history has attracted much attention in recent years. Nor should it be forgot that Hume – who, incidentally, is identified in the catalogue of the Cambridge University Library simply as 'historian' – wrote in the mid-eighteenth century a *Natural History of Religion*. This widespread concern with history was sufficiently well established by the close of the century for Friedrich Schlegel to have made reference in 1797 to the new *Historismus*, a term which had become common currency by the middle of the nineteenth century, but which to this day has eluded precise definition.[3] A number of disparate influences were at work in the nineteenth-century's preoccupation with history, but the Romantic rebellion against the Enlightenment must surely be reckoned as having been decisive.

The Romantics and their kin felt strongly that the world of the Enlightenment's *philosophes* and *Weltweiser* was far too narrow. It was felt to be too narrow both in the sense that reason had been emphasized at the expense of other sorts of human experience and in the sense that their world had been cut off from the richness and diversity of other ages and other cultures. Such writers as Hegel, Möhler and Coleridge reacted against what they saw as the dry rationalism and excessive individualism of the eighteenth century, and stressed those features which help to form nations and cultures and to differentiate them from each other: language, literature, national temperament and, above all, history and tradition. Reason's construct, 'natural religion', was also repudiated in favour of 'positive religions', the actual traditions which exist or have existed in space and time. The Romantics regarded the Enlightenment as having had an a-historical and rootless view of the 'rational man'. Such an appeal to history is not without ambiguity: for if man is essentially an historical being, moulded by his past and developing in new ways, may not this relativize the claims of every religion? This was certainly one worry expressed time and again in the nineteenth century, culminating in the 'crisis of historicism' which all but defeated the likes of Dilthey and Troeltsch.

This relativizing of the absolute truth-claims of individual religions had also another consequence. 'Other' religions became potential sources of divine wisdom comparable to one's own, and not merely examples of wilful idolatry and blind superstition or living museums of strange customs and beliefs to be visited occasionally by the curious or the dilettanti. In respect to religion, as well as other interests, Lord Acton was right to observe that the Romantics 'doubled the horizon of Europe' by their openness to 'the whole inheritance of man'. The increasingly professional study of Indian and other Eastern languages blossomed as a result of the Romantics' discovery of 'the orient', leading eventually to the development of the comparative study of religions as a separate discipline. One thinks especially of the pioneering work of Friedrich Max Müller at Oxford. Sociologists like Max Weber also took a keen interest in Indian (and other) religions. During the nineteenth century it can be observed that non-Western religions began to make their first real impact in modern times on the European mind. Adopting the Upaniṣadic formula *tat tvam asi* (Chāndogya VI.viii.7), Schopenhauer made the metaphysical unity of all that is a fundamental premise of his own philosophy. The diversity of religions was welcomed by many of the Romantics, including the youthful Schleiermacher, as indicative of the diversity of humankind and of the multiplicity of possible relations to the One or the Whole. The more mature Schleiermacher, however, worked out a sort of hierarchy of religions, with the monotheistic faiths of Judaism, Christianity and Islam occupying the highest plane and, of these, Christianity was regarded 'in fact' as 'the most perfect of the most highly developed forms of religion'.

The idea of religions' developing from simpler and more primitive to more complex and higher forms squared well with the Romantic stress on organic development or unfolding in the history of human spirit. The purest expression of this feature of Romanticism is perhaps Hegel, who transformed reason into a world-historical process. Hegel defined religion with disarming simplicity as 'the consciousness of God'. Viewed *phenomenologically*, 'consciousness of God' refers in Hegel's writings to man's coming to be aware of his essential unity with the divine Spirit. The emergence of his consciousness may be traced in the history of religions, from the most primitive to the more advanced, culminating in Christianity, which is termed the 'revelatory' or 'absolute' religion. In it alone God is known 'as He is'. Viewed *speculatively*, however, 'consciousness of God' refers at the same time to God's own self-consciousness. The history of religions is likewise the means of God's own coming to 'be-for-himself' (*Fürsichsein*) in and through man's ever-developing consciousness of Him. For both God and man, therefore, the historical unfolding of religion is *Heilsgeschichte*. Hegel's handling of the history of religions is clearly suspect. He appears to make what are properly speaking historical decisions on philosophical or even theological grounds, and his knowledge of individual religious traditions (especially Buddhism) is sometimes embarrassingly thin. Yet, he epitomizes the Romantic concept of 'development' and his influence in the nineteenth century was considerable within both Christian and Jewish attempts philosophically to comprehend the historical development of religious consciousness. Toward the end of the century, for instance, Edward Caird employed a modified version of the Hegelian schema in his two-volume account of *The Evolution of Religion*. Again, like Hegel, he considered a suitably distilled version of Christianity as final or absolute religion: the 'objective' religions of Greece and Rome and the 'subjective' religion of Judaism are interpreted as merely preparatory for the final Christian synthesis. Not surprisingly, the Jewish philosophers Samuel Hirsch and Nachman Krochmal told the Hegelian tale with a different ending: Judaism represents for them the highest possible development of religious consciousness, of which Christianity must be regarded a corruption. All such schemata, but specifically the Christian variations, were repudiated by Ernst Troeltsch, who toward the end of his life felt compelled to draw the full and radical consequences of historical relativism. Not everyone felt under a similar compulsion. Well into the twentieth century, for example, Ritschl's intellectual offspring, both legitimate and natural, were continuing to insist in the face of the obvious that Christianity is not a religion alongside other religions, nor is its revelatory foundation subject to weakening by the ravages of historical relativism. Even if allowed as logically coherent, such a position is factually untenable. The fears it masked were nonetheless genuine.

For much of the nineteenth century, the facts of history seemed to offer a refuge to faith which had been denied it by the demolition of natural theology and the collapse of the religion of reason. Historical fact, not speculative theory, was thought by many to constitute the sure foundation of religions such as Judaism and Christianity. The Darwinian controversy may have cast doubts on the creation stories of Genesis, but recent finds by the burgeoning science of archaeology seemed at first to give 'scientific' confirmation of specific claims found in the sacred scriptures of Judaism and Christianity. As the textual-critical study of those scriptures got underway, however, matters seemed less clear. Today's new 'theories' (!) called into question yesterday's 'assured results of historical investigation'. The discovery in concert with archaeology of the true extent of 'pagan' influence on the growth of Israel's religion called into question for many devout Jews the revelatory claims of Torah. Debates about the historical reliability of the Fourth Gospel, the authorship of certain letters traditionally ascribed to Paul, and the intricacies of 'the Synoptic problem' raised similar problems for Christians. By the beginning of the twentieth century it had also become clear that 'the Jesus of history' and his simple message were neither more accessible nor less problematic than 'the Christ of faith' and the richly elaborated christology handed on by tradition. The assurances of 'history' seemed at least for theology as empty as had been those of 'metaphysics' and as unwarranted as those of 'dogmatics'. In any case, no one since the time of Lessing had been able to certify how one could ever move from the contingent facts of history to the sort of certainty on which faith could properly rest. It was not clear to the theologians of the nineteenth century whether one should attempt, with Kierkegaard, to get across this 'ugly ditch' with a single heroic leap or, with those engaged in the quest of the historical Jesus, simply to fill it piecemeal with gradually accumulated historical detail. Others tried to bridge the gap by commitment to a strong and continuous tradition which was said to stretch securely from one side to the other. In addition to the Tractarians in Britain, one thinks of Chateaubriand, de Lamennais and de Maistre in France.[4] The contribution of Rabbi Samson Raphael Hirsch to the revival of Jewish Orthodoxy serves to remind that the effects of the Romantic respect for the authority of tradition were by no means restricted to Christianity. Nor were all those concerned with tradition 'traditionalists'. Whether or not they may be said to have been largely successful or even be adjudged to have been sufficiently faithful to their respective traditions, a carefully measured effort to adapt that tradition to the needs of the present characterized Reform Judaism, Protestant Liberalism, and Roman Catholic Modernism alike.

Reason and rationality, 'humanity' and human nature, history and 'historicism' – these three themes dominate nineteenth-century religious thought and give it unity. Variations on these themes feature centrally in the twentieth century as well. But, that is another story.

NINIAN SMART
Professor of Religious Studies, University of Lancaster and the University of California, Santa Barbara
JOHN CLAYTON
Principal of Cartmel College and Lecturer in Religious Studies, University of Lancaster
STEVEN KATZ
Professor of Near Eastern Studies, Cornell University
PATRICK SHERRY
Lecturer in Religious Studies, University of Lancaster

Notes

1 The distinction between 'left-wing' and 'right-wing' agnostics is developed by James Livingston in his contribution on 'British Agnosticism', in volume II.

2 Peter Hünermann, *Der Durchbruch des geschichtlichen Denkens im 19. Jahrhundert* (Freiburg, Basel, Vienna, 1967).

3 Compare, for instance, the diverse use of the term in the following articles: Georg Iggers, 'Historicism', *Dictionary of the History of Ideas*, edited by P. P. Wiener (New York, 1973), pp. 456–64; Maurice Mandelbaum, 'Historicism', *The Encyclopedia of Philosophy*, edited by Paul Edwards (New York and London, 1967), vol. IV, pp. 22–5; and G. Scholtz, 'Geschichte, Historie' and 'Historismus, Historizismus', *Historisches Wörterbuch der Philosophie*, edited by Joachim Ritter and Karlfried Gründer (Darmstadt and Basel, 1974), vol. III, cols. 344–98, 1141–7.

4 Unfortunately, it has not been possible to include a chapter on these three thinkers. The reader is referred instead to B. M. G. Reardon's useful survey *Liberalism and Tradition: Aspects of Catholic Thought in Nineteenth-Century France* (Cambridge, 1975).

I

Immanuel Kant

EMIL L. FACKENHEIM

Kant wrote extensively on the subject of religion. Although a child of the Age of Enlightenment and as such suspicious of, if not hostile to, all religious orthodoxies, he could not leave religion alone, whether 'within the bounds of reason' or even beyond it, touching on (if not actually dealing with) the Christian revelation. His three *Critiques* all end with religious questions, and one work – *Religion Within the Bounds of Reason Only* – deals with nothing else.

Despite an air of deceptive obviousness, the religious issues in question, as dealt with by Kant, almost all raise complex questions for the interpreter. Among these are the relation between ritual and morality, between political and religious authority, and – most obscure but surely also most important – the room, if any, left by 'reason only' for the Christian revelation.

However, one problem in Kant's philosophy of religion surpasses all others in significance. In Kant's view, morality is the highest sphere of rationally accessible truth. It also must be autonomous, i.e., unlimited in scope and authority by a sphere beyond it. Despite all this he asserts the necessity of a 'transition' from 'morality' to 'religion'. Kant must explain and justify the necessity of this 'transition'. In case he fails, his philosophy of religion fails as a whole. His 'moral religion' – as well as any other form of supposedly justified religion – reduces itself, in that case, to morality pure and simple. As for religion – *all* religion as such and in principle – it is, in that case, at best useful humbug. Such, however, was not Kant's view.

I

On frequent occasions Kant defines religion as the interpretation of our moral duties as divine commandments. This definition, while authoritative, is not without difficulties. For if the religious interpretation adds grounds or motives to the moral ones already present in the concept of duty, it threatens moral autonomy; and if it does not, it threatens to make religion itself into a redundancy. It would seem that these difficulties can be removed only if one turns from this first definition to a second and considers this latter as the more fundamental. Kant asserts that 'morality necessarily leads to religion'.[1] An inspection of Kant's first definition, already referred to, would have to ask how this transition is possible. An inspection of Kant's second, more fundamental definition must ask why the transition is necessary. This second definition identifies religion as justified hope.

In a celebrated passage in the *Critique of Pure Reason* Kant writes: 'All the interests of my reason, speculative as well as practical, combine in the following three questions: 1. What can I know? 2. What ought I to do? 3. What may I hope?'[2] The third question is answered by religion. It does so not by exercise of an additional capacity, over and above the capacities for knowledge and moral action, but rather by somehow conjoining these two, and by recognizing a limitation in their conjunction.

'Reason' is not 'interested' in religious hopes which men happen to have but only in such as are justified. The justification itself cannot consist in the demonstration of a human tendency to hope, for this could be mere wishful thinking even if it were more or less or even altogether universal. Nor is it sufficient to demonstrate that the religious hope in question does not contradict the laws of logic or morality. To be sure, a restriction of this sort is necessary. (In Kant's view there can be no rationally justified religious hopes for supernatural events which would shatter the laws of nature, or for divine acts of Grace which would shatter the laws of morality.[3]) It is not, however, sufficient. Since Kant has confined knowledge to the realm of appearance, it is quite possible to have non-contradictory opinions about whatever may transcend appearance; but the mere logical tenability of such opinions is not enough to make them part of a rational hope. Again, it is equally possible to find examples of religious hopes which are morally unobjectionable. Such could include even the crude kind of religious thought which expects of heaven no more than just rewards for earthly virtue. But once more the fact that such hoping may be morally unobjectionable does not mean that it is rationally justified.

How then *can* the religious hope be rationally justified? Not by a theoretical necessity, for knowledge is confined to the phenomenal world. Nor is there a moral necessity for religious hoping.[4] For while it may be morally necessary *for us* to mete out reward in accordance with moral desert, no such necessity exists for believing that the universe will do the same. Indeed a religious hope which springs from nothing more than a cosmic projection of the idea of justice simply begs the question. But if the religious hope cannot spring from either a theoretical or a moral necessity how can it nevertheless be rationally justified? For according to Kant, reason has no more than these two functions.

With this question, we have come upon the most critical and most profound aspect of Kant's religious thought. It is the most critical, because on his ability to answer this question the transition from Kantian morality to religion wholly depends. It is the most profound, because his answer revolutionizes religious thought, substituting as it does 'moral theology' for the traditional 'natural theology' which Kant has seen himself compelled to discard. Unfortunately, this aspect of his thought is also one of the most obscure parts of Kant's teaching. Indeed, it is only fair to confess that a host of critics have dismissed it in despair, and that the following attempt to understand it is not made without trepidation.[5]

II

In view of the importance of the subject, we begin with an extensive summary. Reason in all its functions is unable to rest satisfied with the relative and the conditioned; it seeks the absolute and the unconditioned. In the sphere of the practical, this is the highest Good. The question facing man, as a rational being is: what is the correct notion of the highest Good?

Two rival views command attention, namely, the Epicurean and the Stoic. For the Epicurean, the highest Good is happiness, while for the Stoic it is the kind of virtue which is acquired by the performance of duty for duty's sake. These two views are mutually exclusive. The Epicurean considers virtue as a mere by-product of happiness, vice being nothing but the result of sickness or unhappiness. For the Stoic, happiness is a mere by-product of virtue; for true happiness consists in the knowledge of duty performed and virtue acquired; to want any other kind of happiness is itself a vice. These views, then, are in sharp contrast. But both are in error, the one because it mistakes man for an animal, the other because it mistakes him for a god.

Epicureanism is in obvious error, for it mistakes all moral autonomy for mere heteronomy. But to act morally is to act because of duty, not for the sake of happiness; and virtue, far from being a mere means to or by-product of happiness, is an absolute Good in its own right. However, the Stoic error, while less obvious, is no less significant. Virtue, while the supreme Good, cannot be the complete Good. Man is a *product* of nature. As such he needs happiness, and this need is not evil but innocent.[6] Hence to consummate human destiny the highest Good must contain happiness as well as virtue; and to consummate it in one synthesis it must contain, not any and all happiness, but happiness in exact proportion to virtue.

Appearances to the contrary notwithstanding, the concept arrived at is in far more radical contrast with the Stoic and Epicurean concepts than these two are with each other. If Stoic or Epicurean are right, man can wholly fulfil the meaning of his destiny.[7] But the ideal now arrived at implies that man cannot do so, at least within the span of earthly life and without the help of God.

According to the Epicurean, to be sure, man cannot hope to attain absolute happiness. But he can accept as his ideal something less because he is not *obligated* to attain absolute happiness: indeed, he is not obligated at all. In the Stoic view, in contrast, man *is* obligated to attain absolute virtue. However, he is capable of attaining it, and to the extent to which he fails he can blame only himself. But if the view now arrived at is correct, man is obligated to attain a Good which he is incapable of attaining. He is obligated to attain it because it is implied in the categorical imperative; yet he is incapable of attaining it. The one component of the highest Good – absolute virtue or holiness – he can aim at but never wholly reach; the other component – happiness in proportion to virtue – he can advance only haphazardly but not systematically. The latter he could do only if 'the maxim of virtue [were] . . . . the efficient cause of happiness'.[8] But since happiness is wholly unlike virtue, this is not the case. In short, 'to realize the highest Good is (i) to aim at moral perfection (ii) to reach it (iii) thereby to merit happiness and (iv) to acquire it, as a necessary consequence of perfect virtue'.[9] But while man even at his best can achieve only the first of these goals he is obligated to achieve all four.

But what man is obligated to achieve he must be able to achieve. It is therefore necessary that the conditions exist by virtue of which he can fulfil his obligation. These conditions are man's immortality and the existence of God.

Absolute virtue or holiness is not a state of successful struggle against conflicting inclination, but a state in which there remains no conflicting obligation and hence no need for struggle. As a moral being, man is obligated to attain this state; but as a finite being, he can only approximate it. This contradiction can be removed only if the approximation can be infinite. But this presupposes man's immortality.

But immortality, by itself, enables man only to achieve absolute virtue, not happiness in proportion to virtue. This is because happiness is wholly unlike virtue, the former belonging to the world of nature, the latter to the moral world; and these two worlds, so far as finite understanding is concerned, are wholly separate. How then can man, by being virtuous, bring about deserved happiness? This is possible only if the two worlds, though apparently separate, are nevertheless ultimately connected; if the same Being is the author of moral law and the natural world: that is, if there is a God who is omniscient, omnipotent and, above all, holy.

Kant concludes that 'morality necessarily leads to religion' because moral obligation necessarily leads to the belief in the conditions without which it cannot be fulfilled. Religion is, on the one hand, the interpretation of moral duties as divine commandments; as such it adds to autonomous morality the belief that moral duties can be fulfilled, because the author of moral law is also the author of nature.[10] On the other hand, religion is the hope for the chance to attain holiness, and for the gift of deserved happiness; as such it is rationally justified because moral reason demands that that can be realized which ought to be realized.

III

This may suffice as a summary of Kant's teaching. We must now consider its significance. And we may begin by stating a number of formidable criticisms which have been directed against it ever since his views first appeared in print:

(i) The argument for immortality rests on mutually exclusive premises. The one asserts that what we are obligated to attain we must be able to attain; the other asserts that we are obligated to attain something which we cannot attain, namely, holiness. Yet if, for the sake of consistency, either of these premises is dropped the argument vanishes.[11]

(ii) The decisive premise in the argument for God is an alien and indeed insufferable intruder into Kant's moral thought. We cannot be morally obligated to bring about the deserved happiness of others, nor morally will to acquire our own; not the former because it is not always within our power; not the latter because we exist in order to do our duty, not in order to become happy. Thus while Kant requires a notion of the highest Good, as the ultimate object of the moral will, this object cannot include happiness.[12] 'The principle of personality alone is the object looked for. Any additional object is not only unnecessary but even detrimental.'[13] But with this conclusion the argument for God loses its force.

(iii) The arguments for immortality and God (provided one is prepared to take them seriously, the above difficulties notwithstanding) are mutually exclusive. Each solves the problem (assuming that there is a problem) in a way which precludes the solution provided by the other. For if (as the argument for immortality asserts) we are able infinitely to approximate holiness, provided only we are given the 'time' to do it, we approximate a state in which we can no longer stand in need of happiness, and the need for a God who dispenses deserved happiness disappears. And if (as the argument for God asserts) the dualism between virtue and the need for happiness persists even in infinity, then immortality is needed, not in order to provide us with a chance to achieve holiness, but merely in order that we might receive the rewards of our earthly goodness.[14]

(iv) The concepts of immortality and God are incompatible with the conclusions of Kant's most fundamental philosophical doctrines. For if temporality and sensuality can belong only to phenomena, they cannot belong to the soul in a non-phenomenal existence. Yet without time and sensual desire how can there be moral struggle and moral progress? But it is precisely the need for infinite moral struggle and progress which gives rise to the belief in immortality to begin with. Again, categories such as causality can apply only to phenomena. How then can they apply to God who is not a phenomenon? Yet if they do not apply to Him how can He be the author of nature and moral law? But it is precisely the need for a cause, linking the worlds of nature and morality, which gives rise to the belief in God at all.[15]

(v) So much for the essence of God and immortality. What about their existence? Do God and immortality exist? But 'existence', for Kant, has meaning only in a phenomenal context. Are they, then, mere ideas produced by our reason? But the problems for the solution of which they are needed are precisely such as cannot be solved by *our* powers of production; and if there are no such problems God and immortality are not needed at all. But perhaps they are ideas to which we – necessarily but mistakenly – ascribe existence, that is, necessary fictions? But then if it *is* true that morality is possible only if God and immortality exist, morality is *itself* a fiction. And if this is *not* true even the fictions are not necessary.[16]

What is one to make of this formidable list of difficulties – a list which, incidentally, could easily be expanded? Is one to conclude that Kant's whole teaching concerning God and immortality must be dismissed, as a hopeless mass of confusion?[17] Yet in so doing one would dismiss what, to Kant himself, was the culminating point of his entire philosophy. For it is a mistaken belief that Kant's *Critique of Pure Reason* aims at the elimination of all metaphysics. Rather, it aims at eliminating the old *kind* of metaphysics in order to prepare the ground for a wholly new kind.[18] And the content of this new kind of metaphysics includes, in addition to freedom, immortality and God. Kant writes: 'God, freedom and the immortality of the soul are the problems to the solution of which, as their ultimate and unique goal, all the laborious preparations are directed.'[19]

IV

It is in this last observation that the key to an understanding lies. Kant's 'theology' or 'metaphysics' is a new *kind* of metaphysics, and it appears as confused and inconsistent only so long as it is mistaken for the old kind. Kant destroys the metaphysics which is based on speculation and replaces it with a metaphysics which is based on moral consciousness. He seeks to prove, not immortality and God, but that the belief in immortality and God is implicit in finite moral consciousness. He seeks to develop, not philosophical concepts of God and immortality, but the concepts of God and immortality which are implicit in finite moral consciousness. If these beliefs are, by certain standards, somehow inadequate, it is not because of incompetent philosophizing on Kant's part, but because of certain characteristics of finite moral consciousness. The task of philosophy is not to change or reject these beliefs, but to show what they are, and why they are implicit in finite moral consciousness. This raises, to be sure, the question why such a philosophical enterprise should be regarded as metaphysics, rather than a mere analysis of the structure of finite moral consciousness. But the answer to this question, while complex in its details, is quite simple in principle: the philosopher too is a finite moral agent; and it is in his latter rather than his former capacity that he is in touch with ultimate moral reality: and as a philosopher he recognizes this fact. This, we contend, is the innermost secret of Kant's 'practical' metaphysics.

V

These contentions must now be demonstrated in detail. And we begin by stressing that they are not wholly unfamiliar to anyone acquainted with Kant's moral thought, even if his religious thought is as yet unknown territory to him. For he has already come upon Kant's doctrine of freedom, the first part of his 'practical' metaphysics and the indispensable basis for all that is to come. Here Kant has proved, not freedom, but that the belief in freedom is implicit in moral consciousness. He has tried to show, not how freedom can be philosophically understood, but that moral consciousness alone can understand it, to the extent to which it can be understood at all. And freedom turns into a metaphysical truth (rather than being a pseudo-moral illusion) through the demonstration that the philosopher *can* accept it as a reality because it does not contradict causality, and that he *must* accept it as a reality because he, too, is a moral agent.

But as we now turn from freedom to God and immortality a new element makes its appearance. The belief in freedom is implicit in moral consciousness insofar as it is moral. The belief in God and immortality is implicit in it insofar as it is *finite* as well as moral.[20] It is implicit in it because the structure of finite morality has certain inner contradictions. The beliefs in God and immortality can resolve these contradictions only by reflecting them.

Philosophy must explicate these beliefs, along with their contradictions; but it must culminate by defining the sense in which the philosopher – who recognizes these contradictions – can nevertheless accept the beliefs which contain them. It is only with the accomplishments of this last task that Kant's 'practical metaphysics' is established.

VI

We begin with Kant's analysis of the structure of finite morality. An infinite moral being would have the notion of moral law but no notion of duty or obligation. Moral law would be the law of its very being; it would necessarily act out of the sheer love of goodness and could not act otherwise.[21] But to a finite moral being – which does not produce itself but is a natural product and as such endowed with natural inclinations[22] – moral law is not the law of its very being. It is not something that *is* but something that *ought to be*. It is present only in the form of obligation; what ought to be can be, in this case, only through obedience and self-constraint.[23] Finite moral existence is struggle and must always remain struggle. Such an existence can achieve virtue, that is, victory in the struggle. But the victory can never reach holiness, that is, a state in which all constraint ceases because nothing remains that needs to be constrained.[24]

But while there is no point at which finite moral existence could cease struggling it is nevertheless obligated to attain a state in which it not only *could* but *would have to* cease struggling because all struggling has become meaningless. This is for three interrelated reasons. Virtue has degrees. Increasing virtue consists of an increasing strength of moral character and a corresponding decrease or transformation of conflicting inclination. Finally, there is no highest degree of possible virtue short of the degree at which the strength of moral character is absolute, and conflicting inclination either vanquished or transformed; that is, short of the point at which virtue passes into holiness.[25]

The contradiction of finite moral existence may therefore be formulated as follows. The more intense a finite agent's moral awareness and effort is, the smaller is his *actual* distance from what he ought to be – and the more acute is his *awareness* of his distance from what he ought to be. If ever his moral awareness and moral effort reached absoluteness, there would no longer *be* a distance, and obligation *as* obligation would vanish; yet if at any state, including the last, he shook off obligation, as *having* vanished, he would, instead of being above the state of moral struggle, forthwith tumble below it.[26]

This contradiction could be avoided only if it could be believed, either that at some conceivable stage obligation could be shaken off, holiness having been achieved, or that there is a degree of virtue short of holiness at which moral reason could rest content. However, both these alternatives represent morally impossible forms of escapism. Moreover, this is not only because they involve illusions about some distant future moment but, more importantly, because they are capable of perverting finite moral existence at any present moment. His own empirical nature can never be wholly transparent to any finite being;[27] hence if it could be believed at *some* moment that holiness is achieved (and the stage of moral struggle superseded) it could be believed at *any actual* present moment. So much for the first above alternative. As for the second, any degree of virtue short of holiness which one may choose to be sufficient, is chosen arbitrarily; hence, once such a choice is allowed, what already *is* may be considered sufficient, and the distinction between 'is' and 'ought' evaporates.

The upshot is that, provided he takes his moral situation seriously, the finite moral agent is forced to believe in his own immortality, understanding this latter as an infinite duration making possible through struggle an infinite approximation of holiness. He need not be *conscious* of this belief. Nor need he actually *hold* it while not morally engaged. *But while he is in actual moral engagement this belief is necessarily implied in his engagement.*

VII

We must now turn to the aspect of the structure of finite moral existence by virtue of which it implies belief in God. This concerns the relationship between moral willing, moral acting and moral ends. An infinite moral being would not, strictly speaking, aim at ends. For there would be, to such a being, no aims as yet unachieved. Since moral law would be the law of its very being, its willing would not be an aiming at something, but identical with its acting. There could be, in the case of such a being, no distinction between its willing – its self-determination – and its acting – its belaboring of an independent external reality. For to such a being there would *be* no independent external reality. In willing it would produce *ex nihilo* what it willed.[28]

The structure of finite moral existence is altogether different. In the first place, all *finite* willing must aim at *ends*. To be sure, if it is moral it is determined not by a desire for ends but by the moral law; but this means, not that finite moral willing can be without ends, but that it aims at these because of duty rather than desire.[29] A finite moral willing which did not aim at ends would not be willing at all.

In the second place, finite *willing* can never be identical with *acting. The finite moral being, while productive of its moral willing, is not productive of its own being.* It is a being which has not made itself, existing in a world which it has not made. Hence its willing, if it is moral willing, is a self-determining; but its acting is a belaboring of a reality independent of it. The dualism between willing and acting, non-existent in the case of an infinite moral being, is, in the case of finite moral beings, inescapable.

This dualism implies a distinction between two kinds of possible ends, namely, those which can be achieved by willing alone, and those which can be achieved only by the kind of overt acting which transforms the world. The question arises whether only the former kind of end, or the latter as well, can be included among moral ends, that is, among such as the finite moral agent can be obligated to realize. The former ends would all come under the heading of promoting his own virtue, the latter, under the head of advancing other people's happiness.[30]

But any attempt to confine moral ends to the former kind would distort the characteristics of finite moral existence. Indeed, to eliminate other people's happiness, as a *morally necessary* end, is in the end to destroy one's own virtue, as a morally *possible* end. A person who attempts, as a matter of duty, to advance the happiness of others succeeds, even if his attempt fails, in strengthening his own virtue. This would not be true if he sought to advance other people's happiness *in order to* strengthen his own virtue. In that case, his willing, instead of being geared to action, would have degenerated into mere self-absorption. Finite willing, while distinct from acting, is not a complete reality devolving upon itself. All serious finite willing is a willing-to-act. And a finite moral willing which does not will-to-act is a mere vague 'meaning well', not serious willing at all.[31]

It follows that the two kinds of end stand or fall together.[32] To be sure, they are distinct kinds of end. But unless the kind of end which can be realized only by acting can be taken morally seriously, the kind of end which can be attained by willing alone becomes unattainable; for in that case willing, (which in the case of finite beings can be serious only if it is willing-to-act), degenerates into a mere concern with self. The conclusion is that the highest Good, as the complex of all moral ends, must contain not only virtue but also happiness; and if the highest Good is to be one whole, this must be happiness in proportion to virtue.

But at this point there arises a problem of the utmost significance. The finite moral agent is always in control of his moral willing, for in this he determines himself. But he is never wholly in control of his acting, for in this he belabors an independent world. Indeed, radically considered – if the consequences of the acting as well as the acting itself are taken into account –

he is never in control at all. This is obvious to anyone who has ever tried to predict all the consequences of his acting prior to acting.

The question is not how the finite moral agent can be responsible for consequences of his acting which he cannot foresee or control. He cannot be responsible for such consequences. The problem is rather how, since the consequences of his acting are ultimately beyond his control, and since all his serious willing is willing-to-act, it is possible for him *even to will*. This would certainly be impossible if external reality were *known* to be systematically obstructive of the finite moral agent's moral purposes, or even if it were indifferent to them. For no one can seriously will to realize ends which he knows to be impossible, or even such as he knows to come into being – if they *do* come into being – by the kind of haphazard chance which is wholly unrelated to his actions.[33] The finite agent does not know, to be sure, that the world is hostile or indifferent. But neither does he have conclusive evidence to the contrary.

So far as the evidence is concerned, the question is open. However, the finite moral agent does not leave it open. He engages in serious moral willing and acting, morally constrained by the categorical imperative, and undeterred by his ignorance of the ultimate consequences of his acting. And this means nothing less than that, whether he knows it or not, he believes in God. He may *be* an agnostic or atheist while not morally engaged; and he may *think* that he is an agnostic or atheist while he *is* morally engaged. But his *actual* moral engagement implies the belief that that which moral law bids him realize in nature can be realized in it because there is a 'common author' of both.[34]

VIII

We have now considered the aspects in the structure of finite moral existence which necessitate the beliefs in immortality and God. We must now consider their relation. This relation is one of contradiction. This contradiction finite moral existence cannot ignore or remove but only accept. Its acceptance – together with the belief that it is not ultimate – is religion.

The contradiction is between two ultimate syntheses required by finite moral existence, the one being holiness, the other, a totality which unites virtue with happiness.[35] This contradiction exists because the finite moral agent cannot, and yet must, take his own need for happiness morally seriously. On the one hand, he cannot take it seriously, for if he regards it as fixed and definable he assumes that there is a fixed degree of virtue which he cannot and hence need not transcend; and if he does not regard it as fixed and definable it is a need destined to gradual elimination. On the other hand, he must take morally seriously at least the need of happiness found in others. For if he does not, he cannot seriously act and will-to-act at all. But how can he accept that *others* need the synthesis of virtue and happiness and yet believe *himself* to be capable of the synthesis of holiness?

The religion of finite moral existence does not supersede but reflect this contradiction. We considered above briefly Kant's definition of religion as the interpretation of our moral duties as divine commandments, along with its difficulties. These difficulties can now be removed. Religion, as so defined, does not add either to the finite agent's moral knowledge or to his moral motivation. It *does* add the belief that the ends which he is obligated to realize in the world *can* be realized in it. However, religion as considered in this aspect only is one-sided, and, if made absolute, self-contradictory. For this reason religion is not only the interpretation of our moral duties as divine commandments (and with it the implied synthesis of holiness). It is also the hope for deserved happiness. But this aspect, too, if made into an absolute, is one-sided and self-contradictory. A *direct* expectation even of deserved happiness would not merely freeze into absolutes arbitrarily chosen degrees of virtue; it also makes impossible all genuine virtue, and hence, all deserved happiness. For genuine virtue can be acquired only if it is sought for its own sake, not for the sake of the reward of happiness; but if the hope for deserved happiness is the ultimate synthesis this is impossible. In short, to make the first aspect of religion absolute (the synthesis of holiness) would be to fall back into the Stoic error, to make the second aspect absolute (the synthesis of virtue and deserved happiness), into the Epicurean error: and all the efforts made to avoid them would be in vain.

Religion in its totality then, includes both these aspects, without yet resolving the contradiction which exists between them. As such it is a focusing, not on the hope for deserved happiness, but on achieving a moral stature which is worthy of happiness. In this focusing, the aim of achieving moral stature is quite independent of whether there is or will be happiness according to moral worth; because of this independence it implies the need for the synthesis of holiness. Yet the hope is inevitably in the background,[36] implying the need for the synthesis of virtue and happiness. Religion culminates at the point at which the finite moral agent recognizes his radical inability to understand the relation between that which must be achieved by himself and that which can be expected only from God.[37]

28

IX

Kant has now completed his analysis of the structure of finite moral existence, and of the religious beliefs implied in it. But this analysis is not, by itself, 'practical metaphysics'. It turns into the latter only by virtue of the thesis that the *engaged* standpoint of finite moral existence is *metaphysically ultimate, for the philosopher no less than for the man in the street*. Kant has already asserted that freedom – which appears as a reality in the moment of moral engagement – is *in fact* a reality rather than a useful or necessary fiction. He now makes the same assertion concerning immortality and God.

But the latter assertion involves far greater difficulties than the former, and indeed can be made only if it is decisively qualified. The belief in freedom was philosophically acceptable (albeit unprovable and even unintelligible) because it was found to be free from contradiction. But the beliefs in God and immortality are *not* free from contradiction, and cannot be made so by a process of philosophical purification. For they necessarily reflect the contradictions of finite moral existence which alone give rise to them. How can these beliefs nevertheless be philosophically acceptable? They are acceptable, Kant replies, if they are regarded as 'symbolic anthropomorphisms'.[38]

The finite-moral concepts of immortality and God are, in the first place, clear anthropomorphisms. Whatever the characteristics of the self apart from its phenomenal existence, temporality and sensibility cannot be among them. And whatever the nature of God – if there *is* a God – will and reason, as we can alone conceive them, cannot be among His attributes.[39]

But, in the second place, to recognize a belief as anthropomorphic is not necessarily to reject it. Only a 'dogmatic anthropomorphism' – which mistakes anthropomorphic beliefs for literal truth – is unacceptable. A 'symbolic anthropomorphism' is not.[40] This latter is an anthropomorphism which is recognized as such and yet not abandoned, first, because it contains truth in however inadequate a form; second, because this truth is inaccessible in a more adequate form.

That the first of these two conditions applies here is understood if some Kantian fundamentals are remembered. Kant teaches a dualism between the empirical and the intelligible-moral self, and between the empirical-natural and the intelligible-moral world. He does not teach that there are two selves and two worlds, but that to our finite standpoint there appear to be two selves and two worlds. The one self and world (which we know) are only appearance; and the other (which are more than appearance) we do not know; they are disclosed to us only in the experience of moral obligation. To an absolute standpoint there would be, not two selves but one self, and not two worlds but one world; and these would somehow contain both our selves and our worlds: for – this is the crucial point – 'appearance' is not illusion;[41] whatever it may be to an absolute standpoint, it would not be sheer nothingness.

It follows that if the standpoint of finite morality is, on the one hand, confined to the dualism of the two selves and the two worlds; and if, on the other hand, it is driven to the belief that this dualism is not ultimate, then it can *represent* this climactic belief only in terms which contain empirical and phenomenal elements. It also follows that, if it is the case that philosophical criticism can *recognize but not transcend* the limitations of the standpoint of finite morality, then it cannot *replace* the beliefs of that standpoint with truth in a higher form; it can only recognize that these beliefs are 'symbolic anthropomorphisms', and that their terms are only of 'analogical'[42] significance.

X

But the question still remains *whether* the standpoint of finite morality can be transcended, either by philosophy itself or in some other way. Kant's 'practical metaphysics' culminates in the demonstration that this is impossible.

Philosophy recognizes as finite, not only the standpoint of theoretical consciousness but also that of finite morality. Does this mean that, in recognizing their finiteness, it can itself attain to an absolute standpoint? On a number of occasions, Kant considers this possibility. But he invariably rejects it.[43]

Human understanding distinguishes between the possibility and actuality of things. But to a reason freed of the finite aspects of human understanding this distinction could not exist. For it would have neither concepts of the merely possible nor sensual intuitions of the merely actual. Being purely intuitive, it would have only the actual; and since the actual could not be distinguished from the possible, it would be the necessary. An absolute or divine reason, and all it knows, would be absolute necessity.[44]

Again, finite moral reason distinguishes between what ought to be done and what is done. But for a moral reason freed of the conditions of finiteness 'there would be no difference between obligation and act'. 'In an intelligible world . . . everything is actual by reason of the simple fact that, being something good, it is possible.'[45] Natural and moral law would coincide. And beings which, being finite, would be under the first law would also be *ipso facto* under the second: they would not merely be capable of conforming to moral law but so constituted as to conform necessarily to it.[46]

This last conclusion is the main reason why the concept of an unconditionally necessary being, while the 'most unavoidable', is also the 'most inaccessible concept of speculative human reason'.[47] It is unavoidable, not only for ordinary speculation in its search for the 'last bearer of all things',[48] but also for the Kantian kind of criticism which, in recognizing the human theoretical and moral standpoints to be finite, gives rise to the problematical notion of an absolute standpoint. Yet this 'unavoidable' concept of the unconditionally necessary is also 'most inaccessible' and a 'veritable abyss' which swallows 'the greatest no less than the least perfection';[49] and among these is the perfection which matters above all, namely, moral perfection. Speculative reason shrinks from the abyss with the assertion that 'God is the Holy One but he cannot create a holy being.'[50] It retreats to the standpoint of finite morality and its symbolic-anthropomorphic truths. The unconditionally necessary is not a reality known from an absolute standpoint, but a problematical concept arising for the finite standpoint. It is a concept by means of which the finite standpoint, becoming philosophical, recognizes its own finiteness.

XI

But perhaps the standpoint of finite morality can be transcended in a non-philosophical way? The claimant which Kant considers is what he calls 'mysticism'. However, for this he reserves some of his sharpest attacks.

It has often been charged that Kant had little or no insight into the nature of religious emotions, and that this failing accounts for the 'narrow moralism' of his religious concepts. But the first charge is manifestly false, and the characterization of his religious concepts as narrowly moralistic reflects obtuseness to the basic Kantian religious problematic. Kant repudiates, not religious feeling and its role in the religious life, but the belief that religious feeling can be speculatively or morally cognitive. And he attacks as 'mysticism' and *Schwärmerei*, not all religious experience, but merely the kind which believes itself in the sort of direct contact with the Deity which would supersede theoretical and moral concepts alike. In its extreme form, mysticism points, as the ultimate Good, to 'a state of absorption in the abyss of the Deity, in which personality is absorbed in the Deity and hence annihilated'.[51] In less extreme forms, it still asserts that the divine essence or the divine will can somehow immediately be felt. However, in the less as well as in the more extreme form, 'mysticism' is a dangerous illusion.

In the first place, even if religious experience were cognitive, it could not be *known* to be so. 'Even if God really spoke to man, the latter could never know that it was God who had been speaking. It is radically impossible for man to grasp the Infinite through his senses, to distinguish Him from sensual beings, and thus to recognize Him.'[52] In the second place, if religious experience were cognitive, it could not be autonomously cognitive. 'If such an immediate intuition happened to me . . . I would still have to use a concept of God as a standard by which to decide whether the phenomenon in question agreed with the necessary characteristics of a Deity.'[53] Even in his most tolerant mood Kant can at most grant that religious experience corroborates the knowledge which reason already possesses. And the reason in question is finite moral reason. But, in the third place, in his less tolerant (and more authentic) mood Kant cannot grant even this much. For the concept of God is that of the Transcendent and the Unconditioned. But the Transcendent and the Unconditioned can only be thought. To claim that It can be immanent and experienced is nothing less than to utter a contradiction in terms.[54] This contradiction is not only speculative but moral as well. 'The question is whether wisdom is poured into man from above, through inspiration, or achieved from below, through the power of his practical reason.'[55] But if Kant has made anything clear, it is that only if it is self-legislating can moral reason be moral at all.

Kant concludes that all forms of religious *Schwärmerei*, far from being forms of genuine religion, are on the contrary indicative of a want of religion. Authentic religion consists in the acceptance of the contradictory condition of moral finiteness, an acceptance made possible by the faith that this condition is not ultimate. It is for want of this faith that religious *Schwärmerei* seeks to escape from the condition of moral finiteness. But its attempt is vain. What it seeks is a divine gift immediately felt; but what it finds are the products of its own imagination mistaken for divine.[56] The mystic believes himself to have risen above the stage of mere religious hope; he believes himself to possess God instead of merely hoping for Him. In fact, he has fallen far below the stage of religious hope; and what he possesses is not God but merely his own inflated, deified self.

Notes

1 Preface, *Religion innerhalb der Grenzen der blossen Vernunft*, Prussian Academy Edition (Berlin, 1902–   ), vol. VI, p. 6. (Henceforth referred to as *Werke*. Unless otherwise noted, all references are to this edition.)

2 *Critique of Pure Reason* B832–3. (Henceforth cited as *Cr.p.R.*) This division also appears in a letter (*Werke* XI 414) and in the introduction to Kant's handbook on *Logic* (*Werke* XI

25). In the last two versions the three questions are 'referred to' a fourth, 'What is man?' Just how seriously one should take this fourth question and if so, what sort of 'anthropology' (*Werke* IX 25) it would involve, are issues beyond the scope of this essay.

3 Scriptural passages such as Romans IX. 18 ('He hath mercy upon whom He will, and whom He will He hardeneth'), if taken literally, are for Kant the '*salto mortale* of human reason' (*Religion innerhalb* [*Werke* VI 121]).

4 Kant asks, and must ask, not 'What *ought* I to hope?' but 'What *may* I hope?'

5 We shall make no attempt to defend Kant's teaching in all its versions, some of which we find frankly indefensible. (See below, n. 34.) We do maintain, however, that the texts justify our interpretation. The *locus classicus* is, of course, the Dialectic of the *Critique of Practical Reason*. (Henceforth cited as *Cr.pr.R.*) But of hardly less great importance would appear to be the following texts: *Reflection* 6173 (*Werke* XVIII 476ff); *Critique of Judgment* ##84ff (henceforth cited as *Cr.J.*); Preface to the first edition of *Religion innerhalb*; *Reflection* 6876 (*Werke* XIX 188ff); *Cr.p.R.* B823–59; *Reflections* 6132, 6454, 6876 (*Werke* XVIII 464, 724ff, XIX 188ff); *Über den Gemeinspruch* (*Werke* VIII 279ff). Especially in view of its late date (1797), a relevant passage in 'Von einem neuerdings erhobenen vornehmen Ton in der Philosophie' (*Werke* VIII 397) is of special significance.

6 To be sure, much obscurity attaches to Kant's concept of happiness. (See H. J. Paton, 'Kant's Idea of the Good', *Proceedings of the Aristotelian Society*, n.s. 14 (1944–5), especially pp. ix–x.) However, these obscurities do not concern our present purpose. Whether happiness can be directly aimed at; if so, whether it is definable (*Grundlegung zur Metaphysik der Sitten* [henceforth *Grundlegung*; *Werke* IV 417ff], also *Cr.J.* #83); if so, whether it is subject to change (*Religion innerhalb* [*Werke* VI 26]): all these are questions outside our scope. What is central to our purpose is solely Kant's certainty – and in this he does not waver – that 'to be happy is necessarily the desire of every rational *but finite* being' (*Cr.pr.R.* [*Werke* V 25]; italics added). Kant *defines* man in terms of this desire, not, to be sure, in so far as he is human, but in so far as he is finite. With this goes his conviction that the inclinations as such are not evil but innocent. (*Religion innerhalb* [*Werke* VI 58]). Unless it is kept in mind that Kant understands man, in these terms, as a rational *but also finite* being, his doctrine of the *summum bonum* will be seen to be unintelligible.

7 Since Kant is often viewed as some sort of modern Stoic it is necessary to insist that the texts bear out the above interpretation. He frequently charges the 'philosophical sects' with the Stoic 'error', and contrasts their view with the Christian which he more or less identifies with his own. See e.g. *Reflection* 6872 (*Werke* XIX 187):

> The highest Good of the philosophical sects could be realizable only on the assumption that man could be wholly adequate to the moral law. Thus one was led, either to adopt a presumptuously flattering view of human actions, or a very lax one of the moral law. The Christian, however, is able to recognize the frailty of his personal value and still to hope, even under the conditions of the holy law, to partake of the highest Good.

See also *Reflection* 6876 (*Werke* XIX 188ff), *Cr.pr.R.* (*Werke* V 85ff, 111ff, and especially 126ff). Kant treats Christian morality 'from its philosophical aspect' only, and credits Christianity with first having recognized the *summum bonum* in its purity (*Cr.pr.R.* [*Werke* V 86]). However, he stresses, on the one hand, that the *summum bonum* is intelligible and acceptable on the basis of reason alone, and, on the other, that Christianity alone cannot be wholly reduced to a religion of reason.

8 *Cr.pr.R.* (*Werke* V 113).

9 Kuno Fischer's formulation, in his *Immanuel Kant* (Heidelberg, 1910), vol. II. I have lost the exact reference.

10 *Cr.pr.R.* (*Werke* V 129ff). This passage ought to be considered as crucial for the whole subject of this essay. Because of its importance we cite it in full, below, n. 12.

11 C. D. Broad, *Five Types of Ethical Theory* (London, 1962), p. 140.

12 Cf. e.g. Arthur Schopenhauer, *Grundlage der Moral*, ed. A. Hübscher (Leipzig, 1938), p. 124:

> This is in the end nothing but a morality aiming at happiness and hence based on selfishness; this eudaimonism which Kant, with much ado, has thrown out of the front door of his system, as being heteronomous, and which now sneaks back in again, through the back door, under the name of the highest Good.

Along the same lines, see also the criticisms of A. Schweitzer, *Die Religionsphilosophie Kants* (Hildesheim, 1974), *passim*; Hermann Cohen (see next note); W. Windelband, *Geschichte der neueren Philosophie* (Leipzig, 1911), vol. II, pp. 131ff; and indeed all the neo-Kantians. Beginning with Fichte, these all attempt to 'purify' Kant's philosophy of its supposed 'eudaemonistic platitudes' (Emanuel Hirsch). This 'purification', however, involves nothing less than the total dismissal of the Dialectic of *Cr.pr.R.* which is not only the climax of that work but may be regarded (and is regarded by this writer) as the climax of Kant's whole philosophy. We shall therefore attempt not to purify Kant's doctrine but rather to understand it. It is summarized by Kant himself as follows:

> In this manner, through the concept of the highest Good as the object and final end of pure practical reason, the moral law leads to religion. Religion is the recognition of all duties as divine commands, not as sanctions, i.e., arbitrary and contingent ordinances of a foreign will, but as essential laws of any free will as such. Even as such, they must be regarded as commands of the Supreme Being because we can hope for the highest Good (to strive for which is our duty under the moral law) only from a perfect (holy and beneficient) and omnipotent will; and, therefore, we can hope to attain it only through harmony with this will. But here again everything remains disinterested and based only on duty, without being based on fear or hope as incentives, which if they became principles, would destroy the entire moral worth of the actions. The moral law commands us to make the highest possible good in a world the final object of all our conduct. This I cannot hope to effect except through the agreement of my will with that of a holy and beneficent Author of the world. And although my own happiness is included in the concept of the highest Good as a whole wherein the greatest happiness is thought of as connected in exact proportion to the greatest degree of moral perfection possible to creatures, still it is not happiness but the moral law (which, in fact, sternly places restricting conditions upon my boundless longing for happiness) which is proved to be the ground determining the will to further the highest Good.
>
> Therefore, morals is not really the doctrine of how to make ourselves happy but of how we are to be *worthy* of happiness. Only if religion is added to it can the hope arise of someday participating in happiness in proportion as we endeavored not to be unworthy of it.

(*Cr.pr.R.* [*Werke* V 129ff]; *Critique of Practical Reason*, transl. L. W. Beck [New York Library of Liberal Arts, 1956], p. 134)

13 See Hermann Cohen, *Kants Begründung der Ethik*, 2nd edn (Berlin, 1910), p. 348. Prior to Cohen Schelling had already written: 'The moral law demands as its object the pure will itself' (*Werke* [Stuttgart & Augsburg, 1856–61], vol. I, p. 429).

14 This is the view of Schleiermacher, see W. Dilthey, *Das Leben Schleiermachers* (Berlin, 1870), Appendix, p. 13.

15 See e.g. F. Paulsen, *Immanuel Kant* (Stuttgart, 1899), p. 323.

16 In connection with the view that Kant's ideas of God, immortality and possibly even freedom are to be understood as necessary fictions it is, of course, especially Vaihinger's work that comes to mind. But whatever may be thought of Vaihinger himself, passages such as *Werke* VIII 136–9 are enough to refute the view that this is Kant's doctrine. For

Kant himself the *summum bonum* cannot be reduced to a 'mere ideal' (p. 139), and God must somehow *exist*. See further below, n. 42.

17 Erich Adickes, the first editor of Kant's *Opus Postumum*, is relieved to discover that in that work 'the whole doctrine of the highest Good, along with the proofs for God and immortality which are based on it, have almost completely disappeared' (*Kantstudien, Ergänzungsheft* 50 (1920), p. 846). He believes that here at last Kant gets rid of the 'standpoint of mercenariness, which in the doctrine of the highest Good became wholly obvious' (*ibid.*, p. 720). Other commentators, such as N. Kemp-Smith, follow Adickes' lead.

But it is doubtful whether too much sense can be made of those sporadic passages in the *Opus Postumum* in which Kant attempts to connect God directly with the categorical imperative. More importantly, it would appear to be illegitimate to place the *Opus Postumum* above the three *Critiques* or even to treat it on a par with them. (The work remained a fragment, and its purpose in Kant's own mind is far from clear.) But the doctrine of the *summum bonum* appears in all three *Critiques*.

18 That elements of the old, pre-Kantian metaphysics remain in Kant's writings to the end would seem to be undebatable. But some recent writers surely overreact to the earlier view that Kant brings about a total break with the traditional metaphysics. Thus we can see no justification for G. Martin's assertion that 'Kant is continuing the tradition of Greek and medieval philosophy without a break' (*Kant's Metaphysics and Theory of Science*, transl. P. G. Lucas [Manchester University Press, 1955], p. 169).

19 *Cr.J.* #91; see also *Cr.p.R.* B395. To suggest that Kant 'takes over' these three doctrines from the enlightenment metaphysics of Wolff and his followers and 'merely gives them a new basis' is no substitute for an exposition. The new basis is not 'mere', and inevitably affects the doctrines themselves.

20 Man's finitude is constituted for Kant by the fact that, though a rational and therefore *self-determining* being he is *not* a *self-making* being. This latter doctrine, essential to Fichte, is so obviously false for Kant as to be disposed of in a subordinate clause, *Grundlegung* (*Werke* IV 451).

21 See e.g. *Cr.pr.R.* (*Werke* V 7k), *Grundlegung* (*Werke* IV 444) *Reflection* 6078 (*Werke* XVIII 443).

22 *Grundlegung* (*Werke* IV 451).

23 *Cr.pr.R.* (*Werke* V 81): 'For man and all other created rational being moral necessity is necessitation, i.e., obligation.' See also *Grundlegung* (*Werke* IV 414).

24 Kant criticizes the belief that such a stage can ever be reached, not only as contrary to all our self-knowledge (*Cr.pr.R.* [*Werke* V 123]) but also as morally dangerous (*Cr.pr.R.* [*Werke* V 83ff]). The belief is morally dangerous, not only because 'man is never more easily deceived than in what promotes a good opinion of himself' (*Religion innerhalb* [*Werke* VI 75]) but also, still more importantly, because the moment he had *in fact* reached such a stage he would no longer *consider* himself in need of moral constraint. This fear on Kant's part may seem paradoxical. If so, it reflects the condition of a being which is obligated to aim at angelic existence and yet cannot attain it.

25 'A duty to love is an *Unding*' (*Metaphysik der Sitten*, henceforth *M.d.S.*, [*Werke* VI 401]). Duty requires restraint while love presupposes absence of restraint. Hence we are obligated to do our duty but not to love doing it. (*Cr.pr.R.* [*Werke* V 83]; *M.d.S.* [*Werke* VI 378H]). Hence also Biblical commandments to love must be interpreted as commandments to act benevolently (*M.d.S.* [*Werke* VI 402]; *Cr.pr.R.* [*Werke* V 83]).

This is not to say, however, that the categorical imperative does not arouse feeling. But the feeling is respect rather than love, and respect is 'the feeling of our incapacity to attain to an idea that is law for us' (*Cr.J.* #27). Thus on the one hand, because of our *distance* from the moral law, this latter is present to us as obligation, and our feeling toward it is respect. But on the other hand, this distance is not absolute or without degrees; for the greater a person's *sense* of distance the less great is his *actual* distance – and the more respect passes into love. 'Reverential awe changes into affection, respect into love, because of the greater ease in satisfying that which we stand in awe of' (*Cr.pr.R.* [*Werke* v 84]). In short, if we consider not only what man ought to do but also what in the 'end' he will do if he does his duty, 'love is an indispensable addition to the incompleteness of human nature' 'Das Ende aller Dinge) [*Werke* VIII 338]).

Since man is a creature who has not made himself he is in principle incapable of wholly reaching the stage of the love of the moral law (*Cr.pr.R.* [*Werke* v 842; *Religion innerhalb* [*Werke* VI 145, 160]). How then can he be obligated even to *aim* at 'being holy' when he *cannot reach* this aim? Kant replies: if the mere striving is confined 'to this life' (*M.d.S.* [*Werke* VI 446ff]). The sobriety manifest in this limitation is still further stressed when Kant defines virtue as 'moral strength of the will', and, since this definition could apply also to a holy or superhuman being, when he qualifies it further as 'moral strength of the will of a *human* being in obeying his *duty*' (*M.d.S.* [*Werke* VI 405]. The emphasis is Kant's).

26 *Cr.pr.R.* (*Werke* v 84): 'The moral state in which a man can be is virtue, i.e., a moral state of mind in struggle. It is not holiness in a supposed possession of a will in total purity. This latter . . . is simply moral *Schwärmerei* and exaggerated self-esteem.'

27 First, man can know only his phenomenal nature (e.g. *Cr.pr.R.* B579); second, when passing moral judgment on himself, he is tempted both by pride (*Religion innerhalb* [*Werke* VI 68]) and a false, self-deprecating humility (*Religion innerhalb* [*Werke* VI 181]; also *M.d.S.* [*Werke* VI 441ff]).

28 See *Vorlesungen über die philosophische Religionslehre*, ed. K. H. L. Politz (Leipzig, 1830), p. 180.

29 Far from holding that the finite moral agent does not aim at ends Kant teaches that 'there can be no free action unless the agent intends a purpose' (*M.d.S.* [*Werke* VI 388ff] also *Cr.pr.R.* [*Werke* v 34]). However, to the extent to which he is moral, this agent aims at ends not because he desires them but because duty directs him (*Cr.pr.R.* [*Werke* v 45ff]; *Cr.J.* 91).

Thus, *for purposes of analysis* one may isolate the moral law as the ground of moral will (*Cr.pr.R.* [*Werke* v 109]), remaining aware that in so doing one reaches the categorical imperative in a form so abstract as to learn no more than 'what obligation as such implies' (*M.d.S.* [*Werke* VI 225]). This must not obscure the fact, however, that any concrete or complete moral willing and acting must include morally commanded purposes. If no such purpose were possible, then, 'since no action can be without purposes, all purposes would only be means to others, and a categorical imperative would be impossible' (*M.d.S.* [*Werke* VI 384ff]).

30 Cf. *Gemeinspruch* (*Werke* VIII 283): 'Happiness contains all those things (but not more than those things) which nature can give us; virtue, all that which none other than a person himself can give to or take from himself.' Because he holds that we cannot but aim at happiness (*Grundlegung* [*Werke* IV 415]; *Cr.pr.R.* [*Werke* v 25]), Kant denies that our own happiness can be among the objects of our duty (*M.d.S.* [*Werke* v 385]). Because of a (possibly exaggerated) emphasis on the need for self-acquisition of virtue, he denies that other people's virtue can be among the objects of our duty (*M.d.S.* [*Werke* VI 386ff]). See Paton, 'Kant's Idea of the Good', p. xxi.

31 H. J. Paton has rightly observed that in asserting that only a good will can be good without qualification Kant does not assert that a good will is the sole good. (*The Categorical Imperative* [University of Chicago Press, 1948], p. 43.) It must be added that only if it is geared to a purpose other than itself can the will be good at all. (See e.g. *Grundlegung* [*Werke* IV 394].)

32 This possibly somewhat daring interpretation is based on passages in which Kant asserts that even though moral willing-to-act is based on the moral law and not on considerations of success, moral reason 'cannot be indifferent' to such success. (E.g. *Religion innerhalb* [*Werke* VI 5], also *Cr.J.* #87.)

33 Kant writes: 'Assume that a person . . . persuaded himself that there is no God: he would still consider himself as unworthy if for that reason he considered the laws of duty as imaginary, invalid, unobligatory and decided to violate them unashamedly' (*Cr.J.* #87). Kant proceeds to take Spinoza as an example of a morally decent atheist and to show – since without an implied belief in God and immortality the moral will cannot believe itself to have the potential of success – that the actions of such as Spinoza belie their theories.

34 In our above account of the *summum bonum* we have been careful to exclude from consideration all passages which Schopenhauer and the neo-Kantians might rightly have regarded as lapses into eudaemonism. See e.g. *Eine Vorlesung Kants über Ethik*, ed. P. Menzer (Berlin, 1924), p. 102: 'Religion is that which is to give weight to morality, it is meant to be its spring. Here we recognize that the person who acts so as to be worthy of happiness may hope to attain it . . .' Having removed these obstacles, we see the Kantian grounds for hope in a share in the *summum bonum* solely in the duty to further it, together with the conditions without which such furthering cannot be done. There is no further reason to wonder why the *summum bonum* should appear in the *Cr.p.R.* primarily as object of (theoretical) hope and in the *Cr.pr.R.* primarily as an ultimate end to be furthered by our actions. Kant conjoins the theoretical and the practical aspects when he defines his three 'postulates' as 'theoretical but as such unprovable propositions which adhere inseparably to an apriori unconditionally valid practical law' (*Cr.pr.R.* [*Werke* V 122]).

35 So far as we know, this contradiction has been noticed only by Hans Urs von Balthasar, *Prometheus* (Heidelberg, 1947), p. 100.

36 See e.g. *Religion innerhalb* (*Werke* VI 133); *Gemeinspruch* (*Werke* VIII 278); *Cr.pr.R.* (*Werke* V 130). A comparison of these three passages shows a significant wavering which is responsible for our cautious formulation.

37 See *Religion innerhalb* (*Werke* VI 139).

38 See *Prolegomena to a Future Metaphysic* ## 57–9; also *Cr.J.*, especially ## 88, 59.

39 See 'Von einem neuerdings erhobenem vornehmen Ton . . .' (*Werke* VIII, 400ff); *Prolegomena* #57.

40 *Prolegomena* #57; also *Cr.J.* #59: 'all our cognition of God is only symbolic. Whoever takes as schematic such attributes as understanding and will . . . lapses into anthropomorphism, while to omit everything intuitive is to lapse into Deism.'

41 See *Cr.p.R.* B69; also *Prolegomena* (*Werke* IV 290ff).

42 See e.g. 'Von einem neuerdings erhobenem vornehmen Ton . . .' (*Werke* VIII 401); *Prolegomena* #58; *Cr.J.* ## 59, 88; *Religion innerhalb* (*Werke* VI 64).
   In the case of immortality, the analogical concept is temporal succession. This is symbolic in that we recognize that a 'future' life is future only *for us* (*Cr.p.R.* B839), i.e., a succession which from a hypothetically adopted divine standpoint does not exist (*Cr.pr.R.* [*Werke* V 123]). On this point see H. Heimsoeth, 'Metaphysische Motive in der Ausbildung des kritischen Idealismus', *Kantstudien, Ergänzungsheft* 71 (1956), p. 224.
   In the case of God, the analogical concepts needed are 'holiness of a legislator (creator) . . . (ii) goodness of a governor . . . (iii) justice as a judge . . .' (*Religion innerhalb* [*Werke* VI 162]).
   More important than a precise identification of the needed analogical concepts is a precise definition of the analogy required. Here the excesses of the recently fashionable ontological interpretation become fully evident. (See above, n. 18.) In criticism of Martin, J. Collins has rightly stressed that Kantian analogy has nothing in common with the Thomistic, if only because Kant rejects any causal inference from nature to God

(*Crosscurrents* 7, 1 (1957), p. 79). Kant himself writes as follows:

It is in a practical respect alone that an analogy between the divine understanding and will and those of man and his practical reason may be assumed, despite the fact that theoretically there is no analogy at all. Through the moral law which our reason prescribes to us authoritatively, not through the theory of the nature of things in themselves, there arises the concept of God which practical reason compels us to *create for ourselves*. ('Von einem neuerdings erhobenem vornehmen Ton . . .' [*Werke* VIII 401]. Italics added.)

Passages such as these necessitate the rejection of the 'ontological' interpretation of Kant's doctrine of analogy. They do not necessitate the acceptance of Vaihinger-style fictionalism. In Kant's authoritative view, we are morally certain of the conditions without which the *summum bonum* would be a 'mere ideal' ('Was heisst: sich im denken orientieren?' [*Werke* VIII 139]), and we are certain of these conditions while engaged in moral action.

As for the 'what' of these conditions, we can understand them only in anthropomorphic terms, but recognize at the same time that they are *only* such terms. As for the 'that' of the conditions, we are certain that they must *be*, not merely be *believed* to be, and this is all 'existence' can mean in this limiting case. Gerhard Krüger has rightly observed: 'Die theoretische Erkenntnis wird nicht dadurch erweitert, dass diese Objekte erkannt werden, sondern dadurch, dass die Ideen überhaupt Objekte bekommen. Nur dass ihnen ein Gegenstand entspricht ist gewiss, nicht was für einer' (G. Krüger, *Philosophie und Moral in der Kantischen Kritik* [Tübingen, 1967], p. 201).

43 See especially the *locus classicus*, *Cr.J.* #76; also the remarkable passage on 'absolute necessity', *Cr.p.R.* B641.
44 *Cr.J.* #76.
45 *Cr.J.* #76.
46 *Cr.J.* #87.
47 Reflection 6282 [*Werke* XVIII 548ff].
48 *Cr.p.R.* B641.
49 *Ibid.*
50 *Op. post.* (*Werke* XXI 66).
51 *Ende aller Dinge* (*Werke* VIII 355).
52 *Streit der Fakultäten* (*Werke* VII 63).
53 'Was heisst . . .' (*Werke* VIII 142).
54 *Streit der Fakultäten* (*Werke* VII 57).
55 'Vorrede zu R. B. Jachmanns Prüfung der Kantischen Religionsphilosophie' (*Werke* VIII 441).
56 *Religion innerhalb* (*Werke* VI 83).

Bibliographical essay

The best general introduction to Kant in English is S. Körner, *Kant* (Baltimore, 1955). See also R. Kroner, *Kant's Weltanschauung*, transl. J. E. Smith (University of Chicago Press, 1956), a work which rightly treats Kant's moral outlook as central to his philosophy as a whole; however, while including religion it does not *show* how 'morality leads to religion'.

Unless Kant's philosophy of religion is to be understood in abstraction from the whole Kantian corpus (a shallow and unproductive approach), pivotal importance attaches to the overall interpretation of his main work, the *Critique of Pure Reason*. The classical 'epistemological' account is H. Cohen's *Kants Theorie der Erfahrung* (4th edn., Berlin, 1925). In recent decades this approach to the first *Critique* has yielded to (or been rivalled by) a 'metaphysical' or 'ontological' one. See two works by H. Heimsoeth, i.e., *Studien zur Philosophie Immanuel Kants: Metaphysische Ursprünge und ontologische Grundlagen* (Cologne 1956), and 'Metaphysical motives in the development of critical idealism', in *Kant: Disputed Questions*, transl. and ed. by M. S. Gram (Chicago, 1967), pp. 158–99. (The essay originally appeared in *Kantstudien* 29 [1924], pp. 121–59.) See also G. Martin, *Kant's Metaphysics and Theory of Science*, transl. by P. G. Lucas (Manchester University Press, 1955); this work is thorough, readable and persuasive. Less persuasive but indispensable is M. Heidegger, *Kant and the Problem of Metaphysics*, transl. by J. S. Churchill (Bloomington, Indiana University Press, 1962). This work (which is often charged with arbitrariness) should be read in conjunction with E. Cassirer's celebrated review, 'Kant and the problem of metaphysics: remarks on Martin Heidegger's interpretation of Kant', in *Kant: Disputed Questions*, pp. 131–57. (This essay originally appeared in *Kantstudien* 34 [1929], pp. 10–26.) The indisputable merit of Heidegger's work is to stress Kant's emphasis on human finitude, played down if not overlooked by the earlier neo-Kantian emphasis on human rationality.

Heidegger does not, however, pursue the theme of human finitude from the cognitive to the moral realm. This task is accomplished superbly by G. Krüger, *Philosophie und Moral in der Kantischen Kritik* (Tübingen, 1931). This work should be read together with H. Cohen's *Kants Begründung der Ethik*, 2nd edn (Berlin, 1910), a profound, if dated, interpretation of the *Critique of Practical Reason*, a work in which the humanistic-idealistic passion inspired in this great neo-Kantian by Kant finds full expression. It is moving to see Cohen reject – with anguish, one feels – as incompatible with just that passion, his master's doctrine of the *summum bonum*, its central place in Kant's entire thought notwithstanding. The best English commentary on the second *Critique* is L. W. Beck, *A Commentary on Kant's Critique of Practical Reason* (Chicago, 1960), a work marked by its author's customary solid scholarship.

To have perceived the transition from morality to religion as the central problem of Kant's philosophy of religion is the merit of A. Schweitzer, *Die Religionsphilosophie Kants in der Kritik der reinen Vernunft bis zur Religion innerhalb der Grenzen der blossen Vernunft* (Freiburg, 1899). A unique study of Kant's religious thought, with a special view to its relation to Christianity, is J. Bohatec, *Die Religionsphilosophie Kants in der 'Religion innerhalb der Grenzen der blossen Vernunft'* (Hildesheim, 1966). This work removes many Kantian obscurities by citing at length sundry theologians of Kant's time, taken seriously by him but now (for the most part justly) forgotten.

The following are other works relevant to Kant's philosophy of religion. (Except for the crucial topic of the *summum bonum*, we confine ourselves to works in English.)

K. Barth, *Protestant Thought From Rousseau to Ritschl*, transl. B. Cozens (New York, 1959), ch. 4

J. Collins, *The Emergence of Philosophy of Religion* (New Haven, Yale University Press, 1967), chs. 3–5

M. Despland, *Kant on History and Religion* (Montreal, McGill-Queen's University Press, 1973)

A. Döring, 'Kants Lehre vom höchsten Gut', *Kantstudien* 4 (1898), 94–101

A. R. C. Duncan, *Practical Reason and Morality: A Study of Immanuel Kant's Foundations for the Metaphysics of Morals* (Edinburgh, 1957)

F. E. England, *Kant's Conception of God* (London, 1929)

E. L. Fackenheim, 'Kant and radical evil', *University of Toronto Quarterly* 23 (1953–4), 339–52

'Kant's concept of history', *Kantstudien* 48 (1956–7), 381–98

R. E. Gahringer, 'The metaphysical aspect of Kant's moral philosophy', *Ethics* 44 (1954), 277–91

T. M. Greene, 'The historical context and religious significance of Kant's *Religion*', in *Religion within the Limits of Reason Alone*, transl. T. M. Greene and H. H. Hudson (New York, 1960), pp. ix–lxxviii

G. E. Michalson, *The Historical Dimensions of a Rational Faith: The Role of History in Kant's Religious Thought* (Washington, University Press of America, 1977)

M. E. Miller, *The Moral Law and the Highest Good* (Melbourne University Press, 1928)

H. J. Paton, *The Categorical Imperative: A Study in Kant's Moral Philosophy* (London, 1946; University of Chicago Press, 1948)

'Kant's Idea of the Good', in *In Defence of Reason* (London, 1951), pp. 157–77

C. A. Raschke, *Moral Action, God and History in the Thought of Immanuel Kant* (Missoula, Montana, American Academy of Religion, Scholars Press, 1975)

J. R. Silber, 'The Copernican revolution in ethics: the Good reexamined', in *Kant: A Collection of Critical Essays*, ed. R. P. Wolff (New York, 1967), pp. 266–90

'Kant's conception of the highest Good as immanent and transcendent', *Philosophical Review* 67 (1959), 469–92

'The importance of the highest Good in Kant's ethics', *Ethics* 73 (1963), 179–97

'The metaphysical importance of the highest Good as the canon of pure reason in Kant's philosophy', *Texas Studies in Literature and Language* 1 (1959), 232–44

'The ethical significance of Kant's *Religion*', introduction to *Religion within the Limits of Reason Alone* (New York, 1960), pp. lxxix–cxlii

W. H. Walsh, 'Kant's moral theology', *Proceedings of the British Academy* 49 (1963), 263–89

C. C. J. Webb, *Kant's Philosophy of Religion* (Oxford, 1926)

A. W. Wood, *Kant's Moral Religion* (Ithaca, Cornell University Press, 1970)

Kant's Rational Theology (Ithaca, Cornell University Press, 1978). These two works, meant to complement each other, break new ground and provoke thought.

Y. Yovel, 'Bible interpretation as philosophical praxis: a study of Spinoza and Kant', *Journal of the History of Philosophy* 11 (1973), 189–212

'The God of Kant', *Scripta Hierosolymitana* 20 (1968), 88–123

'The highest Good and history in Kant's thought', *Archiv für Geschichte der Philosophie* 54 (1972), 238–83

Kant and the Philosophy of History (Princeton, 1979).

M. B. Zeldin, 'The *summum bonum*, the moral law, and the existence of God', *Kantstudien* 62 (1971), 43–54

The standard edition of Kant's collected *Schriften* is the so-called 'Prussian Academy Edition' (Berlin, 1902–   ), work on which is continuing under the sponsorship of the Deutsche Akademie der Wissenschaften in the German Democratic Republic. A softcover edition of the first nine volumes, comprising all of Kant's published works, has been issued by de Gruyter under the title *Kant Werke: Akademie-Textausgabe* (Berlin, 1968). Students will find the following translations generally reliable. *Critique of Pure Reason*, transl. N. K. Smith (2nd ed.; London, 1964); *Critique of Practical Reason*, transl. L. W. Beck (Indianapolis, 1956); *Critique of Judgment*, transl. T. M. Greene and H. H. Hudson (New York, 1960); *Perpetual Peace*, transl. L. W. Beck (Indianapolis, 1957); *Lectures on Philosophical Theology*, transl. A. W. Wood and G. M. Clark (Ithaca, New York, 1978). Two translations of the *Grundlegung zur Metaphysik der Sitten* can be commended: *Foundations of the Metaphysics of Morals*, transl. L. W. Beck (Indianapolis, 1959), and *Groundwork of the Metaphysic of Morals*, transl. H. J. Paton (New York, 1978).

2

Fichte and Schelling

J. HEYWOOD THOMAS

The public controversy concerning Fichte's religious outlook and his condemnation as an atheist make the connection between him and Schelling doubly interesting. It is as interesting to see the tension between idealist philosophy and theology[1] in both as the seedbed of modern atheism as it is to see in Schelling's development of Fichte's philosophy of religion the decisive formulation of those insights which idealism was to contribute to modern theology. Also interesting is the question of the relation between this emergent idealism and the philosophy of Kant whose spectre haunts all modern philosophy and theology. If it is in Fichte that one sees the obvious effect of the importance Kant gave to morality there is also a clear connection between Schelling's metaphysics of freedom and Kant's intuition that in dealing with the problem of freedom one was approaching the heart of the matter in metaphysics. In his masterly survey of post-Kantian idealist systems Frederick Copleston has aptly characterized them as not only continuing Kant's understanding of a possible metaphysic but inflating his theory of knowledge into a metaphysics of reality.[2] It will be particularly important for us in this context to see how this metaphysics accommodated religion; for, as we have said, one of the reasons why both Fichte (1762–1814) and Schelling (1775–1854) are interesting to the modern historian of religious thought is that each is so far from being a crypto-theologian that his thought can be interpreted as posing the question of what sense can be given to the fundamental ideas of Christianity, God, creation, revelation and redemption. Thus one can appreciate from a study of Schelling's enormous influence on Tillich, which the two dissertations reveal, that Tillich had seen the significance of Schelling for the twentieth century – and one can say that Fichte's significance can in like manner be appreciated. That it has not been appreciated is perhaps due to the fact that there has been no theologian of similar stature to Tillich whose thought has reflected the influence of Fichte.

Nevertheless the influence of Fichte could well be said to be as pervasive as that of Kant – and indeed the Kantianism of so much German theology at the turn of this century may have in fact reflected the influence of Fichte more than that of Kant himself. It is certain that Fichte and Schelling represented two types of thought sufficiently well for E. Hirsch in the 1930s to attribute much of the disagreement between himself and Tillich to the fact that he was attracted to Fichte and Tillich to Schelling.[3] Nor was it only in Germany that Fichte was still read. From the middle of the nineteenth century until the second decade of this one, Fichte's stock was high with the British philosophical public. In the 1860s few educated men in Britain had not heard or read something of Fichte: and, because of T. H. Green's debt to him,[4] the first generation of twentieth-century readers of philosophy would have been familiar with his thought.

Fichte

To grasp anew what Fichte did in the Philosophy of Religion one must recall the achievement of Kant. One of the main questions which Kant had posed for philosophy of religion was not merely the relation of faith to knowledge but the very possibility of conceiving the object of faith. Side by side in the critical philosophy there is an equal stress on the significance of the idea of God as the warrant for morality and the problematic character of the idea which is the Ideal of Reason. In a sense, one can say that Fichte followed the moral emphasis purely and simply and developed in his theory of the absolute ego something which may perhaps properly be called a religious outlook but can hardly be described as orthodox Christianity. Schelling's philosophical development, by contrast, could perhaps be understood as the progression from a purely metaphysical and religiously sterile outlook to a metaphysics of religion or a metaphysical theology that is responsive to revelation and the religious experience.[5] We have, then, two examples of a common problem but two very different solutions despite their close historical connection.

Fichte's first philosophical publication was the *Essay towards a Critique of all Revelation* (1792) which he had written partly out of his anxiety to please Kant and in which he developed the Kantian view of faith as finding its warrant in practical reason. In the years that followed his appointment to the Chair of Philosophy at Jena in 1794 Fichte set about developing an idealist system on the basis of the critical philosophy – a critical idealism rather than a mere synthesis of realism and idealism. Not only did he publish a theory of science which expounded his theoretical deduction of consciousness but he published also his works on natural right and ethics both of which are said to be 'according to the principles of the theory of science'. The importance of these works is twofold. In the first place, they illustrate the way in which Fichte sought a better appreciation of the final unity of theoretical and practical reason. The famous *Essay* of 1792 takes this as its point of departure and reveals a concern with the more metaphysical aspects of Kant than the problems of practical reason as such. This stance which characterizes Fichte's earliest work is both described and emphasized in his lecture *On the Vocation of a Scholar* where he speaks of this highest good, the unity of practical and theoretical reason.

The perfect harmony of man with himself, – and that this may be practicable, the harmony of all external things with his necessary practical ideas of them, – the ideas which determine what these things *should be*; – this is the ultimate and highest purpose of human existence. This harmony is, to use the language of the critical philosophy, the Highest Good; which Highest Good, *considered absolutely*, as follows from what we have already said, has no parts, but is perfectly simple and indivisible, – it is the complete harmony of a rational being with himself. But in reference to a rational being who is dependent on external things, it may be considered twofold; – as the harmony of the Will with the idea of an Eternal Will, or, *moral goodness*; and as the harmony of external things with our Will (our rational will, of course), or *happiness*.[6]

The problem which occupied Fichte in the 1790s, then, was the harmonization of our ideal unity of being with the assertion by Kant of human freedom. This problem was to remain one of the mainsprings of his philosophy.

The nineteenth century opened to the reverberations of the atheism controversy which had brought his Jena career to an end.[7] To understand his position, however, it is necessary to emphasize that he clearly had no intention of developing an atheist philosophy. Rather he had been trying to develop a philosophy of freedom starting out from the recognition by the self of its autonomy. This was for him as invigorating an experience as Wordsworth's 'very heaven' of being young in the morn of the Revolution. That assertion of pure autonomy may or may not be a tacit atheism in Kant. However, in the very Kantian piece written by Fichte's colleague, Forberg, concerning the 'evolution of the concept of religion' there was no doubt about the secularization of religion. It is for Forberg nothing but a practical belief in a moral world government, a living faith in the Kingdom of God that will come upon earth. By this 'moral government of the world' (*moralische Weltregierung*) Forberg means simply an empirical warrant for the final triumph of the good. Religion is identified with duty, the duty not of believing in God the moral governor of the world, but of acting as if one believed this. Puzzled and more than a little embarrassed by all this polemic which echoed so much of his own vigorous language Fichte wrote and published his essay 'On the Foundation of our Belief in a Divine Government of the Universe' (1798). Here he sets out both his agreement with Forberg and his more speculative understanding of the problem. Like Forberg he sees no other source of the certainty of God's existence than faith and conscience and like Kant he sees faith as the expression of freedom.[8] As has been said already, Fichte had sought a fundamental unity of theoretical and practical reasons. He came to realize that this was inadequate as a bridge between the two apparently independent reasons of determination, nature and morality. Now in the essay on divine government he views the 'world' not merely as something simply given, different from mind, but as a reality that arises from the inner sense of freedom. Everything, that is, had to be understood as originating from the same source which disclosed to us our moral commitment. The true reality of things is this moral order which Fichte speaks of as 'the divine that we accept'. Fulfilment of duty makes this divine real to us. 'Real atheism . . . consists in . . . refusing to obey the voice of our conscience until we believe that we can see a happy outcome.'[9] Fichte clarifies this moral interpretation of atheism further by saying that the moral order of the world of which he has spoken cannot be conceived as a particular being (*ein besonderes wesen*) with the attributes of personality and consciousness. Did God possess such attributes he would be finite and no longer God. His conclusion is somewhat paradoxical. On the one hand, he insists that God's existence is the source of all other certitude and goes on to use biblical language to speak of the relation between God and the world. On the other hand, however, he insists as before that 'the concept of God as a particular substance is impossible and contradictory'.[10] As a result of this publication Fichte was charged with atheism and he was obliged to leave Jena. But not before he had vigorously defended himself against a charge which to him seemed plainly wrong. So far from being an atheist he was, he thought, a veritable defender of faith. These polemical pieces of which the most important is the *Appellation an das Publikum* do not add anything substantial to the article. He repeats his distinction between the theoretical and the practical as two areas of knowledge with two quite different ways of knowing. The object of theoretical knowledge is the finite world of the sensible whereas the area of the practical is the suprasensible world of moral feeling. In this sense morality and religion are identical: what distinguishes them is that morality is the expression of this suprasensible relation in action and religion expresses it in faith. 'The relation of the deity to us, as moral beings, is the immediately given; a particular being of this deity comes to be conceived merely as a result of our finite imagination.'[11] His rejection of the idea of God as substance Fichte defends as a means of asserting God's transcendence and seeks to take the battle into his critics' camp by saying that it is no more than a rejection of idolatry. 'What they call God is to me an idol . . . For me God is simply and solely the ruler of the suprasensible world. Their God I deny . . . and this makes me in no sense an atheist but rather a defender of religion.'[12] Christianity, says Fichte is addressed not to speculation but the moral sense of man. His critics would make rational knowledge the principle of life whereas for him the primary thing was the vital system of feelings. It was the transcendent character of feeling which made the assertion of the suprasensible possible and faith expressed the certainty of that awareness.

It will be useful to ask how seriously we ought to take Fichte's self-portrait because it will help us understand in what sense the religious elements of his later writings are to be construed. There can be little doubt that Fichte was perfectly sincere in his claim that he was defending religion. This certainly was the view of Schlegel who also agreed with Fichte's identification of his philosophy and the Christian viewpoint in his defence of Fichte published in 1799 as an open letter, *To the Germans*.[13] Moreover, if Fichte has not been sincere in his claim why should he continue in 1806 to show such a keen desire to relate his theory to the Christian tradition?[14] His anxiety to defend true religion is the key to our understanding of the early writings. Taken merely on its own *The Science of Knowledge* of 1794 could be read as an existentialist celebration of the absurdity of human existence, thrown into the world and cursed to finitude by a God who does not appear. Not only does the passion of Fichte's self-defence betoken a missionary zeal but the cast of his whole thinking shows how wrong it would be to read the development of his thought as the deliberate elaboration of an atheistic solipsism which then masquerades as religion. How far removed it was from solipsism has already been obvious from the reference to the lectures on the vocation of the scholar.[15] Frederick Copleston and others have pointed out how Fichte's thought develops in an increasingly religious direction after the atheism controversy.[16]

In the light of his 'defence of religion' one must take at more or less its face-value the discussion of the idea of 'church' in *The Science of Ethics* (1798). The absence of any notion of church was one of the notable features of the *Critique of all Revelation* which seems to have dispensed with the Kantian view of the church as the extra incentive which was needed in the struggle for moral progress. For Fichte in 1792 the church would have smacked too much of a heteronomous determination of man. Yet what this must mean is that though this talk of 'church' is to be regarded as indeed a religious theory there is nothing here which goes beyond a humanist ideal of social unity. It is, says Fichte, 'an ethical commonwealth', a 'reciprocity amongst all rational beings for the purpose of producing common practical convictions'.[17] This idea of 'church' is both an implication of the first principle of the *Wissenschaftslehre*, that 'the ego absolutely posits itself' and a development of it in the sense that it is here transformed by his theory of interpersonality. That is to say, the practical conviction is merely an expression of the ego's absolute positing of itself; but the theory of interpersonality means that such a conviction is consistently involved in a ceaseless dialogue. There is, in a word, a mutual struggle for truth. This, says Fichte, can only be achieved if there is a common ground of agreement and to this he gives the ecclesiastical name of 'symbol' without suggesting that it has either the revelatory or the institutional character of creed. Even more significant is the fact that for Fichte the most important function in society is fulfilled by neither this 'church' nor the State but by a third institution which ensures that both are open to progress. This third institution he calls the 'republic of scholars'. His picture of this university is both idealistic and realistic. It is realistic in so far as he clearly understands that the ideal of dialogue is incapable of being achieved by many citizens and its idealism lies in its view of the function of the University as the only hope for progress from general ignorance and the means in fact of producing both Church and State.

It is clear from the account that Fichte's religious thought underwent a significant development in the period from 1792 to 1800 which could be briefly characterized as the development of a transcendental moralism against the background of a Kantian doctrine of religion as based on morality. The *Critique of all Revelation* was, as we have seen, a thoroughly Kantian work which seemed to make explicit the religious implications of Kant's philosophy. The existence of morality presupposes the existence of God not only as the reconciliation of the orders of nature and morality, the Power who can grant happiness proportionate to virtue but also as the perfect expression of the moral ideal itself. So beginning from the foundation of Kantian ethics Fichte proceeded to the concept of God as to the deduction of the concept of revelation. The consciousness of the moral law is a divine proclamation of that law. That moral law as God's law is what indeed gives religion its character as something which *binds* us.[18] Like Kant, Fichte speaks not only of the holy will but also of man's radical evil which is what could be called the presupposition of revelation. However he went on to transform the critical philosophy which had insisted on the primacy of the practical reason into an ethical idealism. By 1798 the moralism which had been characteristic of Fichte's thought from the 1792 *Essay* had become more severe and the writings of the atheism controversy are a condemnation of eudaemonism as 'radical blindness' and 'alienation' from God's law, as idolatry and the denial of all true religion. The identification of God and the moral order and of religion and morality which was clear enough in the article 'On the Foundation of our Belief in a Divine Government of the Universe' is given strident emphasis in *Appellation an das Publikum*. There Fichte says 'The man who wants pleasure . . . has no religion . . . A God who is supposed to aid lust is a despicable being.'[19] Similarly, in two unpublished lectures which belong to this period[20] he says 'The true faith is the belief in the possibility of a realization of the moral law: there is no other faith . . . Any faith which does not flow from moral conviction and persuasion is a pseudo-faith, a superstition.' From this we can see that whereas in 1792 Fichte agreed with Kant that religion was an indispensable aid to morality by 1799 he was prepared to claim for duty a validity of its own with no reference at all to God. He refers, in a letter of 5 November 1799 to his wife, to the benefits of the controversy which he had understood as he was writing *The Vocation of Man*, a work of the important transitional period. 'In the course of the composition of this present work', he says, 'I have taken a closer look at religion than ever before. I am emotionally moved only by total clarity; the clarity I have achieved here could not fail to grip my heart.'[21] He speaks of the absolute ego as the Absolute and eventually as Life and Light and finally as God.

Fichte's theory of interpersonality has certainly been important in this development of a moralistic view of religion. It is much more obviously so in his theory of history.[22] The point is that the entire dialectic of history is interpreted as a twofold relation, the self-same relation of free response which is characteristic of recognizing someone else as a person. In *The Science of Rights* he emphasizes this need for individuals to be educated to be men and in this context he refers to the Book of Genesis as 'an old and venerable chronicle, which, indeed, contains throughout the profoundest, sublimest wisdom, and establishes results, to which all philosophy must, after all, return'.[23] As far as he himself was concerned, Fichte seems to have turned again in 1797 to consider the Genesis story and he interprets it as historical, following in all probability the lead of those pioneer biblical scholars, Eichhorn and Gabler.[24] However, he handles the myth with great freedom, assuming that God has not merely called a first pair of men to freedom but endowed a whole people with a particular knowledge and morality. As well as this *Urvolk* a second people quite devoid of culture was created. Thus the dialectic spoken of already becomes possible because these two races meet. In other words, history is produced by the interaction of these two races. We must note this peculiar view of history not so much because it is what gave rise to Fichte's nationalism but because it is the source also of his strange view of the origin of Christianity. The *Urvolk* lived in Asia and from there the original message of religion was somehow transmitted to Jesus and to the author of the Fourth Gospel without any Jewish mediation whatsoever. More significant is the general theory of the nature of history that he developed. In *Characteristics of the Present Age* (1806) he defines the purpose or end of mankind's life as the ordering of 'all their relations with freedom according to reason'.[25] He then proceeds[26] to distinguish two main epochs or ages: the one when there is not as yet a voluntary and reasonable ordering of relations and the one when this is achieved. This basic distinction, however, yields the following five-fold division of history:

1   the age of the pure domination of the instinct of reason
2   the age of a first revolt of freedom against this authority
3   the age of a gradual release of freedom from the mere instinct of reason
4   the age when consciousness is first achieved and a consistent attempt is make to order everything according to this reason in freedom
5   the age when everything is ordered according to reason in freedom.

It is with the third of these ages that Fichte was concerned as 'the present age'. Similarly, he seems to have abandoned his hypothesis of the *Urvolk* when in *Staatslehre* (1813) he developed a new understanding of the relation of receptivity and spontaneity. Fichte had always understood that pure spontaneity is merely formal and, if it is to be active and concrete, needs content. However, the hypothesis of the two original people representing receptivity and spontaneity was an inadequate answer to the problem of how freedom gains this content. Shortly before his death, as a result of reflecting on the problem of miracles, Fichte came to the conclusion that besides the original infusion of meaning in history from time to time the Absolute was at work in history. This was the significance of heroic individuals like Jesus. Consequently in the *Staatslehre* Jesus no longer figures as a recipient of some original Asian revelation but as a new, indeed ultimate, image which absolute reason has introduced into this world. This image is the solution to the problem of spontaneity and receptivity in that this image is both the indispensable authority for man and yet is nothing but the call of all men to freedom. What faith here received from Christ must therefore be expressed in human action. Men must recognize each other as images of absolute value.

We have seen how Fichte's declared aim in his later writings was the clarification of his religious ideas. In no respect is this more true than the way in which those writings reveal what he understood by spirituality. For it has been well said by C. K. Hunter[27] that the recent investigation of Fichte which uses the theory of interpersonality as the interpretative key has shown how little he has to say in his earlier work about the experience of love. It is only in the popular writings of 1805–8 – particularly in *Characteristics of the Present Age* (1800) and *The Way towards the Blessed Life* (1806) – that he describes the phenomenon of love. In the period immediately following the atheism controversy Fichte had insisted that he regarded the moral world-order which is God as an *ordo ordinans*[28] and this was the way he continued to speak of God in the *Wissenschaftslehre* of 1804.[29] However, once again it is instructive to consider *The Vocation of Man* which belongs to the transitional period of 1800. Here Fichte uses language which is almost personal – 'the eternal and infinite Will', 'creative Life', even 'the sublime and living Will, named by no name and compassed by no concept';[30] but there is also a clear insistence that personality as something finite does not apply to God. The work has a distinctly theistic tone not only because of the language used of God but also because the doctrine of the infinite will is a matter of faith. However, idealism it still remains because everything is 'a wonderful dream'.[31] The tone is, nevertheless, important in that it represents the task of the later works which was that of giving this vision of faith a clear philosophical expression. In Fichte's early work all theoretical and practical knowledge is founded in and through free activity. Viewed theoretically it is intellectual intuition of the act whereby the absolute self posits itself: practically it is known in our experience of longing for absolute autonomy. In the later work, however, human life is fundamentally love of 'God' – which makes it particularly important to see what Fichte understands by the idea of God. We have seen both the development of Fichte's philosophy and its very strong sense of consistency. That is, Fichte never consciously rejected his early thinking, however much he modified it. Nevertheless in *Darstellung der Wissenschaftslehre* (1801) he asserts the primacy of Being and he speaks of Absolute Being coming to a knowledge of itself in human knowledge of reality. Even more mystical – or at least Platonic – is the language of the 1804 lectures on the theory of science. There the divine Being is spoken of as Light which divides itself into Being and Thought. Yet once again Fichte insists that God transcends our conceptual grasp. The care with which Fichte here draws the parallel between himself and Spinoza is very revealing. Both he and Spinoza, he says, have one absolute substance and for both finite knowledge is an absolute accident of this substance, absolutely determined by Being itself. The two systems, however, differ radically on the question of the transition from substance to accident. Since the question is never really raised by Spinoza there is no definition of this transition. Now, because Fichte was posing the problem of the critical philosophy for this monistic philosophy he insists that there are two principles to be asserted – Absolute

Being and absolute freedom. So his intention could be said to be an attempt at correcting Spinoza by means of Kant's philosophy and correcting Kant by means of Spinoza. Thus *The Way to the Blessed Life* defines the idea of God as Being, Absolute Being but identifies Being and Life. It is true that this Life is one and indivisible; but it is expressed in the distinctions of its external manifestation. That manifestation is possible because of God's *Dasein* in consciousness. 'What does this consciousness contain?', asks Fichte and he replies that it is nothing but the world. 'In consciousness the divine Life is inevitably transformed into an abiding world.'[32] We cannot understand this language as expressing any traditional doctrine of transcendence, as is clear from the way in which Fichte speaks of this love as manifested by life. For at least the whole of his life after the period of *The Vocation of Man* Fichte thought of God as the immanent creativity of human imagination and spirituality. What is so intriguing is the fact that he does not regard the transcendental structures of consciousness as subject to historical processes. Once again, however, it must be insisted that we are not dealing with anything other than the way in which man can be Shelley's Prometheus. Thus spirituality is a matter of proper self-relation. Life can become real rather than apparent through aspiration towards the eternal: love divides the apparent being and reunites this divided being of the self.[33] The basis of all finite existence is therefore to be found in this love of God because as phenomenal that is the 'feeling of being as being', felt as a 'holding together on one's own'. Thus man knows the 'original image of his true and proper being'.[34]

As we have seen, *Characteristics of the Present Age* offers not so much a metaphysic of love as one of a 'world-plan' for history. Even so, it is worth emphasizing that such a view of history as governed by the production of harmonious, free, rational relations does express very clearly the interpersonal nature of human history. And what is especially significant is that the only sense given here to the notion of an eternal rational existence is that of the human species. That is to say, it is the life of men in 'all their relations' which is seen as the goal so that it is neither a question of the individual in his empirical solitariness nor of some transcendent non-empirical existent. Similarly in *Addresses to the German Nation*[35] the history of culture in the modern world is described as a religious progress; but it is the development of a consciousness of 'clear knowledge' in three stages. The first step was to rid religion of the external form of authority which deprived it of freedom; the second step was to discover this religion within ourselves; and the final step is perfectly to educate 'the nation to manhood'. Now, though the history of culture is thus interpreted as in some sense a religious phenomenon there are two respects in which Fichte seems to be moving away from orthodox theism, if not indeed religion. In all three of the works we have considered the later stages of Fichte's fivefold division of history are described in religious language and indeed Fichte asserts at the end of *Characteristics of the Present Age* that his view of history is 'a religious theory' recognizing all earthly life as the necessary development of the one good and perfectly blessed divine life. However, the emphasis on 'clear knowledge' suggests that the religious character of this philosophy is from beginning to end an emphasis on the immanence of the divine life in knowledge and action. Secondly, the emphasis on religion becomes noticeably less in the writings of the period after 1806 so that the relative importance of these expressions of Fichte's religious thought is open to question. If, then, we ask finally whether Fichte did indeed move away from the moralism of his early treatment of religion it would seem difficult to escape von Baader's conclusion that Fichte by his refusal to attribute personality to God failed to overcome 'baneful spiritualism and baneful naturalism'.[36] The relevance of Fichte for our own thinking on religion and theology has been attacked only obliquely; but it cannot be denied that there have been and are contemporary theologians who find in Fichte intimations at least of a basis for theism. The central theme of his thinking is his stress on the common origin of freedom and determination, and nobody who has read such widely different thinkers as Tillich and Berdyaev can fail to recognize therein a theme of modern theology which is indeed metaphysical but in no sense empty. Moving backwards, as it were, in Fichte's thought, the interpretation he gives of history likewise strikes readers of Niebuhr as speaking a similarly realistic message though in very different and indeed essentially abstract language. But for all the nobility of his view of history there will remain in it a fatal weakness for the generation of theologians who have learned from Kierkegaard and Heidegger that we deceive ourselves if we think of the human consciousness as non-historical. Fichte speaks of unity and wholeness in a peculiarly non-human because non-historical fashion. This is why the *Critique of All Revelation* both poses a central problem of philosophy of religion and yet fails to do full justice to the concept of religion. Fichte saw clearly enough that revelation was a central issue for the understanding of religion and its claim to our assent. Not only was he thus continuing a dominant theme of eighteenth-century religious controversy but he was articulating this notion in a way which was to prove more characteristic of the nineteenth and twentieth centuries. Like Kant Fichte saw religion as essentially morality but his appreciation of a consequent difference between the realm of theological propositions and a religious life was more the perspective of Schleiermacher and nineteenth-century liberalism if not indeed Feuerbach. Even so, the identification of religion and morality must result in a neglect of the positivity of religion which for our historically-minded age must represent the starting-point for any investigation of religion. Doubtless we find Fichte's legacy essentially problematic because it is as difficult to grasp as it is abstract: what we must not forget is that it is a legacy that has at least in part also formed us and the theological concern of our time.

Schelling

To many of his contemporaries Schelling was seen as Hegel had portrayed him and, for the most part, scholars both in the nineteenth century and well into the twentieth century treated him as the link between Fichte and Hegel.[37] Indeed Schelling himself contributed to this kind of misunderstanding because the bulk of his writing was published before 1804. So the general impression among his contemporaries in the nineteenth century that he was the first heir of the Fichtean legacy has been repeated by scholars who look to his early work for the evidence of his lasting contribution to the history of philosophy. There is no denying the fact that it was Fichte's influence which turned this 'superior exemplar of a superior class'[38] into a rebel. As Nauen says, 'Schelling from the outset rejected the moderate Kantianism prevalent at Tübingen' and 'preferred the intellectual integrity of Fichte's radical Kantianism to the uncertainties of Christian orthodoxy'.[39] True, Schelling had clearly hoped when he published his work on myths (*Über Mythen Historische Sagen und Philosopheme der ältesten Welt*) in 1792 that he would be able to revolutionize Tübingen from within; but even so his aim was to fight 'the philosophers in sheep's clothing'.[40] Two years later, however, he abandoned his exegetical work and devoted himself to the new Kantian philosophy developed by Fichte. His paper 'On the possibility of a form for all philosophy' (1794) shows him to be for the most part a faithful disciple of Fichte acknowledged indeed by the mentor as a new and brilliant follower.[41] Yet from the beginning there were some very significant differences between them which only gradually became obvious and which were later to become a source of contention and a matter for public comment. In the first philosophical publication Schelling had not accepted Fichte's estimate of moral thinking as the paradigm for all thought. What for Fichte was a mastery to be extended from the moral sphere to that of human knowledge was for Schelling man's total awareness of himself as the free cause of all things.[42] Whereas Fichte had spoken of the present age as the period of increasing freedom Schelling felt that the discovery of human freedom implied a revolutionary attitude to the *status quo*.[43] There was too a fundamental difference of opinion about the nature of man's knowledge of the ground or basis of science (*Grundsatz*). For both Fichte and Schelling this could be conceived; but for Fichte such knowledge was abstract and purely formal while for Schelling there was what he calls in 'On the possibility of a form for all philosophy' an 'absolute in human knowledge'.[44] Fichte regarded the deduction of the foundation of science as the highest form of knowledge.[45] In Schelling's eyes, however, the highest form of knowledge transcended both theoretical and practical knowledge and unified both. What was in Fichte an epistemological theory was now being transformed by Schelling into a metaphysical view; for Schelling argues in 'On the possibility of a form for all philosophy' that as well as being the source of scientific and moral meaning man was the source of the world's 'objectivity'. *On the Ego* (1795) was intended, he tells us at the outset, to free men from their 'slavery to objective truth' and to convince them that they were the source of all truth and reality.[46] He distinguishes between the empirical and the absolute ego, saying 'The completed system of science starts with the absolute ego.'[47] The absolute ego which is grasped only in intellectual intuition is the first principle of all truth and ultimate source of all reality. With this new philosophical achievement went the vision of an ideal society where freedom was achieved and right being identical with duty there was no need for coercion.[48] This drew from both Hölderlin and Hegel the criticism that Schelling was being distracted from their common revolutionary educative purpose by his mystical tendencies. It may well be that the unknown correspondent of the *Philosophical Letters on Dogmatism and Criticism* (1795–6), as Nauen maintains,[49] was Hölderlin. If so, then the letters show Schelling defending Fichte against Hölderlin whose enthusiasm for Fichte's thought did not extend to those features which appealed especially to Schelling. Nevertheless Schelling became convinced of the danger of quietism and agreed with Hölderlin that it was a mistake to base moral and political freedom in a doctrine which by its mysticism suggested such quietism. He acknowledged the truth of Hegel's criticism of his earlier mysticism that it was more suitable for gods than for men.[50] The *Philosophical Letters* were written, then, in defence of criticism (Fichte) against Spinozistic dogmatism; but they evince an elitism foreign to Fichte. Only the philosopher is fully conscious of his freedom.[51]

In his writings prior to 1801 Schelling concerned himself with two problems – that of making human freedom the science of all human experience and that of integrating this freedom and nature. Nauen remarks that momentarily Schelling tried to make out the connection between these two lines of thought:

Reflecting the influence of Hölderlin on his thinking, convincing neither himself nor his reader, Schelling argued that in the course of its own self-discovery the human spirit would eventually discover in the beautiful the means whereby it could find itself in the world, and that it was in art that human freedom and nature reached a state of perfect equipoise.[52]

The philosophy of identity which Schelling developed in the opening years of the nineteenth century is his attempt to answer the question of the nature of the absolute and its relation to particulars. In *Darstellung meines Systems der Philosophie* (1801), a work which is Spinozistic certainly in its form and possibly also in its content, he tried to show that 'the highest law of the existence of Reason, and so of all existence, is the law of identity'.[53] Subject and object unite in absolute Reason 'the total indifference of subjective and objective'. Schelling was becoming increasingly conscious of his need to elaborate a philosophy of nature which would completely overhaul Fichte's transcendental idealism. As the new century began Fichte and Schelling were taking different paths and Schelling's philosophy of nature did not meet with Fichte's approval. Though the differences between them were hardly known by the public the philosophers themselves were in no doubt as several texts of the period show.[54] Indeed the disagreement between the two philosophers could be noticed by the attentive (as early as 1798–9, the winter when Henrik Steffens was a student in Jena).

What was so pleasant at that time in Jena was the agreement which reigned between the authors of so important a transformation in literature. Just as in an organic development the most varied forms have a common point of departure . . . so then everyone thought they were undertaking a common task; from that was born a spiritual alliance which was to have an important effect. Fichte and Schelling had well understood their differences but they had not expressed it. However, they did not see one another often; though Fichte could believe that Schelling's speculative point of view started from a position like his own, he could not stomach Schelling's philosophy of nature. There indeed remained hidden a difference and even a hostile separation. But because Fichte moved only in ethics and the related realms of jurisprudence, Fichte and Schelling travelled together for a while and did not enter into conflict because they did not meet one another.[55]

If we follow Steffens' suggestion that beginning from a common point of departure they took their separate routes we can usefully note the difference between their philosophies of nature by noting first their agreement. Following Fichte Schelling maintained that nature is a positing (*Setzung*) of the ego. He also agreed with Fichte that the forms of nature could be deduced *a priori* and that nature could only exist in these forms. Finally he, like Fichte, sees in each determined natural phenomenon a determination

(*Bestimmung*) of the ego's freedom. However, whereas Fichte could not see this determination as the basis of my being myself, Schelling thought that we can intellectually intuit ourselves and deduce the fact as fact. Fichte regarded factual necessity as the immutable character of fact. Nature determines us according to a factual necessity; we do not possess an intuition which enables us to perceive a free movement in it from one moment to another. Schelling, on the other hand, saw nature as a subject-object which is itself spontaneous, which freely poses the forms it invents. Nature itself forms consciousness. The formative principle of nature is then to be found objectively in nature itself and is not, as Fichte thought, simply subjectively transposed into nature. This principle Schelling regards as an unconscious Ego, a 'soul of the world'. According to Fichte finality in nature rests on reciprocal causality and is explained only by presupposing certain factually necessary forces. For Fichte what is factual, purely factual, can never be deduced but can only be experienced. The science of nature must proceed inductively. By contrast Schelling knew nothing that was not deducible: for him the science of nature is an *a priori* deduction. Both nature and spirit, in his view, equally take as their necessary point of departure an ultimate unity which is an objective, self-realizing, reason. Fichte, however, insisted that a unity of nature and spirit is only produced by the activity of a moral order to the world. Consequently according to Schelling the absolute is unknowable while for Fichte it can be known by the intellect. In a sense, what Fichte has done is to apply the principle of natural necessity as strictly as Kant and in exactly the same way to leave room for freedom and a suprasensible order. Lauth shows that this difference between Fichte's and Schelling's views of nature which had been clarified by 1801 was precisely the point made by Fichte many years later in the Eighth Lecture of his *Grundzüge des gegenwärtigen Zeitalters*.[56] There Fichte concludes:

After all, that seems clearly to be the spirit of the particular period of our epoch in which we live: the system of well-balanced experience, alone worthwhile, seems to be in a fair way of disappearing and in opposition to it is the system of a delirium which, thanks to a pretended speculation, will throw out experience itself from the domain which belongs to it alone and will end by introducing disorder.[57]

Well could Fichte have remarked that he did not need Hegel's *The difference between the systems of Fichte and Schelling* to tell him that they were in fact different.[58]

What is much more difficult to decide is where we are to locate Schelling's contribution and importance. His significance for the development of a literary theory of Romanticism makes him indeed the 'Prince of Romantics'; but Gutman's point is then well taken, that the Prince is in fact to be found in the years before 1810.[59] On the other hand, is it more likely that Tillich[60] is correct in his judgment that Schelling's important achievement was the 'positive philosophy' of his later years? This seems as much of a conundrum as the related question of the number of periods – five (Windelband), four (Zeller and Fischer) or just two (von Hartmann and Drews).[61] Perhaps the wisest response to both is the suggestion made by Tilliette that this major problem of Schelling *forschung* is a false problem.[62] For however useful and indeed necessary it is to consider Schelling's work in different periods, to make that division an interpretation of his philosophy is a quite erroneous elevation of an exegetical device. Tilliette's description is most apt – Schelling's thought is a philosophy in process of becoming; and this is as true of his philosophy of religion as of the system as a whole (if indeed we do attribute such a final unity to his philosophy). Tillich has emphasized the development of religious categories in Schelling's thought and this means that religion was not a topic to which he turned only with the publication of *Freedom* in 1809. From the beginning he had shared the contemporary enthusiasm for Greek culture and especially Greek mythology and religion. It would be useful to consider for a moment this interest in myth as an example of the relation of Schelling's early and late periods and the consistent concern therein with the problem of religion. Besides his earliest writings on myths there are references to the problem in *Philosophical Letters on Dogmatism and Criticism* (1795), in the article 'Is a philosophy of history possible?' (1797), in the main work of the Jena period, *System of Transcendental Idealism* (1800) and above all in *Philosophy of Art* (1802–3). The importance of myth as a problem for thought in this period is evident from the material which was to hand – Kant's *Conjectures on the beginning of the history of humanity* (*Mutmasslicher Anfang der Menschengeschichte*) and Herder's *The most ancient documents of the human race*. As Steffen Dietzsch has pointed out in emphasizing the importance of myth for Schelling, 'at this time mythology was not at all purely an academic question but it constituted a deep-rooted cultural heritage'.[63] Therefore we must see in Schelling's early interest in mythology not simply an accident of his seminary context but indeed an engagement with one of the most powerful cultural influences to which he was then open, an influence which, as Dietzsch says,[64] is to be put alongside that of transcendental philosophy. Together these made up the elements of the young Schelling's vision of the world. He 'proclaimed that the astonishing faculty of imagination is the intermediary which ties together theoretic and practical reason to make of them . . . the peculiar organ of philosophy. On it rests his new mythology . . . The understanding of the world which took mythology for its form of expression is entirely the

Kantian idealism.'[65] This is a nice point; for Schelling's philosophy of identity is certainly based on the Kantian doctrine of transcendental schematism just as his philosophy of nature is a development of Kant's transcendental deduction. What is particularly important is that Schelling also regarded this as the significant element in mythology: mythology is essentially a work of art in which the natural is mixed with the historical. This was, he thought, the great discovery of K. P. Moritz who, as he says in *Philosophy of Art*, had 'the great merit of showing for the first time the absolute poetical character of myth'.[66] What would give such an analysis of myth its plausibility would be the common element of symbolism in both mythology and works of art.

This excursus on myth had served to show the kind of interrelation between Schelling's 'positive' or 'negative' philosophy (as he characterized the thought of his early and late periods) which since W. Schulz's 1955 study of Schelling's late philosophy has been a central issue of all Schelling scholarship. The later philosophy of revelation was to be described as a philosophy of mythology; but the philosophy of identity had already sought the reconciliation of nature and history in mythology. Schelling's aim had been to show the indestructible connection between the ego and the external world in a *transcendental* part of the ego. In his article on the possibility of a philosophy of history he described mythology as being 'originally nothing but a historical schematism of nature': it is indeed a resurrection of nature – for in myth nature and art are identical.[67] Thus, in the celebrated phrase of Walter Benjamin, the young Schelling's understanding of mythology is the claim that 'On the face of nature in the hieroglyphics of the past is written "History".'[68] Myth, that is to say, was for Schelling the most radical expression of the identity of the ego and the non-ego because there is already in myth an eternal identity of the objective and the subjective which, he says, is personified in the old mythological gods.[69]

Schelling's later philosophy can be said to arise from the dissatisfaction he felt not only with what he called his earlier negative philosophy but more particularly with the Hegelian resolution of its problems. Of the lectures he delivered in Munich in the winter semester of 1832–3 the first eleven are devoted to a preliminary explanation of the opposition between 'logical' and 'historical' systems of philosophy.[70] All previous attempts at developing a philosophical system were unsatisfactory because they were basically unhistorical and did not do justice to the basic contingency of the world as grounded in the brute fact of creation. Moreover they did not give the concept of God its proper place in the system since these logical explanations of reality put it at the end rather than at the beginning of the system.[71] As

Tillich has pointed out, Schelling had resolved the Kantian impasse in Philosophy of Religion by asserting an absolute identity of experience and reality: absolute consciousness was identical with absolute reality.[72] If the philosophy of identity is to be justified then experience itself must be seen to yield an absolute system. It was precisely the failure of Hegel's contradictory attempt to do this which led Schelling to develop his 'positive philosophy'. Tillich's description of that is interesting. 'It is no accident', he says, 'that Schelling overthrew the system of identity by means of a "doctrine of freedom".'[73] For Schelling, 'idealism leaves us completely bewildered' about freedom;[74] for in a system such as Hegel's freedom can only mean obedience to a higher necessity. It is ironic that one of the first reactions to Schelling's concept of freedom as he developed it in *Of Freedom* (1809) was F. H. Jacobi's *Von den göttlichen Dingen und ihrer Offenbarung*, published in 1811, where the charge of pantheism was emphatically and even virulently expressed. Before considering the work on freedom let us look, then, at the account given in *Philosophy and Religion* (1804) of the theory of Creation as Fall. There Schelling had expounded the doctrine of the Absolute as pure identity which can be apprehended only in an intuition.[75] This intuition cannot be achieved by instruction. The Absolute is expressed in the eternal ideas or, more properly for Schelling, in the one Idea which is the ground of all things. This Idea is the divine eternal self-knowledge.[76] The origin of the world as such is explained not simply in terms of this necessary self-knowledge but of 'a complete breaking-away from Absoluteness by means of a leap'.[77] This is no temporal event but is as 'eternal as the Absolute itself'.[78] Neither can the Fall be made a simple deduction from the Absolute and its eternal Ideas. It cannot, says Schelling, be explained. However, this doctrine of a cosmic fall should not perhaps be regarded as having any great significance for Schelling's theism or even his philosophy of time as the category of finitude – this for two reasons. In the first place, since it is not something we can deduce from the Absolute then the event is in a real sense outside the Absolute. Now philosophy properly so called cannot for Schelling be concerned with anything other than the Absolute. Therefore this idea can in a very clear sense be described, as indeed it is in texts after 1805, as an idea that derives from a different philosophy, in short a negative philosophy. Secondly, the doctrine of cosmic fall could be said to be merely a device whereby Schelling solves the problem of the contradiction between absolute identity and *human* freedom. This is Fackenheim's view of the function of the doctrine in Schelling's philosophy of religion. 'Since absolute identity and human freedom cannot exist together and yet since both are real, the only possible solution is that an original cosmic identity has been shattered by an original act of finite freedom.'[79] In writing *Philosophy and Religion* Schelling was trying to reconcile this earlier Philosophy of Nature with the growing interest in a general theory of history and culture. Arthur Lovejoy puts the matter very succinctly: 'In much of his philosophizing between 1800 and 1812 . . . he has still two Gods and therefore two religions – the religion of a time-transcending and eternally complete Absolute, an "Identity of Identities", the One of Neoplatonism – and the religion of a struggling, temporally limited, gradually self-realizing World-Spirit or Life-Force.'[80]

It was clear, then, before 1809 that freedom was a recurrent theme in Schelling's work and that more especially the relation of individual freedom to God is an important *Leitmotif*. *Of Human Freedom* is, says Schelling, an attempt to remedy the deficiency of 'faulty presentation' because of which 'the beginning made in the essay on *Philosophy and Religion* . . . remained obscure'.[81] Instead of the old distinction between nature and spirit he wants to posit and expound the proper distinction between necessity and freedom. The 'chief points' of this new exposition of his thought were freedom, good and evil and personality. By using the distinction between subject and predicate as antecedent and consequent Schelling wants to show not only 'the real meaning of the law of identity'[82] but also that 'pantheism does not make . . . freedom . . . impossible'.[83] Spinoza's error is in fact not his pantheism but his determinism, 'the abstract conception of the world and its creatures, indeed of eternal substance itself, which is also a thing for him'.[84] Schelling's dissatisfaction with 'idealism' is due to the fact that it yields 'only the most general conception of freedom and a formal one. But the real and vital conception of freedom is that it is a possibility of good and evil.'[85] This is, of course, the most serious problem for Schelling's system; for if everything positive in reality itself is derived from God – which is the principle of identity – then it must be possible for God to do evil. This apparently inescapable conclusion Schelling is able to avoid because he distinguishes between God and the inner basis of his existence, in the same way as he distinguishes between light and its ground in gravitation and human personality and the dark ground or basis. Reflecting the influence of Boehme, whose work he had been reading since 1804 and had known since 1799,[86] Schelling says that God's freedom is to give birth to himself. The basis of God's personal existence is the impersonal longing for personal existence. This is the difference between God and man just as the structure of personality is the similarity between them. 'Without the preceding gloom, creation would have no reality; darkness is its necessary heritage. Only God – the Existent himself – dwells in pure light; for he alone is self-born.'[87] In

59

positing himself as the unconscious will God also posits himself as the rational will of love. It is because this unity which in God is indissoluble is dissoluble in man that there is a possibility of evil. Schelling had been encouraged in his reading of Boehme by Franz von Baader and he commends von Baader as the author who had especially emphasized this correct understanding of evil as the reversal of the principles.

The importance of the work on Freedom not only for understanding Schelling's own development but indeed for the very development of modern philosophy has been emphasized by Tillich in his second dissertation on Schelling.[88] What was achieved, he argues, was that the problem of freedom was raised to a higher level of synthesis beyond the dichotomy of determinism and indeterminism. However, he insists that freedom is possible 'only where there is contradiction between freedom and necessity'[89] and this means that freedom is not an indeterminable, groundless choice. Likewise there is no transition from the absolutely undetermined to the determined. Man alone can determine himself. But the act 'which determines a man's life in time does not belong in time but in eternity . . . That Judas became a traitor to Christ, neither he nor any creature could alter; nonetheless he betrayed Christ, not under compulsion but willingly and with full freedom.'[90] With the Reformers in mind Schelling says that he too declares a predestination but only in the sense that as a man acts here so he has acted since eternity. This is an all-important clarification (if that is not too ironic a word) of Schelling's view of freedom and the origin of evil. For as he rightly contrasts Kant's doctrine of radical evil with Fichte's version of that view he makes it quite clear that there is a certain *a priori* quality in this view of determination and that it is not merely a matter of observing what comes within the range of senses. Schelling shows himself hardly concerned finally whether his system will be called pantheist or not. The reason for this is that he is emphatic in his claim that the theory he has outlined explains both the general possibility of evil and the distinctive nature of the divine identity of necessity and freedom. 'The will to creation was . . . only a will to bring light to birth and, therein, goodness. Evil, however, did not come into consideration for this will . . . It was neither the object of a divine decree, nor – and still less – of a permission.'[91] The closing words of this work[92] confirm the significance Tillich gives to the ideas of will and the irrational in his interpretation of Schelling:

Now in the present construction, irrationalism attains the greatest import, because the irrational principle is concerned within God as his *prius*, which precedes his being as God. The 'that' is given primacy over the 'what' . . . The universal does not individualize itself; the individual generalizes itself, makes itself comprehensible. *The irrational is* not subordinate to the idea, in the manifold of *individuals; rather it is first of all* above the idea, in the absolute individual.[93]

This voluntaristic metaphysics of freedom was indeed what Schelling had in mind as the basis of his positive philosophy.

Tillich's interpretation of the development of Schelling's philosophy as a movement from mysticism to morality, though too simplistic to be correct, does have the merit of emphasizing by its reference to guilt the essentially religious character of Schelling's later philosophy. This is very clear in the work which he called his 'favourite child', *The Ages of the World*[94] which is an extension of his earlier work, *Of Human Freedom*. This was meant to be a work in three parts and probably the fragment we have does not extend beyond the first part. Though its problem is the basic metaphysical problem which Tillich thinks was most clearly articulated by Schelling – Why is there anything rather than nothing? – the point of departure is the epistemological problem posed by science. 'What we call knowledge is just striving after conscious recollection, thus more an aspiring after knowledge than knowledge itself.'[95] Everything must be made inward and until it has become inward remains incomprehensible for man.[96] There is a recurrent blessedness for man in thus feeling the unity of his nature. Later, however, Schelling was to speak of his philosophy as 'metaphysical empiricism'. As Copleston judiciously remarks, Schelling's use of the word 'empiricism' must be understood in a relative sense.[97] This is at once obvious when we read the text of *Ages*; for what is remarkable about this is that we are immediately transported from epistemology to mythology. Not only is the beginning of history the first topic mentioned but we are soon told that 'God is the oldest of beings'.[98] This religious and distinctly mythological language is necessary, in Schelling's view, because the philosophical problem of the meaning of being finds its answer in what lies beyond human experience. Thus the work begins with the discussion of the idea of God. God is the most spontaneous being – the necessary who is also free. Corresponding to the duality are the dual principles of God's necessity: 'the outflowing, outspeading, self-giving essence, and an equally eternal power of selfhood, of return into self, of being-in-self'.[99] Rejecting the idealist tendency to fasten on the positive aspect merely, thereby transforming God into an empty infinite, Schelling insists on the two aspects of God. This doctrine of God, he says, is so far from being invalidated by any supposed law of contradiction that it is in fact an application of it.[100] For God is both the Yes and the No and 'just as eternally the third principle or unity of the Yes and the No'. This persistence of the idealist resolution of contradiction is also an interesting development of the theme.

When Schelling refers to God's 'nature' he means the necessary aspect of God and this is what he expounds in his doctrine of potencies. Just as in the divine nature the eternal affirmation overcomes the negating power so in the first potency something is but is posited as not being. The first potency is $A = B$. It is that which is potential because though it is not it is capable of being. B is 'the negatory' which disappears when the first potency generates the second. This generation, however, is possible only because the negatory power is overcome. So, says Schelling, 'that original No is the beginning and the first'.[101] It is the unconscious ground of personality and the basis of religion. The second potency is A^2 'that in which the negatory, B, now disappears'. That is, there is here no negation because the second potency appears when something is generated by the first potency and when that happens something *is*. It is that which is, pure being.[102] The second potency is thus the principle of reality according to which organic structure is dependent on something more than the rational. The picture that we have, then, is one of a pre-temporal development of God himself which presumably was Schelling's way of combating the reductionist influence of idealism in the doctrine of God. Thus he thought that he was restoring the real notion of God as transcendent. The divine evolution which we have described is completed in the third potency which is necessarily posited by the other two as their unity. 'This third must in itself be outside of and above all antithesis, the purest potency, that which is free of both, and most essential . . . From the first potency to the third there is a continual progression, a necessary concatenation.'[103] The whole idea of God is the unity of these concepts of a necessary nature and freedom, a structure of being and a principle of being. God is the indissoluble unity of the potencies, the eternally living one who is both his beginning and his end. Nature 'belongs only to what is necessary in God, and, taken strictly, God is called God only with respect to his freedom'.[104] Clearly, then, God in himself neither is nor is not.[105] Having so far expounded only the eternal life of the godhead, Schelling indicates that the crucial point in his doctrine of God is the identity of the unity and duality that characterize him. Typically Schelling turns to the history of religion and of language and makes his point by referring to the two names of God in the Old Testament. 'Elohim' expresses the divine substance in 'pure aspirates', 'mute letters' and indeed a movement from 1 to 4 in the tetragrammaton. Misleadingly Schelling adduces the opening words of Genesis – 'bara Elohim' – as evidence that the unity of the divine essence is a duality, reading them as 'he who created is Elohim' rather than simply 'Elohim created'.[106] Equally there is in God a duality of 'an eternal present and eternally (or eternally becoming) past' and this Old Testament doctrine is presupposed in the New Testament. Nature is for Schelling an organic process neither purely material nor purely spiritual.[107] It is an evolution in which both necessity and freedom play an equally important part. It is indeed the evolution towards the unity of spiritual and corporeal being. This analysis of the process of nature is, however, not to be understood as separate from or replacing the notion of divine act in creation. The function of such analysis is merely to show that if we are to understand nature we need a dynamic rather than a mechanistic logic. So, despite the fact that nature exists only after a decisive act as the part of the supernatural, the natural and supernatural are closely linked. To understand anything in nature is to see it as the coarse vessel for the spiritual.[108] The concept of spirit world is for Schelling not only the inner reality of anything which exists but also the historical finality of the development of spirit through the process of nature and history. It is in this eschatological context that Schelling uses his favourite notion of the world-soul which unites all beings.

Using Schelling's distinction between negative and positive philosophy we can call this first part of *Ages of the World* negative philosophy concerned only with the analysis of essence whereas the remainder of the book deals with the way in which existence comes to have presence for us. The fact that he speaks of nature in these dynamic terms does not, as was said earlier, minimize Schelling's emphasis on divine creation. The godhead is the ground of the world 'by the most divine free will'. It is 'always the eternal No to all external being' and yet 'also necessarily eternal Yes'. This contradiction is resolved by Schelling's theory of time as a succession of eternities. Both in his view of the derivation of being and in his analysis of the revelation of the godhead in being Schelling has now abandoned a rational dialectic, giving prime importance to the fact of a divine decision to create which both grounds existence and is its meaning. He insists that the creation of the world is in time and explains it as the process of the sequence of potencies in Godly nature becoming a succession of principles of real being of increasing potency. Schelling takes great delight in the way what one might call the first-order religious language fits this philosophical scheme of his. Equally he indulges in some symbolical formulation of the principle of the ultimate unity of God. 'God leads human nature through no other course than that through which his own nature must pass.'[109] All this is finally made an explicit rejection of idealism which was itself 'only the expressed secret' of the prevailing tendency to idealize and empty Christianity.[110]

What emerges from this account is such a division of Schelling's philosophy into a positive philosophy following the negative philosophy which characterizes the period up to 1820 as is proposed by Tilliette, for instance.[111] But what did Schelling mean by 'positive philosophy'? First and foremost it would seem he means a knowledge of the being of Identity as distinct from Fichte's self-styled philosophy of reflection which yielded only the knowledge of Being reflected in the ego. This positivity is characterized by the essential determination of an apprehension of determined being as that is revealed in experience. Reason reaches only the *concept* of Being-itself: it knows Being-itself only negatively as a pure possibility – that is the necessary being of the medieval *non posse non esse* – not as something which *exists*. The philosophy of reason therefore remains a negative philosophy – 'it operates negatively or better it takes up an attitude of neutrality in relation to the real and to existence – because it proceeds to the successive elimination of the contingent in order to extract, to detach being-itself in thought . . . because in the end it reaches only the negative concept of its object . . . possessing it only as a concept'.[112] Thus it is that Heidegger takes Schelling as seriously as he does Plato and Kant; for he discovers in him a line of thought which leads ontology away from the formalism of logical categories such as identity to categories of concrete human existence. For Heidegger Schelling is attempting to move away from a logic of human existence as the hermeneutical tool of Philosophy.[113] Schelling's thought is, he says, thus an authentic ontological system.[114] This emphasis helps us appreciate the difference Schelling sees between negative and positive philosophy – that the former is unable to explain the existent world. It deals only with the idea of ultimate reality; but there is no deduction of a *That* from a *What*. Consequently the deduction of the world in the negative philosophy of idealism is only a deduction of essences, of what things must be if they exist. The negative philosopher can only say of the world as an extra-divine reality that 'if it exists it can exist only in that way and only as such and such'.[115] The positive philosopher, on the other hand starts with God 'as a pure That' and shows that He is a creative personal Being, the existing 'Lord of Being'.[116] In an important sense, then, the distinction between negative and positive philosophy relates to a fact the explanation of which presents philosophy with its task. Knowledge for Schelling is enriched only by acquaintance with a fact so that we need an eye trained to see the event which is produced or produces itself in the phenomena rather than merely the phenomena themselves. When in 1827 Schelling reappeared on the philosophical scene he had no need to seek this fact in his own philosophical construction because he was able to point to it as already in evidence in the philosophy of nature which he had elaborated in *Ages of the World*.

Another way of understanding the difference between positive and negative philosophy, would be to distinguish between the two kinds of knowledge of God. In negative philosophy God is known only *in* reason or more precisely in the immediate content of reason, Being; whereas positive philosophy knows God as He is in Himself and outside any thinking. Negative philosophy is thus concerned not with existence proper, the *seyend-seyn* of God, but only with His Being, a necessary general existence.[117] The scientific nature of positive philosophy also demands that it must show that its object not only *exists* but that it is something specific, not indeed *a* being but Being. Only thus can it show that the existent with which it deals is God because God alone is the existent, the individual, who is at the same time the Whole.[118] In the negative philosophy God was a purely illusory priority whereas in the positive philosophy He is to be found in His proper place. The task of positive philosophy is to show that what necessarily exists if it is God must contain within itself the three elements which constitute the idea of Being. After establishing that God *must* be Being in idea it will establish that He remains Lord of existing empirical Being. The distinction between negative and positive philosophy is thus for Schelling a distinction between a subjectivist and an objectivist theology. Yet another way in which the distinction can be made is in terms of revelation; for in negative philosophy God is hidden and positive philosophy is a philosophy of revelation. It is important to note, however, that this revelation is not direct – God is present in positive philosophy as in Christianity by means of a mediator. This led Schelling in his last years to contemplate a higher wisdom in which God would Himself be present as spirit. Such a theory would have developed the dream expressed as early as 1802, that the conflict between paganism and Christianity would disappear in a common spiritual perception. Indeed even before 1800 Schelling had affirmed that the Absolute is 'the indifference of the ideal and the real'.[119] It is not surprising, then, that in his later thinking though Schelling distinguished between negative and positive philosophy as operating within the realm of the ideal and real respectively he could quite easily go on to maintain their ultimate perfect unity. So he insists that we must 'assert the connection, yes the unity between the two'.[120] It is also worth noting that Schelling regarded the positive philosopher as standing on the boundary between theosophy and philosophy, entering into the tension between them and from his standpoint of rational knowledge transcending them both. Though theosophy does not, he says, assume scientific, that is rational, form, yet it is not irrational. It 'makes claims to speculative content', he says,[121] if this claim by a genuine theosophy is valid. Thus he comments in *Philosophy and Revelation* that the teachings of the theosophists, reaching their peak in Jacob Boehme, had never been scientifically expounded before his own work. In this way, theosophy made positive philosophy necessary – 'these teachings imply the necessity of a Positive Philosophy even if they do not realize it themselves'.[122] To this task of developing a positive philosophy in which the truth of revelation would be presented as truths of reason Schelling devoted the latter half of his life and it is this which forms the substance of *Philosophy of Mythology* and the *Philosophy of Revelation*.

This connection with theosophy is worth emphasizing. In 1806 Schelling wrote of the 'mystics' or 'enthusiasts': 'If, up to now, I have not seriously studied their writings, this has not been at all due to contempt, but to carelessness which should be reproved, and of which, in the future, I will no longer allow myself to be guilty.'[123] It appears that it was the poet Tieck who first made Schelling aware of Boehme[124] but there can be no doubt that his great interest in Boehme was mentioned and developed by Franz von Baader, that 'very learned man and great lover of mystical and theosophical writings'.[125] Though we know that he did not possess a copy of Boehme until 1804[126] it is not at all unlikely that Schelling knew his work at quite a tender age because the works of Oetinger, Boehme's interpreter, were available to him in his father's library. Marquet points out that Schelling's interest in Boehme and Oetinger is particularly evident at three points in his career, each of them being significant dates: 1802 when he was writing *Philosophy of Art*, 1806 when he was settled in Munich and in contact with von Baader, and 1809 when he started thinking of *Ages of the World*.[127] An examination of Schelling's developing philosophy confirms the impression that the philosophy of identity was influenced by theosophical thought. There is a very obvious similarity between the view of Schelling and those of von Baader on the 'forces', that of attraction and that of repulsion, which are combined by a third principle (the earth) to form a relative equilibrium or the basis of all the potencies and manifestations of these principles. In themselves the two principles yield nothing but chaos. So the schema of chaos, the life of mutual opposition and the principle of light which is the legacy of Boehme, appears in both von Baader and Schelling. Again, to move to the second significant date – by 1802 the early interest in myth which we have noted culminated in a theory of ideas as a world of its own in which the immanent revelation of the Absolute to itself is accomplished. It is likely that by the summer of 1802 Schelling had read Boehme's *Aurora*. When therefore one reads in the Würzburg lectures a reference[128] to the movement by which man brings the near and the distant together on the earth just as God does so by his immobility, the echoes of Boehme are quite unmistakable. Whether one should see such direct influence in the case of

66

Schelling's doctrine of the Fall is perhaps debatable;[129] but there can be no denying the distinct echo of Boehme's emphasis on the root of evil in man's I-ness (*Ichbert*) which makes him 'the enemy of the Nothing'.[130] The 'system' or 'architectonic' of Boehme's theology is precisely the structure of Schelling's *Ages of the World*.[131] Though after 1820 other influences such as Pascal and Hamann play an important role in Schelling's thought, the positive philosophy inaugurated in *Ages of the World* carried marks of theosophical influence to the end. Also it ought to be said that if von Baader was the inspiration of Schelling's positive philosophy and the original link between him and Boehme, Schelling exercised an equally powerful influence on von Baader's development of a true philosophy of faith with its theosophical doctrine of God and Fall and its religious theory of social and political existence.

For Schelling only the positive philosophy can produce understanding of religion and this is done by means of its elaborating a philosophy of mythology and of revelation. Indeed when in 1821 he went to Erlangen he set about transferring the schema of the history of nature developed in *Ages of the World* to the realm of nature. The contrast between the negative and positive philosophy is indeed one between a philosophy that does not make room for religion and one that is truly religious. What, then, does Schelling mean by religion? To begin with, the meaning of history is for Schelling religious because the focal point of his positive philosophy is, as Tillich showed, the construction of the history of religion. Schelling begins the exposition of the nature of religion given in *Philosophy of Revelation*[132] by making a distinction between two types of religion, scientific and unscientific. Scientific religion is an entirely rational religion manifesting the original unity of the intellect and the object, and as such is completely unhistorical. Unscientific religion, on the other hand, is so thoroughly historical a phenomenon that it is based on a pre-rational consciousness of God. Its historical manifestation or development is in the three forms of mythology, revelation and philosophical religion, 'the religion of free philosophical knowledge'. In mythology we have a sequence of gods (i.e. paganism) but, false as they are, these gods yet express the original relation of consciousness to God through the first potency. God is here presented as nature or wrath so that we are not dealing with God as He is in Himself but outside His divinity. Mythology develops into revelation because the natural religion of mythology is complemented by the supernatural religion of revelation. Obviously we are no longer dealing with God outside Himself but with the fulness of the divine Being in His freedom. As we have said, for Schelling unscientific religion, which is really religious rather than a mere expression

67

of a rational principle, manifests a pre-rational consciousness of God. As a result there is in it a free relationship of the consciousness to God, the Lord of being. This living personal relationship is effected by the second potency, incarnate in Christ as the Son. Predictably, philosophical religion manifests the age of the Spirit. This analysis of the history of religion attempts to present religion as the revelation of God by Himself which is in a sense controlled by the Christian claim of a specific complete revelation. It would be very easy to take Schelling's views as some kind of Christian apologetic. He does indeed show in the history of religion the self-revelation of the one personal God whose unity includes the three potencies: this general revelation is the inner truth of mythology. Also he says that this inner truth first finds concrete expression in Christianity. Just what, then, is the connection that this metaphysical deduction of a historical progression of revelation establishes between mythology and Christianity? In so far as Christianity as a revelation presupposes a free act of God in self-disclosure Schelling cannot identify the two concepts; but he clearly regards the connection between them as logical or it would not be possible to make the deduction. So Schelling seems to hover between asserting a necessary connection between the two and emphasizing the distinction between them. One possible way of reconciling this contradiction is to understand both concepts as relating to God's volition. In which case we must take the mythological description of God's history in terms of unconscious and conscious activity in a literal sense. The only other way of removing the tension is to say that the revelation in Christ is the truth to which mythology points or what could be said to be the real meaning of mythology. The difficulty with this interpretation is that it makes Schelling's view rather too Hegelian. However, in either case, Schelling's view of the relation between Christianity and mythology can hardly be reconciled with a full theology of revelation as the unique act of God in Christ. Moreover, Schelling's metaphysical framework for his theory of a history of religion would equally take him away from such a theology. For though the positive philosophy was very definitely a philosophy of revelation this positive philosophy does represent a viewpoint that transcends both mythology and Christianity. Thus in his *Deduction* of 1841 he says both that this philosophy cannot exist without Christianity and that it cannot be simply identified with empirical Christianity. Philosophical religion is free religion and not an acceptance of Christian faith on authority. 'The free religion is only *mediated* through Christianity; it is not immediately posited by it.'[133]

There can be no clearer exposition of Schelling's attitude towards orthodox Christian dogmatics than his own words in *Philosophy of*

Revelation where he rejects the 'reproach' of being called orthodox. 'The Philosophy of Revelation', he says, 'is not concerned with orthodoxy – I reject it because it would give the Philosophy of Revelation an entirely false point of view.'[134] Though its task is that of explaining Christianity and its central concern is therefore the event of the Incarnation, the characteristic idea of Christianity, the kind of explanation he seeks to offer is what he calls a historical explanation of Christianity. This includes, as we have seen, 'inner, divine and transcendent history', history in the strict sense, and not a 'merely external' history.[135] But just as he both insists on the crucial importance of christology for Christianity and yet says nothing about the life of Christ so he completes his christology with a satanology. The significance of this is that in *Philosophy of Revelation* Schelling was, then, developing a new understanding of Christianity which was in clear opposition to traditional theology and orthodox dogmatics.

How, then, are we to understand Schelling's religious thought as a whole? Indeed is there a whole? This debate, which occupied so many scholars so greatly, can now perhaps be said to be finished if not actually settled. For the truth of the matter is that even those scholars who have insisted that there are so many changes in Schelling's work have nevertheless spoken as if there were some golden thread or threads running through all his writings. In his dissertation *God in the Philosophy of Schelling* (1933) Rowland Gray-Smith remarks that the change in Schelling was no more essential a change than a snake casting its skin.[136] But what is the real philosophy, the heart of the matter? It is all too easy to be struck by the echoes of Schelling in Kierkegaard and to be so misled by the known historical connection between them as to claim Schelling was the first existentialist philosopher of the modern period. This was the view Tillich took and here in all probability he was following Heidegger. Tillich expounded this view of Schelling's influence with enthusiasm and consistency[137] though not with any clear detail. It is an interpretation that seems very convincing because, as both W. Kasper and H. Fuhrmans would accept, it is the religious theme that is dominant in Schelling's philosophy from beginning to end.[138] This makes it all the more important that we should see this religious motivation for what it is. The conclusion that Tilliette reaches in his meticulous and huge study is that Schelling is his own first exegete;[139] and though he indicates that caution is needed in handling that exegesis it must be said that Tilliette's general attitude is that Schelling understood himself better than anyone. Since, then, in his exegesis of Schelling's philosophy of religion and his interpretation of Christianity Tilliette makes no critical comment we must assume that he regards them as adequate. We have no right, he contends,[140] to doubt the sincerity of Schelling's religious concern during his later years. However, this is to pose the wrong question and Schelling's sincerity does not answer the question whether his theory of the history of religion and in particular of Christianity is true and whether his understanding of its nature is correct. It seems undeniable that in the last analysis Schelling's understanding of God and of religion tends inevitably towards pantheism, and Jacobi's critique of him on that score is right. Perhaps it is significant that Schelling never really regarded Judaism as part of revelation so that it is no surprise that the Old Testament stress on the holiness of Yahweh is something quite alien to Schelling's understanding of God. Thus, though it is true that the emphasis of Schelling's later work is more theistic than pantheistic and his intention in the positive philosophy is to develop a speculative theology that does indeed accommodate Christianity one comes to the conclusion that Schelling's work is so much of a piece that it never quite escaped the grasp of his earlier pantheism.

That we cannot dismiss this speculative theology as unworthy of theological consideration is evident from the fact that some very different theologians in the nineteenth and twentieth centuries are heavily in Schelling's debt. I refer first to Franz von Baader who, as we have seen, received as much inspiration as he gave. Both through von Baader and directly Schelling influenced Søren Kierkegaard. Indicating this debt in my study of Kierkegaard I commented that the extent of Schelling's influence has not been fully analysed:[141] this regrettably remains the case. Having started to read Schelling in 1837 Kierkegaard was, in my view, so impressed by what he read and what he heard of Schelling through Danish reports that he decided in 1841 to go to Berlin to hear him. What attracted Kierkegaard in Schelling's thought was his anxiety that philosophy should be a philosophy of existence and reality and the clear recognition that the only way in which philosophy could deal with religion was by taking revelation as its point of departure. As far as historical evidence of the connection between them is concerned the most important point to note is that despite his well-known disappointment in Schelling's lectures which occasioned the remark in 1842 'Schelling drivels on intolerably'[142] we find Kierkegaard reading Schelling once more in 1843 and the years immediately following. This is why I think that the echoes of Schelling in Kierkegaard, while not in any way suggesting the necessity of seeing Schelling as an early Kierkegaard, do indicate motifs which were more clearly and critically expressed by Kierkegaard. Coming now to the twentieth century, Process Theology is a type of theology which Schelling can be said to have anticipated even if the school is not an example of what Hartshorne has called the 'immense array of internal differences' in idealism.[143] Schelling's description of consciousness as a history and his insistence that God reveals himself and becomes existent in history are sufficiently close to Whitehead to give Process Theology the appearance of reflecting Schelling's panentheism. Finally, I must refer to Paul Tillich, whose close relation to Schelling I pointed out in one of the earliest discussions of his theology.[144] This has been argued in greater detail by scholars such as Kenan B. Osborne;[145] but it was put beyond any doubt by Tillich himself. There is not only the evidence of the two dissertations which are in such obvious ways the earliest expression of much that remains characteristic of Tillich but also the evidence of Tillich's early 'revolutionary' theology. Moreover, we have Tillich's own recognition of the debt.[146] Though accepting the description of his approach and position as essentially Kantian, Tillich was so close to Schelling that he was in his latest years prone to quote Schelling's words as his own. Thus Schelling's religious thought is indeed our legacy – both historically and for its intrinsic fruitfulness.

Notes

1 J. Macquarrie, *Twentieth-Century Religious Thought* (London, 1963), p. 23 defines idealism thus: 'The term "idealism" is used to describe a variety of philosophies which all in one way or another regard physical objects as existing only in relation to an experiencing subject, so that reality is conceived in terms of mind or experience.' For a fuller definition of idealism see Paul Edwards, *Encyclopedia of Philosophy* (New York, 1967), vol. IV pp. 110–18. A. C. Ewing's fine work, *Idealism* (London, 1934), remains an invaluable aid to the understanding and appreciation of idealism – see especially his comments on the definition of idealism (pp. 2ff) and his distinction (p. 5) between epistemological idealism, Kantian idealism and the panpsychism of source, kinds of idealist metaphysics. Macquarrie's discussion of the influence of Hegelianism on English theology reflects the common, though not entirely accurate, understanding of the theology of the *Lux Mundi* group.

2 F. Copleston, *A History of Philosophy* (London, 1963), vol. VII, p. 7f.

3 This remark, of which Dr J. P. Clayton made me aware, is here quoted merely to exemplify the typology.

4 For Green see Nettleship's memoir published in London in 1906 and H. D. Lewis's valuable essays in *Freedom and History* (London, 1962) as well as his contribution in volume two of the present work. Melvin Richter in *Politics of Conscience, T. H. Green and His Age* (London, 1964) comments on the influence of German thought on Green.

5 Cf. P. Tillich, *Mysticism and Guilt-Consciousness in Schelling's Philosophical Development*, transl. V. Nuovo (Lewisburg, Bucknell University Press, 1974), p. 53: '. . . the radical development of the principle of identity leads through itself to the full affirmation of the concept of guilt. Schelling entered upon this path, and without stopping pursued it to its end.'

6 *The Popular Works of Johann Gottlieb Fichte*, transl. W. Smith (London, 1889), vol. I, p. 155 (Sämmtliche Werke, vol. VI, p. 299).

7 The documents concerning it have been collected by H. Lindau in his *Die Schriften zu Fichtes Atheismus-Streit* (Munich, 1912).

8 H. Rickert has pointed out in his article 'Fichtes Atheismusstreit und die Kantische Philosophie', *Kantstudien* 4 (1900), pp. 148ff the increasing difference between Fichte's position and that of Forberg.

9 'On the foundation of one belief in a divine Government of the Universe', *Nineteenth Century Philosophy*, ed. P. G. Gardiner (New York, 1969), p. 26.

10 *Ibid.* Cf. Hirsch, *Geschichte der neueren evangelischen Theologie*, vol. IV, (Gütersloh, 1952), pp. 340 and 352.

11 *Appellation an das Publikum* in Lindau, *Fichtes Atheismus-Streit*, p. 119. Cf. G. R. Preul, *Reflexion und Gefühl. Die Theologie Fichtes in seiner vorkantischen Zeit* (Berlin, 1969).

12 Lindau, *Fichtes Atheismus-Streit*, p. 130.

13 F. Schlegel, *Werke* (Munich, 1963), vol. XVIII, Appendix 3, pp. 521ff.

14 In the work, *The Way Towards the Blessed Life or the Doctrine of Religion*, *The Popular Works of Johann Gottlieb Fichte*, vol. II, pp. 289–496.

15 Vide *The Popular Works of Johann Gottlieb Fichte*, vol. I, pp. 147–205.

16 Vide Copleston, *History of Philosophy*, vol. VII, pp. 83–93. Cf. M. Wundt's comment 'The Atheismusstreit inevitably imparted a powerful impulse to Fichte's religious thought, concentrating the whole power of his mind more and more upon the religious question' (*J. G. Fichte* (Stuttgart, 1927), p. 268).

17 *Science of Ethics*, p. 248.

18 *S.W.* V 43.

19 Lindau, *Fichtes Atheismus-Streit*, p. 125.

20 *Ideen über Gott und Unsterblichkeit, Zwei religionsphilosophische Vorlesungen aus der Zeit von dem Atheismusstreit*, ed. Büchsel (Leipzig, 1914), p. 49.

21 *Fichtes Briefe*, ed. Berman (Leipzig, 1919), p. 111.

22 Cf. his discussion of the origin of language in his lectures on Logic and Metaphysics (*Vorlesungen über Logic and Metaphysik*, 1797, in *Nachgelassene Schriften*, vol. II, especially pp. 147–59). See also C. K. Hunter's important book, *Die Interpersonalitätsbeweis in Fichtes früher angewandter praktischer Philosophie* (Meisenheim, 1973).

23 *The Science of Rights*, transl. A. E. Kroeyer (London, 1889) p. 61 (*S.W.* III 40f).

24 On the contribution of these see J. W. Rogerson, *Myth in Old Testament* (Berlin, 1974), pp. 3–7 and also R. Clements' essay on Old Testament criticism in volume three of the present work.

25 *The Popular Works of Johann Gottlieb Fichte*, vol. II, p. 5. (*S.W.* VII 7).

26 *Ibid.*, p. 6f (*S.W.* VIII 8).

27 C. K. Hunter, *Die Interpersonalitätsbeweis*, p. 180.

28 *S.W.* V 261.

29 *Ibid.*, p. 382.

30 *S.W.* II 303.

31 *Ibid.*, p. 245.

32 *Op. cit.* in *Popular Works*, 3rd edn., p. 394.

33 *Ibid.*, p. 390.

34 *Ibid.*, p. 494.

35 *Addresses to the German Nation*, ed. G. A. Kelly (New York, 1968), pp. 87–8.

36 F. von Baader, *Vorlesungen über speculative Dogmatik* (Munster, 1830), vol. II, p. 82.

37 Cf. X. Tilliette, 'La nouvelle image de l'idéalisme allemand', *Revue Philosophique de Louvain* 71 (1973), 46–61.

38 F. G. Nauen, *Revolution, Idealism and Human Freedom* (The Hague, 1971), p. 27.

39 *Ibid.*, p. 32.

40 G. L. Plitt (ed.), *F. W. J. Schelling, Aus Schellings Leben in Briefen* (3 vols., Leipzig, 1869–70) vol. I, p. 40.

41 Cf. Nauen, *Revolution, Idealism and Human Freedom*, p. 34. He refers to Schelling's letter

to Fichte of 26 September 1794 (J. G. Fichte, *Briefwechsel*, I, 403), Fichte's letter to Reinhold of 2 July 1795 (*ibid.*, 481) and Schelling's letter to Hegel, January 1795 (J. Hoffmeister (ed.), *Briefe von und an Hegel* (Hamburg, 1969), vol. I, pp 13–15).

42 Fichte, *S.W.*, vol. I, p. 60, n. 1.

43 *Ibid.*, pp. 80–1. Vide Fichte, *S.W.*, vol. VI, pp. 5–6 for his somewhat conservative attitude towards institutions.

44 Schelling, *S.W.*, vol. I, p. 52, n. 1.

45 Fichte, *S.W.*, vol. I, p. 202.

46 Schelling, *S.W.*, vol. I, pp. 79–82.

47 *Ibid.*, p. 100.

48 *Ibid.*, p. 157, n.

49 Nauen, *Revolution, Idealism and Human Freedom*, p. 41. He refers to H. Fuhrmans (ed.), *F. W. J. Schelling Briefe und Dokumente* (Bonn, 1962), vol. I, pp. 55–9 and Ernst Müller, *Hölderlin: Studien zur Geschichte seines Geistes* (Stuttgart, 1944), pp. 159–67.

50 Schelling, *S.W.*, vol. I, p. 248.

51 *Ibid.*, p. 257.

52 Nauen, *Revolution, Idealism and Human Freedom*, p. 48. He refers in the note to F. Rozenweig, *Kleinere Schriften* (Berlin, 1937), pp. 271–3. Müller, *Hölderlin: Studien*, pp. 146–73, J. Hoffmeister, *Hölderlin und die Philosophie* (Leipzig, 1942), pp. 58–86.

53 Schelling, *S.W.*, vol. IV, p. 115.

54 Reinhart Lauth has examined these in 'Le deuxième conflit entre Fichte et Schelling (1800–1)', *Archives de Philosophie* 38 (Paris, 1975), pp. 177–200 and 353–77.

55 H. Steffens, *Was ich erlebte* (Breslau, 1841), vol. IV, pp. 122–4. Born in Norway, Henrich Steffens (1773–1845) came to Germany to study and later became a German citizen. He is generally mentioned, if at all, by historians of philosophy as a follower of Schelling though Harald Høffding also mentions his influence on the line of philosophy from Sibbern through Møller to Kierkegaard (*Danske Filosofer* (Copenhagen, 1921), vol. III, p. 47). This is very evident from Kierkegaard's own references to Steffens in the Journal and the connection has been usefully discussed by Helge Hultberg in 'Steffens und Kierkegaard', *Kierkegaardiana* 4 (1977), pp. 190–9. Both Steffens and Schelling wanted to develop an evolutionary chemistry which would explain the universe's evolutionary processes. This Steffens did in his *Anthropologie* (1822) which sketches a picture of the past geological history of the earth. Man, says Steffens, has lost his innocence as a creature of nature and is now regaining it through *Naturphilosophie*.

56 Lauth, 'Le deuxième conflit', p. 375. Cf. Fichte, *S.W.*, vol. VII, pp. 123–4

57 Fichte, *S.W.*, vol. VII, p. 125.

58 H. Schulz (ed.), *Fichte in vertraulichen Briefen seiner Zeitgenossen* (Leipzig, 1923), pp. 189–90, quoted by Lauth, 'Le deuxieme conflit', p. 373.

59 Schelling, *Of Human Freedom*, transl. J. Gutman (Chicago, 1936), p. xiv.

60 See P. Tillich, *Perspectives on 19th and 20th Century Protestant Theology* (London, 1967), pp. 142ff and his two dissertations on Schelling, *Mysticism and Guilt-Consciousness in Schelling's Philosophical Development* (Lewisburg, 1974), and *The Construction of the History of Religion in Schelling's Positive Philosophy* (Lewisburg, 1974).

61 Cf. Gutman's edition of Schelling's *Of Human Freedom*, pp. xxviiff.

62 Xavier Tilliette, *Schelling: Une philosophie en devenir* (Paris, 1970), vol. I, p. 16.

63 S. Dietzsch, 'Le problème du mythe chez le jeune Schelling', *Archives de Philosophie* 38 (Paris, 1975), pp. 395–400.

64 *Ibid.*, p. 396.

65 Fritz Strich, *Die Mythologie in der deutschen Literatur von Klopstock bis Wagner* (Halle, 1910), vol. I pp. 375ff, quoted by Dietzsch, 'Le problème du mythe', p. 397.

66 Schelling, *S.W.*, vol. V, p. 412.

67 Schelling, *S.W.*, vol. I, p. 472.

68 Walter Benjamin, *Gesammelte Schriften* (Frankfurt am Main, 1972), vol. I, p. 353, quoted by Dietzsch, 'Le problème du mythe', p. 399.
69 Schelling, *S.W.*, vol. V, p. 415.
70 Vide Fuhrmans' note in the Introduction (p. 21) to *Grundlegung der positiven Philosophie*.
71 *Ibid.*, p. 77.
72 Tillich, *Mysticism and Guilt-Consciousness*, p. 49.
73 *Ibid.*, p. 89. Cf. E. Fackenheim, 'Schelling's Philosophy of Religion', *University of Toronto Quarterly* (1952–3), p. 5.
74 Schelling, *S.W.*, vol. I, p. 351.
75 Cf. Schelling, *S.W.*, vol. IV, p. 16.
76 Cf. *ibid.*, pp. 21ff.
77 *Ibid.*, p. 28.
78 *Ibid.*, p. 31.
79 E. Fackenheim, 'Schelling's Philosophy of Religion', p. 7.
80 Arthur O. Lovejoy, *The Great Chain of Being* (New York, 1965), p. 317.
81 Schelling, *Of Human Freedom*, transl. Gutman, p. 4.
82 *Ibid.*, p. 14.
83 *Ibid.*, p. 22.
84 *Ibid.*
85 *Ibid.*, p. 26.
86 Plitt (ed.), *Aus Schellings Leben in Briefen*, vol. I, pp. 246–7, 376.
87 *Of Human Freedom*, p. 34.
88 Tillich, *Mysticism and Guilt-Consciousness*, pp. 89ff, 138.
89 *Ibid.*, p. 91.
90 *Of Human Freedom*, pp. 63–4.
91 *Ibid.*, p. 82.
92 *Ibid.*, p. 98.
93 Tillich, *Mysticism and Guilt-Consciousness*, p. 98.
94 Plitt (ed.), *Aus Schellings Leben in Briefen*, vol. II, p. 256, quoted by Bolman, *op. cit.*, p. 67. The lectures on the positive philosophy (1827–33) bear the title 'System of the Ages of the World' (cf. H. Fuhrmans, *Schellings letzte Philosophie* (Berlin, 1940), p. 307).
95 *Ages of the World*, transl. F. de Wolfe Bolman (New York, Columbia University Press, 1942), p. 86.
96 *Ibid.*, p. 88.
97 Copleston, *op. cit.*, p. 138.
98 *Ages of the World*, pp. 93–5.
99 *Ibid.*, p. 97.
100 *Ibid.*, pp. 103–4.
101 *Ibid.*, p. 113.
102 *Ibid.*, p. 114.
103 *Ibid.*, pp. 114–15.
104 *Ibid.*, p. 133.
105 *Ibid.*, pp. 144–5.
106 *Ibid.*, p. 161.
107 Cf. *Ibid.*, p. 164.
108 *Ibid.*, p. 171.
109 *Ages of the World*, p. 225.
110 *Ibid.*, p. 234.
111 Tilliette, *Schelling: Une philosophie en devenir*, vol. II, p. 42. Cf. p. 233.
112 *Ibid.*, p. 49.
113 M. Heidegger, *Schellings Abhandlung über das Wesen des menschlichen Freiheit* (Tübingen, 1971), pp. 16ff.

114 *Ibid.*, pp. 39f and 55f.
115 *S.W.*, vol. v, p. 558.
116 *Ibid.*, p. 746.
117 Cf. *S.W.*, vol. v, p. 455.
118 *Ibid.*, vol. vi, p. 274.
119 *S.W.*, vol. iii, p. 400.
120 *S.W.*, vol. v, p. 746.
121 *Ibid.*, p. 255.
122 *Ibid.*, vol. xi, p. 120.
123 *S.W.*, vol. iii, p. 714.
124 Vide Gutman's edition of Schelling's *Of Human Freedom*, p. xlv.
125 Plitt (ed.), *Aus Schellings Leben in Briefen*, vol. ii, p. 101.
126 *Ibid.*, p. 10.
127 J.-F. Marquet, *Liberté et existence* (Paris, 1973), p. 573.
128 *S.W.*, vol. viii, p. 419.
129 Cf. E. Benz, *Les sources mystiques de la philosophie romantique allemande* (Paris, 1967) and his earlier study of Schelling, *Schellings theologische Geistesahnen* (Wiesbaden, 1955).
130 Boehme, *De signatura rerum*, vol. ix, p. 63.
131 Marquet argues (*Liberté et existence*, p. 581) that this identity results from Schelling's discovery of a dramatic and mythical expression in Boehme of what is for Marquet the central problem of Schelling's philosophy – the articulation of existence in freedom. What is particularly interesting is that he shows Schelling's debt to Boehme by a textual analysis of Boehme's *Aurora* and Schelling's *Ages of the World* (*op. cit.*, pp. 584–5).
132 *S.W.*, vol. xii, pp. 189ff.
133 *S.W.*, vol. v, p. 440.
134 *S.W.*, vol. vi, p. 472.
135 *Ibid.*, p. 612.
136 Philadelphia, 1933, p. 99.
137 Vide *Theology of Culture* (New York, 1959), pp. 77–8 and *Perspectives on 19th and 20th Century Protestant Theology*, pp. 142ff. Cf. Heidegger, *Schellings Abhandlung* and *Nietzsche*.
138 H. Fuhrmans, *Schellings Philosophie der Weltalter* (Dusseldorf, 1954), pp. 238ff. Cf. 'Der Ausangspunkt der Schellingschen Spätphilosophie', *Kant-Studien* 48 (1956–7), pp. 302ff (*G.W.*, vol. iv, pp. 133–44) and W. Kasper, *Das Absolute in der Geschichte* (2 vols., Pfullingen, 1961), p. 124.
139 Tilliette, *op. cit.*, vol. ii, p. 503.
140 *Ibid.*, p. 396.
141 *Subjectivity and Paradox* (Oxford, 1957), p. 51. Pages 50–4 sketch this influence. Von Baader played as important a part as Fichte in Kierkegaard's development away from Romanticism.
142 *Papirer* IIIA 195 (A. Dru, *Journals of Kierkegaard: a Selection* (London, 1938), 399).
143 Charles Hartshorne, 'The case for Idealism', *The Philosophical Forum* (Fall 1968), p. 8.
144 *Paul Tillich: An Appraisal* (London, 1963), *passim*.
145 Kenan B. Osborne, *New Being: A Study of the Relationship between Conditioned and Unconditioned Being according to Paul Tillich* (The Hague, 1969). Cf. Kenneth Hamilton, *The System and the Gospel* (London, 1963). The fullest argument is that of D. J. O'Hanlon in his doctoral dissertation (Gregorian University, Rome, 1957), 'The influence of Schelling on the thought of Paul Tillich'.
146 *On the Boundary: an Autobiographical Sketch* (London, 1967), pp. 51ff.

Bibliographical essay

Fichte

The existing edition of Fichte's collected works is that prepared by his son, I. H. Fichte: *Johann Gottlieb Fichtes Sämmtliche Werke* (Berlin 1845–6; reprinted, Berlin, 1971) (*S.W.* I–VIII) and *Johann Gottlieb Fichtes Nachgelassene Werke* (Bonn, 1834–5; reprinted Berlin, 1971) (*S.W.* IX–XI). A critical edition is being prepared under the editorship of R. Lauth and Hans Jacob, *J. G. Fichte: Gesamtausgabe der Bayerischen Akademie der Wissenschaften*. This edition has three sections, *Werke, Nachgelassene Schriften*, and *Briefe*: twenty volumes have already been published. English translations of these works are not numerous and probably the largest collection is *The Popular Works of Johann Gottlieb Fichte*, a translation by William Smith of several shorter works (of which the most important perhaps is *The Vocation of the Scholar*), and some substantial works like *The Way toward the Blessed Life or the Doctrine of Religion* (vol. II, pp. 277–505). Both *The Science of Knowledge* and *The Science of Rights* and also *The Sceince of Ethics* were translated into English by A. E. Kroeger and were published in London in 1888, 1889 and 1907 respectively. Cambridge University Press has in recent years published fresh translations of two important works by Fichte: *The Science of Knowledge*, edited and translated by Peter Heath and John Lachs ('Texts in German Philosophy Series', 1982) and *Fichte's Critique of All Revelation*, edited and translated by Garret Green (1978).

A most comprehensive and probably well nigh exhaustive list of the works of Fichte which were published before 1968 is given in Hans Michael Baumgartner and Wilhelm G. Jacobs' *J. G. Fichte: Bibliographie* (Stuttgart-Bad Camstadt, 1968). Surprisingly one of the earliest works on Fichte was that of R. Adamson published in London and Edinburgh in 1881. This, like all Adamson's work, is now of historical interest merely and of little use to the contemporary student of idealism. Since the turn of the century a certain impatience with the nationalism of which Fichte was hailed as a herald by German philosophers in the first two decades has worked together with a dissatisfaction with idealism in general to make Fichte rather a neglected figure. Until the rediscovery of Fichte in the 1960s there were very few significant works on him. Of these very few without doubt the outstanding ones are those of Heimsoeth and Léon. Heinz Heimsoeth's book, *Fichte*, published in Munich in 1923 is perhaps the very first book which can be described as a scholarly and faithful account of the most significant aspects of Fichte's thought. It antedates Gurvitch's *Fichtes System der konkreten Ethik* (Tübingen, 1924) which, as one would expect from Gurvitch, is a most penetrating analysis of Fichte's moral and social philosophy and as such gives a valuable survey of the fundamentals of Fichte's thought. As for Xavier Léon's *Fichte et son temps* (Paris, vol. I, 1922; vol. II.1, 1923; vol. II.2, 1924) it is nothing short of a monumental work which remains the most informative and authoritative single study of Fichte. It has been most enlighteningly supplemented, nevertheless, by the work of Reinhard Lauth who has enabled us to see Fichte in terms of his own philosophical development rather than in relation to the rest of the idealist movement. His *Zur Idee der Transzendentalphilosophie* (Munich, 1965) and his earlier article 'Le problème de l'interpersonnalité chez J. G. Fichte', *Archives de Philosophie* 25 (1962) are particularly noteworthy. For not only does Lauth in a real sense rediscover Fichte himself: he has been the first to show that this notion of interpersonality is the key to Fichte's view of history. Thus he has inspired the work of people like Adolph Schurr (*Philosophie als System bei Fichte; Schelling und Hegel*, Stuttgart, 1974) and that of the late C. K. Hunter whose *Der Interpersonalitätsbeweis in Fichtes früher angewandter praktischer Philosophie* (Meisenheim, 1973) is the most thorough and comprehensive study of Fichte's 'archaeological' approach to the theory of interpersonality. Special mention must be made of Professor Frederick Copleston's beautifully lucid and compact survey of Fichte in his *A*

History of Philosophy, vol. VIII (London, 1963) which is the only comprehensive account of Fichte in English. Finally there is the important work of the distinguished Kierkegaard scholar, Emanuel Hirsch. In his *Geschichte der neueren evangelischen Theologie*, vol. IV (Gütersloh, 1952) Hirsch summarised his previous two studies, *Fichtes Religionsphilosophie im Rahmen der philosophischen Gesamtentwicklung Fichtes* (Göttingen, 1914) and *Christentum und Geschichte in Fichtes Philosophie* (Tübingen, 1920). These remain important works despite the fact that there have been some studies of Fichte's philosophy of religion among the many books on Fichte published since the centenary. Of these perhaps the most useful contribution, not least because of renewed interest in the theology of feeling is Reiner Preul's *Reflexion und Gefühl. Die Theologie Fichtes in seiner vorkantischen Zeit* (Berlin, 1969).

Schelling

Just as Fichte's works were collected and published in a complete edition of fourteen volumes by his son so were F. W. J. Schelling's by K. F. A. Schelling: F. W. J. Schelling, *Sämmtliche Werke* (Stuttgart and Augsburg, 1856–61). The Jubilee edition begun by Manfred Schröter in 1927 and completed for the centenary of Schelling's death is a rearrangement of the *Werke* in twelve volumes. A new critical edition, modelled on Lauth's edition of Fichte, which will extend to some eighty volumes is being published by the Bavarian Academy of Sciences under the editorship of H. Fuhrmans and H. Zeltner. Publication began in 1975 and the Historisch-Kritische Ausgabe will appear in four series: (i) the published works (ii) the unpublished manuscripts (iii) the correspondence (iv) the records of his lectures by his hearers. Comparatively little of Schelling's work has been translated into English, and during his lifetime only two pieces were published one of which was the 'Introductory Lecture at Berlin', the inaugural lecture in Berlin of 15 November 1841, which Kierkegaard, Engels and Bakunin would have heard. The other was *The Philosophy of Art*, translated by A. Johnson and published in London by Chapman in 1845. Apart from some shorter pieces such as 'On the possibility of a form for all Philosophy' published in Fritz Marti's translation as recently as 1975, there are only five works of Schelling's in English. The earliest was E. S. Morgan's translation of *On University Studies*, which appeared between 1877 and 1881 and which was published in a new edition by N. Guterman (Athens, Ohio, Ohio University Press, 1966). The first really substantial text to appear in English was James Gutman's translation of *Of Human Freedom* (Chicago, Open Court, 1936). This was followed in 1942 by F. de Wolfe Bolman's translation of *The Ages of the World* (repr. New York, AMS Press, 1967). The University Press of Virginia has published Peter Heath's edition of *Schelling's System of Transcendental Idealism* 1978). These three volumes all contain useful introductions and notes. Finally, the celebrated *Die Nachtwachen des Bonaventura* (1804–5) has been translated and edited by Gerald Gillespie and published by the University of Texas Press in Austin in 1971. Though Gillespie follows the traditional ascription of this text to Schelling it ought to be said that this ascription is very much in dispute.

One of the oldest studies of Schelling is that of the renowned historian of philosophy, Emile Bréhier whose book, *Schelling* was published in Paris in 1912. Until the revival of interest in Schelling after the centenary of his death this was a very important work partly because there was so very little other assistance available to the student of Schelling. However, already in 1940 H. Fuhrmans had shown the importance of Schelling's final period in his significant book, *Schellings letzte Philosophie, Die negative und positive Philosophie im Einsatz des Spätidealismus* (Berlin, 1940). He followed this with a masterly detailed study of Schelling's move into the world of theosophy in the book *Schellings Philosophie der Weltalter* (Dusseldorf, 1954) so that Tilliette has called him 'le maître des études schellingiennes' (X. Tilliette, *Schelling: Une philosophie en devenir* (Paris, 1970), vol. I, p. 38). For Fuhrmans the centre of gravity of Schelling's work is to be found in *Of Human Freedom* and *Ages of the World* and the key to the interpretation of Schelling in the antinomy of necessity and freedom from which polarity all others are derived. Diametrically opposed as it would seem to Fuhrmans' interpretation is that of Walter Schulz. The revolutionary aspect of Schulz's book, *Die Vollendung des deutschen Idealismus in der Spätsphilosophie Schellings* (Stuttgart, 1955) was that he was the first to insist on the unity of Schelling's philosophical production and its essentially rectilinear development. Schulz aimed at recovering the proper appreciation of Schelling's negative philosophy and establishing that Schelling remained a transcendental idealist so that the progression from negative to positive philosophy is the very key to the interpretation of Schelling's philosophy as a development. Precisely because he was the logical conclusion of the philosophical development initiated by Kant he was the precursor of the philosophies of existence.

This conclusion of Schulz's reminds one of Tillich's favourite theme, that existentialism began with Schelling, and it is perhaps particularly appropriate at this point to mention the two studies Tillich published on Schelling because they were notable contributions in their day which remain interesting anticipations of later scholarly opinion and also because they were published in 1974 in an English translation by Victor Nuovo. *The Construction of the History of Religion in Schelling's Positive Philosophy* is the 1910 doctoral dissertation submitted to the University of Breslau and published in the same year; *Mysticism and Guilt-Consciousness in Schelling's Philosophical Development* is the 1912 Halle licentiate dissertation which was published that year. Both English texts were published in Lewisburg by the Bucknell University Press. In the introduction to his first dissertation Tillich describes his task thus: to present the construction of the history of religion as the focal point of Schelling's positive philosophy. His interpretation of Schelling is based on the doctrine of being and potencies. In his view Schelling had become an irrationalist in his later period – the sense that he regards everything that is as having a relation to the idea but that primacy in this relation must be given to being. The history of religion is the focal point of Schelling's positive philosophy. Interestingly enough, it was only the second dissertation which Tillich included among his collected works and there is no doubt that this was the more original work of the two. Typically Tillich sought to paint Schelling's development and his significance on a very large canvas in the sense that he tries to show its place not merely in modern European philosophy but in the whole tradition of philosophy since Parmenides. Much more emphatically than before Tillich emphasizes the unitary development of Schelling's thought and the polarity he now turns to consider is mysticism and the inescapable moral element of guilt-consciousness. His argument is that the antithesis of mysticism and guilt-consciousness, of the realization of theoretical reason in an identity and the realization of practical reason in a differentiated practical reason, can only be overcome by making will an ultimate metaphysical principle. This is achieved by an irrational act of God, overcoming sin with the superabundance of grace. In the Christian reconciliation mysticism triumphs not as mysticism but as a victory of personal community over contradiction.

Without any doubt the greatest work on Schelling, like the greatest study of Fichte, comes from France and Xavier Tilliette's magisterial two-volume study. *Schelling: Une philosophie en devenir*, (Paris, 1970) gives the lie to Père Tilliette's excessively modest disclaimer of any comparison with Léon's *Fichte et son temps*. The very size of the work and its ample survey of texts and literature make any brief account impossible. The first volume discusses 'the living system' as it was developed in the years 1794–1821 and though Tilliette says that his rule is to follow Schelling's intention and sketch the fundamental form of his work rather than its detail the volume is a cosmos of minute research. Thus the second volume devoted to 'the later philosophy' (1821–54) gives an exposition of the positive philosophy in its genesis and total developments. In this context perhaps the most important point to note is the amazing sympathy Tilliette shows which perhaps does not allow the tension between a biblical monotheism and Schelling's pantheism to emerge as a critical problem. In the wake of Tilliette's work there has appeared another important work which must be briefly mentioned, *Liberté et existence* by Jean-Francois Marquet (Paris, 1973). It is sub-titled 'a study of the formation of Schelling's philosophy' and argues that Schelling exemplifies a philosopher's destiny. His true 'system' was written bit by bit in a space which was other than that of the history of his works. It makes much of Schelling's connection with Boehme and there is a useful appendix on Schelling and the Germanic theosophy. Regarding Schelling's influence on German Catholic thought, see Thomas O'Meara, *Romantic Idealism and Roman Catholicism: Schelling and the Theologians* (Notre Dame, Indiana, 1982).

Finally, one of the most instructive books on idealism is F. G. Nauen's *Revolution, Idealism and Human Freedom* (The Hague, 1971) which treats as a unit the early thought of Schelling, Hölderlin and Hegel during the 1790s. Nauen shows that their early thought is affected not only by shared cultural and intellectual attitudes and political expectations as members of a Württemberg élite, but also by their relationship to one another as friend and critic.

3
Georg Wilhelm Friedrich Hegel

PETER C. HODGSON

Hegel envisioned his philosophical enterprise as a 'System of Science' that would encompass all finite realities in a systematic grasp of absolute reality.[1] He also envisioned, initially at least, two points of entry into this system. The first would be the 'The Science of the Experience of Consciousness' – the *Phenomenology of Spirit* of 1807, described as a 'pathway to science' or as a 'ladder' to the absolute standpoint.[2] The second would be the *Science of Logic*, published during the period 1812–16. These represent, respectively, the phenomenological and the logical (or speculative) entrées to the system.

These two 'sciences' were combined in the *Encyclopedia of the Philosophical Sciences* (1817),[3] which included not only a 'Science of Logic' (Part I) and a 'Philosophy of Spirit' (Part III), but also a 'Philosophy of Nature' (Part II) – Hegel's only published work on this subject, although manuscripts from the Jena period containing the rudiments of a *Naturphilosophie* have been edited posthumously. The third part of the *Encyclopedia*, the 'Philosophy of Spirit', encompassed not only materials found in the *Phenomenology of Spirit*, but also those covered by the *Philosophy of Right* (1821) – the fourth and last book published by Hegel during his lifetime – and by his great Berlin lecture cycles, all published posthumously shortly after his death of 1831, on the *Philosophy of Religion* (1832), the *History of Philosophy* (1833), the *Philosophy of History* (1837), and on *Aesthetics* (1835).[4] Hegel's thought about religion was not limited to the lectures on this subject but in fact pervades his entire corpus of works, since in his view all human cultural and intellectual activities find their ultimate center in religion – i.e., 'in the thought, the consciousness, and the feeling of God. Thus God is the beginning of all things, and the end of all things.'[5]

Before turning directly to the subject of his religious thought, it will be helpful to gain a broader perspective on the structure of Hegel's philosophical system. This system is elaborated in terms of Hegel's famous doctrine of the *triple mediation* between the three branches of philosophy, which correspond to three fundamental moments of reality itself: the *logical idea*, *nature*, and *finite spirit*. By 'logical idea' Hegel intends a Platonic-like notion of the pure idea subsisting in the abstract medium of thought, the 'realm' of purely logical relations and concepts, or in theo-logical terms the eternal essence of God before the creation of the world. 'Nature' refers to the natural world (physical, chemical, biological), while 'spirit' in this context means finite human being (as an intersubjective reality, not merely a collection of individual subjects). 'Spirit' or 'mind' (*Geist*) is in fact the ultimate Hegelian category, descriptive of that process of embodied consciousness which encompasses finitude and sublates it, yet is itself intrinsically infinite, universal, and absolute. God is spirit but so also is human being in the modality of finitude and differentiation. Spirit first *appears* in the form of finite consciousness, but the task of philosophy is to show spirit in its rise to its absolute essence as idea, while conversely it demonstrates that the logical idea is actualized by means of its embodiment in nature and finite spirit. The telos of both logical idea and finite spirit is the reality of God as Absolute Spirit, a theme to which we shall return shortly.[6]

The three branches of philosophy are related to each other by a set of syllogisms in which each moment assumes in turn the middle, mediating position between the other two:

... first, nature is the mediating member. Nature, that immediate totality, unfolds itself into two extremes, the logical idea and spirit. But spirit *is* spirit only insofar as it is mediated by nature. Secondly, spirit – known by us as individual and active – is the middle, and nature and the logical idea are the extremes. For it is spirit which recognizes the idea in nature and raises nature to its essence. Thirdly, the logical idea is itself the middle. It is the absolute substance of both spirit and nature, that which is universal and all-penetrating.[7]

The three figures of any syllogism according to Hegel are the individual subject (I), the particular quality (P), and the universal substance or principle (U) (*Enc.*, §§ 181–7). For example, in the syllogism

All human beings are mortal
Socrates is human
Therefore, Socrates is mortal

human beings = U, mortality = P, and Socrates = I. In this form of the syllogism, U is the middle or mediating term, but all syllogisms can be varied so that P and I in turn assume the middle position. While the syllogisms are valid in form, the premises of each syllogism are true only if it can be shown that they derive in turn as conclusions to the other two, in which case we would have a logically necessary system, as Hegel thought to be the case with the system of philosophy. Assuming for the moment that the logical idea = U, nature = P, and spirit = I, Hegel's mediation of the branches of philosophy may be expressed as follows:

1 The natural mediation: U–P–I. The logical idea is the principle of nature; spirit is embodied in nature as pre-self or other-than-self; therefore spirit is founded not in itself but in the logical idea, and the logical idea is the principle of spirit. (This is the form of the mediation represented by the order in which the branches of philosophy are treated in the *Encyclopedia*.)

2 The spiritual mediation: U–I–P. The logical idea is the principle of spirit; nature has its telos in spirit; therefore nature is raised to its essence in the logical idea, and the logical idea is the principle of nature.

3 The logical mediation: P–U–I. Nature has its principle in the logical idea; spirit has its principle in the logical idea; therefore nature and spirit are co-extensive in the sense that nature is the pre-self of spirit, and spirit is the telos of nature.

Now, as is already apparent, the critical assumption underlying the whole of Hegel's philosophical system is that it is the logical idea rather than nature or spirit that is defined as the universal principle, while nature is identified with particularity and spirit with individual subjectivity. If nature were to become the universal principle, then spirit would be mediated with its particular (now merely logical) qualities by means of nature itself, and the resulting system would be *naturalism*. If finite spirit were to become the universal principle, then nature would be mediated with its particular (logical) qualities by means of spirit itself, which would be an instance of *subjective idealism*. Both naturalism and subjective idealism are monisms that tend to reduce everything to one principle: matter or mind. The alternative requires the transcendence of the logical idea as the universal principle rather than its immanence in nature and finite spirit as their particular logical qualities; this transcendence of the idea yields Hegel's *absolute* or *objective idealism*. If nature and spirit are to be mediated in such a way that neither is to be reduced to the principle of the other – and Hegel contends that only this mediation conforms to lived experience – then they must be mediated by a middle term that is the universal principle of both, the logical idea. Nature, in turn, when it assumes the middle position in the triple mediation, prevents finite spirit from collapsing into undialectical identity with pure rationality by disclosing spirit's embodied character and demonstrating that it is not its own principle, while spirit in middle position 'raises nature to its essence' in the sense that it recognizes nature to be the appearance of the idea in the mode of particularity, immediacy, externality.

Although Hegel describes this process as a 'circle of mediations' (*Enc.*, § 189), his thinking is not simply circular. Philosophy does not circle back to the beginning in endless repetition; rather it comes back to the beginning enriched and changed. The concept of philosophy, he writes at the end of the *Encyclopedia* (§ 574), 'is the self-thinking idea, the truth aware of itself – the logical system, but with the signification that it is universality *approved and certified in concrete content as in its actuality*. In this way science has gone back to its beginning: its result is the logical system but as a *spiritual* principle.' Thus the movement of Hegel's thought is both circular and linear; it is, in other words, that of a helix or helical spiral. He stands between the Greek and Romantic fascination with the circle and the biblical view of salvation-history as a linear, teleological process. The two perspectives are reconciled in and transfigured by the Christian doctrine of the Trinity: the triune God is eternally self-complete, yet continually enriches or 'spiritualizes' himself in the world-historical process.

Hegel's system may be viewed against the backdrop of a number of 'undialectical' philosophical positions, all of which he associated with a form of thought described by Kant as *Verstand* ('understanding' or 'intellect'). *Verstand* is undialectical in the sense that it apprehends objects in terms of their specific, abstract, separate, often contradictory qualities, each of which it treats as having a subsistence and being of its own. It is unable to grasp the identity that underlies the different aspects in which things show themselves, and thus it remains trapped in immediacy, unable to mediate between disparate elements rationally. What Hegel means by genuinely mediating or dialectical thought will be noted shortly.

Now, when traditional *metaphysical dualism* employs *Verstand*, it 'takes the infinite only as something negative and so as something "beyond," [supposing] that it is doing all the more honour to the infinite, the more it pushes it into the distance away from itself and removes it from itself as something alien'.[8] Despite the dualism, it was believed possible to have objective knowledge of the transcendent other world by means of revelation and the categories of understanding. This sort of metaphysics was exposed by Kant as 'transcendental illusion'. Although Hegel accepted Kant's critique, he did not agree with the latter's restriction of pure reason to the *a priori* categories of the mind, which are properly applied only to empirically based experience. This position led to an *agnosticism* with respect to things as they are in themselves and to non-empirical realities, such as the soul, freedom, and God (which can be understood only as postulates of practical reason). Hegel contrasted his own 'absolute' or 'objective idealism' to Kant's 'subjective idealism': the 'idea' in which the phenomena of consciousness have their existence is not merely the idea of finite human minds but the 'universal divine idea' (*Enc.*, §§ 40–52).

Another undialectical way of understanding the relation between the infinite and the finite was that of *pantheistic monism* in both atheistic and acosmic forms. Pantheism either takes finite things in their finitude and interconnection to be God, and the world alone really exists: its atheistic form, as in Feuerbach. Or it denies the finite world all reality and truth in differentiation from God, and God alone really exists: its acosmic form, as in Spinoza and the early Schelling. Hegel was forthright in his rejection of pantheism and sought many times to distinguish his own position from it – a position that can be characterized as 'panentheistic' (although he himself did not use this term) rather than as pantheistic (*Enc.*, §§ 50, 151, 573; *L.P.R.* 1: 96–7, 214–18).

Finally, Hegel questioned the adequacy of religious 'intuitionism', according to which God, because he cannot be thought, is given to us only in the *immediacy* of intuition, feeling, or experience. He lamented the poverty of an age that can count it as gain to secure the bare belief that there *is* a God, without concern for the truth or content of such belief. Hegel here referred to Jacobi and Descartes, but he may also have had in mind his colleague and adversary Schleiermacher (*Enc.*, §§ 61–78).[9]

In contrast to dualism, agnosticism, monism, and religious immediacy, Hegel proposed a *speculative dialectic of identity and difference*. 'Dialectic' describes a way of speaking or reasoning (*lektikē*, from *legein*, 'to speak') that pits word against word or thought against thought (*dia* as 'separation') in order, by means of a necessary and mutually negating conflict, to find a way or to indicate a direction toward a mediating, synthesizing position (*dia* as 'transition'). True dialectic involves both separation (negation) and mediation (synthesis, negation of the negative). It is based, not on 'pure' or 'abstract' negation, which would come to a standstill in irresolvable or total conflict, but rather on 'determinate' negation, 'which cancels in such a way that it preserves and maintains what is sublated, and thereby survives its being sublated' – lending 'determinacy' or content to the new form (*Phen.*, 137, 234).

The instrument of this dialectic is 'reason' (*Vernunft*), which is the cognitive process that unites all the contradictions of the intellect (*Verstand*) and is constitutive of the very structure of actuality itself, the 'soul of the world', its moving, vital principle (*Enc.*, §§ 6, 24, 45, 81–2). 'Precisely by pushing a position to the point of self-contradiction', rational or speculative dialectic 'makes possible the transition to a higher truth which unites the sides of that contradiction: the power of spirit lies in synthesis as the mediation of all contradictions'.[10] By means of reason, the difference between experience and thought, being and knowing, finite and infinite is taken up into a dialectical identity in which difference is both annulled and preserved (*aufgehoben*).[11] Philosophy, writes Hegel, is a 'system of identity'. 'Everything is ultimately identity, unity with itself.' But there are many different kinds of unity – abstract and concrete, immediate and mediated, substantial and spiritual – and it is essential to recognize 'the difference in the character of the unity'. Thus 'the whole of philosophy is nothing else than a study of the nature of different kinds of unity' (*L.P.R.* 1: 99–100).

We are prepared now to examine Hegel's religious thought as it develops in accord with the major themes of the *Lectures on the Philosophy of Religion*, although references to earlier works will be included as well.

I. The concept of religion

1. Phenomenological and speculative approaches to religion

We have suggested that there are two points of entry to Hegel's system. The first can be described as a *phenomenological* approach, which takes its start with the crystallization of consciousness out of lower forms of life and traces its 'rise', through various stages of consciousness, to the absolute ground and telos of its being. The analysis would show that, at each stage of consciousness, spirit remains unfulfilled and is constantly drawn beyond itself in the quest for a more adequate and encompassing reconciliation of estranged antitheses – the antitheses of nature and spirit, of consciousness and its objects, of lordship and bondage, of the individual and society, of immanence and transcendence, etc. The fragmentary and alienated character of all forms of subjective and objective human spirit finally propels spirit beyond itself to its home in Absolute Spirit. Ricoeur points out that for Hegel the rise of consciousness entails a movement in which each figure or form of consciousness finds its meaning not in what precedes but in what follows; consciousness is drawn forward toward a meaning in motion, by which each stage is sublated in the following stage. In that sense Hegel offers not an 'archaeology' but a 'teleology' of consciousness: spirit is constituted *as* spirit in the very dialectic of transition from one figure to the next.[12] This 'teleology' is pursued above all in the *Phenomenology of Spirit* but also in the third part of the *Encyclopedia* and in the *Philosophy of Right*.

Now this quest of spirit, this *erōs* for the Absolute, is intrinsically a religious quest. Mark Taylor describes it as the 'itinerarium mentis in Deum' and suggests that for Hegel the rise of consciousness to the Absolute constitutes a form of the proofs for the existence of God, namely, of the cosmological and teleological proofs.[13] Thus it is not surprising that Hegel should recapitulate this phenomenological approach at the beginning of the *Lectures on the Philosophy of Religion* in a section called 'The Necessity of the Religious Standpoint'.[14] The demonstration of the 'necessity' of something implies that one starts from something else, which in this case is the finite world, finite consciousness. The movement of the finite *itself*, not merely our study of it, shows that it raises (*erheben*) and sublates (*aufheben*) itself into something higher than itself. We follow the odyssey of consciousness as it returns of itself to the fountain of its true being. The task of the 'whole circle of the philosophical sciences' is to show how 'the natural and spiritual universes return to their truth in the religious standpoint' (*L.P.R.* 1: 106–9).

Hegel goes on to suggest that this 'return' actually corresponds to the inner dialectic of the divine life. The dialectic of differentiation and return that abides within the pre-worldly Trinity is the *truth* of this dialectic as it appears in the form of the finite world and consciousness. Thus the necessity of the religious standpoint that appeared to be *deduced* from the preceding stages of the natural and spiritual worlds is now seen to be *inherent* in itself. Or, expressed metaphorically, the 'advance' or the 'rise' is like 'a stream flowing in opposite directions, leading forward to what is other than itself, but at the same time working backwards in such a way that what appears as the last, as founded on what precedes, shows itself rather to be the first – the foundation' (*L.P.R.* 1: 109–15).

The metaphor brings us to the point of the peculiar 'reversal'[15] that is so characteristic of Hegel's thought – the reversal from a phenomenological to a *logical* or *theo-logical* perspective, which Hegel also epitomizes as the *speculative* concept of religion in a section so titled at the beginning of the first part of the philosophy of religion lectures. From this point of view it becomes evident that the rise of finite spirit to the Absolute is *at the same time* the return of Absolute Spirit to itself, or the *self*-consciousness of Absolute Spirit (*Phen.*, 685; *L.P.R.* 1: 205–6). Religion entails a relation of finite spirit to Absolute Spirit in which the latter's knowledge of itself is mediated through the former. In its highest form, 'religion is not the transaction or affair of a human being but is essentially the highest determination of the absolute idea itself' (*L.P.R.* 1: 206, cf. 33). Or as Hegel expresses it in the *Encyclopedia* (§ 564), referring to the theologian Göschel: 'If the word

"God" is taken in earnest in religion at all, it is from him, the theme and center of religion, that the method of divine knowledge may and must begin . . . God is God only so far as he knows himself: his self-knowledge is, further, a self-consciousness in man and man's knowledge *of* God, which proceeds to man's self-knowledge *in* God.'

This speculative approach to religion is described by Taylor as the 'descensus Dei in mundum' and coincides with the ontological proof of God's existence. Its logical form is expostulated in both the *Science of Logic* and the *Encyclopedia* 'Logic', whereas the theo-logical form is articulated by the doctrine of the Trinity, which forms the very heart of the Christian religion. By contrast with the various finite or 'determinate' religions, which share in the rise of consciousness to the Absolute, the Christian religion is the 'consummate' or 'revelatory' religion because it is based on the self-disclosure of the Absolute.

Before moving on to a more detailed investigation of Hegel's conception of religion, it will help to ask what he means by the notion of 'Absolute Spirit'. Despite the dialectical relationship of finite and infinite spirit, it is clear that 'Absolute Spirit' cannot refer simply to the absolute primacy of finite consciousness, as the left-wing and atheistic interpreters of Hegel have claimed. It is the logical idea that is absolute (*Enc.*, § 213). Although the idea in its absoluteness stands over against nature and finite spirit, it nonetheless 'goes forth freely' into nature and *actualizes* itself *as* spirit, i.e., as a process of embodied consciousness (*Enc.*, §§ 244, 381). Thus we may conclude that 'the *Absolute is Spirit* – this is the supreme definition of the Absolute' (*Enc.*, § 384). In fact, the terms 'absolute' and 'spirit' reciprocally define each other. Spirit raised to its rational essence is *absolute* because it is the actualization of the logical idea, of pure, self-thinking thought. And the Absolute (God) can be actualized only as *Spirit*. 'The spirituality of God is the lesson of Christianity.' 'Christian theology . . . conceives of God . . . as Spirit and contemplates this, not as something quiescent, something abiding in empty identicalness but as something which necessarily enters into the process of distinguishing itself from itself, of positing its other, and which comes to itself only through this other, and by positively overcoming it – not abandoning it' (*Enc.*, § 381). The Absolute is not 'spirit in general' but 'spirit which is absolutely manifest to itself, self-consciousness, infinitely creative spirit' (*Enc.*, § 384).

Does this identity of the Absolute and Spirit exist from the beginning or is it achieved only at the end of the world-historical process? The proper interpretation, in our view, is that the identity of the Absolute and Spirit, while *implicit* at the beginning, is *actualized* through the historical process and is fully accomplished only at the end. One may appropriately employ the Whiteheadian distinction between the 'primordial' and 'consequent' natures of God, and in fact Hegel himself distinguishes the 'abstract' from the 'spiritual' God (*Enc.*, § 384). Yet for him this 'end' is also the true beginning: 'Absolute Spirit is in reality the true, the positing of the idea, as well as the positing of nature and of finite spirit . . . Absolute Spirit, self-conscious of itself, is the first and the alone true, in which the finite world which is thus something posited exists as a moment' (*L.P.R.* 1: 207).

2. *God as abstract and as related*

The threefold structure Hegel gave to 'The Concept of Religion', especially in his 1827 lectures, is significant because it established the pattern by which he analyzed each historical religion, including Christianity. As we shall see, this structure corresponds to the trinitarian dialectic of the divine life.

First, the idea of 'God' can be *abstracted* from the religious relationship in which it occurs and conceptualized purely in and for itself as the religious 'object'. Here we encounter the 'well-known and familiar idea' of God as the absolute, self-subsisting being, *causa sui*, the abstract universal comprehending and containing everything, God as *absolute substance*. This by itself is an impoverished and inadequate notion of God, for it has not yet advanced to the insight that God is also Absolute Spirit – that *substance* is *subject* and vice versa (*Phen.*, 80) – for such an insight requires the mediation of God with the otherness of the world by which he is spiritualized (*L.P.R.* 1: 61–2, 90–100).

In the second moment a *religious relationship* is established by focussing on the religious subject in whom this relationship transpires. The religious relationship has two aspects, a *theoretical* and a *practical*. The theoretical aspect of the relationship subsists in the several forms of religious consciousness: feeling, intuition, representation, and thought. In Hegel's view, these aspects of religious consciousness correspond to the second moment of the divine life, in which differentiation, diremption, and estrangement occur – the 'representation' (*Vorstellung*) of God in the world, symbolized by the figure of the Son. The third moment comprises the practical aspect of the religious relationship, *cultus* or *worship*, through which the difference between finite and infinite is sublated and reconciliation is brought about. Here we find a correspondence to the third moment of the trinitarian process, the divine return-to-self in the figure of the Spirit.

Formally, the abstract concept of God corresponds to the immanent Trinity, the being of God in and for himself, represented by the figure of the Father. But in point of fact when Hegel took up the immanent Trinity in his treatment of the Christian religion, he did so not under the abstract concept of God but as the first of the 'concrete representations' of God on the part of Christian faith. In other words, the doctrine of the Trinity already presupposes the identity of substance and subject that is lacking in the abstract concept. Thus in the 1821 lectures on the Revelatory or Consummate Religion, the section on the 'abstract concept' was limited primarily to an elaboration of the ontological proof for the existence of God. By 1827 this section had been removed from the Revelatory Religion to the Concept of Religion, where it was treated along with the other proofs. Because the ontological proof is characteristically Hegelian, we shall provide a brief summary of it here, using as our source the version found in the Revelatory Religion.[16]

Whereas the cosmological and teleological proofs begin with finite being and attempt to show a necessary transition to 'infinite universality' or to the concept, the ontological proof moves in just the reverse direction, demonstrating the transition from concept to being (or existence). Both ways are necessary, says Hegel, and the truth is to be found in their identity.[17] The ontological argument is developed in two phases, although the distinction does not stand out very clearly in the text. First, *any true* concept must have reality or being, for the concept without objectivity is only an empty image (*Vorstellen*) or opinion, while being (or reality) without a general concept disintegrates into externality and appearance; or, more simply, 'in the concept being is contained' (*C.R.*, 49, 56). Kant criticized the ontological proof by arguing that being or existence cannot be abstracted ('unpacked') from the concept. Existence is not a predicate and nothing is added to the concept of a hundred dollars if in addition they also *exist*. This is true, says Hegel, only because existence is *already* contained in the concept itself. The *true* concept of a hundred dollars includes the being or reality of these dollars. What Kant intends, however, by thinking in terms of abstract understanding (*Verstand*), is to distinguish *mere subjective* concepts from other, more real human activities, such as intuition, feeling, willing. This is what has led to the general disparagement of the concept as 'only' a concept, which exists subjectively in the heart and has no reality. 'We know quite well, of course', says Hegel, 'that one can build castles in the air, which have no existence in reality.' But such castles are not true concepts, they are merely images or fancies (*C.R.*, 47–9, 101 n. 13, 54–9).

Likewise – and this brings us to the second phase of the argument – the true concept *of God* is of the One who exists *necessarily* because he is not merely *a* concept but *the* concept, the concept of the all-real, the most-real, the perfect. At this point Hegel is able to embrace Anselm's version of the proof: God is by definition 'perfect' ('that than which nothing greater can be conceived'), and *perfection requires the unity of concept and being*. God would be less than perfect if he did not actually exist. This assumption concerning the meaning of perfection, says Hegel, is present in the imagination of all men and lies at the basis of all philosophy. It is assumed by reason and common sense, and only understanding attempts to deny it. However, Hegel develops this aspect of the argument in his own distinctive way. Concrete existence belongs necessarily to the concept of the Absolute because in order to be itself it has to become something other than itself, positing an actual world into which it dirempts itself and from which it returns to itself, enriched, spiritualized, 'existentialized' (*C.R.*, 47–9, 53–8).

3. Religious representation and religious thought

The religious *subject*, to which the focus now shifts, includes within *itself* the relationship of the two sides: the active universal and the immediate subject, the infinite and the finite. 'In thinking I lift myself up to the Absolute . . . and am infinite consciousness, while I remain at the same time finite self-consciousness . . . Both sides seek each other, and both flee from each other . . . It is in myself and for myself that this conflict and this conciliation take place' (*L.P.R.* 1: 63–64). Hegel notes that this focus upon *religion*, or the religious relationship, is the characteristic preoccupation of modern theology, while in the Middle Ages it was the essence of *God* that was thematized and defined. The truth of the modern view is that God is not to be considered apart from subjective human spirit. However, this is not because God remains *unknown*, as in the modern view, but because God himself is essentially *Spirit* and can be known only in terms of a relationship of spirit to Spirit: this relationship *is* religion (*L.P.R.* 1: 101, cf. 258).

The forms of religious consciousness include feeling (*Gefühl*), intuition (*Anschauung*), representation (*Vorstellung*), and thought or conceptual knowledge (*Denken, Wissen*). Although Hegel analyzes all these forms in detail in both the *Encyclopedia* (§§ 445–68) and the *Lectures on the Philosophy of Religion* (1: 115–99), we shall focus our discussion on the latter two and their interrelation.

Vorstellung – a term that resists adequate translation into English, its meaning not being really conveyed by the commonest rendering, 'representation' – is a mode of reflection or intelligence that mediates between sensible intuition and thought. Hegel distinguishes between three moments of representation: recollection (*Erinnerung*), imagination (*Einbildungskraft, Phantasie*), and memory (*Gedächtnis*). Its operations can be described roughly as follows.[18] The imagination produces synthetic representations out of recollected images derived from sensible intuition, under the categoreal forms of the intellect or understanding (*Verstand*). These synthetic images remain abstract and partial, describing things in terms of distinct, contradictory qualities or attributes, but unable to grasp their conceptual unity. To think in terms of examples or pictures rather than definitions, as children often do, is to think representationally. Imagination issues in language that utilizes the intellective categories to produce signs by which represented images are named. These signs are taken up into memory, which reduces them to universal, permanent syntheses or 'words' in which sign and meaning are objectively united, thus rendering the intuition into a representation proper or a *verbal* image. As such, representation is an essential part of the cognitive process. Difficulty emerges only when an attempt is made to render trans-empirical, non-finite, non-ostensive realities in terms of the finite, abstractive categories of the intellect. For example, *Vorstellung* thinks of God as a quasi-sensible object with distinguishable attributes, which fall into contradiction (He is both 'one' and 'three', present in a particular place yet omnipresent, etc.). It is said of human beings that they are both good *and* evil, free *and* dependent. Or infinitude is thought of in spatio-temporal terms as the mere 'beyond' of what is present to hand. *Vorstellung* is unable to work dialectically through these apparent contradictions, and thus it issues in what would be Hegel's version of the Kantian 'transcendental illusion'.[19]

It is important to note that *Vorstellung* is already a form of cognition and that it is in process of resolving itself into thought proper (*Gedanke, Denken*), in which the sensuously based images of representation are sublated – annulled *and* preserved in a strictly rational grasp of actuality (*Enc.*, §464; *L.P.R.* 1: 24–5, 155–8). This movement is already taking place in religious representation and does not merely describe the transition from religion to philosophy. The goal of religion is to attain *knowledge* (*Wissen*) of God, not merely feeling or personal conviction. Such knowledge involves not only an element of *immediacy* (Plato was right in saying that the truth lies implicitly within human being and has only to be aroused by appearing) but also a *mediated* relation to an object or content other than oneself, a relation that posits both identity and difference between the knower and the thing known. Knowledge of God entails an 'elevation' (*Erhebung*) to God; religion is essentially this 'passing over' or 'transition' (*Übergehen*) from one content to another, from the finite to the absolute, infinite content (*L.P.R.* 1: 160–7). When it makes this transition, it must finally leave behind representations of the infinite based on external, sensible apprehensions.

In many respects the question of the relation between *Vorstellung* and thought is *the* problematic issue in Hegel's entire speculative system. On the one hand, thought moves *through* representation *to* conceptual knowledge; on the other hand it *passes back and forth between* representation and concept.[20] As Yerkes points out, Hegel recognized 'the *external temporal priority* of sensuous experience as the initiating occasion of all thinking reflection', and 'the *internal temporal priority* of representational thinking . . . "on the way" to pure thought about God'. The human being *remains* a finite, sensible, historical creature, while at the same time being 'essentially' a thinker. Hence the absolute truth must exist for us historically, and *Vorstellung* is a necessary moment in the rise of consciousness to the Absolute, being preserved as well as annulled by its speculative transformation.[21] Hegel's point seems to be that religious consciousness errs when it merely *rests* with *Vorstellung* and does not *move* back and forth *between* and ultimately *to* conceptual knowledge of God. But he is not finally clear about the modality in which *Vorstellung* is preserved at the conceptual level or how it in fact continues to fructify speculative thought about God. We shall return to this issue in our concluding remarks at the end of the chapter.

4. Religious cultus

Hegel by no means neglects the *practical* form of the religious relationship as constituted by the activities of cultic life. Indeed, he places great emphasis upon the cultus because here the telos of religion is attained, namely, a return to the Universal mediated through the subjectivity and intersubjectivity of worship and the religious community. The subject recognizes the absolute substance in which it is to sublate itself as being at the same time *its* essence, *its* substance, in which self-consciousness is implicitly contained. It is this unity and reconciliation, this feeling of partaking in the Absolute, that constitutes the sphere of cultic life. Hegel insists that the object of worship, God, is by no means a subjective projection, although he does not stand over against the subject as an alien other. Worship consists in the partaking and enjoying (*Genuss*) of something higher than ourselves; it is a liberation from finitude (*L.P.R.* 1: 66–9, 210–11, 221–9).

With reference to each of the historical religions, Hegel treats several topics under the theme of 'cultus': its faith (the form of knowledge associated with worship, the *certainty* of absolute truth), its determinate character and special forms, and its relation to the political sphere. The latter is of special significance because the movement of cultic life leads outwardly into worldly or secular life. This going out into the actual world is essential to religion, which forms the basis for the true liberation of a people.[22]

II. *Determinate religion*

1. The character and structure of determinate religion

Hegel's approach to the study of religion in its determinate historical forms was innovative because he was the first to articulate a history of religions based on the principle of development. Prior to him the religions had simply been classified into three great divisions and evaluated according to certain formal criteria within these divisions: fetishism (animism), polytheism, and monotheism.[23] As we shall see, Hegel took over this classification but he worked it into an ingenious developmental schema that brings to light parallel phenomena at different stages of development. The stages of the consciousness of spirit supply us with the determinate forms of religion. Hegel is quite insistent that 'the religions, as they have followed upon one another, have not arisen accidentally. It is spirit which rules inner life, and to see only chance here, after the fashion of the historical school, is absurd.' We have started, he notes, with the *concept* of religion, but this is the concept as it exists *for us*, in thought. This concept, which is the truth of religion, must also take on *objective* form; it must actually rise to *consciousness*, become explicit in human history. The task of the history of religion is to trace the course by which *true* religion (the concept of religion) takes its *rise* and becomes *actual*. All religions participate in and contribute to this process of actualization; this means that all religions *contain* the concept of religion, but in limited, finite, determinate ways. They do not yet *correspond* adequately to the concept, which attains full actualization only in the Revelatory Religion. Thus Hegel is able to say that all religions possess rationality and truth, and although they 'are not indeed *our* religion, yet they are included in ours as essential though subordinate moments, which cannot fail having in them absolute truth. Therefore in them we have to do not with what is foreign to us but with what is *our own*' (*L.P.R.* I: 76–7, 262–3).

The suggestion that all religions mediate the truth and that they are all included in 'our' religion as 'essential though subordinate moments' amounted to a revolutionary insight. Although ultimately it did not transcend a grandiose Christian imperialism, it led Hegel to consider all expressions of religion with the utmost seriousness, and he developed a vast knowledge of world religions, flawed only by the inadequate scientific basis for the study of religions that prevailed in his time. His analyses were remarkable for their penetrating, non-prejudicial character, for the passion to *understand* the phenomena in question and to *appreciate* their particular mediation of truth, while at the same time locating them in a larger interpretive framework that perceived how the limitations of each preceding stage were transcended by the next. To a considerable degree he approximated the phenomenological ideal of pure description, although what he offered, of course, were not straightforward historical accounts. Rather he sought to isolate what he took to be the essential features of each religion and to redescribe these philosophically; as Fackenheim points out, Hegel's major writings on the subject 'all treat religion *as it is already reenacted and transfigured by philosophic thought*'.[24] This accounts for his very free approach to historical data, his tendency to juxtapose facts without reference to context, to disregard the internal historical development of the particular religions, and to designate the religions by their philosophical rather than their historical names. We should also note that Hegel considered all the world religions except Christianity to be essentially phenomena of the past, living on only in so far as they have been sublated in the Revelatory Religion – a limitation to which we shall return at the conclusion of the essay.

The underlying developmental thesis is that of an advance from the natural immediacy of religious consciousness to the religions that posit the divine as substantial power, thence to those which focus upon spiritual subjectivity (either of God or of human being), finally to the knowledge of Spirit in its absolute truth – a rising up to God in which God brings Himself into relation with the subject (*L.P.R.* I: 263–4; cf. the summary of the entire development provided on 265–9). Thus Hegel divides Determinate Religion into two major parts – the Religion of Nature and the Religion of Spiritual Individuality, in relation to which the Revelatory or Consummate Religion is able to assume the third, mediating position. The developmental schema discloses parallels between the tripartite divisions internal to each of these major religious groups, and the whole is subsumed under an essentially trinitarian view of divine self-manifestation.[25]

2. The Religion of Nature

The most primitive form of religion is *animism*, the belief that all things are immediately indwelt by spiritual powers. Human beings, however, are able to control these powers and make use of them to advantageous ends: this is the purpose of *magic* (shamanism) (*L.P.R.* I: 270–316). Already the utilitarian or expedient function of religion is evident and becomes more so in the emperor-cult of *Chinese state religion*, which anticipates Roman religion. At the same time, however, animism is a primitive form of the religion of Spirit because of its belief in universal spiritual presence, which pervades all things and empowers human beings. Hence a parallel exists between the most primitive religion and the consummate or final religion:

'This idea [of spiritual presence] necessarily belongs to the oldest class of principles. It is present in the Christian religion too, but in a higher form, and, as it were, transfigured' (*L.P.R.* I: 311).

An advance occurs when human beings become conscious of a *substantial power* outside themselves and of their own powerlessness in relation to it. A distinction now arises between the natural and the spiritual, but the latter is still conceived in substance terms. God is the universal absolute substance in which all finite reality is immersed. Thus we arrive at the *pantheism* classically represented by *Buddhism* (the Religion of Being-within-Self) and *Hinduism* (the Religion of Fantasy) (*L.P.R.* II: 1–65).

The final step within the sphere of nature religion is to a conflict between the natural and the spiritual and a resultant *dualism*, but with the spiritual still represented by at least quasi-sensuous images such as 'light'. A movement toward an understanding of the subjectivity and individuality of God occurs with the introduction of the ethical category of the 'good'. Here we find *Persian* religion (Zoroastrianism, Parseeism, the Religion of Light) and *Egyptian* religion (the Religion of Enigma) (*L.P.R.* II: 65–122).

3. The Religion of Spiritual Individuality

The religions included by Hegel under the category of 'spiritual individuality' or 'free subjectivity' *correspond in reverse order* to those preceding them (*L.P.R.* II: 169–70). This is a most important point for the proper understanding of Hegel's architectonic and for the correlation between his treatment of Determinate Relation and Revelatory Religion in the context of the systematic structure of the philosophy of religion as a whole.

It means that the first of the spiritual religions to be considered is the one that parallels the highest of the nature religions. This is *Jewish* religion or the Religion of *Sublimity*, which advances beyond dualism to a genuine *monotheism* and understands God as 'spiritual subjective unity' (a conception which for the first time rightly merits the name 'God'), in radical distinction from the finite, created, natural world. Because God remains abstract subjectivity with no internal relations (he is not yet properly conceived as 'Spirit' but only as 'Father'), the world is not a moment of divine self-othering and has no essential relation to God, hence no genuine self-existence; it remains prosaic, undeified, negated. The term that best describes the relation between the holy, exalted God and the inessential, powerless, negated world is that of 'sublimity'. The human condition is one of servitude: service to the Lord and fear of him, which is the beginning of true wisdom. This religion generates *anguish* (*Schmerz*), which arises out of the knowledge of the irreconcilable estrangement between the divine and the human, as well as *hope* for a future reconciliation (*L.P.R.* II: 170–224). Hegel's treatment of Judaism is not as prejudiced as if often claimed, but the essential inadequacy of it is that he neglects the post-biblical development of Judaism and does not consider it as a continuing, living religion. In this respect he shares the anti-Judaism of European Christendom, which ghettoized Jewish culture and religion and then proclaimed that Judaism was a thing of the past.[26]

In sharp contrast to the transcendence of Jewish religion stands the immanence of *Greek* religion, the Religion of *Beauty*, which is also a religion of humanity and freedom. Here nature is transfigured into the multiple outward forms of spirit, and the one infinite subjectivity of Jewish religion particularizes itself into a number of finite divine subjects. This is a spiritualized pantheism or *polytheism* and hence, from a religio-historical perspective, parallels the Religions of Substance (Buddhism, Hinduism). These finite gods are formed by the human imagination: they are 'invented', Hegel says, but not 'fictitious', because they are projections or representations of the *implicit* divinity of human spirit. In them are expressed the nobility and freedom of the human spirit and the beauty of its bodily form. The defect with these gods, however, is not that they are *too* human; rather they are insufficiently so because the sensuous form in which they necessarily appear cannot yet be set free as sensuous but remains 'blended' with the gods. Absolute Spirit cannot yet appear in a particular, empirical individual but requires for its appearance a multiplicity of quasi-sensuous gods. In the birth of these gods, nature is subdued but not yet overcome, sublated. Finally, over the entire circle of the gods prevails the sphere of necessity or fate (*Ananke*) – ultimate, impenetrable power (*L.P.R.* II: 224–88; cf. Hegel's extolling of the 'Religion of Art' in *Phen.*, 709–49).

The relation between Jewish and Greek religion is a reciprocal one, as signalized by the fact that in 1827 Hegel varied the order in which he treated them, taking up Greek religion first and Judaism second.[27] In the 1827 lectures it becomes clear that from the point of view of *theology* Jewish religion is superior because its God is *one* and *holy*, whereas from the point of view of *anthropology* Greek religion is superior because of its celebration of human subjectivity and freedom. The more complex and innovative history of religions structure adopted by Hegel in 1824 (by way of contrast with 1821 and 1827) required that Jewish religion be treated first and Greek religion second, as, respectively, religions of transcendence and immanence, monotheism and polytheism, paralleling the religions of light and substance, anticipating the kingdoms of the 'Father' and the 'Son'. But there is no simple evolutionary progression from Jewish to Greek to Roman religion, as though each were superior to its predecessor. Rather the strengths and weaknesses of Jewish and Greek religion complement each other, while Roman religion represents a collapse into decadence.

In *Roman* religion we find a reversion to the *expedient* or *utilitarian* function of religion first evident in the Religion of Magic. The ends sought after by religious means are at first immediate, finite, particular: the desires and needs of private individuals, the quest for pleasure, good fortune (hence this is also a religion of egoism or selfishness). But the universality of these ends is happiness, and the content of this happiness is the *state*. The well-being of the state in its universal, worldly sovereignty becomes the ultimate end of Roman religion. However, this universal state remains finite, devoid of divinity – a collectivized manifestation of merely human amoral self-seeking. In Hegel's view the most demonic form of power is that of a state without God, a state that pretends to *be* God. The decadent animism of this religion is reflected by the fact that the Romans were avid inventors and collectors of gods; they had expedient finite gods for every occasion, public and private, and thus were seemingly very pious. But in fact by collecting all the gods they had plundered from Greek and Egyptian temples and setting them up side by side in the Roman Pantheon, they allowed the gods mutually to extinguish one another. Out of this demise of the gods emerges the true Roman god, *Fortuna publica*, cold, unsympathetic, empty fate, which is a mask for death – the death celebrated by the violent slaughters of the religious games, the tyranny of the emperors, and the *virtūs* of suicide (*L.P.R.* II: 288–315).

Thus the religion whose end is happiness culminates in the absolute *unhappiness* of spirit – an unhappiness that results from an infinitizing of the finite, a finitude without measure or standard. The truth of the reconciliation of finite and infinite could arise not in the Greco-Roman world but only among a people who possessed the pure idea of the One, yet were painfully separated from it. The confluence of Jewish anguish (vis-à-vis the unattainable transcendent God) and Greco-Roman unhappiness (vis-à-vis the unredemptive character of finitude) defines the moment when 'the time had fully come . . .' (*L.P.R.* II: 316–23; *C.R.*, 147–52).

III. The Consummate or Revelatory Religion[28]

1. The character and structure of the Revelatory Religion

Christianity is the *consummate* religion because it is the religion of *revelation*. '*What* God is, and the fact that he is known *as* he is . . . is made manifest in it. Open manifestation is its character and content, namely, the revelation, manifestation, being of God for consciousness.' Revealedness constitutes the very essence of God, who discloses himself eternally in and as the process of self-diremption and return-to-self. 'A Spirit that is not open or manifest is no spirit' (*C.R.*, 11–13; cf. *L.P.R.* 1: 83–5). It must be acknowledged that Hegel evidences a tendency toward an all-consuming, enthusiastic revealedness that leaves nothing concealed or mysterious: God makes himself utterly open and is rationally comprehensible (*C.R.*, 78–9, 91).[29] Hence the consummate religion is also the *absolute* religion in the sense that absolute knowledge of the Absolute is attained, at least in the mode of religious representation.

Hegel enumerates other characteristics of Christianity, including truth, freedom, and reconciliation (*C.R.*, 12–15), but the most important of these is that the *revelatory* (*offenbar*) religion is also the *revealed* (*geoffenbart*) religion, which is to say that it is a *positive* religion, given to consciousness in a sensible, historical fashion (*C.R.*, 16). It was only by means of considerable intellectual struggle that Hegel came to appreciate the 'positivity' of the Christian religion,[30] although it remained a stumbling block for him to the end. He acknowledged the necessity of positivity because 'everything must come to us in external fashion', and external authority plays an essential role in human affairs, as the function of positive law indicates. Yet the essential, rational truth of the Revelatory Religion, while mediated positively, derives solely from its spirituality and can be verified only by the witness of the Spirit, not by historical proofs (*C.R.*, 16–26). The tension in Hegel's thought on this point, and his antihistorical impulse, become especially evident in the last section of the Revelatory Religion, where he takes up the question of the verification of the faith of the community that Jesus was the Christ. After a rather extended discussion of miracles, he concludes with a generalized critique of the 'historical [*historisch*], juridical method of confirming a fact', which leads to the famous statement that spiritual content 'is to be justified by philosophy, not by history; what the Spirit does is no history [*Historie*]'. However, in the more fundamental sense, Spirit *is* historic (*geschichtlich*) in its process of self-distinguishing and self-redintegrating; and Hegel insists with equal rigor that the 'eternal divine history' (*Geschichte*) is empirically, sensibly present in Jesus of Nazareth. His point seems to be that what is *in fact* sensibly present and positively revealed in Christ – the divine reconciling idea – can be recognized *as such* only by faith, spiritually, not by miraculous proofs or historical investigation. The divine idea precisely 'as realized in this individual' can be *properly* verified only by the 'witness of the Spirit' after the death of Christ and his removal from the temporal sphere (*C.R.*, 243–54).[31]

In the 1821 lectures Hegel's treatment of the Revelatory Religion followed the familiar division of 'abstract concept of God', 'concrete representation', and 'cultus', established in the Concept of Religion and applied to each of the Determinate Religions. But beginning in 1824 this schema was modified in such a way as to make the trinitarian structure underlying it quite explicit. The Christian religion was now set forth in terms of three 'spheres', 'moments', or 'elements' in the 'development of the idea of God'. These moments are not simply contingent occasions in the outward manifestation of God but rather have their basis in the immanent trinitarian life of God, i.e., in the 'divine history' itself. In 1831 Hegel made this even more explicit by referring to the moments as three determinations of the divine 'self-revelation'; and they were now given the specific trinitarian designation of the three 'kingdoms' of the 'Father' (the being of God in-and-for-itself, the immanent Trinity), the 'Son' (divine self-differentiation and incarnation), and the 'Spirit' (divine self-reconciliation and spiritual presence).[32] The next three sections of our presentation will allow this structure to unfold.

2. The idea of God in and for itself: the immanent Trinity

The doctrine of the Trinity, in Hegel's view, is the 'central point' and 'absolute truth' of the whole of philosophy, the 'fundamental determination' of the Christian religion (*C.R.*, 79–80; *L.P.R.* 1: 39). When Hegel uses the word 'Trinity', he ordinarily means the immanent, logical, or pre-worldly Trinity, i.e., the *actus purus* of the inner divine life, the process of diremption and return contained *within* the eternal concept. 'God in his eternal universality is the one who distinguishes himself, determines himself, posits an other that is his own, and likewise sublates the distinction, thereby remaining present to himself, and is Spirit only through this process of being brought forth' (*C.R.*, 94; cf. 67–8, 73, 78–9, 86).

The immanent character of this process is brought out by the suggestion that what is involved is a 'play' or 'show' of distinction and sublation, 'a play of love with itself in which no seriousness is attributed to other-being'. Love is in fact the most intrinsic attribute of the triune divine life. Love entails both a distinguishing of two and a sublation of the distinction, so that the two are actually one. Love means to have one's self-consciousness not in oneself but in another, to find oneself in the *other* as one's own. It describes a *union mediated by relationship and hence difference*.[33] This union is what constitutes personhood or personality. To be a person means to be reflected into self through distinction, to find one's self-consciousness in another, to give up one's abstract existence and to win it back as concrete and personal by being absorbed into the other (*C.R.*, 72, 80–3, 94–5). Hence God's being is intrinsically personal: He is the one true and perfect person. However, there are not three 'persons' in God as represented by traditional Church dogma, for this notion, when pursued literally, leads to three Gods and the loss of divine subjectivity and unity. The names 'Father', 'Son', and 'Spirit' are figurative, childlike ways of expressing the three moments constitutive of the interior dialectic of the divine life – unity, differentiation, return; or universality, particularity, and individuality. In truth, all three are 'Spirit', and Spirit represents the result or totality, the end of the divine life that is also the beginning. The three-in-oneness of the Trinity can be properly grasped only speculatively, not by means of *Verstand*, which attempts to count and thus falls into contradiction.[34]

Implicit throughout Hegel's work, although rarely discussed explicitly as such, is the correspondence between the immanent and the economic Trinities. The spheres of the immanent divine life are the same as those of worldly life, and the otherness within God's life is the *truth* of otherness as it appears in the form of the finite world and consciousness. To become a concrete, spiritual, actual God, the logical or immanent Trinity (the 'primordial' nature of God in Whiteheadian language) must be reenacted in the economic Trinity (the creation of the world and finite spirit as other-than-God and the sublation of the difference). In this sense God is dependent or 'consequent' upon the world to become God in the true and actual sense. God is God-in-process: 'Without the world God is not God' (*L.P.R.* 1: 114–15, 200). Yet this dependence is already posited in the immanent intermediation of the logical Trinity; and the dependence of God upon the world is therefore independence, the necessity of creation is the purest freedom, the divine self-othering is gratuitous love. An ultimate harmony prevails between the primordial and consequent natures of God – or, in more classical language, between the inward 'processions' and the outward 'missions' of the Trinity – without the two being collapsed into an undifferentiated identity (*Enc.* §§ 381, 383, 384). Fackenheim brings this out clearly:

> The preworldly trinitarian play is complete, apart from its worldly manifestation; yet this latter – no mere repetition of the play – is as real for philosophic comprehension as it is for Christian faith. The trinitarian God is wholly real apart from the world and wholly real in it, and only because of His preworldly reality can His worldly manifestation be complete. *The two Trinities of Christian faith, then, do not reduce themselves, in one of two opposite ways, to one: they remain two, for philosophic thought as much as for Christian faith. And philosophy accepts what faith has asserted: that their relation is Love.*[35]

In terms of the architectonic of Hegel's system, the 'Kingdom of the Father' is clearly coterminous with the logical idea of the *Encyclopedia* and represents figuratively the immanent or preworldly Trinity, God as absolute, abstract idea. However, the 'Kingdom of the Son' encompasses both nature and finite spirit (the second and third parts of the system), since it represents divine self-differentiation, including the creation of the world (natural and human), the fall, the incarnation and the beginning of reconciliation. And the 'Kingdom of the Spirit' corresponds to Absolute Spirit (the end of the system that constitutes a return to the beginning), since it represents divine self-redintegration and the consummation of reconciliation in the community of Spirit. Thus the trinitarian structure of the divine life modifies in certain respects the triadic structure of the system: nature and finite spirit correspond to the second 'person' of the Trinity, while Absolute Spirit corresponds to the third.[36] Moreover, the economic Trinity, which really includes the whole *plērōma* God and world, *encompasses* the immanent Trinity as the first of its moments – the divine subject that goes forth into the world and returns to itself.

3. Divine self-differentiation: creation, fall, incarnation, redemption

The second moment in the development of the idea of God is subdivided into two themes: creation and fall, and incarnation and redemption. We shall have to treat the first of these quite briefly. Creation *corresponds*, to be sure, to the second moment of the inner dialectic of the divine life. But Hegel makes it clear many times that the created world is not simply *identical* with God in the moment of self-differentiation: there is a difference between 'the eternal Son of the Father' and 'the physical and spiritual world'. Such an identification would entail a crude pantheism, which Hegel consistently avoids.[37] His position may rather be described as *panentheism*: the world exists *in* God but is not identical *with* God. The 'in' suggests that the divine differentiation *ad intra* constitutes the condition for the possibility of other-being *ad extra*. While *implicitly* and *teleologically* one, both God and the world *need* the moment of *explicit*, *actual* difference. Hegel's position can best be understood if it is recognized that he shares with Augustine, Aquinas, and the medieval and German mystics the great Neo-Platonic schema of *exitus et reditus*, emanation and return. In such a schema, nature and the created order may be understood to be *genuinely* different from the creative ground of being but not *radically* or *wholly* different. For Hegel the difference is to be understood dialectically, because the truth and telos of the world remains the divine idea.[38]

Hegel describes human being as 'finite and natural spirit' and focuses on what he calls the 'natural man', who exists 'according to nature'. To exist in such a way means to establish the criteria for one's life according to the immediacy, particularity, and externality of physical nature; it means to allow one's desires, appetites, physical needs, and private self-seeking to dominate the will rather than thought. Nature itself is not evil, but when it is allowed to serve as the criterion and telos of human being it becomes an occasion for the actual occurrence of evil. The precondition of evil is knowledge, and Hegel appears to be fascinated by the contradiction and ambiguity of knowledge as depicted by the story of the fall. On the one hand, it is precisely knowledge that constitutes the essence of human spirit, the *imago Dei* in humanity; yet on the other hand Adam is forbidden to eat of the tree of knowledge of good and evil because the serpent knows, and God knows, that it will make man 'like God', capable of infinite knowledge and eternal life. Knowledge is the precondition of evil in the sense that one cannot *do* evil, either in the sense of existing according to nature or of projecting oneself into divinity, if one does not *know* what the possibilities of evil are (*C.R.*, 122–61).

Despite the central importance of the second theme, *incarnation*, as 'the speculative midpoint' of philosophy (*L.P.R.* 1: 151), Hegel never discusses it in terms of the language and problematic of classical christology: two natures (divine and human), one person (of the incarnate Logos), hypostatic union, *communicatio idiomatum*, etc. He does not need to because he is operating with an anthropology of divine-human union that avoids the conventional aporia of incarnationist christology. He offers rather a speculative transfiguration of this doctrine in terms of an argument for the possibility, necessity, and actuality of the incarnation (or 'appearance') of God in a single individual.

The *possibility* of such an incarnation is based on the general concept of 'incarnation', meaning, in Hegel's view, the ideal unity or implicit identity of divine and human spirit, the idea of reconciliation, the 'universal divine idea' (*C.R.*, 46, 170, 174–5; *Phen.*, 760). This is what Hegel intends by twice quoting the line of Schiller: 'From the chalice of the entire realm of spirits foams forth to God his own infinitude' (*Phen.*, 808; *C.R.*, 172). On the one hand, God is not abstract infinitude, cut off from the possibility of appearing, but is a concrete God, capable of entering into finitude, negation, and suffering, as connoted by the image of the chalice. On the other hand, humanity is capable of receiving this appearance, of being assumed into communion with God, recognizing the Universal as *its* goal, as *its own essence* (*C.R.*, 169, 171–4, 191).

The *necessity* of the incarnation is grounded, first, in the process of self-othering intrinsic to the divine life, which we have considered already. But in addition, the consciousness of reconciliation can first arise not in the form of philosophical speculation but rather in that of empirical certainty. 'Only what exists in an immediate way, in inner or outer perception, is *certain. In order for this divine-human unity to become certain for man, God had to appear in the world in the flesh*' (*C.R.*, 181). Hegel stresses not only the sensible, positive way that consciousness of divine-human unity must be mediated, but also the fact that this consciousness must *come to* humanity. In view of the estrangement into which the human condition has fallen, the truth must *appear* in order for it to be *recollected*, and incarnation characteristically takes on the aspect of 'appearance' (*Erscheinung*) for Hegel.[39]

How does the idea of divine-human unity *actually* appear in history? It does so, according to Hegel, not in a multiplicity of incarnations but in *one particular individual*, who is not merely a divine teacher or a teacher of morality but the 'God-Man', the 'Son of God', because in him the divine idea is realized *explicitly* and in its *consummate development*. Why should this be the case? Because it is only in a single individual that we find the *concrete* unity of universality and subjectivity, of infinitude and finitude. The individual represents the final pinnacle, the fullest actualization, of spirit in its subjectivity: 'Once is always' (*Einmal ist allemal*).[40] This does not seem quite to settle the matter, because it is conceivable that such a concrete unity could be differently manifested in several individuals. Perhaps principles of efficiency and sufficiency are operative here in an unspoken way, together with the assumption that ultimacy is in some sense exclusive or unitary. Moreover, if there were several God-men, each equally consummate, they would have to be compared under an abstract category (such as God-manhood) and the concreteness associated with the appearance of the truth would be lost.

How are we to determine whether any particular individual is *this* individual, the one who stands over against all the others as the ground of their certainty? This determination, says Hegel, is a matter for history to make, not philosophy (*C.R.*, 191, 242). But *how* is history to be read? How is the claim of the Christian community that Jesus of Nazareth is this individual, the Christ, to be verified? At this point Hegel is not entirely consistent, although his dominant emphasis is clear. The verification that Jesus was the one in whom the divine idea was concretely and consummately actualized is a matter of the *witness of the Spirit* to the community of faith; it is a proof of the Spirit, not a proof by miracles or any other sort of merely historical evidence. Indeed, apart from the witness of the Spirit, Jesus may be viewed only as an ordinary man in accord with his external circumstances – a Socrates, a martyr to the truth (*C.R.*, 193, 239–56). But there is another, less dominant motif that surfaces when Hegel takes up the teaching of Jesus and his passion and death. Here he purports to give an account of how the idea of divine-human unity takes its course in the history of this individual such that his temporal presence is able to be a *presentation* (*Darstellung*) of the idea – indeed a presentation that is '*absolutely adequate to the idea*' (*schlechthin der Idee gemäss*). 'It is the divine idea that courses through this history.' Moreover, the words of Jesus, his teachings, 'confirm the truth of the idea of what he has been for his community'.[41] Statements such as these reflect the utter seriousness with which Hegel, at least during his Berlin period, affirms the factual positivity of the incarnation of the divine idea in the historical Jesus. It would be wrong to suggest that he equivocates on the question as to whether Jesus was *in fact* or was only *believed* to be the God-man. Rather, as we pointed out earlier, his position is that the *facticity* of Jesus' identity as the consummate appearance of the divine idea can be *properly* perceived and affirmed not in a merely historical but rather in a spiritual mode, by faith, after his death and removal from the immediacy of apprehension.

Thus the actual life-history or 'story' of Jesus is a matter of central importance for Hegel. Although his exegetical procedure is utterly uncritical, his theological insight is striking. For example, his discussion of the teaching of Jesus focuses on the themes of the kingdom of God and love – themes inherited from his early writings and presented with great religious power. He is sensitive to the revolutionary, world-transforming character of Jesus' proclamation, which announces the condition for the possibility of a new modality of human communion and freedom, a new way of being in the world (*C.R.*, 184–199). This revolutionary proclamation led directly to Jesus' crucifixion, which 'sealed the truth of his teaching'. Death represents the extreme limit of the finitude and negation of ordinary human life. Thus to say that 'God himself is dead' on the cross of Christ is to refer to the pinnacle of divine self-divestment, the uttermost proof that God took on human form.[42] Death, however, also represents the 'highest love' that arises out of 'deepest anguish'. By the very intensification of finitude to the limit, the latter is sublated and redemption is accomplished. God is not literally 'satisfied' by a price that has been paid; rather reconciliation is shown to be his eternal nature, the fundamental law of reality (*C.R.*, 199–221).

4. Divine self-reconciliation: the community of the Spirit

The resurrection of Jesus from the dead signifies that the divine 'process' does not come to a halt with the death of God; rather God 'maintains himself in this process, and the latter is only the death of death. God rises again to life, and thus things are reversed' (*C.R.*, 212). Obviously, the sensible, representative form in which this doctrine is couched must be philosophically transfigured, for the reality of the resurrection has nothing to do with empty tombs and physical appearances. It is a reality for faith alone, not for external history, as signified by the fact that Christ appeared only to his friends. In fact, the resurrection-event constitutes a transition from the sensible presence of God in a single individual to the spiritual presence of God in the community of faith. It can be treated under the figures of both 'Son' and 'Spirit', and thus the boundary between these two 'kingdoms' remains blurred for Hegel.[43] He uses a revealing expression when he says that the 'sensible history' of Christ has been 'sublated to the right hand of God'. The *Auferstehung* (resurrection) of Jesus entails an *Aufhebung* (sublation) – an annulling of his sensible presence, yet a preservation of real presence and its transfiguration into the modality of Spirit (*C.R.*, 246, 248). The resurrection *means* the spiritual presence of Christ in the community, Christ's presence *as* Spirit, the universal actualization of the redemption accomplished definitively in him (cf. *C.R.*, 236–7, 252).

Thus God himself is no longer present in the form of historical objectivity but rather in that of inwardness or subjectivity, for which faith is the appropriate mode of apprehension. However, this is a peculiar form of subjectivity: it is a *renewed, transfigured, communal* subjectivity, in essence a unique and unsurpassable *inter-subjectivity*, engendered by the 'infinite love that arises from infinite anguish', distinguishable from all other forms of human love and friendship. Privatistic and exclusivistic modes of existence are set aside, as are all distinctions based on mastery, power, position, race and wealth, and in their place is actualized a truly universal justice and freedom (*C.R.*, 235–6, 238–9). The community in which God dwells is the community of faith, the community of the Spirit. The name 'Holy Spirit' refers to the unifying and liberating power of divine love arising from infinite anguish – the same love that was objectively represented on the cross of Christ but that now works inwardly, subjectively, building up a new human community. 'This is the Spirit of God, or God as present, actual Spirit, God dwelling in his community.' The community of Spirit is identical with the Kingdom of God proclaimed by Jesus. The Kingdom of God *is* the Spirit, or more precisely, 'the Kingdom of the Spirit', which is the name for the third sphere of the Consummate Religion (*C.R.*, 217, 235–8).

Following a section in which he argues that the community of faith *originated* in the verification that Jesus was the Christ by the witness of the Spirit (to which we have already referred in our discussion of positivity), Hegel takes up the question of the *existence* of the community. Although it is essentially a spiritual community, it must also assume the form of a worldly organization or institution. It becomes the *Church*, which subsists in a number of determinate forms: faith (the credo), doctrine, repentance (spiritual rebirth), and cultus (*C.R.*, 256–70). The latter is the most important, constitutive of the very essence of the Church, and with regard to it Hegel makes a seemingly un-Protestant move, for the focus of Christian worship is to be found not in preaching or prayer but rather in the sacrament of Holy Communion. By eating and drinking the body and blood of the Lord, the communicant actually partakes of and enjoys the reconciling union of God and humanity. In this sense the communion entails an eternal repetition of the life, passion, and resurrection of Christ in the members of the Church, and it represents a consummation in praxis of the truth of the Christian faith.[44] Hegel's tendency to downplay the actual post-biblical development of Christianity is reflected in his argument that the only significant difference among the Christian confessions arises at the point of interpreting the sense in which Christ is present in the eucharistic elements. Between the Catholic veneration of the host as the prolonged sensible presence of Christ, and the Reformed reduction of the sacrament to a mere memorial, stands the authentic Lutheran view of the spiritual presence of Christ, not in the elements as such, but in the act of partaking, which is an act of faith (*C.R.*, 271–2, 274–6).

IV. Religion, philosophy, and modern secular culture

1. The relation of religion and philosophy

Hegel includes under the cultic aspect of religion its relation to secular life and the actualization of reconciliation not only in the community of faith but also in the cultural and political forms of the secular world. He believed that such an actualization had come about in Western culture with the creation of what Fackenheim calls a 'final secular-religious world', which recognizes the immanence of the divine in three major spheres of ethical activity: the family, economics, and the state. The sanctity of these spheres is pointedly affirmed vis-à-vis the monastic vows of chastity, poverty, and obedience.[45] In the Philosophy of Religion lectures Hegel takes up this theme in a section called 'the realization of the spirituality of the community in universal actuality', the culminating modality of which is the transfiguration of faith into philosophy. The goal of these lectures, he says, has been to reconcile reason with religion, to show the rationality and necessity of religion in its manifold forms, and thereby to advance the cause of religious faith. This reconciliation is based on the conviction that religion and philosophy, while assuming different *forms*, have the same *content*, which is the truth of the self-revealing God and of divine-human union. On the one hand, Christian faith has the true content but lacks the form of thinking, while on the other hand philosophy recognizes the necessity and temporal priority of the imaginative, figurative forms of religion while at the same time transcending them in the true form, which is the form of truth, the concept (*C.R.*, 289–92; *Phen.*, 797–8, 805–6).

There is a sense in which Hegel intends to maintain a reciprocity in the relationship between religion and philosophy. He points out that religion can exist without philosophy, since its forms are adequate to the content and are available to all persons, but that philosophy cannot exist without religion, since it has access to its content only through religion, which it encompasses. He once remarked that 'a philosophy without heart and a faith without understanding are abstractions from the true life and being of knowing and believing . . . Thought and faith are part of a living whole, each fragmentary by itself.' If philosophy is 'higher' than religion, this is only because the form of the concept is higher than the form of faith. The 'reciprocal relation' between the two suggests that the religious image gives rise to the speculative concept, while the latter in turn articulates the true meaning of the former.[46]

But in the final analysis Hegel is not as clear about the reciprocity as he is about the sublation of religion in philosophy. 'Philosophy', he says, '*is* theology' in the sense that it presents the reconciliation of God with Himself and the world and re-establishes the significance of the classical dogmas. 'Philosophy is itself, in fact, worship' (*L.P.R.* I: 20, 37–40; *C.R.*, 289–90, 292). It appears to have the capacity to take over the function of religion, although Hegel is careful never to draw the conclusion that religion, like art, has become 'for us a thing of the past'.[47] Religion remains a living, vital reality alongside philosophy. Nonetheless, Lauer and Fackenheim are right in suggesting that Hegel's philosophy of religion produces something like a 'philosophical religion', which transfigures all determinate historical religions and purports to grasp the divine-human relationship *sub specie aeternitatis*.[48]

2. *The twilight of Christendom*

When Hegel concluded his lectures in 1821 he experienced a rather frightful vision of contemporary Christian decadence and of the collapse of the very secular-religious world into which he believed the community of faith was in process of being 'transformed' or 'realized'. As in the age of the Roman Empire, so now, he says, everything has been profaned and there is no true belief in God. A mania spreads abroad for private rights, goods, enjoyments; the religious basis of political life, of objective veracity and truth, has been lost. The clergy and teachers have abandoned their responsibilities, and the speculative truth of the Gospel is no longer heard, having been replaced by dead and merely historical modes of cognition. The salt has lost its savor; love *without* anguish is proclaimed. All that remains is 'finitude turned in upon itself' – a prevailing scepticism, subjectivism, privatism. (*C.R.*, 294–6.) Apparently the vision did not recur because in subsequent years the ending to the philosophy of religion lectures was completely different; but it is difficult for the reader at least to shake the vision off.

If we are in fact experiencing 'the twilight of Christendom' (Crites), does this not imply that the community of faith will 'perish' or 'pass away'? Yet 'to speak of a passing away would mean to end on a discordant note'. At this point divergences occur between Hegel's own lecture manuscript and the *Werke* (*L.P.R.* III: 149–51), whose version apparently draws on the now-lost transcript of the 1821 lectures by Leopold von Henning. In the manuscript certain qualifications are immediately introduced. The passing away in fact means only a 'passing over' to the kingdom of heaven. Moreover, the passing away applies only to individual subjects, not to the community, and it concerns only the external, contingent forms of religion, not its true substance. None of these qualifications is found in the *Werke*, which goes on to read: 'Only, how can it be helped? This discordant note is present in actuality.'

Thus we are left wondering whether the twilight of Christendom in fact spells an end to the Christian faith. As we have pointed out, Hegel regarded religion as a necessary and inexhaustible expression of human spirit. If so, two possibilities would appear to be open. One would be to replace the outmoded religions of the past by a new secular, humanistic religion 'within the limits of reason alone', a *Volksreligion*. But that option, explored by the young Hegel, was excluded by the mature thinker; in any case it would have no effect against the cultural decadence to which he pointed. The other possibility would be that Christian faith is capable of assuming new historical or philosophical forms, of being reborn out of the 'cross of the present' (*Right*, p. 12). 'The gates of hell', he writes, misquoting the words attributed to Christ in Matthew xvi. 18, 'shall not prevail against my teaching' (*C.R.*, 294). Perhaps Hegel intended to contribute to the rebirth of this teaching by means of his speculative transfiguration, which would bring to light the purely revelatory, consummate nature of the Christian religion, no longer hindered by its figurative, finite forms. Alongside the discordant note, Hegel sustained a prevailing ontological and historical confidence, which encompassed the destructive power of the negative but was never destroyed by it.[49]

3. The limits of Hegelian philosophy: fragmentariness and forgetfulness
It may appear surprising that so inclusive and unitary a philosophical system as Hegel's should be subject to the criticism of fragmentariness and forgetfulness. But Hegel himself hinted at the *fragmentary* character of his attempted philosophical resolution of the present-day discord. Religion, he says, must take refuge in philosophy, but philosophy 'is partial: it forms an isolated order of priests, who hold sway in their sanctuary, who are untroubled by how it goes with the world, who must not mix with it, and whose work is to protect this possession of truth. How things turn out in the world is not our concern' (*C.R.*, 297). Even if one follows the reading of the *Werke*, which qualifies the last sentence by adding the word 'immediate' before 'concern', it is clear that the *primary* responsibility of philosophy in Hegel's view is to protect the possession of truth, not to spell out its practical implications. Of course the truth has such implications and they must be spelled out, but this task appears to exceed the capability of philosophy. At precisely this point Kierkegaard and Marx were critical of Hegel, for they proposed to extend the responsibility of philosophy to include existence and praxis. 'The philosophers have only *interpreted* the world in various ways; the point is, to *change* it.'[50] But for Hegel there was a sense in which the philosophical comprehension of life can come only *after* the fact and is able only to interpret the world, not change it: precisely this is its fragmentary, partial character. 'When philosophy paints its gray in gray, then a shape of life has grown old, and with gray in gray it cannot be rejuvenated but only understood: the owl of Minerva begins its flight only with the gathering twilight.'[51]

Ricoeur suggests that despite the teleological character of Hegel's thought as it follows the forward-moving dialectic of spirit, philosophy has for him basically a *retrospective* vantage point, which tends to absorb all that has happened and can happen into an already accomplished rationality: 'for us' the process has already reached its telos and thus everything can be viewed in its proper place. Hegel's thought is teleological but not eschatological; it is not genuinely open to the novelty, vitality, and unfinished character of history.[52] Philosophic reason ultimately wins out over worldly, historical positivity, reducing the latter to a necessary moment in the dialectic of thought, not recognizing the validity of any facticity that radically transcends reason. In this respect Hegel's philosophy contains the seeds of its own destruction, for reality constantly outstrips reason and is never capable of being totally comprehended by it. The philosopher seems to have sensed the 'partiality' of his philosophy at this point.

Hegel's thought not only is fragmentary but also has experienced *fragmentation*. Fackenheim suggests that today we face a pervasive and inescapable cultural fragmentation, which calls radically into question any philosophical attempt to mediate between God as 'absolute idea', the natural world, and human being, and that therefore 'were he alive today, so realistic a philosopher as Hegel would not be a Hegelian'.[53] Although the latter judgment may be questioned, there is no doubt but that the disciples of Hegel immediately split into warring factions and that the controversy over the proper interpretation of his thought has not ceased until this day. We shall provide a brief survey of the range of interpretations in the Bibliographical Essay.

H.-G. Gadamer in his essay on 'Hegel and Heidegger' points out that Heidegger advanced the notion, first formulated by Nietzsche, that Hegel represents the consummation and collapse of Western metaphysics. By this Heidegger intended to point to the 'forgetfulness' of metaphysics – above all, the forgetfulness of its own primary theme, Being – and to suggest that we can move beyond Hegel only by remembering what he has forgotten. To do so, however, we must remember *why* and *how* he has forgotten what he has, and this means to stay with him in a special way, for he is the most comprehensive and radical thinker of modernity.[54]

We shall develop this insight in a way not pursued by Heidegger or Gadamer, namely, by indicating four sorts of 'forgetfulness' that bear especially on Hegel's religious thought. Here we have found the recent work of Paul Ricoeur quite suggestive.

The *forgetfulness of evil*. Can radical evil be incorporated into the Hegelian vision? Hegel's tendency is to dissolve the problematic of evil into dialectic, to regard it as a moment in the achievement of absolute knowledge. Evil is a by-product of the negation, separation, estrangement occasioned by knowledge and in this sense it is a dialectical necessity, not an inscrutable, absurd force. The problem of evil, suggests Ricoeur, requires us to return from the Hegelian theodicy to the Kantian appreciation of radical evil and its tragic dimension.[55]

The *forgetfulness of transcendence*. Although transcendence clearly is present in Hegel's thought – the transcendence of the logical idea vis-à-vis nature and finite spirit, the transcendence of God as Absolute Spirit vis-à-vis the rise of consciousness to the Absolute – the great stress on the *revealedness* of the Absolute, its rational comprehensibility, its implicit identity with the human subject, means that Hegel inevitably downplays the mysterious, violating, numinous, revealing/concealing power of Being vis-à-vis human consciousness. Hegel certainly does not forget the Absolute, but he tends to forget the transcendence of the Absolute, confident that the Absolute can be known *absolutely*. Thus as Ricoeur suggests, he ultimately sacrifices faith in the sacred to absolute knowledge of the Absolute, and this in turn led to 'the collapse of the Hegelian system itself – by this I mean the absolute incredibility of the notion of absolute knowledge in a time of a hermeneutics of suspicion'.[56]

The *forgetfulness of the living religions*. Hegel shared the imperialism of Western European Christianity and its blindness to other living religions as serious options for belief and practice. In the early nineteenth century, knowledge of African and Asian religions was both prejudiced and imprecise; Hinduism and Buddhism, in which there was a growing interest, were studied primarily in their classic representations. Since the ghettoization of European Jews in the late Middle Ages, very little was actually known of Judaism as a living religion, and its validity was challenged on theological grounds. Islam was viewed in terms of its historic rivalry with Christian culture, and it is notable that Hegel's scheme has no real place for it. The sole validity of Christianity was culturally self-evident to 'Hegel's Christian', and thus to affirm even the relative truth of other religions, as Hegel did, amounted to a revolutionary insight. Although Hegel's philosophy provided a great impetus to the history of religions, this discipline as a 'science' soon surpassed him. However, the Hegelian vision of a *theology* of the history of religions has yet to be attained on a contemporary methodological basis.[57]

The *forgetfulness of the unsurpassable power of religious symbols*. Hegel rightly recognized and described the process by which the representative, symbolic, imaginative language of religion gives rise to, is both annulled and preserved in, conceptual philosophical discourse. Such an *Aufhebung* is required in order to save the meaning of religious language in the face of reductionistic, 'scientific' explanations. The philosophical transfiguration preserves and interprets the referential world of religious discourse, which is the nonostensive world of poetry, narrative, parable and metaphor, not the objective world of modern science or the everyday world of human intercourse.[58] In this respect Hegel rose to the challenge of defending the truth and rationality of religion in general and the Christian religion in particular to its cultured and scientific 'despisers.' He knew that it was impossible to return to a precritical naïveté or dogmatic authority with regard to the reading of religious texts.[59]

But the defense threatened to destroy what was being preserved by taking it up into a 'higher' philosophical conceptuality that cut itself off from the symbolic matrix out of which it had arisen and from which it must continue to be fructified. The validity of concepts can be threatened in two ways. On the one hand, just as metaphors can 'die' without conceptual transform-ation, so also concepts can 'die' without being forced to 'think more', to engage in a constant process of reconceptualizing, by the religious and poetic imagination. On the other hand, concepts can fall into 'transcendental illusion' by forgetting their limited character and function: while consti-tuting the 'horizon' or 'logical space' for the clarification of meanings, they cannot provide *objective* knowledge of the Absolute. Rather they remain bound to the indirect discourse of metaphor, which demands that knowledge of the Absolute be formulated in terms not of a logic of identity but rather of the 'odd' logic of 'superabundance'.[60] Precisely in the attempt to 'recollect' everything (*Phen.*, 807–8), Hegel 'forgot' the inherent limits of philosophy and the unsurpassable power of the primary religious symbols.

In the light of these and other criticisms of Hegel's thought, one may legitimately wonder what it is that remains valid and compelling about his philosophy of religion. Perhaps the answer may be sought at two levels. On the first, one cannot help being impressed by Hegel's extraordinarily sharp observation and description of the elements of religious experience. One might describe it as his phenomenological rigor, which allows religious realities to appear as they show themselves in the constitution of meaning for consciousness. He penetrates beneath surface impressions and received wisdom, and things are often brought to light by means of striking new metaphors. Secondly, there is Hegel's evident passion to understand, to think through, to penetrate the meaning and truth of religious phenomena, and above all to render conceptually intelligible the doctrines of Christian faith. For Hegel this required the construction of a total philosophical world view, the cognitive presuppositions of which are no longer valid. But the system does not stand or fall as a whole. One can still be profoundly instructed by individual elements of this philosophical vision and by Hegel's clarification of specific religious and theological meanings. And one can appreciate that Hegel achieved for his day what is urgently needed for ours, on different and presently unattainable grounds, namely, a coherent unification of the disciplines of knowledge, and a systematic articulation of the ultimate purposes of human life in the context of the natural world and before God.

Notes

1 Emil Fackenheim, *The Religious Dimension in Hegel's Thought* (Bloomington, Ind., 1967), pp. 31–2.

2 *The Phenomenology of Mind*, transl. J. B. Baillie, rev. 2nd ed. (London, 1949), pp. 87–8, 144. Hereafter cited as *Phen*.

3 Hegel issued a second edition in 1827 and a third in 1830. For information on English translations of this work, see the Bibliographical Essay. In some cases I have modified the translation of quoted passages. Hereafter cited as *Enc*.

4 For information on English editions of these works, on additional writings of Hegel that have been edited and published posthumously, on the several collected editions of his works, and on major secondary studies, see the Bibliographical Essay at the end of the chapter.

5 *Lectures on the Philosophy of Religion*, transl. E. B. Speirs and J. Burdon Sanderson (3 vols., London, 1895), vol. I, p. 2. For references to the introduction and the first two parts of the *Philosophy of Religion*, I make use of the Speirs–Sanderson translation, based on the second German edition contained in vols. XI–XII of the *Werke* (Berlin, 1840), hereafter cited as *L.P.R.* I or II. For references to the third part, see n. 17. All citations from *L.P.R.* have been checked against the original, and in many instances I have altered the translation.

6 On Hegel's notion of the 'logical idea' or 'logical realm' (*das Logische*), see esp. *Enc.*, §§ 19–25, 41–2, 45, 236; and Hans-Georg Gadamer, *Hegel's Dialectic: Five Hermeneutical Studies*, transl. P. Christopher Smith (New Haven, Conn., 1976), pp. 76–8, 93–6, 99. On the notion of 'spirit', see R. C. Solomon, 'Hegel's concept of "Geist"', in *Hegel: A Collection of Critical Essays*, ed. A. MacIntyre (New York, 1972), pp. 125–49. Solomon argues that Hegel's *Geist* is a reinterpretation of and improvement on Kant's 'transcendental ego', offering a solution to the problem of methodological solipsism, i.e., the problem of the knowledge of self and of other minds. *Geist* is not identifiable with individual persons but is the underlying, unifying principle of consciousness or subjectivity. Solomon's analysis is helpful as far as it goes, but it does not explain how *Geist* can, and indeed must, be predicated of divinity as well as of humanity. In other words (to put the point in Solomon's terms), ultimately *God*, and God alone as *absolute* Spirit, is the answer to the problem of solipsism according to Hegel.

7 *Enc.*, § 187; cf. §§ 567–71, 575–7. Translation quoted from Fackenheim, *Religious Dimension*, p. 84; Fackenheim offers a brilliant exegesis of this passage, pp. 85–112. See also Malcolm Clark, *Logic and System: A Study of the Transition from 'Vorstellung' to Thought in the Philosophy of Hegel* (The Hague, 1971), pp. 201–2.

8 *Hegel's Philosophy of Right*, transl. T. M. Knox (Oxford, 1952), § 22. Hereafter cited as *Right*. Cf. *Enc.*, §§ 26–36.

9 On Hegel's critique of all these positions, and especially pantheism, see Emanuel Hirsch, *Geschichte der neuern evangelischen Theologie* (Gütersloh, 1954), vol. V, pp. 239–43.

10 Gadamer, *Hegel's Dialectic*, pp. 105, 107. In another context Gadamer helps to interpret the meaning of 'speculative', which, he points out, connotes a relationship of 'mirroring' (*speculum*). Speculative thinking is opposed to the dogmatism of everyday experience, for it recognizes that non-finite, trans-empirical realities cannot be sensibly perceived but rather appear only reflectedly in the process of thinking dialectically, by means of which thought is drawn beyond every finite perspective into an 'infinity of meaning' and its self-mediation. Speculative thinking recognizes that the event of interpretation 'is not our action upon the subject matter, but the action of the subject matter itself (*das Tun der Sache selbst*)'. Gadamer here refers to Hegel's discussion of true method as 'the movement of the concept itself' in *Wissenschaft der Logik*, II: 330 (*Werke*, vol. V [Berlin, 1834]). At the

same time there are significant differences between Hegel and Gadamer in the use of speculation, since the latter insists on the finitude of all human experience and rejects the possibility of achieving absolute knowledge. See *Truth and Method* (New York, 1975), pp. 421, 423–31.

11 Fackenheim, *Religious Dimension*, pp. 76–7, 229–33; Clark, *Logic and System*, pp. 142, 146–7, 182, 196.

12 Paul Ricoeur, *Freud and Philosophy: An Essay on Interpretation*, transl. Denis Savage (New Haven, Conn., 1970), pp. 459–72.

13 Mark C. Taylor, 'Itinerarium mentis in Deum: Hegel's proofs of God's existence', *The Journal of Religion* 57 (1977), 211–31. On the Hegelian proofs, see also Bernard M. G. Reardon, *Hegel's Philosophy of Religion* (London, 1977), pp. 88–99.

14 The precise structure of the first part of the *Philosophy of Religion*, 'The Concept of Religion', is very difficult to determine because Hegel followed a completely different order each of the times he lectured on the subject. The order is not properly represented in either the original *Werke* (1832, 1840) or the edition by Georg Lasson (1925). For our purposes it is enough to say that the two sections entitled 'The Necessity of the Religious Standpoint' (*L.P.R.* I: 105–15) and 'The Speculative Concept of Religion' (*L.P.R.* I: 204–10) ought to precede the three main divisions of the 'The Concept of Religion' – namely, 'The Abstract Concept of God', 'The Religious Relationship', and 'The Cultus' – and to be considered as an introduction to this subject as a whole. Cf. Walter Jaeschke, *Der Aufbau und die bisherigen Editionen von Hegels Vorlesungen über die Philosophie der Religion* (Master's Thesis, Free University of Berlin, 1970), pp. 11–23, 62–4. Although in these lectures Hegel apparently took up the 'Speculative Concept' before he did the 'Necessity of the Religious Standpoint', I have reversed the order, as Hegel himself did in other contexts, to conform to the phenomenological-logical sequence.

15 Martin Heidegger points to this 'reversal' in Hegel's thought by indicating that the progression of consciousness is not 'driven' by the given shapes of consciousness but is 'drawn by the pull of the goal' – the 'arriving presence' of the Absolute or Being – that 'brings itself forth in appearance' (*Hegel's Concept of Experience* (New York, 1970), pp. 30, 69, 79–80).

16 The 1827 series of lectures actually took up the matter of the proofs in the section on religious thought or knowledge (*L.P.R.* I: 168–71), but the *Werke* transposed most of this material to an appendix following the *Lectures on the Proofs of the Existence of God* (*L.P.R.* III: 328–67). For the sake of brevity we shall limit our discussion to the ontological proof.

17 *The Christian Religion: Lectures on the Philosophy of Religion, Part III*, edited and translated by P. C. Hodgson, based on the edition by G. Lasson (American Academy of Religion Texts and Translations Series, 2; Missoula, Mt., 1979), pp. 45, 51–3. Hereafter cited as *C.R.* Hegel lectured on the philosophy of religion in Berlin four times over a ten-year span: 1821, 1824, 1827, and 1831. The original *Vorlesungen über die Philosophie der Religion* contained in vols. XI–XII of the *Werke* (Berlin, 1832, 1840) was an editorially constructed text, produced by blending together student transcripts or notebooks from different years and, in the second edition, including passages from Hegel's own difficult-to-decipher lecture manuscript of 1821. Lasson (1925–29) distinguished the sources to some degree and gave special prominence to Hegel's own manuscript, but his rearrangement of the texts and general editorial principles created more problems than they solved. My edited translation of the third part corrects some of these problems, but it is intended only as a study edition until a completely new edition can be prepared. Work on such an edition is well underway. The texts of the 1821, 1824, and 1827 lectures are being reconstructed and published as separate though parallel units, together with 'special materials' from the *Werke* that cannot be identified with any of the extant manuscripts. These include fragments from the 1831 lectures, which cannot be reconstructed because the original notebooks have all been lost. This new edition is being published by Felix

Meiner Verlag, jointly edited by Walter Jaeschke, Ricardo Ferrara, and myself. The new English translation of Hegel's *Lectures on the Philosophy of Religion*, which I am also editing, is being published in three volumes by the University of California Press. Volume I (Introduction and The Concept of Religion) is scheduled for 1984; volume II (Determinate Religion) is planned for 1986 or 1987; and volume III (The Consummate Religion) is due to appear in 1985. Volume III, a completely revised version of Part III of Hegel's lectures, will replace my 'study edition' of *The Christian Religion* which was used in the preparation of the present chapter.

18 This summary is based on *Enc.*, §§ 451–64; *L.P.R.* I: 142, 144, 148, 151, 154, 157–8; Clark, *Logic and System*, pp. 55–67; and James Yerkes, *The Christology of Hegel* (American Academy of Religion Dissertation Series, 23; Missoula, Mt., 1978), pp. 89–93.

19 Cf. *L.P.R.*, I: 157–8, 172–204; and Yerkes, *Christology of Hegel*, pp. 110–12.

20 *L.P.R.* I: 24–6, 156–60; *Enc.*, § 573; *Berliner Schriften, 1818–1831*, ed. Johannes Hoffmeister (Hamburg, 1956), p. 318; Yerkes, *Christology of Hegel*, pp. 94, 113–15; Clark, *Logic and System*, pp. 24–6.

21 Yerkes, *Christology of Hegel*, pp. 113–15.

22 *L.P.R.* I: 69–70, 248–57; *Right*, § 270.

23 Hirsch, *Geschichte*, vol. V, pp. 246–9.

24 Fackenheim, *Religious Dimension*, 117–18.

25 This analysis of the structure of Determinate Religion will require some modification when volume II of the new critical edition has been completed. (See above, note 17; see also below, p. 121.) The most adequate study to date of Hegel's treatment of non-Christian religions is Reinhard Leuze, *Die ausserchristlichen Religionen bei Hegel* (Göttingen, 1975). Being dependent on the *Werke* and Lasson, however, Leuze failed to grasp Hegel's overall structure. He nonetheless usefully provides information about the sources upon which Hegel relied and critically evaluates the adequacy of Hegel's interpretation in the light of contemporary history-of-religions research.

26 Fackenheim remarks that the charge of prejudice against Judaism 'must primarily be leveled *against Hegel's Christian*', not Hegel himself (*Religious Dimension*, p. 136).

27 *Die Religionen der geistigen Individualität*, ed. Georg Lasson (*Vorlesungen über die Philosophie der Religion*, vol. II.1; Hamburg, 1927), pp. 57, 245–51. This fact is concealed by the *Werke* edition.

28 In all of the extant sources, Hegel's preferred title for Part III of the lectures is 'The Consummate Religion' (*die vollendete Religion*) or 'The Revelatory Religion' (*die offenbare Religion*); the latter is the same title as that used by the *Phenomenology*, while the *Encyclopedia* employs 'The Revealed Religion' (*die geoffenbarte Religion*). 'The Absolute Religion' is not used as a title by Hegel himself, although it appears in the text of the lectures along with the other terms; it was adopted as the title by the 1st edition of the *Werke* (1832) and was continued by Lasson. *Offenbar* is translated as 'revelatory' or 'manifest' to distinguish it from *geoffenbart* ('revealed'), since Hegel intended a distinction as well as a relation between the terms (*C.R.*, 16), the latter referring to the positive, historical character of the divine manifestation. Hegel also designates this religion by its historical name, 'the Christian Religion', which I adopted as the title of my study edition, while indicating the several philosophical names in the subtitle. (See *C.R.*, xxi–xxiii.) Some materials in this and the next section are similar in content to portions of the Appendix to my translation of *The Christian Religion*, which provides a more detailed commentary on the text of that work. This duplication is with the consent of Cambridge University Press and Scholars Press (the publisher of the translation).

29 Cf. Jörg Splett's criticism of this tendency in *Die Trinitätslehre G. W. F. Hegels* (Freiburg/Munich, 1965), pp. 150–4.

30 In one of his earliest works, *The Positivity of the Christian Religion* (1796), written from the

point of view of Kantian rationalism, Hegel was harshly critical of the way in which the purely moral religion of Jesus was transformed into 'positive' Christianity. See especially the introduction by Richard Kroner to *Early Theological Writings*, transl. T. M. Knox (Chicago, 1948), which contains the *Positivity* text.

31 Stephen Crites brings out the tensions in Hegel's thought on the issue of positivity. 'The problem of the "positivity" of the Gospel in the Hegelian dialectic of alienation and reconciliation' (Ph.D. Dissertation, Yale University, 1961), pp. 197–204, 235.

32 Hegel summarizes the 'division of the subject' in *C.R.*, 35–9; see also the section on 'the development of the idea of God', *C.R.*, 60–7. On the intricacies of the structural variations between the several lecture series, see the introduction and notes to *The Christian Religion*, especially the table, 'Comparative Analysis of the Structure of the Text' (pp. xxx–xxxi). Detailed information is also available in Jaeschke, *Aufbau*, pp. 28–39.

33 *C.R.*, 68, 72, 86–7, 117–18; cf. the fragment on *Love* (1797) in *Early Theological Writings*, pp. 302–8.

34 *C.R.*, 67–9, 71–5, 78–99; cf. also Hirsch, *Geschichte*, vol. v, p. 255; and Splett, *Trinitätslehre*, pp. 121–6.

35 Fackenheim, *Religious Dimension*, p. 205; cf. pp. 149–53, 202–5.

36 Clark notes this modification, *Logic and System*, p. 160.

37 As evidence for the difference: *C.R.*, 109–10, 114–19; *Phen.*, 776–7. Contra pantheism: *Enc.*, §§ 50, 151, 573. See also Fackenheim, *Religious Dimension*, p. 130; and Hirsch, *Geschichte*, vol. v, pp. 238–9.

38 *C.R.*, 109–13, 117–19. The proper interpretation of Hegel on this point has been much disputed: cf. Crites, 'Positivity', pp. 82–9, 91–4, 101–3; Reardon, *Hegel's Philosophy of Religion*, pp. 100–4; Splett, *Trinitätslehre*, pp. 141–2.

39 *C.R.*, 174–7, 255; *L.P.R.* I: 165. Hirsch believes that in this regard Hegel's position has evolved from that expressed in the *Phenomenology*; see *Geschichte*, vol. v, pp. 239, 255–6. For further discussion of the issues involved here, see Crites, 'Positivity', pp. 236–7; and Yerkes, *Christology of Hegel*, pp. 164–8, 171–2, 177–8, 189–95.

40 *C.R.*, 171–4, 177, 180–2, 242; *Right*, § 348. Cf. Crites, 'Positivity', pp. 217–20; Yerkes, *Christology of Hegel*, pp. 169–70, 170–3.

41 *C.R.*, 184, 190, 199–200, 224 n. 15, 242–3. An excellent discussion of the issues involved here is provided by Yerkes, *Christology of Hegel*, pp. 173–205. See also Crites, 'Positivity', pp. 213–16. It is this second motif that is lacking from the *Phenomenology of Spirit*.

42 The cross also puts an end to all notions of a transcendent, other, impassible God, and thus it assumes philosophical significance. This is what Hegel means by his reference to the 'speculative Good Friday' in *Faith and Knowledge*, transl. Walter Cerf and H. S. Harris (Albany, 1977), p. 191, and to the 'Golgotha of Absolute Spirit' in *Phen.*, 808.

43 *C.R.*, 207–10, 212–14, 221; *Phen.*, 762–3, 780–2. See also Stephen Crites, *In the Twilight of Christendom: Hegel vs. Kierkegaard on Faith and History* (American Academy of Religion Studies in Religion, 2; Chambersburg, Pa., 1972), pp. 47–8; and Crites, 'Positivity', pp. 222–7.

44 *C.R.*, 268–70, 274–5. Cf. *Early Theological Writings*, pp. 248–52. We should recall the high significance Hegel accords the cultus as the 'practical' form of the religious relationship in the Concept of Religion.

45 *Enc.*, § 517; *Right*, §§ 142–57, 257–70; Fackenheim, *Religious Dimension*, pp. 206–13, 232–3; Crites, *Twilight*, pp. 43, 51–4.

46 *C.R.*, 289–90, 292–3; *L.P.R.* I: 19–22, 154–5; *Enc.*, Preface to the 2nd edition, § 573; *Berliner Schriften*, pp. 325, 328; Fackenheim, *Religious Dimension*, pp. 116, 192; Hirsch, *Geschichte*, vol. v, p. 250.

47 *Aesthetics*, transl. T. M. Knox (2 vols., Oxford, 1975), vol. I, pp. 11, 103. David Friedrich

Strauss and other left-Hegelians drew precisely this conclusion and attempted to substitute philosophy for religion.

48 Quentin Lauer, 'Hegel on the identity of content in religion and philosophy', *Hegel and the Philosophy of Religion*, ed. D. E. Christensen (The Hague, 1970), pp. 265–8, 273–5; Fackenheim, *Religious Dimension*, pp. 185–92.

49 Yerkes, *Christology of Hegel*, pp. 228–31. On the issues raised here, see also Crites, *Twilight*, pp. 56, 101–3.

50 Karl Marx, 'Theses on Feuerbach', *Writings of the Young Marx on Philosophy and Society*, transl. L. Easton and K. Guddat (New York, 1967), p. 402.

51 *Right*, p. 13; cf. Crites, *Twilight*, pp. 102ff.

52 Paul Ricoeur, *The Conflict of Interpretations: Essays in Hermeneutics*, ed. Don Ihde (Evanston, 1974), pp. 21–2, 414ff, 422; *Freud and Philosophy*, pp. 459–61, 468–72. See also Crites, 'Positivity', pp. 239–45; and John E. Smith, 'Hegel's reinterpretation of the doctrine of Spirit and the religious community', *Hegel and the Philosophy of Religion*, p. 174.

53 Fackenheim, *Religious Dimension*, pp. 224, 235–6.

54 Gadamer, *Hegel's Dialectic*, pp. 101–4.

55 Ricoeur, *Conflict of Interpretations*, pp. 312–13; *Freud and Philosophy*, pp. 526–7.

56 Ricoeur, *Freud and Philosophy*, p. 526; 'Biblical Hermeneutics', *Semeia* 4 (1975), p. 141.

57 Wolfhart Pannenberg is attempting to work toward such a theology, with considerable indebtedness to Hegel. See *Theology and the Philosophy of Science* (Philadelphia, 1976), pp. 358–71; and 'Toward a theology of the history of religions', *Basic Questions in Theology*, vol. II (Philadelphia, 1971), pp. 65–118.

58 See Paul Ricoeur, *The Rule of Metaphor*, transl. Robert Czerny et al. (Toronto, 1977), pp. 286–94.

59 Hirsch, *Geschichte*, vol. V, pp. 253, 266–7.

60 Ricoeur, *The Rule of Metaphor*, pp. 295–303; 'Biblical Hermeneutics', pp. 138–45.

61 Both Fackenheim, *Religious Dimension*, pp. 77–84, 235–42, and Reardon, *Hegel's Philosophy of Religion*, pp. 135–9, follow the left-center-right schema, as does George Kline, 'Some recent interpretations of Hegel's philosophy', *The Monist* 48 (1964), 34–75. Franz Gregoire, *Études hegeliennes: les points capitaux du system* (Louvain, 1958), proposes five types on a right to left spectrum. On the left-right schematization, see *Die Hegelsche Linke*, ed. Karl Löwith (Stuttgart, 1962); *Die Hegelsche Rechte*, ed. Hermann Lübbe (Stuttgart, 1962); and W. R. Beyer, *Hegel-Bilder: Kritik der Hegel-Deutungen* (Berlin, 1967). I have been helped by Warren McWilliams' detailed analysis of the conflict of Hegel interpretations in 'Hegel and transcendence: the riddle of the Phenomenology' (Ph.D. Dissertation, Vanderbilt University, 1974), pp. 11–95. Mention should be made of the following collections of essays, which offer a variety of views and help to bring the reader up to date on the state of research: *Hegel-Studien*, ed. F. Nicolin and O. Pöggeler (Bonn, 14 vols. and 20 Beihefte since 1962); *Hegel and the Philosophy of Religion*, ed. D. E. Christensen (The Hague, 1970); *New Studies in Hegel's Philosophy*, ed. W. E. Steinkraus (New York, 1971); *Hegel: A Collection of Critical Essays*, ed. A. MacIntyre (New York, 1972); *Hegel-Bilanz: Zur Aktualität und Inaktualität der Philosophie Hegels*, ed. R. Heede and J. Ritter (Frankfurt, 1973).

Bibliographical essay

At the beginning of the chapter we described the four works published by Hegel during his own lifetime and the Berlin lecture series edited and published by former students shortly after his death. These works are available in English translation as follows: (a) *Phenomenology of Mind*, transl. J. B. Baillie (rev. 2nd ed., London and New York, 1949); *Phenomenology of Spirit*, transl. A. V. Miller (Oxford, 1977). (b) *Science of Logic*, transl. W. H. Johnston and L. G. Struthers (2 vols., London, 1929); transl. A. V. Miller (London, 1969). (c) *Encyclopedia of the Philosophical Sciences*, (3rd ed., 1830, with *Zusätze* based on student notes added to the edition of 1845): Introduction and Part I (§§ 1–244): *The Logic of Hegel*, transl. William Wallace (2nd ed., Oxford, 1894; reissued 1975); Part II (§§ 245–376): *Hegel's Philosophy of Nature*, transl. A. V. Miller (Oxford, 1970); Part III (§§ 377–577): *Hegel's Philosophy of Mind*, transl. William Wallace and A. V. Miller (Oxford, 1971). (d) *Hegel's Philosophy of Right*, transl. T. M. Knox (Oxford, 1952). (e) *Lectures on the Philosophy of Religion*, transl. E. B. Speirs and J. Burdon Sanderson (3 vols., London, 1895) soon to be superseded by the new edition and translation mentioned above in note 17. (f) *Lectures on the History of Philosophy*, transl. E. S. Haldane and F. H. Simson (3 vols., London, 1892–5). (g) *Lectures on the Philosophy of History*, transl. J. Sibree (London, 1899), transl. D. Forbes and H. B. Nisbet (Cambridge, 1975); Introduction only: *Reason in History*, transl. R. S. Hartman (New York, 1953). (h) *Aesthetics*, transl. T. M. Knox (2 vols., Oxford, 1975).

During the course of the twentieth century a large number of additional manuscripts never published by Hegel have been edited and made available to the public (English translations cited when available). (a) From the Tübingen, Bern, and Frankfurt periods, 1788–1800: *Hegels theologische Jugendschriften*, ed. H. Nohl (Tübingen, 1907); partially translated as *Early Theological Writings*, transl. T. M. Knox (Chicago, 1948). See the excellent study by H. S. Harris, *Hegel's Development: Toward the Sunlight, 1770–1801* (Oxford, 1972). (b) From the Jena period, 1801–7: *The Difference between Fichte's and Schelling's System of Philosophy*, transl. W. Cerf and H. S. Harris (Albany, 1977); *Faith and Knowledge*, transl. W. Cerf and H. S. Harris (Albany, 1977); *Jenenser Realphilosophie*, I & II, ed. J. Hoffmeister (Leipzig, 1931–2); *Jenenser Logik, Metaphysik and Naturphilosophie*, ed. G. Lasson (Leipzig, 1923). (c) From the Nürnberg period, 1808–16: *Nürnberger Schriften*, ed. J. Hoffmeister (Leipzig, 1938). (d) From the Berlin period, 1818–31: *Berliner Schriften*, ed. J. Hoffmeister (Hamburg, 1956); *Lectures on the Proofs of the Existence of God*, which Hegel was editing for publication when he died in 1831 and which were appended by the original editors to the *Lectures on the Philosophy of Religion* (III: 155–327; newly edited by G. Lasson, Leipzig, 1930). See also *Briefe von und an Hegel*, ed. J. Hoffmeister (3 vols., Hamburg, 1952–4).

Collected editions: (a) *Werke: Vollständige Ausgabe durch einen Verein von Freunden des Verewigten* (18 vols., Berlin, 1832–45). Some volumes issued in second editions. (b) *Sämtliche Werke: Jubiläumsausgabe in zwanzig Bänden*, ed. H. Glockner (Stuttgart, 1927–30). A reprint of the original *Werke*. (c) *Sämtliche Werke: Neue kritische Ausgabe*, ed. J. Hoffmeister (32 vols. projected, Hamburg, 1923–56). A 'Kritische Gesamtausgabe' was begun by G. Lasson in the early twenties. His death in 1932, followed by the Second World War, meant that the project had to be reconstituted by his co-editor, J. Hoffmeister. However, Hoffmeister's death in 1955 left the 'Neue kritische Ausgabe' also incomplete. (d) *Gesammelte Werke* (30–40 vols. projected in two series; Hamburg, 1968–). This will be the definitive critical edition, sponsored by the Deutsche Forschungsgemeinschaft, edited by the Rheinisch-Westfälische Akademie der Wissenschaften at the Hegel-Archiv in Bochum. The project will take two or three decades to complete. The volumes published thus far include: *Jenaer kritische Schriften*, ed. H. Buchner and O. Pöggeler (1968); *Jenaer Systementwürfe* I, ed. K. Düsing and H. Kimmerle (1975); *Jenaer Systementwürfe* II, III, ed. R. P. Horstmann and J. H. Trede (1971, 1976); *Wissenschaft der Logik*, I, II, ed. F. Hogemann and W. Jaeschke (1978, 1981).

The range of secondary literature on Hegel is extraordinarily wide and growing at an enormous rate in view of the current renaissance of interest in Hegel studies. For an exhaustive survey of the literature, see *Hegel Bibliography: An International List of Works by and on Hegel and His Philosophy, 1797–1973*, ed. Kurt Steinhauer (Munich, 1977). Our essay can only skim the surface. D. F. Strauss was the first to suggest that immediately after Hegel's death his followers and interpreters divided into three groups: left-wing, right-wing, and center. This typology, despite its limitations, has endured and remains a convenient way to categorize the range of Hegel studies down to the present day, although obviously some works fit the categories more precisely than others.[61]

The *left-wing* interpreters have in effect denied the necessity of Hegel's 'logical mediation' (the transcendence of the logical idea vis-à-vis nature and finite consciousness as the universal principle of both) and thus were drawn to one of two options: (a) A form of *naturalism* or *materialism*, according to which matter is the universal principle of reality. This was the position of most of the 'young Hegelians' (cf. W. J. Brazill, *The Young Hegelians* [New Haven, 1970]) from Ludwig Feuerbach and Bruno Bauer to Karl Marx, and it is continued by contemporary Marxist interpreters of Hegel such as Roger Garaudy, *Dieu est mort: étude sur Hegel* (Paris, 1962); Alexandre Kojève, *Introduction to the Reading of Hegel* (New York, 1969); Georg Lukács, *The Young Hegel, Studies in the Relations between Dialectics and Economics* (Cambridge, Mass., 1976); and Herbert Marcuse, *Reason and Revolution: Hegel and the Rise of Social Theory* (Boston, 1960). (b) A *humanistic subjectivism*, according to which finite mind is the universal principle. This position was first hinted at by D. F. Strauss and was then developed in radical form by Max Stirner. It is represented by contemporary humanistic interpreters of Hegel such as Jean Hyppolite, *Genèse et structure de la Phénoménologie de l'Esprit de Hegel* (Paris, 1948); Walter Kaufmann, *Hegel: A Reinterpretation* (New York, 1966); Karl Löwith, *From Hegel to Nietzsche* (New York, 1967); Theodor Litt, *Hegel: Versuch einer kritischen Erneuerung* (Heidelberg, 1953); and Charles Taylor, *Hegel* (Cambridge, 1975). Both forms of the left-wing interpretation are immanentistic, secular, and at least implicitly atheistic, questioning the reality of transcendence both in Hegel's thought and in human experience as such.

The *right-wing* interpreters have tended to deny the naturalistic or realistic mediation and thus were led to downplay the independent reality of nature and finite spirit and to reify logic into a panlogical transcendent metaphysics or theistic pantheism. Here we find a flight from the world and a tendency toward acosmism. Representative of this position were the original theological right-wing interpreters of Hegel such as C. F. Göschel and G. A. Gabler, as well as several later British Idealists; the Russian metaphysician Iwan Iljin, *Die Philosophie Hegels als kontemplative Gotteslehre* (Bern, 1946); and the French philosopher Henri Niel, *De la médiation dans la philosophie de Hegel* (Paris, 1945). Other theological interpreters of Hegel, while not espousing this view themselves, believe that Hegel was guilty of it: Theodor Haering, *Hegel: Sein Wollen und sein Werk* (2 vols., Leipzig, 1929, 1938); Jörg Splett, *Die Trinitätslehre G. W. F. Hegels* (Freiburg and Munich, 1965).

Finally, a group of interpreters, both philosophical and theological, argue that Hegel's actual intention was to hold to a *middle position* in terms of the triple mediation of the logical idea, nature, and spirit, and that the intention was admirable even if not finally sustainable in light of the centrifugal forces of modern society. This would include the original Hegelian 'center' (P. K. Marheineke, Karl Daub, Karl Rosenkranz, and F. C. Baur), the nineteenth century American idealist Josiah Royce, and the German historical theologian Emanuel Hirsch, *Geschichte der neuern evangelischen Theologie*, vol. v (Gütersloh, 1954), chap. 50. Important recent studies of Hegel's philosophy belong here, such as those by Malcolm Clark, *Logic and System: A Study of the Transition from 'Vorstellung' to Thought in the Philosophy of Hegel* (The Hague, 1971); J. N. Findlay, *The Philosophy of Hegel: An Introduction and Re-Examination* (New York, 1962); Hans-Georg Gadamer, *Hegel's Dialectic: Five Hermeneutical Studies* (New Haven, Conn. and London, 1976); G. R. G. Mure, *The Philosophy of Hegel* (London, 1965); as do a number of contemporary theological interpreters: Stephen Crites, 'The problem of the "positivity" of the Gospel in the Hegelian dialectic of alienation and reconciliation' (Ph.D. Dissertation, Yale University, 1961); Crites, *In the Twilight of Christendom: Hegel vs. Kierkegaard on Faith and History* (American Academy of Religion Studies in Religion, 2; Chambersburg, Pa., 1972); Emil Fackenheim, *The Religious Dimension in Hegel's Thought* (Bloomington, Ind., 1967); B. M. G. Reardon, *Hegel's Philosophy of*

Religion (London, 1977); James Yerkes, *The Christology of Hegel* (American Academy of Religion Dissertation Series, 23; Missoula, Mt., 1978); and Mark C. Taylor, *Journeys to Selfhood: Hegel and Kierkegaard* (Berkeley, 1980). Especially helpful for interpreting Hegel's philosophy of religion are the works by Crites, Fackenheim, Hirsch and Yerkes.

A second edition of Yerkes' study of Hegel's christology has appeared under the same title in the recently-inaugurated State University of New York Series of Hegelian Studies. Several other important new works on Hegel's religious thought have also appeared in that series: Quentin Lauer, *Hegel's Concept of God* (Albany, 1982); Paul Lakeland, *The Politics of Salvation: The Hegelian Idea of the State* (Albany, 1984); Raymond K. Williamson, *Introduction to Hegel's Philosophy of Religion* (Albany, 1984).

NOTE: By the time this chapter is published, volume I of the new edition and translation of *Hegel's Lectures on the Philosophy of Religion* will have appeared, to be followed shortly by volume III. (See above, note 17.) Owing to overlapping production schedules of these two projects, however, it has not been possible here to include page references to the new edition. Nor has it been possible here to take full account of the substantial differences between the four separate series of lectures (1821, 1824, 1827, 1831), which have only recently come to light and which will be elucidated for the first time in the new edition. In particular, it should be noted that Hegel did not arrive at the form of the Concept of Religion that we describe until 1827, and that, contrary to the impression created by the *Werke* and Lasson, upon which we have relied, Hegel did not give a two-fold structure to Determinate Religion, but a triadic structure, according to which the Religion of Expediency (Roman religion) constitutes a third, distinct moment. On the basis of a recently discovered set of excerpts made by D. F. Strauss from a transcript of the 1831 lectures, the new edition is now able to provide an outline and synopsis of the whole of the last lecture series, which offers a quite different schema for treating the determinate religions. When it is finally complete, the new critical edition will – in short – both stimulate and facilitate a thorough reassessment of current views about Hegel's philosophy of religion.

4

Friedrich Schleiermacher

B. A. GERRISH

The publication of Schleiermacher's anonymous book *On Religion: Speeches to its Cultured Despisers* (1799) has been hailed as the birth of a new theological era. But even his friends found it, in some respects, a puzzling work. Friedrich Schlegel, for instance, as we know from an amusing letter of Schleiermacher to Henriette Herz (19 June 1799), demanded to know where the new author's 'centre' was. Over the years, as the first book grew into the collected works, the answer to Schlegel's question did not become any easier. And yet it is obviously crucial for any attempt to sum up Schleiermacher's lifetime achievement. The task calls, not for an inventory of all his writings and ideas, but for the courage to single out dominant motifs that seem to determine, if by no means to exhaust, the thoughts that have to be left out.

I. A pietist of a higher order

As the first division of the collected works indicates (it was planned in thirteen volumes, of which eleven were published), Schleiermacher concerned himself with virtually every branch of theological studies except Old Testament. There are titles on philosophy of religion, systematic theology, New Testament, church history, Christian ethics, and practical theology. He was, besides, a busy preacher, and the entire second division of the works consists of ten further volumes of sermons. The third division, entitled 'philosophy' (in nine volumes), embraces studies in the history of philosophy; in dialectic (epistemology and metaphysics), ethics, politics, psychology, aesthetics; in philology and education. In addition, Schleiermacher was an amazingly prolific letter-writer and – through his labours on Plato's dialogues – one of Germany's most eminent classical scholars. Although much more still remains in unpublished manuscripts, it is a formidable corpus; and it is not difficult to understand why he was accused of carrying on his private education in public. Even so, to represent him only as a preacher and a professor would still be to miss his full significance as a public figure in church, academy, and nation.

If, however, one's interest is not in the man as such but in his contribution to religious studies, there can hardly be any doubt where his significance is to be sought: in the determination and skill with which he took up again the specifically *dogmatic* task. He lavished immense care on the publication of his dogmatics, whereas his philosophy survives largely in the form of unpublished lectures; and the manuscripts of his *Dialectic* betray the fact that philosophically he had difficulty in making up his mind. His dogmatics remained, in his own estimate at least, independent of philosophical influences. True, it can be fully understood only from its place in a total theory of the sciences, and the content he gave to it brought the subject closer to what we should today call the 'humanistic study of religion'. Indeed, Schleiermacher's theology exercised a powerful influence on the development of self-consciously non-theological ways of studying religion that do not always admit their parentage. His dogmatics was neither narrow nor conventional. But it *was* dogmatics. He took up once more an enterprise that had languished in the Age of Reason, and he developed it in ways that quietly acknowledged the impossibility of older models.

The result was a reconstruction of the theological tradition so brilliant and subtle that one does not know which to marvel at more: the startling creativeness of his innovations or the ingenuity of his carefully-forged links with the past. For sustained systematic power and intellectual penetration, his dogmatic masterpiece *The Christian Faith* (1821–2; 2nd ed., 1830–1) is unsurpassed in Christian theological literature. Anyone sufficiently familiar with both will be struck by the parallels between Schleiermacher's *Glaubenslehre* (as he liked to call it) and Calvin's 1559 *Institutio*. But the classical Reformation system is more loosely organized; and if Calvin's rigour is sometimes sacrificed to his rhetoric, it must also be admitted that the artistry of his design suffered from his inability to ignore his opponents. Perhaps it is only with the much earlier masterpiece of Western theology, the *Summa Theologiae* of Thomas Aquinas, that the *Glaubenslehre* can be justly compared. At any rate, this – from the other side, so to say – was the verdict pronounced by Johannes Evangelist von Kuhn, of the Catholic Tübingen School, who wrote: 'Among all the later and present-day theologians, only Schleiermacher can be compared with him [Thomas] as far as scientific force and power are concerned.'[1]

No summary account of a work so densely packed as *The Christian Faith* can possibly do it justice. But we may take our bearings from

Schleiermacher's own remarks in his oft-cited letter to F. H. Jacobi (30 March 1818). The philosopher had described himself as a pagan in intellect but a Christian in feeling. To Schleiermacher, this was a confusion of categories: paganism and Christianity, he insists, can only run into conflict in the same sphere, the sphere of religion; and religion (or, better, 'religiousness') is a matter of feeling. All the intellect can do is to reflect on this feeling and interpret it. If Jacobi's feeling is Christian, how can his intellect put a pagan interpretation on it? Rather than any such conflict of feeling and intellect, Schleiermacher wants to speak of nothing more than a 'polarity'. Jacobi's metaphor for his predicament was of two bodies of water that never come together: Schleiermacher cheerfully accepts the separation but changes the metaphor, for the things that are here separated belong indispensably together in a 'galvanic pile', in the operation of which the innermost life of the human spirit consists.[2] In Schleiermacher's own experience, the religious feeling remained relatively constant; what changed was his explication of it. Consequently, if conflict is plainly to be read in his early biography, it can in principle have been only a conflict between old interpretations and new as he sought to attune two sides of his personality.

The contrast drawn in Schleiermacher's response to Jacobi was correctly specified by A. E. Biedermann. What one might expect as the companion of deep religious feeling (*Gefühl*), he points out, is speculative profundity; but what one finds in Schleiermacher is keenness of intellect (*Verstand*), turned in critical inquiry precisely upon the centre of his feeling. Biedermann is again exactly right when he says that, if religion was the centre of Schleiermacher's feeling, it took the quite specific form of a *Heilandsliebe* ('love of the Saviour'), given to him from beyond anything the human spirit could generate for itself. At least, that was Schleiermacher's own judgment: the fact that he took the unusual risk of subjecting so delicate an experience to critical scrutiny was what made him, as he said of himself, a 'pietist (*Herrnhuter*) of a higher order'. Or, as Biedermann puts it, it was the union in him of two strikingly different characteristics, commonly encountered separately in sharply antithetical individuals, that made Schleiermacher the 'regenerator of modern theology'.[3]

Perhaps the mystery of Schleiermacher's centre is not incorrectly resolved, then, if one locates it in a distinctive type of Christian sensibility – but only if one immediately adds that this centre stands in a kind of dialectical tension with his critical intellect. It is easy to see why Schleiermacher himself writes to Jacobi, not about his 'centre', but about 'the two foci of my own ellipse'. More important, the Christian sensibility itself, as he sees it, is not simple but compounded of two elements. It is clear that for Schleiermacher an awareness of God is a datum of human consciousness as such: all it takes to recognize it is 'a little introspection'.[4] What remains axiomatic for him, on the other hand, is that in the specifically Christian awareness of God everything is related to the redemption accomplished by Jesus of Nazareth (*Gl.* 11). Whatever may be the exigencies of abstract exposition, in the actual life of the Christian there is a mutual penetration of two moments, a 'general God-consciousness' and a 'relation to Christ', neither of which is reducible to the other (*Gl.* 62.3). Hence we may fairly concentrate our own exposition on these two themes. And this will once again have the merit of corresponding closely with Schleiermacher's own remarks to Jacobi.

His goal, he remarks, though never finally attainable, is simply to comprehend the deliverances of the Christian consciousness and to find their place alongside other regions of human experience.

If, then, my Christian feeling is conscious of a Divine Spirit in me that is something other than my reason, I will never give up searching for it in the deepest depths of the nature of the soul. And if my Christian feeling becomes conscious of a Son of God who differs from the best of us otherwise than by a 'better still', I will never cease to search for the begetting of this Son of God in the deepest depths of nature and to tell myself I shall as soon comprehend the Second Adam as the first Adam, or first Adams, whom I must likewise accept without comprehending them.[5]

To a quite remarkable degree, this confession summarizes the theological quest of a lifetime. The reflective activity of the intellect upon religiousness Schleiermacher calls, in the same passage, 'dogmatics'; what it seeks to interpret, if it is a Christian dogmatics, is Christian feeling. And he clearly picks out the two principal objects that he seeks to grasp as the content of the Christian consciousness: the Divine Spirit and the Second Adam. Even what is perhaps the main difficulty for his dogmatic task is at least touched on: how the contents of the Christian consciousness are to be related to the concept of 'nature', which the intellect acquires partly from other sources. He acknowledges that the two functions of feeling and intellect give rise to an oscillation, a constant effort to attune the two never-completed activities of philosophy and dogmatics. Finally, he goes on, in the same paragraph, to indicate that his enterprise maintains continuity with the language of tradition, but is not tied to the letter. The dogmatic language shaped by Augustine is rich and deep enough to be still serviceable if handled with discretion. But the original and in this sense 'fixed' interpretation of Christian feeling is the Bible, which may only be better understood – and developed. 'As a Protestant theologian, I shall let no one curtail my right of development.'

Schleiermacher was convinced that his link with the Protestant Reformers

[handwritten: "theology is a daughter of Religion"]

lay, not only in the right of development which he claimed for himself, but also in the experiential nature of his entire procedure. As he asks his friend Lücke: 'Was it not the case with our Luther . . . that his theology was manifestly a daughter of his religion?'[6] He could equally well have appealed to John Calvin, the principal doctor of his own Reformed tradition, for whom the only knowledge of God with which theology was to concern itself was given in 'piety', much else being firmly excluded as 'speculation'. A characteristically Protestant style of descriptive theologizing lay behind both of the two determinative themes of Schleiermacher's dogmatics: he himself spoke of it as 'empirical'.

[handwritten: empirical dogmatics]

II. Glaubenslehre: *dogmatics for a new age*

The task Schleiermacher set himself in his dogmatics can be stated readily enough: he intended to give a disciplined account of the distinctively Christian way of being religious, more particularly as it appears in the 'evangelical' (Protestant) church. Concerning the first edition of *The Christian Faith*, he wrote to Friedrich Lücke that 'the presentation of the peculiarly Christian consciousness was . . . the actual aim of the book' (*Sendschr.*, p. 33). He was fully aware that such a programme, however secure its links with the past, betokened a new direction in Christian theology; it even invited a new designation, *Glaubenslehre* or 'the doctrine of faith'. In practice, Schleiermacher found it convenient still to use the old term 'dogmatics', but he knew he was venturing on something different from orthodox and rationalist theologies alike. Against the orthodox Protestant tradition, the enterprise of *Glaubenslehre* is not defined as essentially exegetical; further, the determination is announced at the outset rigorously to exclude the philosophical elements that had intruded even into orthodoxy, but still more into the rational theologies of the eighteenth century. 'The fundamental thought of the inquiry before us', Schleiermacher writes, 'is that the philosophical and the dogmatic are not to be mixed' (*Gl.*[1] 2, note b). Dogmatic science has an 'empirical' character that distinguishes it both from a biblical theology and from philosophical speculation; and it is this same empirical character that lies behind the requisite ordering of the dogmatic materials.

*[handwritten: * dogmatic science → empirical not rat'l specul.]*

1. Theology as science

Schleiermacher furnished a general guidebook to the theological terrain in his remarkable *Brief Outline on the Study of Theology* (1811; 2nd ed., 1830), still perhaps the best work of its kind.[7] In the *Outline*, dogmatics is not identical with theology but is only a part of it. Christian theology is the sum total of the scientific studies and rules without which church leadership would be impossible: it is constituted as a distinct field, not simply by its content (although all the parts do have a common relationship to a particular mode of faith), nor by a uniform method, but precisely by its practical goal of equipping Christian leaders. Its main divisions are philosophical, historical, and practical theology; and dogmatics – surprisingly, at first glance – is assigned to the second division along with exegetical theology and church history.

The divisions Schleiermacher makes within the total field of Christian theology are only to be fully understood by their place in his general scheme of the sciences, which is simply presupposed in the theological writings but can readily be extracted from the lectures on philosophical ethics, dialectic, and aesthetics. First of all, theological studies belong to the general *domain* of 'ethics', by which Schleiermacher means the science of reason – of all that pertains to the human spirit, its history and culture. Next, within ethics so defined two *kinds of knowing* are distinguished: the 'speculative' kind is directed to essence and works with concepts, while the 'empirical' kind is directed to existence and works with judgments.[8] But the individual sciences do not all belong wholly to one or other of these two kinds: some sciences combine the two, or combine their results. Thirdly, then, Schleiermacher distinguishes these hybrid disciplines by their respective *goals* as either 'critical', if they issue in knowledge, or 'technical', if they issue in rules of action.

In this overall scheme, the place of the three main divisions of theology can be roughly determined if we say that philosophical theology is a critical discipline, historical theology is empirical, and practical theology is technical. Only it must immediately be added, by way of qualification, that the three theological disciplines are not to be isolated from one another but coexist in a continuous exchange. So, for instance, a genuinely historical view of Christianity presupposes the findings of philosophical theology (*K.D.* 65, 252). Exactly what it is that historical theology owes to philosophical theology is a question that can be postponed (until sec. 2). For now, we have the epistemological location of dogmatics: it belongs to historical theology in the sense that its concern is with a particular aspect of concrete human existence – namely, a specific, historically given mode of believing (a *Glaubensweise*). It is, in short, 'ethical' knowledge of the 'empirical' kind; and, so understood, it plainly has the same general subject-matter as church history, from which it is distinguished simply as historical knowledge of how the church and its faith are now, in the present. If allowances are made for eccentricities of terminology, Schleiermacher's placement of dogmatics on the scientific tree is clear enough, and it has some important methodological consequences.

As a historical–empirical discipline, dogmatics does not have to establish its object of inquiry; it takes it as given and only seeks to explicate its content. In this sense, *Glaubenslehre* 'presupposes' faith, and there is no need to inflate the discipline with attempted proofs of, for instance, the existence of God (*Gl.* 33.3). Christian piety is a fact: dogmatic inquiry exfoliates as it seeks to trace the ways in which this fundamental fact enters into relation with other facts of consciousness. To be sure, the fundamental fact (*Grundtatsache*) of dogmatics must be described as an *inward* fact; and in this respect dogmatics differs, not only from deductive sciences that begin with a fundamental *principle* (*Grundsatz*), but also from those disciplines that are historical in the sense of embracing a definite field of *outward* perception (*Gl.* 28.2).

Schleiermacher's recognition that dogmatics is not history as ordinarily construed did not incline him to abandon its classification as historical theology. But the inwardness of the fundamental fact does mean, so he believed, that dogmatics can only be pursued from the inside, by one who has had the inner experience for himself. This, of course, has nothing to do with any special miracle of grace: it is simply a general epistemological principle (*Gl.* 13, postscript). Hence the Anselmian motto inscribed on the title page of *The Christian Faith*: 'Qui expertus non fuerit, non intelliget' (no one will understand unless he has experienced). In particular, the way the church's teaching 'hangs together' (its *Zusammenhang*) can be convincingly presented only by someone who starts from personal conviction. Dogmatics is historical theology by reason of its historical *datum*; yet a dogmatic treatment of doctrines is not a purely historical *report* such as anyone with the requisite information could give of any system whatever (*K.D.* 196; cf. *Gl.* 19.1).

Nowadays, we would be less likely to call the analysis of self-consciousness 'empirical' (*Sendschr.*, pp. 20–1) or to classify dogmatics as 'historical theology' on the grounds that its data belong to historical existence. In some of its stages, as we shall see, Schleiermacher's procedure has plain affinities with what we would rather call 'phenomenological' method. But, despite the terminological obstacles, the general character of the approach he adopted need not be unclear to us, especially when contrasted with the alternatives. To begin with, if dogmatic propositions arise solely out of 'logically ordered reflection on the immediate utterances of the devout self-consciousness' (*Gl.* 16, postscript), and if it is specifically the Protestant self-consciousness that is made the datum of dogmatic inquiry (*Gl.* 23), then the task plainly cannot be carried out through direct scriptural exegesis: the more immediately pertinent texts are in fact the Protestant creeds or confessions (*Gl.* 27.1–2).

It would be a total misunderstanding of Schleiermacher, however, if one were to infer either that he was a Protestant confessionalist (an unlikely inference!) or that he was indifferent to the Scriptures. The point is a strictly methodological one. Of the three types of dogmatics that he mentions – scriptural, scientific, and confessionalist (*Gl.* 27.4) – he was naturally attracted to the second by his strong systematic drives. But he did not believe that a scientific dogmatics should diverge too far from the other two types, nor that dogmatics of *any* kind could relegate the autonomous task of exegetical theology to a merely subordinate role (*Gl.* 19, postscript; *Gl.* 27.3). More important, the specific mode of being religious which constitutes the subject of his discipline, and of which the confessions are simply historical expressions, is a consciousness of being under the Word of God. If Schleiermacher found no place for the proclamation of the Word or the unparalleled authority of Scripture, then it would not be the evangelical consciousness that he was talking about. In actual fact, while he can see the point of the old dogmatic preambles on Scripture as the norm of authentic Christian piety, he sets his doctrine of Holy Scripture where the Reformers had in part already placed it: under ecclesiology. There the New Testament acquires the primary character of a preaching by and about Christ that generates faith (*Gl.* 128.2–3). And one should not be surprised to find in this segment of *The Christian Faith* the plainest affirmations of scriptural authority and sufficiency (*Gl.* 129.2, 131.2) or of the absolute centrality of the ministry of the Word (*Gl.* 134.2, 135.1; cf. *Gl.* 15.2).

2. *Theology and philosophy*

Schleiermacher's theoretical veto of speculative intrusions into dogmatics should not be taken as antimetaphysical; nor, on the other side, does his actual use of speculative categories betray an inconsistency. Once again, as with his views on the appeal to Scripture, it is all a question of methodological uniformity (*Gleichförmigkeit des Verfahrens*: *Gl.* 33.3). Speculation has its own legitimacy, but it belongs on the scientific tree at another point than dogmatics. And if the dogmatician finds it useful to appropriate speculative categories, he may do so only insofar as their content is determined by his own science, not by that of the philosophers.

The fundamental question concerns the way in which talk about God is *generated*. The dogmatician's sole concern is with statements that arise out of the immediate religious consciousness (in a manner to be specified more exactly in due course: see part III below). It may well be that the path of speculation also leads to statements about a Supreme Being that look very like dogmatic statements. But precisely because they arise from a different activity of the human spirit, it is imperative not to confuse them with genuine dogmatic statements; otherwise, the consistency of the dogmatic method will be impaired. If, then, the dogmatician chooses to borrow the language of some philosophical school, he takes it in freedom to shape only the *form* of his propositions. The extraordinary question whether a proposition can be true in philosophy and false in theology, or *vice versa*, cannot properly arise: the proposition, despite similarities of form, simply could not have the same meaning in the two different contexts (*Gl.* 16, postscript).[9] By 'scholasticism', a term he uses as pejoratively as did the Protestant Reformers, Schleiermacher means exactly the confusion of dogmatics and speculative philosophy (*Gl.* 28.3).

It does not follow, of course, that dogmatics and philosophy are mutually opposed, only that they are different. Each has its roots in human nature, and an actual conflict between them would have to presuppose an unthinkable disharmony in human nature itself (*Gl.* 28.3). Besides, as we have noted, dogmatics is not the whole of Schleiermacher's theology: it is expressly linked with ethics (in his peculiar sense) and with the philosophy of religion by the critical discipline of philosophical theology, which serves to locate the language of evangelical faith on the language map. For if we are to talk coherently about the distinctive faith of the Christian church, we must be able to specify in general what is a 'church' (i.e., a religious community) and what is a 'faith' (i.e., what is religion). Hence the introduction to the *Glaubenslehre* proceeds, first of all, to anchor the language of dogmatics in a definition of the essence (or determining characteristics) of Christianity. The closely-woven argument, culminating in proposition eleven, first decides what a religious community is (with propositions borrowed from *ethics*); second, how the various religious communities may be related to one another (propositions borrowed from *philosophy of religion*); and, third, what is the Christian religious community's distinctive essence (propositions borrowed from *philosophical theology*). In this manner, Schleiermacher's preamble to dogmatics sets out, not to demonstrate anything (seeing that the discipline begins with actual facts of experience), but simply to find the place of evangelical faith among other modes of being religious and the place of religiousness itself among the diverse functions of the human spirit (*Sendschr.*, pp. 20–1, 54–5; *K.D.* 21). And this, naturally, can be accomplished only with the assistance of speculative and critical disciplines that work with general concepts, not exclusively with concrete individuals. 'Philosophy', in Schleiermacher's usage, covers the activity of just these disciplines, along with the epistemological inquiry of what he calls 'dialectic'.

3. The shape of the new dogmatics

If Christian doctrines are individually accounts of Christian religious affections (*Gl.* 15), dogmatic theology is the science that *systematizes* the total doctrine prevalent in a particular church at a given time (*Gl.* 19; *K.D.* 195). But *how* exactly is the mass of doctrinal material to be reduced to a systematic order? Special care was bestowed by Schleiermacher on the architectonics of his *Glaubenslehre* because he recognized that the meaning of a proposition is determined in part by its context or location; indeed, he held that the arrangement, along with the precision of its language, is what gives a dogmatics 'scientific form'. It is not sufficient to move the immediate utterances of religious feeling out of their original poetic and rhetorical form into technically correct ('dialectical') language, unless the resulting propositions are brought into a definite relationship with one another (*Gl.* 28.1–2). Schleiermacher's own arrangement was an ingenious combination of a traditional twofold division of 'parts' and a threefold division of 'sections' that was uniquely his own.

Since Calvin, Reformed dogmatics had commonly moved from the knowledge of God as creator to the knowledge of God as redeemer; and in Calvin himself, at least, Adam's fall meant that the second kind of knowledge, though treated later, must in actual experience now come first. Schleiermacher adopts the inherited two-part scheme, drawing out its plain implication that the doctrine of God is given in the system as a whole, not in a single *locus de Deo* that can be disposed of early in the presentation (see *Gl.* 31.2). And in him, too, the order of exposition reverses the order of experience, but not quite for Calvin's reason. The logical movement of Schleiermacher's system is from the abstract to the concrete. Everything in a Christian dogmatics turns strictly on the fact of redemption, and his thinking is therefore wholly misconstrued if it is not recognized that the explication of the consciousness of grace in Part II of *The Christian Faith* is the determinative point of reference for the entire system (*Gl.* 84.4; cf. *Gl.* 90.2). 'Piety', isolated in the introduction for separate consideration, is the irreducible abstraction that places religious language on the language map. The doctrines of creation and preservation in Part I present next, not the full Christian consciousness, but the religious consciousness still in abstraction from the antithesis of sin and grace (*Gl.* 50.4, 62.1, 64.2) or, as Schleiermacher puts it in his heading, 'that religious self-consciousness which is always both presupposed by and contained in every Christian religious affection'. Only in the doctrine of redemption in Part II does he turn to the fully concrete evangelical consciousness. And even within Part II the passage from the abstract to the concrete is invoked to explain the separate treatment of sin: if we consider the consciousness of sin *per se*, we are still moving in the region of the abstract since the full Christian understanding of sin, as of everything else, is given only by reference to the decisive fact of redemption (*Gl.* 66.2, 79.1).

The originality of Schleiermacher's order lay still more in his combining the inherited twofold scheme with a threefold distinction between different 'forms' that dogmatic propositions may take (*Gl.* 30). In the primary and strict form, they are *descriptions of human states*: that is, they are about the religious consciousness, which we may consider either abstractly in itself (Part I) or concretely as subject to fluctuation (Part II). If we take account of the subdivision of Part II, which considers sin and grace separately as two aspects of a single antithesis, we shall then find ourselves speaking of the religious consciousness under three headings: as a consciousness of the general relationship between self, world, and God (Part I), as a consciousness of sin (Part II, first aspect), and as the full Christian consciousness of grace (Part II, second aspect). Under each heading, the dogmatic inquiry is turned directly to certain 'human states'. But if the religious consciousness is of the self in relation to God and the world, it is entirely possible to shift the focus from the self-consciousness as such to one or other of these two elements disclosed in it. If we focus our attention on the presence of God to the religious consciousness, our dogmatic propositions will be formed as *concepts of divine attributes and modes of action*. Similarly, if we focus on the self's awareness of the world, they will become *assertions about characteristics of the world*. And since propositions of the second and third forms can likewise be developed under the three headings already mentioned, the structure that emerges may appropriately be pictured as a three-by-three grid.[10]

Here, then, is the shape of the new dogmatics: after the introduction, it falls into two parts, one of which is subdivided and each of which contains separately-grouped propositions in three forms. The arrangement is not obscure, but it is certainly complex and perhaps strikes the reader as even a little artificial. Yet the methodological principle behind it is crucial. The 'empirical' procedure that Schleiermacher proposes requires everything in the system to be presented as a modification of the immediate self-consciousness. Now this immediate self-consciousness, analysed in his introduction (as we shall see), discloses the self as coexistent with the world, and both as co-posited by God. But if the analysis thus provides a warrant for distinguishing three forms of proposition, it is not difficult to see that all three forms cannot possibly have the same status: the second and third are expressly distinguished as 'secondary'. And even in the secondary forms, which could in principle be dispensed with, nothing is to be asserted that cannot be 'developed out of propositions of the first form' (*Gl.* 30.2). Dogmatic statements about the world and God emphatically do not pretend to offer either a natural science or a theistic metaphysics. Rather, they express the way in which the religious consciousness – or, more specifically, the sinful consciousness or the redeemed consciousness respectively – *perceives* the world and God. The intrusion of additional matter that originates either in natural science or in metaphysical speculation would only dilute the purely dogmatic method.

It does not follow that a system of Christian dogmatics says nothing at all about the kind of a world we live in, or that Christian faith is compatible with any state of affairs whatever. Schleiermacher certainly admits that not every view of the world is compatible with the religious consciousness (*Gl.* 28.1) and that the dogmatician has a responsibility so to express the content of the Christian consciousness that no conflict with natural or historical science will arise (*Sendschr.*, p. 40). His *Glaubenslehre* is dogmatics for a new age, not only by reason of its affinity with the subjective and historical turn in modern thinking, but also because it fully accepts the obligation to adjust its formulas to the current state of knowledge. And just there, of course, lie many of the problems with respect to our two determinative themes: the Divine Spirit and the Second Adam.

III. The Divine Spirit and natural causality

In his brilliant apology *On Religion* Schleiermacher, then a Reformed chaplain in a Berlin hospital, tried to induce his cultured friends to take a second look at the religion they despised. They were accustomed to the view that religion means, above all, the beliefs in a personal deity and a personal immortality, together with the prudent behaviour these beliefs recommend; and they found that they were more interested in other things. Schleiermacher's strategy was to show them that religion is in actual fact a 'sense and taste for the infinite' which gives a deeper worth to the things they valued most. It is reducible neither to beliefs nor to morals, yet it inspires the quest for knowledge and accompanies morality like sacred music. It ought, besides, never to have been missed by those who cherish art, imagination, individuality, and spontaneity.

However astute, the argument pleased hardly anyone. The cultured despisers were disappointed to find, in the final address, that it was the *Christian* religion they were supposed to embrace. And yet Schleiermacher's fellow-churchmen had already decided, by the time they had finished the second address, that what he commended was not Christianity at all. In *The Christian Faith*, written after he had returned to Berlin and had been appointed to a theological chair at the new university, he perhaps tried harder to reconcile the churchmen than to appease the despisers. At least, he sought to remove the suspicion of pantheism that had hovered over his talk about God, but uncompromisingly heightened – indeed, absolutized – the redemptive activity of Christ.

1. God and the feeling of absolute dependence

Schleiermacher was convinced that many who think themselves opposed to belief in God are only repelled by the standard presentations of the subject and are by no means strangers to the affections of the God-consciousness (*Gl.* 172.2). The task he set himself was to develop his own concept of God solely by analysis of the religious self-consciousness, moving (in the manner we have noted) from the most abstract to the fully concrete. As in the *Speeches*, so also in *The Christian Faith* he held that the *essence* of 'piety', the irreducible element in every religion, must be sought neither in beliefs nor in behaviour but in 'feeling', by which he meant the immediate self-consciousness underlying all our knowing and doing. It is 'immediate', and so assigned to 'feeling', in the sense that the self has not yet made itself the object of its own contemplation (*Gl.* 3.2, 3.4).

A little introspection, Schleiermacher holds, can catch the original polar structure (*Duplizität*) of self-consciousness as a consciousness of self and other together. It is a consciousness, as he puts it, of the 'being of the subject for itself' and 'its coexistence with an other', which in its totality is 'the world'. The relation of self and other revealed in self-consciousness is one of reciprocal influence: introspection discloses the self both acting upon the other and being acted upon by it or, what is the same thing, as conscious of its partial freedom and partial dependence. In short: 'Our self-consciousness, as a consciousness of our being in the world or of our being together with the world, is a series divided between the feeling of freedom and the feeling of dependence' (*Gl.* 4.1–2). But look again, Schleiermacher bids us, and you will find in addition a feeling of *absolute* dependence – unqualified, that is, by any reciprocal influence from the self. And *this* feeling cannot arise from the influence upon us of anything presented to us in the world, nor from the influence of the world as a whole (in the sense of the totality of temporal being); for on any such object we would in fact exercise a counter-influence.

The feeling of absolute dependence is the consciousness that even the entirety of our *activity* is 'from somewhere else'. And this is what is meant by 'piety' (*Gl.* 4.3–4).

Observation of immediate self-consciousness thus shows it to have a necessarily religious 'determination'. Plainly, it is misleading when Schleiermacher's term 'feeling' is taken for the emotional side or faculty of human life. For what appears to observation, he thinks, is something fundamental about the structure of our personal life as such. Piety is not relegated to one department of life but is understood to pervade life in its entirety and in each moment. In response to the critics of the first edition of his *Glaubenslehre*, Schleiermacher stressed that he had meant our consciousness of the actual way in which our being is determined. But because this consciousness does not depend on any previously grasped ideas, he did not like to term it a 'knowing'. 'What I understand by "pious feeling" by no means proceeds from conceptions (*von der Vorstellung*)', he explained, 'but is the original attestation of an immediate existential relationship' (*Sendschr.*, pp. 13, 15). Not that there cannot be an original concept of God, arrived at by another route (i.e., philosophically): it is simply that such a concept would be of no concern to dogmatics, which must begin from piety (*Gl.* 4.4).

For dogmatics, the original use of the term 'God' is to denote the 'whence', given in self-consciousness, of our receptive and active existence. And the *most* original conception (*Vorstellung*) with which we are concerned can be nothing more than articulation of the feeling of absolute dependence. Made into the object of reflection, the feeling of absolute dependence 'becomes', as Schleiermacher has it, a consciousness of *God*. And whatever more is put into the conception of God must be developed out of the fundamental content given in immediate self-consciousness. In this sense, dogmatics starts not from a rationally established *idea* but from an original *revelation* of God (*Gl.* 4.4).

2. God-talk and world-talk

In a striking departure from the dogmatic tradition, Schleiermacher turns immediately from his prolegomena to the doctrines of creation and preservation; he simply passes over the doctrine of the Trinity, which appears only in the famous appendix to the work as a whole. The reason for postponing his remarks on the Trinity is made transparently clear, and it once again expresses the cardinal dogmatic rule. As ordinarily understood, the term 'Trinity' has reference to eternal distinctions in the Godhead (*Gl.* 170.2); but in dogmatics, since we have to do only with the consciousness of God that is given in our self-consciousness along with the consciousness of the world, we have no formula for the being of God in itself as distinct from the being of God in the world. We should have to borrow any such formula from the province of speculation, and so become unfaithful to the nature of our discipline. (*Gl.* 172.1)

It is easy to see for ourselves, without any explicit guidance from the author, that the doctrines of creation and preservation, by contrast, follow naturally enough upon the introduction: as Schleiermacher understands them, they are simply explications of our feeling of absolute dependence.

To begin with, it may seem as if he has laid a quite insufficient foundation for a doctrine of God. For what, after all, can be said of God on the slender basis of the feeling of absolute dependence, especially if, as he insists, the feeling is something simple and unchanging? The problem is resolved by further analysis of self-consciousness. Our language about God does not simply assert that self-consciousness points to a 'whence' of the feeling of absolute dependence: rather, it is about the ways in which this fundamental feeling coexists with what Schleiermacher calls the 'sensible self-conscious-ness' – that is, with our experience of nature and of other selves (*Gl.* 5.3; cf. *Gl.* 5.1). The feeling of absolute dependence never fills a moment of consciousness but accompanies our entire existence as the consciousness that all of our 'self-activity' comes from somewhere else (*Gl.* 4.3). And this consciousness, while always there for deliberate observation to uncover, varies in strength precisely because of its union with the sensible self-consciousness, which does not uniformly encourage the emergence of the 'higher' consciousness (*Gl.* 5.5) – although we must obviously avoid any suggestion that awareness of God is compatible only with moments of pleasure in our perception of the world (*Gl.* 5.4).

If for the moment, however, we set aside the fluctuations of the God-consciousness and inquire only about its relation to the sensible self-consciousness as such, what we have is nothing other than the doctrines (in Part I) of creation and preservation, both of which are about the feeling of absolute dependence or about the divine causality disclosed in it. But in taking his stand on the usual methodological point, Schleiermacher now has something more than procedural purity in mind: the ideas of God and nature are also at stake. In the first place, he wants so to interpret 'creation' that nothing is said about a supposed temporal beginning of the world and men, since any such notion would make the divine causality too much like a human work in the realm of reciprocity (*Gl.* 36.2, 39.1, 40.2, 41). What we must rather assert, on the basis of our feeling of absolute dependence, is that the realm of reciprocity itself (including ourselves) has a 'whence' which is *not* subject to reciprocity. Similarly, in the second place, Schleiermacher wants so to interpret 'preservation' (or providence) that nothing is said about God's intervening in the closed causal system of nature, but that God is identified as nature's timeless and spaceless ground (*Gl.* 34.2, 47.2, 54). To his way of thinking, there is therefore a close connection between the consciousness of God and our consciousness of being placed in an all-embracing system of nature (*Gl.* 34, 46.1); and he can conclude that the divine causality, though not identical with natural causality, must be equated with it *in scope* (*Gl.* 51). The only God-talk possible for the dogmatician is a particular kind of world-talk.

That these are not exactly the traditional Christian doctrines of creation and providence, needs no emphasis. True, Schleiermacher leaves no room for the cry of 'pantheism' thrown at the earlier *Speeches*. Given his analysis of the feeling of absolute dependence (in his introduction) and his characterization of divine causality as the world's eternal ground (in Part I), there is simply no way in which God-consciousness and world-consciousness could be logically confused: his annoyance with the critics on this point was fully justified.[11] But in at least three respects his conception of God's relation to the world remained unconventional, not to say heretical. First, the object of providential care is for him the system, not directly the individual, and any thought of God's making ad hoc decisions or performing isolated acts for anyone's benefit is firmly excluded (see, e.g., *Gl.* 46.1). Though he spoke freely of divine 'preservation' (*Erhaltung*), Schleiermacher disliked the very term 'providence' (*Vorsehung*), which seemed to him, in comparison with the biblical term 'foreordination' (*Vorherversehung*), to give inadequate expression to the connection of the part with the whole (*Gl.* 164.3). Second, while in a sense he did set 'God' and 'nature' over against each other as antithetical concepts (*Gl.* 96.1), he also treated them as correlative (*Gl.* 46.2, 54). In *The Christian Faith*, as in his *Dialectic*, the world is not without God, nor is God without the world. Thirdly, he resisted any attempt to include 'personality' among the dogmatic attributes of the world's ground. The divine causality may be termed 'spirit', and it is said to be 'omniscient', but in order to deny that it is a lifeless mechanical force rather than to assert that God has a consciousness like ours (*Gl.* 51.2, 55).

To many of Schleiermacher's contemporaries, it was astonishing that anyone who had so transformed the traditional picture of God could fulfil the office of an evangelical preacher. D. F. Strauss, for instance, in his reflections on prayer and the personal God,[12] asserted that for Schleiermacher prayer could be only 'the expression of a conscious illusion', retained partly out of habit and partly for the sake of his congregation. About this, however, Strauss was entirely mistaken. In the very first collection of his printed sermons, Schleiermacher included one entitled 'The Power of Prayer in Relation to Outward Circumstances',[13] which is the exact homiletical counterpart to what was later asserted, as a forthright doctrinal conclusion, in *The Christian Faith*: 'Our proposition sets prayer, too, under divine preservation, so that prayer and its fulfilment or non-fulfilment are only parts of the same original divine order; consequently, that something might otherwise [i.e., in the absence of prayer] have turned out differently is only an empty thought' (*Gl.* 47.1). As a pastor, Schleiermacher did not conceal this conclusion from his flock, although he naturally set it in the context of a more naive and direct religious discourse. In the sermon, he remarks that of course children may tell their father what it is they desire. In Gethsemane Christ himself laid his longings before his heavenly Father. (Anthropomorphism, we infer, is entirely proper at the immediate religious level.) But just there, in the experience of Christ, lies an important admonition: what he wanted was not granted him, but his wishes had to be bent to the will of God. (So the text itself invites dogmatic controls on naive anthropomorphism.) It is a rule of prayer that God is to be approached as the Unchangeable Being,

in whose mind no new thought and no new decision can arise since he said to himself, 'All that I have made is good' [Gen. 1.31]. What was decreed then will come to pass . . . If, because of the way he has ordained the tissue of events, you must do without what you wish for, you have your compensation in all the goodness that you see in the world . . . But the Wise One is also kind. He will not let you suffer and do without solely for the sake of others. His will is that for the justified man everything should work together for his own good [Rom. VIII.28]. So arises trust that, within the whole, notice has been taken of us, too, however small a part we may be.

What strikes one most about this homiletical exercise is perhaps the ease with which Schleiermacher can avail himself of the inherited Reformed or Calvinistic vocabulary (with its strong sense of an elaborate divine 'plan' in which the individual must seek his place). Very little adjustment seems to be needed, to say nothing of any dissembling. Of course, 'translation' takes place, but Schleiermacher was perfectly open about that, too. In a moment of gratuitous candour he admits what must be obvious to any reader of *The Christian Faith*: that dogmatic language, though expressly pointed towards ministry, is not immediately available for preaching but has to be thought through and reworded (*Sendschr.*, p. 59). In his own sermon on prayer, what is reworded is in part a theme contained already in his first book. To be religious and to pray, says the preacher, are one and the same thing; but the 'prayer without ceasing' which the Apostle commends (1 Thess. V.17) consists in the art of combining every thought of any importance with thought about God. In other words, as the apologist had said already, it is to have the sense of the infinite in every moment of one's finite existence. This the Christian consciousness certainly presupposes. But it is not, of course, the specific content of the Christian consciousness.

IV. The Second Adam and the consciousness of grace

Sent to school with the Moravian Brethren at Niesky (in 1783), the young Schleiermacher had brought happiness to his family with his letters home about the love, the peace, and the mercy of the Saviour. Although there is plain evidence of earlier spiritual disquiet, his troubles only reached the turning point after he had transferred to the seminary at Barby (1785). In the short autobiographical sketch he later prepared for the church authorities (1794), he spoke of 'companionship with Jesus', commended to him by his teachers, as something he longed for rather than had. No doubt, its cultivation was inhibited partly by the questioning spirit that had begun to awaken in him (no thanks to his environment). Finally, in a letter of 21 January 1787, he shattered his father's illusions about him: he had lost his faith and could no longer believe in the deity of Christ or his vicarious sacrifice. And yet anyone who looks back on the letter from the vantage point of *The Christian Faith* will be bound to feel that what Schleiermacher lost was not (or not for long) his faith but his first interpretation of it – if, indeed, he ever did appropriate for himself the lessons he was taught in the Brethren's classroom. Although estrangement from the orthodox doctrines, begun even before he entered the seminary, culminated in a systematic critique of dogma, everything in the *Glaubenslehre* still hung on the picture of the Saviour and its compelling attraction. And one can well understand Strauss's nettling remark that 'Schleiermacher's Christology is a last attempt to make the churchly Christ acceptable to the modern mind.'[14]

1. The ideal made historical

By postponing his discussion of the Trinity, Schleiermacher hoped he might avoid some of the wrong turnings taken on the road to Nicaea (cf. *Gl.* 172.3). But he did not simply ignore the differences between his own christological doctrines and the inherited dogmas: the central division on the person and work of Christ in *The Christian Faith* was interlaced with some vigorous polemic. He was able to appropriate a tradition of criticism going back from the Enlightenment Neologists to the Socinians of the Reformation period. More important, he was also a debtor to more positive attempts at reformulating the christological problem, among which Kant's *Religion*

Within the Limits of Reason Alone (1793) had been a penetrating and influential example. For Kant, the question was not: How could two whole natures, the one human and the other divine, have been united in the person of the incarnate Son? but rather: What is the religious idea (or ideal), and how was it related to the historical individual, Jesus of Nazareth? And the problem so formulated was made all the more urgent by developments in historical criticism that raised doubts about the nature of the New Testament documents: whether they could be trusted as sources of genuine information about the historical Jesus.

Whatever he learned from others, however, Schleiermacher's *approach* to the problem was entirely his own, rooted in the distinctive methodological principles we have already explored. The first clear traces of the fresh approach made their appearance not in the *Speeches* but in a relatively minor product of his tenure at the University of Halle: the little dialogue *Christmas Eve* (1806). Partly perhaps for apologetic reasons, the fifth speech had remained tentative and even ambiguous in its statements about Christ; and the uncertainties were not entirely resolved by the explanations added to the third edition (1821). The significance of Christ had certainly been located in the idea he embodied, the idea of mediation; but he had not been presented as the only mediator, nor had finality been claimed either for his person or for his idea. In other words, the defence of Christianity in the *Speeches* falls short of traditional Christian sentiments, despite one or two more generous phrases that do not seem quite to harmonize with the rest.

The *Christmas Eve* dialogue, on the other hand, plainly indicates that the Christian consciousness is where christological reflection must actually *begin*. Leonard's cynical opinion is that nothing more can be discovered in the historical documents than conflicting christologies. The counter-arguments of Ernest and Edward do not deny the historical difficulties, but they suggest that it is not with the Gospels that we have to begin – unless perhaps we turn (with Edward) straight to the mystical evangelist John, who was the least interested in particular events. We take our point of departure preferably from the actual Christmas joy of the Christian community, its experience of a heightened sense of existence that can only be traced back to the appearance of the Redeemer.

The christological assignment for *The Christian Faith*, then, is this: so to speak of Christ that we can account for his perceived effects on the consciousness of the Christian community. Only within these parameters, we may say, can Kant's question be answered. And criticism of church dogma immediately takes on a quite different significance than it had for the Neologists: its role is to conform the trinitarian and christological formulas to the Christian self-consciousness, a task which the Protestant Reformers unfortunately neglected (*Gl*. 95.2, 96.3, 172.3). The formulas required for an adequate christology will be the results of arguing back from the observed effect to its sufficient cause. It must be admitted that, as time was to show, the structure of this christological argument landed Schleiermacher in difficulties that even his closest disciples found embarrassing: Schweizer, for instance, pointed out that a Roman Catholic dogmatics could establish, by an exactly parallel argument, the Roman Church's belief in Mary as the Sinless Queen of Heaven.[15] Others less sympathetic to Schleiermacher's christology, such as Wilhelm Dilthey, pointed out that the alleged historical cause seemed *more than* sufficient to account for the religious consciousness observable in the Christian church. In view of the difficulties, it is hardly surprising when the attempt is made (by Redeker, for example)[16] to deny that Schleiermacher's procedure really did follow an effect-to-cause pattern. For the moment, I am not concerned to evaluate the soundness of this procedure but only to state what I think it was. And I am bound to conclude that, if allowance is made for the un-Kantian, putatively historical content of Schleiermacher's 'postulate', D. F. Strauss understood him correctly: just as the existence of God was for Kant a postulate of the practical reason, so the dogma of Christ was for Schleiermacher a postulate of Christian experience.[17]

It was not, however, the *old* dogma that Schleiermacher wanted to reestablish by this route, though one is surprised to find just how close, in the end, he came to it. Beginning with the approximations to blessedness that occur in Christian experience, he first establishes that these are always associated with a new 'collective life' (*Gesamtleben*) which works against the 'collective life' of sin. And since this consciousness of grace is always referred to the redemption accomplished by Jesus of Nazareth, we must affirm that the new collective life goes back to the influence of Jesus, who effects redemption by the communication of his own God-consciousness (see esp. *Gl*. 87–8).[18] The train of argument then culminates in proposition 93:

If the spontaneous activity of the new collective life is taken to be originally in the Redeemer and to proceed from him alone, then as an individual historical being he must have been at the same time ideal (*urbildlich*): that is, the ideal must have become fully historical in him, and his every historical moment must at the same time have carried in it the ideal.

In short, that 'the Word became flesh' (probably Schleiermacher's favourite text) means that in Christ the ideal became historical. For Kant, by contrast, who in this respect was a forerunner of the Hegelians, the ideal is always immanent in human reason as such, and the historical Jesus may at most have given it a 'public foothold'; it is besides, quite unlike the God-consciousness of the *Glaubenslehre*, a purely moral ideal.[19] It hardly needs to be pointed out that Schleiermacher was much better able than Kant (as well as more eager) to preserve the link with orthodox Christian tradition: his Christ is perfect, sinless, utterly unsurpassable, and precisely because of his perfect God-consciousness there was an 'actual being of God in him' (*Gl.* 93.2, 94.2).

Such a generous claim on the Redeemer's behalf, even if not quite the orthodox *vere Deus*, immediately poses again the problem of the natural. For how can the perfect realization of the ideal in Jesus possibly be compatible with the *vere homo*, his genuine humanity? Schleiermacher's ingenious reasoning has here two sides to it. On the one hand, since the God-consciousness is something human, even the perfect God-consciousness of Jesus cannot as such be termed supernatural; it is, after all, nothing other than the *human* ideal (*Gl.* 13.1; *Gl.* 14, postscript; *Gl.* 22.2). And the God-consciousness of Jesus both developed naturally in him and is transmitted naturally to others (*Gl.* 89.2, 93.3). (As far as the miracles reportedly *worked by* Jesus are concerned, Schleiermacher sets them aside as a merely historical or scientific problem of no pertinence to dogmatics: *Gl.* 47.3, 103.4.) But the *appearance* of the perfect God-consciousness in history, Schleiermacher thinks, was certainly supernatural, if only in the carefully circumscribed sense that we cannot explain it by its environment in the collective life of sin but must assume a creative divine act (*Gl.* 88.4, 89.1, 93.3). And even the emergence of such novelties in nature is not without scientifically attested analogues (*Sendschr.*, p. 40). The important thing, as Schleiermacher remarked to Jacobi, is not to let anyone prescribe the limits of nature.

2. *The world as theatre of redemption*

Even the historical novelty of a unique revelation cannot, *sub specie aeternitatis*, be construed as an arbitrary divine intervention: if it is a divine act, it must be eternal (*Gl.* 13.1). And so the doctrine of timeless causality lies behind the doctrine of Christ, too. Conversely, christology completes what Part I has taught us about the divine causality. For what is omnipotence to me if I do not know its goal (*Ziel*)? All the propositions of Part I are empty frames until filled with the content of Part II (*Sendschr.*, p. 32; cf. *Gl.* 167.2, where the equivalent term is *Motiv*). Of course, it cannot be said that one event is any more or any less the effect of omnipotence than another (*Gl.* 57.1); even sin cannot have been smuggled into the world by some accident that escaped the divine causality. But what can and must now be said is that the total unbroken fabric of events has a pattern. With complete logical consistency, Schleiermacher embraces (carefully qualified) the formula thrown at the old Reformed divines as the supposed *reductio ad absurdum* of their belief in the sovereignty of God: that God is 'the author of sin' can be given an acceptable sense once it has been understood that God ordains sin, like everything else, for the sake of redemption (*Gl.* 79–81). All the divine activities in the old ecclesiastical mythology – with its narrative of a temporal creation, a temporal fall, an incarnation to restore mankind, and so on – are collapsed into a single divine 'decree' to raise humanity to a higher level of consciousness:

> There is only *one* eternal and general decree to justify men for Christ's sake. It is the same as the decree to send Christ; otherwise, the sending of Christ must have been conceived and determined in God without its outcome. This decree, once more, is *one and the same* with the decree to create the human race, inasmuch as in Christ first is human nature completed. (*Gl.* 109.3)

The proper title for *Christ* in this scheme is 'the Second Adam' precisely because in him the creation of man is perfected: in the unity of the divine decree everything, from the beginning, has pointed towards the appearance of the Redeemer (*Gl.* 89.1, 89.3, 94.3, 97.2, 164.1, 164.2). And Schleiermacher can unroll a historical tapestry as remarkable as any in the more conventional Christian theologies: Christ is the absolute centre of history; all mankind is related to him, though many do not know it; and all religions are destined to pass over into Christianity (*Gl.* 13.1, 86.1, 93.1; cf. *Speeches*, fifth speech, explanation 16). The church, in which Schleiermacher detects a 'being of God' analogous to the being of God in Christ, is the locus of Christ's continuing influence and the historical means by which the Kingdom of God must be extended and the divine election consummated (*Gl.* 123–5, 119–20; cf. *Gl.* 87.3).

Similarly, the only attribute of *God* that answers to the experience of redemption is 'love'. For the work of redemption has been shown to turn upon the union of the divine essence (*Wesen*) with human nature in Christ, and by God's 'love' is meant that in God which corresponds with the human inclination to want union with another; it is the underlying divine disposition (*Gl.* 165.1, 166.1). Now, everything that is truly predicated of God as a divine attribute must be an expression for the divine essence. And yet neither in Scripture nor in the teaching of the church do we in fact find propositions that are parallel to 'God is love': love alone is equated with the being or essence of God (*Gl.* 167.1). Of course, the divine love may not be so construed that it negates the attributes already specified. Yet all the attributes pertaining to creation and preservation and even those related to the consciousness of sin are no more than provisional and preparatory, finally gaining their full significance only in relation to the love of God (*Gl.* 56, postscript; *Gl.* 64.2, 167.2, 169.3). Nevertheless, Schleiermacher finds that he has one last attribute to discuss.

Accompanying the divine love, but not quite of equal status with it, is the 'wisdom' of God, which is 'the art of (so to say) perfectly realizing the divine love' (*Gl.* 165.1). That wisdom does not fully share the favoured rank of love is clear, Schleiermacher thinks, from the fact that we do not say 'God is wisdom', and he offers an explanation on the basis of his distinctive method. The forgiven man is directly conscious of *himself* as the object of the divine disposition of love; but only by an extension of self-consciousness does the experience of redemption lead him to affirm the perfect harmony of *all* things (*Gl.* 167.2, with the parallel passage in *Gl.*[1] 183.3, cited in Redeker's edition). But it is with the divine wisdom that Schleiermacher's dogmatics concludes. *The Christian Faith* culminates in an essentially aesthetic vision of the world as 'the theatre of redemption'. In other words, it ends on a note much loved by the old Reformed divines: the world is *manifestatio gloriae Dei*.

What follows from the fact that we take the divine love to be also wisdom is first of all this: that, whatever else we think of in the term 'world', we cannot possibly view the totality of finite being in its relation to our consciousness of God as anything other than the absolutely harmonious work of divine art. (*Gl.* 168.1)

The divine wisdom is the ground by virtue of which the world, as the theatre of redemption, is also the absolute revelation of the Supreme Being – and therefore *good*. (*Gl.* 169)

All that remains is the epilogue on the need to rethink the doctrine of the Trinity as an affirmation of the being of God in Christ and the church, so making it what in intention it originally was: the actual copestone of Christian doctrine (*Gl.* 170.1).

V. The reference of Christian language

The leading criticisms that have been brought against Schleiermacher have always tended to cluster around the two major themes I have singled out. It has been alleged, first, that he loses the *divine* referent of Christian language in a subjective theory of religion as feeling; secondly, that he sacrifices the *historical* referent of Christian language to his subjective Christ of faith. At first it was the 'speculative theology' of the Hegelians that was the chief, though by no means only, rival to Schleiermacher's system. But the dominance of a very different variety of Protestant liberalism at the other end of the century – the school of Ritschl – did not entirely break the original lines of criticism. Neither did the dialectical theology's assault on Schleiermacher in the early twentieth century. The explanation for this surprising continuity lies partly in the critics' propensity, seemingly incurable, to read him as a speculative thinker; one can then oppose him either with a more satisfactory system of speculation or else with the call to return to a more purely biblical and Reformation faith. Writing in 1933, Wobbermin identified as the fundamental error (the *proton pseudos*) of Schleiermacher criticism the assumption that his theology must be approached from the perspective of his philosophy; and he found this tradition of interpretation going back to the influential work of Bender, written under Ritschlian auspices, and even beyond – to Schleiermacher's first Hegelian critics. 'One can bluntly describe Brunner's Schleiermacher book', he remarked, 'as a modernized new edition of Bender's work.'[20]

1. Schleiermacher and the speculative theology

In actual practice perhaps, Schleiermacher's procedure of moving from figurative to scientifically exact language resembled the Hegelian programme of transposing 'representations' into 'concepts'. But there was a significant difference of principle: for the Hegelians there was always the temptation to presume that philosophical reflection superseded religion by grasping its conceptual core, whereas for Schleiermacher the core of religion was not conceptual, and reflection could never be more to him than interpretation of what is 'original' in the figurative form (*Gl.* 17.2).

The fact is that the followers of Hegel and the followers of Schleiermacher started from two quite different intellectual visions. The *ewiger Vertrag* (usually translated 'eternal covenant') of which Schleiermacher wrote to Lücke was a kind of non-aggression pact: not, that is, a unification of Christian faith with scientific inquiry, but an agreement on the part of each to let the other go its own way unhindered. Where Jacobi saw only conflict, Schleiermacher discovered at most an oscillation – and the Hegelians looked for a synthesis. Biedermann, for instance, insofar as he was critical of Schleiermacher, followed the Hegelian line. He admitted that religion and philosophy are autonomous domains of the human spirit, yet not in such fashion that they simply 'lie outside each other', to be related only as polar opposites. The interpretation of piety in doctrines does not pass out of the domain of religion proper, as though religious feeling itself remained wholly unaffected; the relation to God, mistakenly held to be pure feeling, already has one foot, as Biedermann puts it, in thinking. His own aspiration was after a consistent philosophical penetration of religion. Hence, although he resisted the common Hegelian tendency to dissolve religion in thinking, he could only deplore Schleiermacher's cheerful philosophical eclecticism.[21] Even the theologian, so the Hegelians insisted (Biedermann among them), had to take a firm philosophical stand. Of course, insofar as Schleiermacher the theologian seemed in practice to be more deeply engaged in speculation than his dogmatic principles allowed, the Hegelians could regard the inconsistency as a happy one (even if he did not seem to speculate very well). Strauss, for example, did not object to the Spinozism he detected in Part I of the *Glaubenslehre*, but only to a certain lack of candour about it: the author, he remarked, threw a cloak of piety over the backs of his philosophical troops, but during the more vigorous manoeuvres their true colours peeked out.[22]

The specific differences between Schleiermacher and the speculative theologians were often concentrated on the concept of God. Symptomatic is the fact that while *he* downgraded the doctrine of the Trinity (in its inherited form) as an obsolete mixture of dogmatics with speculation, the Hegelians found themselves nowhere more at home than in trinitarian speculation (although their thoughts on the subject were unconventional). But the philosophy of Hegel, if preeminently speculative, was also emphatically historical, and it is not surprising that christology became a second focus of disagreement. F. C. Baur, who found Schleiermacher's concept of God excessively abstract,[23] also argued that he failed to establish the identity of his religious ideal with the historical Christ.[24] True, Schleiermacher did not argue for the sinless historical Redeemer solely by a dogmatic deduction from the church's consciousness; he accepted the obligation to look at the Gospel sources, launching in 1819 what is said to have been the first course of academic lectures ever devoted to the life of Jesus. But there the problems were, if anything, still more acute. Strauss, who exposed the logical structure of Schleiermacher's *dogmatic* argument, also subjected his *historical* lectures to ruthless criticism and showed convincingly that what he found in the Gospels was exactly what he was looking for: the 'Saviour' of his Moravian religious experience.[25]

Criticism of Schleiermacher from the standpoint of historical thinking proved more durable than the Hegelian philosophy that first produced it. We now have access, for instance, to Dilthey's interesting argument that he unjustifiably tied the universality of the ethical-religious ideal (the 'Kingdom of God') to the historical particularity of Jesus, whom he burdened with greatly inflated predicates.[26] During the first quarter of the present century, the signs were nonetheless favourable for a fresh development of Schleiermacher's revolutionary insights. The flaws exposed in the Ritschlian theology seemed to invite a return to the enterprise of the *Glaubenslehre*, at least insofar as its philosophical foundations had apparently been made secure. And, interestingly, some of the most historically-minded thinkers were among the new admirers of Schleiermacher, including Troeltsch, who came to view the dominant Ritschlianism as a reactionary form of biblical positivism. Although Troeltsch associated himself with the history-of-religions school, it was to Schleiermacher that he turned as the master of modern dogmatics – if only by reason of his programme and not his doctrinal formulations.[27] So Troeltsch announced in 1908, and he was only one of several theologians and scholars who contributed to what was greeted as a 'Schleiermacher renaissance'.[28] But then came the Barthian deluge.

2. *Schleiermacher and the dialectical theology*

With the rise of the dialectical theology in the present century, Dilthey's criticism was turned upside down. Something very like the dualism he had detected in Schleiermacher's theology reappeared as the main object of disapproval in Emil Brunner's *Mysticism and the Word*; only now the universally religious was rejected in favour of the uniquely Christian, and it was flatly denied that Christianity could properly be treated as one of the religions of mankind. Brunner granted that faith in Christ determined Schleiermacher's personal *piety*: his point was, however, that this faith could only be considered an alien intrusion in his dogmatic *system*, which made the initial blunder of not starting from the Christian revelation but from a general theory of religion as mystical union with the All. Once Schleiermacher was trapped in the little garden of the pious, so Brunner tells us, there was no way out: mystical religious experience lacks reference to Another. Against this mysticism, clearly documented in the *Speeches* and supported by the identity philosophy of the *Dialectic*, the 'Word about Christ' could only be spoken in contradiction.

In his review of Brunner's vigorous indictment, Karl Barth found some features of his associate's critique to be objectionable, but he fully shared the verdict that the defendant's theology subjected the Word of God to an intolerable bondage. And in a number of essays he suggested that the reason for the root methodological error lay in Schleiermacher's apologetic stance: at the very beginning, he subordinated the positive dogmatic task to the role of the apologist, who is not a servant of Christianity but a master of it – a virtuoso. It took two 'Assyrians' to call Jerusalem to order by exposing the fatal consequences of the initial flaw: Ludwig Feuerbach showed how the transcendent reality of the theologians could now be viewed as an illusion, and D. F. Strauss showed what happens if you venture to read the New Testament as history. In sum, from merely human religious experience you cannot get either to God or to the real Christ. So, at least, Barth argued, and in the middle third of our century the theological world was widely, though by no means universally, dominated by his reading of Protestant history.[29]

The dialectical theology's estimate of Schleiermacher and Protestant liberalism no longer carries immediate assent. I hope my exposition will have made clear, without the further argument which I have attempted elsewhere, at least that what Schleiermacher *intended to do* and what Brunner *says he did* are two utterly antithetical operations. And I do not myself believe that Brunner took his adversary's programmatic statements seriously enough. Neither can I see sufficient reason to hold that Schleiermacher's undoubted concern to avoid conflict with science led him, as Barth thought, to relegate the dogmatic task to a secondary rank. There can, of course, be no question of just setting the neo-orthodox criticisms aside; and if there are occasional signs at the present day that it has become possible to dismiss them without engaging in detailed argument, that is cause for regret – just as, not so many years ago, one could only regret the dissemination of poorly substantiated, ritualistically repeated stereotypes about Schleiermacher. This does not alter the fact, however, that there is a real need to rediscover the theological generation that was swamped in the deluge. Thinkers like Mulert and Wobbermin were not only sophisticated Schleiermacher scholars who immediately perceived the flaws in the dialectical theology's historiography, but also astute theologians in their own right who had sound reasons for believing that Protestant theology was on the verge of taking a wrong step.

The first line of Schleiermacher criticism had become, in Brunner, the accusation of 'psychologism' or 'agnostic expressionism'. But Wobbermin, at least, recognized the possibility of a fresh defence that would draw out the affinities between Schleiermacher and Edmund Husserl. The basic aim of the *Glaubenslehre*, he suggested, was to develop a phenomenological theology in line with Luther's existential thinking, but also in anticipation of Husserl's notion of the intentionality of consciousness. And the givenness of God in the feeling of absolute dependence, Wobbermin pointed out, is something quite other than the inferential proof of God's existence that it has often been mistaken for.[30] The double comparison suggested by these remarks – with the Reformation (or at least Luther) and with phenomenological philosophy – is, I think, a programme worthy of further exploration. Only, I would myself insist that the Reformation comparison must be made more with Calvin than with Luther, and I am not persuaded that the feeling of absolute dependence is the only or the best point at which to anchor our talk about God.

On the second line of criticism, Wobbermin's theological generation may have seen the way, not to defend Schleiermacher's christology (in the final analysis it may not be defensible), but to develop it and to pare off its objectionable features. If the history prerequisite to the occurrence or survival of evangelical faith had to consist of verifiable conclusions from life-of-Jesus research, Schleiermacher's christology would indeed be in serious trouble (and he would have a lot of company). But if we are to follow through his own method consistently, then the directly pertinent history can only be the event in which Christ is proclaimed. Recognition of the need to relocate the 'fact' on which faith depends lay behind the attempt to differentiate between *Historie* and *Geschichte*. On this discussion, too, Wobbermin made some exceptionally discerning remarks.[31] Although he was not entirely liberated from the temptation to move back from confidence in the proclaimed Christ to confidence in the historicity of the Synoptic Jesus, he did affirm the point – fundamental to Schleiermacher's theology – that the hallmark of the historical (i.e., of *Geschichte*) is not pastness but the reference to human existence in its 'becoming'. And he proposed that by *Historie* we should understand nothing other than researched *Geschichte*, this human existence made into the object of inquiry. Something like this lay behind Schleiermacher's conception of dogmatics as *historische Theologie*. The christological section of dogmatics, if its object is the impression made by the portrayal of Christ in the Christian proclamation, should be so conceived (to echo Schleiermacher's phrase) as not to get us entangled with science – in this instance, historical science.

Finally, the liberal rearguard was entirely capable of some counter-sallies of its own. As Mulert prophetically observed in 1934, it remained open to question whether Schleiermacher's critics would have any greater success in grasping the objective reality of God without being led astray by subjective presuppositions of their own. Some of what they characterized as 'psychologism' and 'historicism', so Mulert suggested, might simply prove attributable to the fact that we can grasp nothing at all except with our psychological faculties and must incorporate everything that happens into the web of history.[32]

It seems, then, that with the waning of the Barthian theology a reappraisal of Schleiermacher is called for. In particular, a second look is needed at just those basic methodological moves of his that have been most fiercely contested. For all Brunner's determination to oppose him with 'biblical-Reformation faith', Schleiermacher's experiential approach actually gave him a strong link with the heritage of Luther and Calvin; it was not simply an accommodation to modern habits of thought. Further, the subtle interweaving of *two* experiential motifs in his dogmatics, the universal awareness of God and the particular influence of Jesus, already transcended in some measure one of the most bitter theological debates of our century. Schleiermacher appears, rightly interpreted, to have worked from a point of view that neither rested on a 'natural theology' (as commonly understood) nor yet hewed to a strictly 'christocentric' line. The 'Word about Christ' was not, for him, the exclusive source of the knowledge of God; but in the Christian it so determined the universally-human awareness of God that Christians, he held, must be said to bear their entire consciousness of God only as something brought about in them by Christ (*Sendschr.*, p. 31). In the apt expression of Richard R. Niebuhr, Schleiermacher's manner of theological thinking was 'Christo-morphic', not in the Barthian sense 'Christo-centric'. And insofar as this makes Christ the 'reformer' of man's knowledge of God, Niebuhr rightly claims that Schleiermacher was more faithful to Calvin than was Barth.[33]

More important perhaps, Schleiermacher's approach does not isolate theology from other ways of studying religion, and yet does not dissolve it into non-theological disciplines either. Questions remain, of course, some of them forcefully posed by the neo-orthodox critics, about the connection between his distinctively theological study of religion and other parts of his own intellectual system: the *Dialectic*, for instance, in which a philosophical doctrine of God is advanced, or the *Hermeneutic*, in which the interpretation of religious texts is subsumed under a general theory of understanding.[34] But here, too, the neo-orthodox critique, notably Emil Brunner's, set the interpretation of Schleiermacher on a wrong track by exaggerating the importance of the *Dialectic* for understanding his dogmatics. A more fruitful inquiry is clearly suggested by the introduction to *The Christian Faith*: To what extent does the relationship of dogmatics to *ethics* (in Schleiermacher's sense) predetermine the interpretation of Christianity? Indeed, it should not be overlooked that Schleiermacher's own intended companion to the *Glaubenslehre* was the *Christliche Sittenlehre*, an unfinished work on Christian 'ethics' in something like our sense of the word. It could well be argued that apart from the Christian ethics even his theology remains truncated; in his recognition of this Barth provided an important corrective to Brunner's *Mysticism and the Word*.[35] Even so, it is unlikely that one would wish to locate Schleiermacher's actual achievement – or his greatest contribution to religious studies – anywhere else but in his dogmatics.

Notes

1 Quoted from the *Tübinger theologische Quartalschrift* (1839) by Robert Stalder, whose *Grundlinien der Theologie Schleiermachers* has been undertaken to justify 'in some measure' von Kuhn's estimate: see vol. 1 (Wiesbaden, 1969), p. ix. Translations are mine unless otherwise stated.

2 The original text of the letter has been reissued by Martin Cordes in 'Der Brief Schleiermachers an Jacobi: Ein Beitrag zu seiner Entstehung und Überlieferung', *Zeitschrift für Theologie und Kirche* 68 (1971), 195–212.

3 Alois Emanuel Biedermann, 'Schleiermacher', *Ausgewählte Vorträge und Aufsätze* (Berlin, 1885), pp. 188–91, 197–8.

4 He uses this expression in the midst of his analysis of immediate self-consciousness, and there is no reason to suppose that the method changes when he goes on to speak of the consciousness of God: *Der christliche Glaube*, 2nd ed. (reproduced in the 7th, critical

edition, ed. Martin Redeker [2 vols., Berlin, 1960]), 4.1. References to the *Glaubenslehre*, abbreviated *Gl.* and cited by paragraph (where appropriate, also by sub-paragraph), will hereafter be given in the text. On the rare occasions when I refer to the first edition (2 vols., Berlin, 1821–2), I use the abbreviation *Gl.*[1]

5 Translated from the text in Cordes, 'Der Brief Schleiermachers an Jacobi', p. 209.

6 *Schleiermachers Sendschreiben über seine Glaubenslehre an Lücke*, ed. Hermann Mulert (Giessen, 1908) (hereafter cited in the text by the abbreviation *Sendschr.*), p. 16. The open letters first appeared in the journal *Theologische Studien und Kritiken* (1829).

7 *Kurze Darstellung des theologischen Studiums*, hereafter abbreviated as *K.D.* and cited by paragraph in the second edition (reproduced in the 3rd, critical edition, ed. Heinrich Scholz [1910; reprint ed., Darmstadt, 1961]).

8 The second of the two domains to which the total body of knowledge is assigned Schleiermacher calls 'physics', the science of nature; and in physics, too, a distinction is made between 'speculative' and 'empirical' kinds of knowing.

9 See also *Gl.* 2.1; the handwritten note to *Gl.* 4.4, cited in Redeker's edition; and the postscripts to *Gl.* 19 and 33.

10 See Horst Stephan, *Geschichte der deutschen evangelischen Theologie seit dem deutschen Idealismus*, 2nd ed., revised by Martin Schmidt (Berlin, 1960), p. 103. A similar diagram will be found in Claude Welch, *Protestant Thought in the Nineteenth Century*, vol. 1 (New Haven, Conn., 1972), pp. 74–5.

11 See the handwritten comment on *Gl.* 4.4, mentioned already (in n. 9 above).

12 David Friedrich Strauss, *The Old Faith and the New*, transl. from the 6th ed. by Mathilde Blind (London, 1873), sec. 35.

13 Reproduced in Schleiermacher's *Kleine Schriften und Predigten*, ed. Hayo Gerdes and Emanuel Hirsch (3 vols., Berlin, 1969–70), 1:167–78. The collection first appeared in 1801 and does not claim to report the spoken word exactly.

14 Strauss, *The Christ of Faith and the Jesus of History: A Critique of Schleiermacher's Life of Jesus*, transl. Leander E. Keck (Philadelphia, 1977), p. 4.

15 Alexander Schweizer, *Die Glaubenslehre der evangelisch-reformirten Kirche* (2 vols., Zurich, 1844–7), 1:94.

16 Martin Redeker, *Schleiermacher: Life and Thought*, transl. John Wallhausser (Philadelphia, 1973), pp. 131–2.

17 Strauss, *Charakteristiken und Kritiken*, 2nd impression (Leipzig, 1844), p. 41.

18 Schleiermacher assumes rather than demonstrates that, through the 'picture' of Jesus transmitted in the Christian community, the impartation of redemption works today just as it did in the days of Jesus's earthly existence, by the impression of his personality. See, e.g., *Gl.* 29.3, 88.2.

19 Immanuel Kant, *Religion Within the Limits of Reason Alone*, transl. Theodore M. Greene and Hoyt H. Hudson (1934; reprint ed., New York, 1960), pp. 113, 143–4.

20 Georg Wobbermin, 'Methodenfragen der heutigen Schleiermacher-Forschung', *Nachrichten von der Gesellschaft der Wissenschaften zu Göttingen aus dem Jahre 1933*, philologisch-historische Klasse (Berlin, 1933), p. 34, referring to Wilhelm Bender's *Schleiermachers Theologie nach ihren philosophischen Grundlagen dargestellt* (2 vols., Nördlingen, 1876–8) and Emil Brunner's *Die Mystik und das Wort* (Tübingen, 1924).

21 Biedermann, 'Schleiermacher', pp. 201–4.

22 Strauss, *Charakteristiken*, pp. 171–2.

23 See, for example, Baur's letter to his brother (26 July 1821) reproduced in Heinz Liebing, 'Ferdinand Christian Baurs Kritik an Schleiermachers *Glaubenslehre*', *Zeitschrift für Theologie und Kirche* 54 (1957), 225–43, esp. p. 238.

24 See esp. Baur's *Die christliche Gnosis* (Tübingen, 1835), pp. 637–56.

25 Strauss, *Christ of Faith*, p. 35.

26 Wilhelm Dilthey, *Leben Schleiermachers* II, ed. Martin Redeker as vol. XIV of Dilthey's *Gesammelte Schriften* (Göttingen, 1966), pp. 473–507.

27 Ernst Troeltsch, 'Half a century of theology: a review', *Ernst Troeltsch: Writings on Theology and Religion*, transl. and ed. Robert Morgan and Michael Pye (Atlanta, Georgia, 1977), pp. 79–81.

28 See Johannes Wendland, 'Neuere Literatur über Schleiermacher', *Theologische Rundschau* 17 (1914), 133–43.

29 See, in particular, Karl Barth, *Protestant Theology in the Nineteenth Century* (Valley Forge, 1973), chaps. on Schleiermacher, Feuerbach, and Strauss; also 'The Word of God in theology from Schleiermacher to Ritschl', *Theology and Church* (London, 1962); 'Evangelical theology in the nineteenth century', *God, Grace, and Gospel* (Edinburgh and London, 1959); and *The Theology of Schleiermacher* (Grand Rapids, Michigan, 1982). The review of Brunner's book appeared in *Zwischen den Zeiten* (1924).

30 Wobbermin, 'Schleiermacher', *Die Religion in Geschichte und Gegenwart*, 2nd ed., vol. v (Tübingen, 1931), cols. 176–7, 172–3. For Schleiermacher, of course, God is never 'given' as an object; and this leads him to deny in *Gl.* 4.4 any *Gegebensein Gottes*, although he does permit the expression that God is 'given to us in feeling'.

31 See Wobbermin's masterful and for the most part convincing study, *Geschichte und Historie in der Religionswissenschaft* (Tübingen, 1911), published as a supplement to the *Zeitschrift für Theologie und Kirche*.

32 Hermann Mulert, 'Neuere deutsche Schleiermacher-Literatur', *Zeitschrift für Theologie und Kirche*, n.s., 15 (1934), 84.

33 Richard R. Niebuhr, *Schleiermacher on Christ and Religion: A New Introduction* (New York, 1964), pp. 161–2, 211–12. Cf. Redeker, who states that Schleiermacher thought 'christocentrically' but not 'christomonistically': *Schleiermacher*, p. 149.

34 The pioneering work on hermeneutics was misleadingly included in the theological division of the *Sämmtliche Werke*, vol. VII.

35 Barth, *Protestant Theology*, p. 436. Unfortunately, the English translation misses Barth's allusion to Schleiermacher's notion of a 'teleological' (not 'theological'!) religion. See also Hans-Joachim Birkner, *Schleiermachers Christliche Sittenlehre im Zusammenhang seines philosophisch-theologischen Systems* (Berlin, 1964), p. 27.

Bibliographical essay

The *Schleiermacher Bibliography* of Terrence N. Tice (Princeton, N. J., 1966) contains no fewer than 1,928 entries, and it already needs to be supplemented by the labours of nearly two more decades. There is no possibility of appraising here a body of literature that required 168 pages simply to list. I must be content to mention at least the primary sources and all the English translations I know of, then to comment briefly on the secondary literature from Britain and America. I am indebted to other German works besides those I have had occasion to cite, but I could not begin to discuss them without making an arbitrary and misleading selection. Those who require only a list will find it in Tice, and they will have suitable guides to German work since his cut-off date (1964) if they look through the bibliographies in the most recent works I list below (sec. 3).

1. The primary sources

The main divisions of *Friedrich Schleiermachers Sämmtliche Werke* (30 vols., Berlin, 1834–64) have been mentioned above. The most conspicuous gap in the collected works is the absence of Schleiermacher's personal correspondence, for which the basic collection is *Aus Schleiermachers Leben: In Briefen*, ed. Ludwig Jonas and Wilhelm Dilthey (4 vols., Berlin, 1858–63). Other collections have been made (see Tice), perhaps the most useful being the two volumes by Heinrich Meisner under the title *Schleiermacher als Mensch* (Gotha, 1922–23).

Among the general anthologies may be mentioned *Schleiermachers Werke in Auswahl*, ed. Otto Braun and Johannes Bauer (4 vols., Leipzig, 1910–13; 2nd ed., 1927–8); *Friedrich Schleiermacher: Kleine Schriften und Predigten*, ed. Hayo Gerdes and Emanuel Hirsch (3 vols., Berlin, 1969–70); and a handy paperback, *Schleiermacher-Auswahl*, ed. Heinz Bolli (Munich and Hamburg, 1968), which includes the two *Sendschreiben an Lücke* among a good sampling of shorter extracts.

Important critical editions include those of the *Reden* by G. Ch. Bernhard Pünjer (Brunswick, 1879), the *Monologen* by Friedrich Michael Schiele (Leipzig, 1902), the *Sendschreiben an Lücke* by Hermann Mulert (Giessen, 1908), the *Kurze Darstellung des theologischen Studiums* by Heinrich Scholz (1910; reprint ed., Darmstadt, 1961), the 1821–2 *Glaubenslehre* by Hermann Pieter (3 part-vols. Berlin, 1980–4), the 1830–1 *Glaubenslehre* by Martin Redeker (2 vols., Berlin, 1960), the *Hermeneutik* by Heinz Kimmerle (Heidelberg, 1959; 2nd ed., 1974), and the *Dialektik* by Rudolf Odebrecht (1942; reprint ed., Darmstadt, 1976). It should be noted that the textual problems posed by the *Dialektik* do not permit one to take Odebrecht's edition (based on the 1822 manuscript) as the sole definitive one.

2. English translations

The translating of Schleiermacher's works into English has had a checkered history, not wholly to be explained by the linguistic and ecclesiastical preferences of the British. More than a century elapsed between the original publication of the reputed masterpiece of modern theology and its appearance in English dress. Even so, over the years a fairly substantial body of Schleiermacher translations has accumulated. In chronological order of appearance, we have the following: *A Critical Essay on the Gospel of St. Luke* (London, 1825), 'On the Discrepancy between the Sabellian and Athanasian Method of Representing the Doctrine of the Trinity' (in *The Biblical Repository and Quarterly Observer*, 1835), *Introductions to the Dialogues of Plato* (Cambridge, 1836), 'On the Worth of Socrates as a Philosopher' (printed in several publications: e.g., with the Eng. transl. of G. F. Wiggers's *Life of Socrates*, London, 1840), *Brief Outline of the Study of Theology* (Edinburgh, 1850), *The Life of Schleiermacher as Unfolded in His Autobiography and Letters* (2 vols., London, 1860), *Christmas Eve: A Dialogue on the Celebration of Christmas* (Edinburgh, 1890), *Selected Sermons* (London, 1890), *On Religion: Speeches to its Cultured Despisers* (London, 1894), *Soliloquies* (Chicago, 1926), 'Catechism for Noble Women' (in *The Hibbert Journal*, 1928), *The Christian Faith* (Edinburgh, 1928), 'Reflections Concerning the Nature and Functions of Universities' (abridged transl. in *The Christian Scholar*, 1965), *Brief Outline on the Study of Theology* (Richmond, Va., 1966), *Christmas Eve: Dialogue on the Incarnation* (ibid., 1967), *On Religion: Addresses in Response to its Cultured Critics* (ibid., 1969), *The Life of Jesus* (Philadelphia, 1975), *Hermeneutics: The Handwritten Manuscripts* (Missoula, Montana, 1977), *On the Glaubenslehre: Two Letters to Dr. Lücke* (Chico, California, 1981). A fresh, or at least revised, translation of *The Christian Faith* itself would be welcome, but it would probably be unrealistic to hope for it. Readers confined to English have no access to the original editions of the *Speeches*, *Brief Outline*, or *Christian Faith* (except through the haphazard footnotes of the scholars).

3. Secondary literature in English

Scarcely anything of the immense German literature on Schleiermacher has been put into English. A notable, if modest exception is Martin Redeker's *Schleiermacher: Life and Thought*, translated by John Wallhausser (Philadelphia, 1973). Although sometimes cryptic by reason of its brevity, it must be rated the best overall introduction to its subject in the English language. Of the older literature, we now have in English D. F. Strauss's *The Christ of*

Faith and the Jesus of History, mentioned already. A few pages from Dilthey's biography of Schleiermacher appear in Wilhelm Dilthey's *Selected Writings*, translated by H. P. Rickman (Cambridge, 1976), but they obviously were not chosen for the light they shed on Schleiermacher. For Barth's estimate of Schleiermacher, see n. 29 above.

Schleiermacher unquestionably made his mark on British, particularly Scottish theologians. But original British works about him are few and general in character, and it would probably be too generous to say of any of them, whatever their pedagogical merits, that they have advanced the state of research. The studies by Munro (a Scot) and Selbie (the English Congregationalist) are still worth reading, and they nicely complement each other: Robert Munro, *Schleiermacher: Personal and Speculative* (Paisley, 1903), combines a short biography with an exposition of Schleiermacher's philosophy (including the ethics), while William Boothby Selbie, *Schleiermacher: A Critical and Historical Study* (London, 1913), gives an overall picture of Schleiermacher's religious thought as well as some indication of the pre-Barthian German debates about it. More recent – and plainly a byproduct of neo-orthodoxy – is J. Arundel Chapman's *An Introduction to Schleiermacher* (London, 1932), which in fact introduces the reader only to the *Speeches* (and a few standard criticisms of them), compares Schleiermacher with Wordsworth (preferring Wordsworth), and reports approvingly on Brunner's *Mysticism and the Word*. Schleiermacher, we are informed, had no doctrine of God, not even in *The Christian Faith*, and must be accounted 'one of the heresiarchs who sent the modern world on the path of subjectivity'. *Friedrich Schleiermacher* by Stephen Sykes (London, 1971) is a very brief but judicious appreciation of Schleiermacher for laymen.

In the English-speaking world, by far the strongest regional interest in Schleiermacher has come from North America. Much of it is unobtrusively shelved away in typewritten dissertations, but the literary genre naturally conveys the intent to contribute to the state of research. It is also from the United States that the last half-dozen translations of Schleiermacher have come, generally furnished with good editorial introductions and annotations. Even before the Edinburgh version of *The Christian Faith* appeared, George Cross had published *The Theology of Schleiermacher: A Condensed Presentation of His Chief Work 'The Christian Faith'* (Chicago, 1911), an abridged translation with a historical introduction and a concluding estimate. Andrew R. Osborn's *Schleiermacher and Religious Education* (Oxford, 1934), printed in England but written in Canada as a doctoral dissertation, ranges more widely than the title suggests but does not start from a correct interpretation of 'immediate self-consciousness'. Richard B. Brandt's *The Philosophy of Schleiermacher: The Development of His Theory of Scientific and Religious Knowledge* (New York, 1941), a revised Yale dissertation by a cosmopolitan scholar, is a very solid piece of work. Its more recent theological counterpart is Richard R. Niebuhr's *Schleiermacher on Christ and Religion: A New Introduction* (New York, 1964). Sharply critical of neo-orthodox prejudice against Schleiermacher, Niebuhr nonetheless adopts the opinion that he did not adequately express the transcendence and personality of God or the character of sin as rebellion; he also offers the homegrown judgment that Schleiermacher was less successful than the American Jonathan Edwards in carrying out the description of Christian religious affections.

The more thematically focussed American studies, if we set aside Jerry F. Dawson's less pertinent essay on Schleiermacher's nationalism (Austin, Texas, 1966), are those by Johnson, Spiegler, Forstman, Williams, Thiel, and Blackwell. In the revised version of his Columbia University dissertation, *On Religion: A Study of Theological Method in Schleiermacher and Nygren* (Leiden, 1964), William Alexander Johnson explored the dependence of Nygren's method on Schleiermacher's, noting also some points of difference. In my opinion, more work still needs to be done on the connection between the transcendental deduction of a category and the phenomenological disclosure of an existential relationship. Schleiermacher is compared with the men of his own immediate world in Jack Forstman's *A Romantic Triangle: Schleiermacher and Early German Romanticism* (Missoula, Montana, 1977), a valuable attempt to specify the shared outlook of the Romantics and to distinguish Schleiermacher's own peculiar standpoint within it. For all of them, the discovery of individuality situated human life precariously between unity and chaos, but for Schleiermacher there was no way to soar, with Novalis and Schlegel, above the polarity to a higher realm.

'Polarities' figure prominently in the studies by Spiegler and Williams, and American 'process theology' lies in their background, too. Gerhard Spiegler's *The Eternal Covenant: Schleiermacher's Experiment in Cultural Theology* (New York, 1967), a welcome guide through the textual and conceptual jungles of the *Dialectic*, argues that the theological enterprise of Schleiermacher founders on his conception of God as absolute (transcendent, *totaliter aliter*) and therefore incapable of relationship to the world, so that theology can in practice only be god-less, a form of cosmology and anthropology. A Barthian conclusion for a strikingly non-Barthian reason! The constructive proposal is that we could secure Schleiermacher's naked assertion of the God-world relationship if we made God himself conform to the dialectical principle of relativity. But is it, I wonder, *Schleiermacher's* assertion that we would then be securing? In effect, Robert R. Williams appears willing to answer yes: his *Schleiermacher the Theologian: The Construction of the Doctrine of God* (Philadelphia, 1978) is critical of Spiegler (even more critical of Barth), but his point is that no drastic revision of Schleiermacher's doctrine of God is needed since it was already bipolar. Amid much that is illuminating in Williams' study and still more that is provocative, readers will work hard to disentangle the interpretation of Schleiermacher from the concepts of all the other thinkers with whom he is compared and from Williams's own constructive recommendations.

Niebuhr, Forstman, and Spiegler reappear, with others, as contributors to *Schleiermacher as Contemporary*, edited by Robert W. Funk (New York, 1970), an international symposium from Vanderbilt celebrating the two hundredth anniversary of Schleiermacher's birth. Finally, the decade of the 1980s has already witnessed further North American interest in Schleiermacher. In a revised version of his dissertation at McMaster University, *God and World in Schleiermacher's Dialektik and Glaubenslehre: Criticism and the Methodology of Dogmatics* (Bern, 1981), John E. Thiel argues that the critical method of Schleiermacher's dogmatics was governed by principles of thinking laid down in his *Dialectic*, specifically by the noetic correlation of 'God' and 'world' (intellection and sensibility), and that Schleiermacher was to this extent justified in acknowledging only a formal influence of philosophy on his dogmatics. One might better reserve the expression 'dogmatic criticism' for Schleiermacher's attempt to assess dogmas and doctrines by their conformity to the Christian consciousness. But *God and World* is an interesting study; and if it does not settle the vexed question of philosophy and theology in Schleiermacher's thought, it does shed light on it. Less systematic, more historical in approach is Albert L. Blackwell's Harvard dissertation, revised and published as *Schleiermacher's Early Philosophy of Life: Determinism, Freedom, and Phantasy* (Chico, California, 1982), which follows its subject through the early part of his career (1789–1804), from the end of his student days at Halle to his return as *professor extraordinarius*. Reading Schleiermacher against the background of his intellectual world – a sound procedure, but not as universal as it should be – Blackwell starts with the unpublished manuscript on human freedom (1792), in which Schleiermacher developed an alternative to Kant's 'transcendental freedom', but shows that for all his early commitment to a deterministic philosophy Schleiermacher still found room for a different kind of freedom and for the liberating role of the phantasy.

Several aspects of Schleiermacher's theology that have been only briefly touched on in the present essay, and others that have not been mentioned at all, are discussed and documented in B. A. Gerrish, *Tradition and the Modern World: Reformed Theology in the Nineteenth Century* (Chicago, 1978), *The Old Protestantism and the New: Essays on the Reformation Heritage* (Chicago and Edinburgh, 1982) and – at a more popular level – *A Prince of the Church: Schleiermacher and the Beginnings of Modern Theology* (Philadelphia and London, 1984).

5

Arthur Schopenhauer

RICHARD TAYLOR

Arthur Schopenhauer, in spite of his considerable and lasting influence outside of philosophy, particularly in literature and the arts, has not had a comparable influence on religious thought. This is not because his philosophy is not a rich and even inspiring source of themes that are of significance to a religious interpretation of life. Rather, it is because of the pessimism that pervades his writing, together with his own unsparing hostility to popular religion, which he thought of as a spurious kind of metaphysics.[1] His attitude towards the Gospels, and the spirit of unselfish love that is found in them, was reverential.[2] And he was, more than any other western philosopher of importance, profoundly influenced by the religions of the East, particularly by Buddhist and Hindu thought.[3] In fact, he thought he found there the confirmation of his own philosophy, the main features of which he had worked out before becoming aware of these sources. Whether this is so or not, there is no doubt that his philosophy is of deep significance to religion, and that his pessimism, properly understood, does not in any way detract from that significance.

A brief biography

Schopenhauer was born in what was then the free city of Danzig, on 22 February 1788, and died in Frankfort on 21 September 1860. He was the son of a prosperous merchant, Heinrich Floris Schopenhauer, and the former Johanna Henriette Trosiener, a woman of considerable style who was well known during her lifetime as a novelist. Most of his youth was spent in Hamburg, however, where he soon manifested an interest in books and a corresponding disdain for business. At fifteen his father offered him an extensive excursion through France and England, but only on condition that, upon completion of the tour, he would devote himself thenceforth to a

157

mercantile career. The offer was enthusiastically accepted, but these travels, instead of diverting the youth from intellectual interests, appeared to nourish them. His capacity for sensitive and penetrating observation, which was to mark his philosophy, was already apparent, and he returned from his travels impressed mainly by the misery and suffering which he saw, barely concealed, everywhere.

When Schopenhauer was seventeen his father died and his mother moved to Weimar, where her house became a gathering place for the cultural elite. The temperamental differences between mother and son were there sharpened to the point that the son was obliged to quit his mother's company altogether. She, of vivacious temperament, quite rightly perceived him as brooding, captious, arrogant, and generally contemptuous of all viewpoints save his own, attitudes which quite regularly emerge in his philosophical writings when commenting on the opinions of his contemporaries.

At twenty-one Schopenhauer came into the inheritance which would provide a fairly comfortable security for his entire life, relieving him of any need to teach or be otherwise gainfully employed, and he at once enrolled at the University of Göttengen, ostensibly in the curriculum of medicine, as a means of gaining admission, but in fact to devote himself to philosophy and classical studies. His philosophical reading was at first virtually limited to the writings of Plato and Kant, on the advice of one of his mentors, and the result was apparent in everything he wrote thereafter. Two years later he transferred to the University of Berlin, and then finally, on the strength of his first book, *The Fourfold Root of the Principle of Sufficient Reason*, he was awarded a doctorate by the University of Jena, in 1813.

It was soon after this that Schopenhauer made his initial acquaintance with the religious and metaphysical traditions of India. *The Upanishads* had been translated into Latin by the orientalist Anquetil Duperron, from a Persian version of the original Sanskrit, and published at Strassburg in 1801–2, and this work came to be a major influence upon Schopenhauer's thinking. He declared it to be the inspiration of his life, and said it would be the consolation of his death. In this complex system, so different from the rationalistic tradition of the West, Schopenhauer thought he perceived insights which he had himself arrived at quite independently. What mostly impressed him was the claim, made in various ways, that the physical world, and with it all living forms, are but appearances of an underlying reality that admits of no division and no individuation. The implication of this is that personal individuality is illusory, and so likewise is every distinction a person makes between himself and the rest of creation. It was from these writings that Schopenhauer lifted the Indian formula, 'tat twam asi', meaning 'this thou art', which he thought encapsulated the fundamental truth of his philosophical system. The underlying identity of all living things which is expressed in that formula became the foundation of Schopenhauer's ethics, as well as his reflections on death, and the meaning of life. Indeed it is, together with his identification of the underlying reality with Will, what distinguishes Schopenhauer's philosophy from all others, and it was clearly the illumination for most of his interpretations of the various aspects of experience.

Most of Schopenhauer's life, after the completion of his formal studies, was marked by what could only be interpreted at the time as failure. His brief foray into teaching, at Berlin, attracted no attention and virtually no students. He had with characteristic arrogance scheduled his lectures to coincide with Hegel's, confident that what he considered the latter's pompous bombast would be eclipsed by the profound and evident truth of his own system. When this did not happen he attributed it to conspiracy on the part of his academic opponents. His philosophical writing went similarly unnoticed. His main work, *The World as Will and Idea*, published in 1819, received only two scant reviews, and sixteen years after publication he was advised that most of the copies had been disposed of at wastepaper prices. He nevertheless managed to bring out a second edition, in 1844, which was considerably enlarged by the addition of numerous essays elaborating upon ideas expressed in the original edition. He did receive a prize from The Scientific Society of Drontheim in Norway for his essay on the freedom of the will, which time has shown to be one of the least important of his writings, but he received no prize from the Royal Danish Academy of the Sciences at Copenhagen for his essay on ethics, in spite of the fact that it was the only one entered in the competition. Ironically, this essay, *On the Basis of Morality*, has turned out to be one of his greatest achievements.

Schopenhauer spent the last twenty-seven years of his life at Frankfort, where he lived a lonely but comfortable and philosophically fruitful life, most of it with little recognition. He adhered to an exact schedule from day to day, which included a two-hour walk with his beloved dog at exactly the same time each afternoon, in whatever weather. His forenoons were spent in creative work. The seemingly endless setbacks to his quests for recognition never hampered his philosophical creativity, or reduced in the slightest his absolute conviction of the truth and importance of his philosophical system. Towards the end of his life, following the publication of a collection of popular essays under the strange title, *Parerga and Paralipomena*, he did begin to receive attention and even acclaim from a few quarters, but not from the universities. This is to some extent true still, for while the academic world has never ceased showering attention upon Kant's works, for example, and others of lesser significance such as Fichte and Schelling, Schopenhauer continues to be regarded there as something of an unaccredited missionary, even as his influence spreads among others. His appeal is not so much to the academic mind, as to the aesthetic, religious and metaphysical, and that great appeal is surely destined to increase.[4]

Schopenhauer's boundless self-assurance and disdain for most of the philosophical work of his own era doubtless saved him from succumbing to intellectual fashions, just as it hindered recognition of his worth among his contemporaries. But along with this somewhat unappealing aspect of his personality must be mentioned the deep love and tenderness he felt towards all living things, together with his acute sensitivity to suffering and evil, whether human or other. These are things that crop up here and there in the works of most philosophers, incidentally and almost parenthetically, but they are at the heart of Schopenhauer's thought, disclosing not only a capacity for observation far in excess of the normal, but a singularly compassionate heart as well.[5]

Schopenhauer and theology

However strange it may seem, Schopenhauer himself apparently never noticed some points of resemblance between his fundamental metaphysical claims and those of the traditional Christian theology which he so detested. He was instead eager to keep the two as far apart as possible, Christianity being, in his view, the source of some of the most revolting errors in history. He did sometimes claim that his doctrine represented the only genuine Christian philosophy,[6] but the aspect of Christianity that he was drawing attention to was its claim that we must renounce the world. Elsewhere he praised the spirit of pessimism that he found in the New Testament,[7] and he sometimes compared the New Testament ethic with his own.[8] His attitude towards traditional theology, however, was one of unmitigated hostility.

The claims of traditional theology that form a significant basis for comparison with Schopenhauer's metaphysics are these:

First, that there exists a creator of heaven and earth, that is, of the whole of phenomenal existence, this creator being Himself no part of that phenomenal realm;

Second, that this creator is Himself uncreated, and subject to no possible diminution;

Third, that He is omnipotent, being subject to no other power in the world but, on the contrary, that of which every other force or power is the expression;

And fourth, that He is eternal and omnipresent, in the sense that He exists beyond all distinctions of time and space, these distinctions being applicable only to creation, that is, to the phenomenal world, and not to its source.

The important points on which Schopenhauer's metaphysics departs from traditional Christian theology, on the other hand, are these two:

First, that while theologians endow this creative being with personality and call it God, Schopenhauer denies it every attribute of personality except will, and accordingly calls it simply *will*. The personal pronoun 'He' is never applied to it, although Schopenhauer does sometimes speak of it in quasi-personal terms, such as those appropriate to motherhood.[9]

And second, that he accordingly denies of it both intelligence and goodness, declaring it to be blind, and indifferent to any purpose whatsoever except existence and, in particular, to be indifferent to the sufferings of living things.[10]

These two differences would to most persons be quite sufficient to render Schopenhauerian metaphysics essentially irreligious, but this would be a hasty judgment. The intelligence and goodness which Christians ascribe to the creator of heaven and earth may very well be prejudices, the first inherited from the Greeks and the second from ancient Judaism. In any case the metaphysical picture of reality that pervades all of Schopenhauer's writings is profound indeed, quite free of the more glaring absurdities of traditional Christianity, and it provides the basis for a deep and meaningful ethic, far more comprehensive than any found in any version of Christianity. Schopenhauer believed that it also provides a basis for a meaningful concept of salvation, quite unlike any envisaged in Christianity, but perfectly confirmed in other religions, especially Buddhism.

What we must do first, then, is set forth Schopenhauer's fundamental metaphysical vision, a vision that can at once be described as both rational and mystical.

The Will

Immanuel Kant's philosophy sundered reality into two realms, that of phenomena and that of the noumenon, or 'thing in itself'. These are not, however, two realities, but rather, two aspects of reality, the phenomenal world being simply the world as it appears to our understanding, or more loosely, the world of appearance, and the noumenal being the world as it is in itself, unconditioned by our apprehension of it. This distinction was not, of course, new in Kant's philosophy. It underlies all the speculations of the ancients, is the cornerstone of Platonism in all its expressions, and it is presupposed in most of the religious systems of civilized cultures everywhere. Indeed any thoughtful person is forced to make such a distinction the moment he notes the implication of the fairly obvious fact that the world as it is experienced by us must be something quite different from the world considered independently of all experience.

Kant claimed that human knowledge is restricted to phenomena, that is, to experience, and that any purported knowledge that goes beyond this, which would be metaphysics as it has traditionally been conceived, is empty. We can never know the underlying reality of things. But at the same time he declared that the knower himself belongs to both realms. That is, a person is to himself a physical object like any other, and capable of being experienced as such. But that is not all he is. He belongs, as well, to the underlying noumenal existence that underlies all phenomena. It is by means of this claim that Kant sought to resolve such longstanding problems as that of free will; the problem, that is, of how a man can be free, and at the same time governed in all his behavior by the laws of causality. It is as a phenomenal being that he is so governed. As a noumenal being he can be subject to laws of reason that he imposes on himself.

Kant did not, however, see in this distinction the possibility that Schopenhauer exploited and made the basis of his philosophy; namely, the possibility that each of us can indeed know the thing in itself, in the most direct manner imaginable, for each of us *is*, in his innermost being, that noumenon. We see ourselves from without, to be sure, just as we see everything else; but we also see ourselves, in a different sense, from within. We do not know ourselves *merely* as appearances, the way we know other physical objects. We know ourselves, too, as that which appears. The knowledge we thus have is direct or intuitive, and not something that can be set forth discursively, in the manner of empirical science.[11]

And what is this inner reality, which Kant declared unknowable, and which Schopenhauer called the will? Schopenhauer's characterization of it is quite clear, and consistent throughout all of his writings.

It is, first of all, not one thing among others. It is the only thing that exists; or in other words, it is reality itself. Other things – bodies existing in space and time – are not really other things at all, but rather manifestations or, as Schopenhauer often calls them, expressions of the will. They are in that sense, from the standpoint of metaphysics, illusory; and Schopenhauer sometimes speaks of the world simply as his 'idea'.

The will is not, therefore, in the ordinary sense, the *cause* of the world, or of anything else. Causation, or what Schopenhauer calls the principle of sufficient reason, applies only to phenomena, that is, to things in space and time.[12] Everything that happens in the realm of experience is related to something else as its causal consequent. The will, however, is not something found in experience, and no distinctions of space and time apply to it. Yet in another sense the underlying will is the cause of the world – in somewhat the sense that droplets of water, for example, are the cause of a rainbow. A rainbow simply is countless droplets of water as they appear to us; and similarly, the physical world is just the manifestation of the will.[13] World and will are each necessary, and sufficient, for the other, which renders them identical, as indeed they are, metaphysically. One is the world as it is, and the other, the world as it appears.

What, then, of the individual will – of an individual person, for example, or any other living thing? Schopenhauer has declared that each of us is, in his inner nature, will, and that the will which constitutes the innermost nature of the world is immediately knowable to oneself. What, then, is the relation of that will which is *myself* to the will of another living being, and to the will which is identical with the world?

Schopenhauer's answer to this is profound and immensely rich in its consequences for religion and ethics. The relationship in question is one of identity.[14] That is to say, reality is one and indivisible. All distinctions between things belong only to the realm of phenomena, and are metaphysical illusions. The distinctions we make between things presuppose space and time. Without these no individuation of things would be possible. But space and time are not real things. They are only conditions for the experiencing of things.[15] They have no application to will, which is beyond every temporal and spatial distinction. The will is not a thing, much less a thing in space or time. It is that of which every thing is a manifestation. So if one asks, What is the relationship between my will and yours, or between my will and the rest of creation? the answer is: They are one and the same will. In one place[16] Schopenhauer uses this analogy to convey this idea: Each of us is related to everything else, and to the world, as the life force of each individual leaf of a tree is related to the life of the tree itself. An individual leaf is not a separate living thing, dwelling parasitically on the tree. Each leaf is the expression of the life of the tree; and if a leaf withers and falls, nothing has really perished. The life that was there before is there still, unabated, undiminished. Therefore no real distinction can be made between the inner nature of one leaf and that of another, or of the tree itself, which expresses itself in visible branching and foliage. Thus is each of us, in our innermost nature, related to the visible world. The implications of this view, which is at once beautiful and overwhelming when it is fully grasped, are enormous. Schopenhauer draws from it a conception of immortality quite unique to philosophy,[17] but not novel to the religions of the East. He also draws from it a profound ethic, which he relates both to the *caritas* of the New Testament,[18] and to the compassionate concern for all living things that is found, for example, in Buddhism.

The relationship between metaphysics and religion

Before considering the implications just alluded to, we should note Schopenhauer's clearly expressed declarations of the role of religion in human affairs. He thought of religion, and especially Christianity, as a surrogate metaphysics.[19] That is, men, as soon as they overcome the demands made upon them for mere survival, begin to reflect on certain questions for which their experience provides no answers – questions such as, Why is there a world? Why am I here? And most pressing of all, Why must I die? In this men differ from all other animals, who live entirely in the present moment and have no conception of non-being, hence no thought of their own deaths. The questions men ask are, in other words, metaphysical ones. But few persons are capable of metaphysical thought, which requires not only great leisure and training, but rare and special qualities of mind. Religion, therefore, emerges as the response to this metaphysical need. It is in that sense a counterfeit metaphysics. The questions it answers are metaphysical, but the answers themselves are not, since they do not rest upon reason. And there are other important differences, too, between religion and metaphysics. The latter, for example, is supposed to be understood as truth, in a strict and proper sense, whereas the doctrines of religion should be understood only in an allegorical sense. Thus religion teaches us that we do not really die, as does, Schopenhauer thought, a true metaphysics. But religion presents this truth to men in a version that they can understand, representing each soul as eligible for eternal life, fabricating imaginative abodes for the departed, and so on. Similarly, religions evolve myths involving the struggles between the forces of good and evil, and usually represent the world as seriously contaminated with evil. In doing so they certainly express deep and important truths, but in forms which, if literally construed, are absurd. They should, therefore, be allegorically construed. What actually happens, however, is that priests present these allegorical truths – along with, of course, a great deal of falsehood – to the masses of men as if they were truths *sensu proprio*, in order that they will be believed by persons lacking the sophistication to understand truth *sensu allegorico*. In this way people's minds become basically corrupted against true understanding, and the two versions of metaphysics – the true and the spurious – come to be fundamentally opposed and hostile to each other.

The main support of religion, Schopenhauer thought, lies in the fear of death, and the means by which religious doctrine gains a hold on men's minds is the privilege the Church always claims of imparting its doctrines to the young, before they have developed any critical power capable of raising doubts. With respect to the former, the gods of mankind, Schopenhauer thought, are invented only to set aside the clear verdict of nature, that each of us is mortal. If they were denied that power, or if our immortality could be shown to be something ensured automatically by nature, then belief in the gods would everywhere quickly evaporate. Still, the doctrines of religion are not all of them false, if understood allegorically; indeed, the most basic claims of religion, with respect to death and to ethics, are fundamentally true. They are merely oversimplified, so that they can be absorbed by the mind in youth and, once planted there, made quite invulnerable to the assaults of reason which develops later.

Schopenhauer's metaphysical theory of death

The original edition of Schopenhauer's *The World as Will and Idea* was supplemented, much later, by two volumes of essays elaborating upon the philosophy contained in the original work, and the longest of these is the one dealing with death.[20] The essay is widely misunderstood by readers who suppose that, by the world and reality, Schopenhauer means the physical world, of which we are individual parts. The imperishability of our true nature follows, of course, as an immediate consequence of Schopenhauer's metaphysics. What perishes in death is a phenomenon, that is to say, a person considered as a physical being, or separate part of the physical world. What perishes with this is, of course, the brain and nervous system, and with these, individual thought, consciousness, intelligence and reason. But these were always adventitious to our true nature anyway. Philosophers are therefore on a wrong track when they identify one's true self with his intelligence or reason. And it is equally wrong to suppose, as most popular religion does, that the individual ego remains, and survives the decay of the body. The concept of the individual ego is that of an inner reality separated from the rest of reality. Separateness, however, presupposes individuation, that is, the possibility of making one thing distinct from another. This, in turn, presupposes individualizing things within the manifold of space and time. Only if we can distinguish *here* and *there*, *now* and *then*, can we also distinguish *this* from *that*. That distinction, however, applies only to physical objects, or in the present instance, to the human body and its nervous system, which are clearly perishable. The only way any individual thing could elude decay would be to last, as an individual thing, forever – and that is, in fact, the manner in which unreflective people conceive of their own survival of death. At the crudest level they imagine that they will live on as individual, recognizable people, and that they will recognize by sight other individuals who are dear to them and who have similarly survived their own deaths. Of course this kind of survival of death is totally incoherent and even inconsistent, and no labors of theologians can possibly make it intelligible. The slightly more subtle view, that the individual consciousness of a person will survive the destruction of his body, is upon reflection hardly more coherent, however. For what escapes death must be precisely what is *not* individual, that is, not tied to the forms of space and time, as consciousness and memory, being functions of the individual brain, must be.

What, then, survives the death of the individual? The question is misleadingly put. What we should say, instead, is that will alone is real, that its manifestations in visible nature arise and perish at each moment, and that death, which is the evaporation of one of these dream-like appearances, can never touch that which is real in a person to begin with. We have, to be sure, no individual immortality, but such a state is nothing a reflective person would covet anyway. The deathlessness that is assured to us is one we share with every living thing or, less misleadingly, one and the same with life itself. Herein lies the truth of Plato's perception, that life itself, or what Schopenhauer calls will, is not subject to death.[21] Plato's mistake was to think of that life as a mere attribute of the rational soul, whereas in fact it is reality itself and not subject to individuation. A person who dreads his own death is, again, like the individual leaf of a great tree which, let us imagine, becomes conscious and reflects: Here I am, an individual and separate living thing, existing in my own right, but faced with my own inevitable decay; would that I might continue as a living leaf forever, even though all these other leaves, and this great tree itself, should become nothing!

Pessimism and evil

Although deathlessness is, in this fashion, assured to us, Schopenhauer's philosophy is not one in which the traditional hopes of religion are promised fulfilment. It is, on the contrary, deeply and notoriously pessimistic. That, however, is a characteristic which Schopenhauer found in most religious systems, including the Christian system, at least so far as their estimate of the world is concerned. What they glorify is not the world, and certainly not mankind.

There was, for Schopenhauer, no problem of evil, in the traditional sense;

that is, no problem of reconciling the evil of creation with the goodness of its source. He presupposed no such goodness in its source. The evil of the world was therefore, to him, a plain and obvious fact, and, reversing the Leibnizian formula, he described it as the worst world possible.[22] This was for Schopenhauer no hyperbole. He meant that, whenever there are competing possibilities for good and evil, it is the latter that always prevails.

The evils of the world, Schopenhauer thought, were, at best, the vanity and meaninglessness of life and, at worst, its suffering. Life's meaninglessness is sufficiently important in this philosophy to receive separate discussion. Here we shall enlarge on Schopenhauer's concept of pain and suffering.

Reversing the classical Augustinian formula, Schopenhauer declared pain and suffering to be what are positive, and their opposites, joy and happiness, to be the mere absence of these. The ancients had sometimes identified goodness with being itself. Indeed, in Plato's philosophy, the Good was the ultimate reality, all other realities being derivative from this. The same idea had been emphasized by Socrates, and the many Socratic schools that emerged in antiquity. St Augustine found in this claim his most famous means of reconciling the apparent natural evil of the world with the goodness of God. All that exists, St Augustine said, is good, and therefore a credit to its maker. What we consider evil is nothing more than the absence, or privation, of that goodness. Evil thus resembles a vacuum – which is real enough, in a sense, but which nonetheless consists of nothing real, and can be understood only as the privation of what truly does exist. Most religious thinkers have felt fairly comfortable with this idea, as being at least a partial solution to the problem of evil.

But, Schopenhauer declared, if we go to experience for our answers instead of turning out agreeable formulas as required by religious presuppositions, what we find is that it is pain that is actually felt, hence pain that is real or positive. To describe it as a mere absence of pleasure is to reverse the testimony of experience. We describe our state as pleasant, on the other hand, when we find ourselves relatively free from pain. Pleasure, therefore, is what is negative, being simply the absence of pain. And so it is, similarly, with happiness and its opposite. A thousand things are at hand all the time to make us miserable, and we consider ourselves happy when these are kept more or less in abeyance. Happiness, therefore, consists simply in the absence of misery and torment, and a happy life, to the extent that it is possible, is nothing more than a life relatively free from suffering. We try to avoid sickness, which is real, and when we succeed in this, we deem ourselves healthy and well. We are aware of hunger and thirst, but not of their satisfaction, except in the negative sense of no longer feeling hungry or thirsty. And thus it is that what is bad is what makes its presence felt, and most of life consists of flight from these positive evils. To the extent that we elude them we consider life good, which shows well enough what is real in the world, and what is illusory.

The same inference, to the positive reality of evil and negative nature of goodness, can be drawn other considerations. Thus a novelist can carry his hero through page after page of pain, anguish and defeat, and the descriptions of these can be varied endlessly; but when it comes time at the end to portray the happiness which is finally won from it all, there is nothing the writer can say. Similarly, Dante had no difficulty describing the contents of hell. Life supplies abundant materials for this. But his description of heaven was basically insipid.[23] Its ingredients have no positive reality in the world that we know. Evils are always at hand and ready to assert themselves at the smallest opportunity. Thus a man can be made wretched by a bacterium, or by accidents arising from the most trivial causes, which can render him blind, or mindless, or inflict upon him any other of the large reservoir of maladies that nature holds always in store; but when he succeeds, for the time being, in avoiding all these, then there is no comparable reservoir of joys to which he can turn. Indeed, Schopenhauer notes, if one wants a clear image of the relative reality of pleasure and pain, he needs only to compare the feelings of two animals, one of which is engaged in eating the other.[24]

The meaninglessness of life

Even if our entire lives were spent in complete freedom from pain and suffering, and could accordingly be deemed to be happy, this would not render them meaningful. A stone, though it feels no pain, may nevertheless exist to no purpose. It is perhaps here that the ingredient essential to every religion is to be found, namely, in the attempt to disclose a meaning or purpose to human existence or, which is part of the same thing, a way of salvation from its evils.

But of course this disclosure of meaning is without significance unless one first sees that life is vain and meaningless without it. And it is here that Schopenhauer's philosophy is particularly eloquent.[25] Not only did his metaphysical concept of a blind and omnipotent will point unmistakably to the meaninglessness of its expression in the world, but he also drew from experience, uncolored by any metaphysics, the same negative view.

The Schopenhauerian will, which brings forth all of nature's forms in such profusion, has no purpose in doing so. It is a will to existence itself or, as Schopenhauer often describes it, a will to live, and no more. This is what is meant by describing it as 'blind'. And if we look at life, and especially at the lives of things other than ourselves, this is what we seem to find. Our own fond hopes and conceits tend to color our view of human existence, and lead us to invest it with meaning in excess of even the slightest hints of it, but we are less likely to be under any such illusion when we contemplate the lives of other things. Insects, for example, arise in countless numbers, then swiftly perish, having accomplished nothing whatsoever in their brief lives but to ensure the repetition of the same cycle, over and over, throughout all time. Some birds span half the globe only to mate and lay eggs, the only point of which is to produce more like themselves to do exactly the same the next season. Thus does the will tirelessly create, and death tirelessly dissolve, in an endless cycle that achieves nothing beyond the pain and travail of what is thus raised up and abolished. This same meaninglessness is found throughout the whole of nature, and human life is no exception. The ground mole, for example, has but one task and that is to burrow in the darkness of the earth, with immense effort, in search of a worm, which will nourish him and give him enough strength to dig in search of another, which in turn nourishes him on to another, and so on and on. Eventually he begets others like himself, who repeat exactly his own history, the entire countless generations of these pathetic animals having no more purpose to their existence than this. To find in such life anything resembling pleasure or joy is to use words without meaning. These animals are not in any real sense in quest of anything. They are not led by hope of reward, but blindly goaded from behind to exist, in themselves and in their offspring, just for the sake of existence itself. And so it is with everything that lives. Life has no meaning beyond life itself, and at every level this presents the picture, not merely of suffering, but of suffering in vain. The details change when we move on to the consideration of human life, the complexities increase, but the overall picture is the same. A vast metropolis, considered from a distance, resembles an anthill, with the comings and goings of its members; and if we imagine that closer inspection will reveal some essential modification of this picture then we are wrong:

All strive, some planning, others acting; the tumult is indescribable. But the ultimate aim of it all, what is it? To sustain ephemeral and tormented individuals through a short span of time in the most fortunate case with endurable want and comparative freedom from pain, which, however, is at once attended with ennui; then the reproduction of this race and its striving. In this evident disproportion between the trouble and the reward, the will to live appears to us from this point of view, if taken objectively, as a fool, or subjectively, as a delusion, seized by which every thing living works with the utmost exertion of its strength for something that is of no value.[26]

The individuals of this ant-like society thus live out their lives, at worst in positive sickness and suffering, and at best in boredom. The boredom is from time to time relieved in what are thought of as the pleasures of life, but which are in fact nothing more than distractions from the endless and invincible meaninglessness of one day following upon another. Schopenhauer, in one of his best similes,[27] likens human existence to the journey of a man riding down a swift river on a raft. The river carries the raft along; its occupant has nothing to say about this. But what he is occupied with at every moment is avoiding, as best he can, with his pole, the rocks and shoals that threaten to destroy him at every moment. And to what purpose? Why this unceasing effort, that claims all his strength? What is the reward that awaits him at the end of it all, and makes it worth his while to sustain his existence at such cost? Only this, that he will at last be thrown over rapids that he can in no way avoid, and be hurled to the very destruction which he has sought so long and hard to put off, but which was always going to win in the end anyway.

It is, certainly, the *raison d'être* of religion to find, or to insert, into this bleak picture some redeeming element. Nevertheless most religions, Christianity in particular, and emphatically the religion of the Buddhists, agree that, without the salvation they offer, the world and life are indeed like this. It is thus a total corruption of the spirit of Christianity to pretend that earthly life is a blessing, or to go about, as some enthusiasts do, viewing the world with a radiant smile. Schopenhauer, with considerable reason, declares that his pessimism represents the only genuinely Christian philosophy there is[28] – which is a reminder of something contented Christians would like to ignore.

Schopenhauerian ethics

The deep and constant pessimism of Schopenhauer's philosophy clearly creates the need for some redeeming claim, some proposed salvation from it all; and this Schopenhauer does attempt to supply. Before considering this, however, we must complete the philosophical background of it through a consideration of his reflections on ethics.

Schopenhauer's ethical writings represent the most inspiring and perhaps the most lasting part of his philosophy.[29] It is here, too, that the inspiration from religion is most obvious. He found his view concerning the role of compassion confirmed by the tradition of Buddhism, and indeed, believed that ancient Buddhism had arrived at its moral view from metaphysical presuppositions much like his own. While far less sympathetic to Christianity, particularly because of its emphasis on the unique worth of man, and positively scornful of Judaism, because of its emphasis on law, he nevertheless thought that what he called the virtue of loving kindness corresponds with the *agape* of the New Testament. And it is, in any case, impossible to read Schopenhauer's *On the Basis of Morality* without being stirred to a sense of kinship and love, not just for one's fellow men, but for all of nature. It is in this work, too, that the reader finds Schopenhauer's suggestion of the possibility of a genuinely noble human nature, so rare in the rest of his writing.

Despite his disclaimers, Schopenhauer's ethical philosophy is Kantian in its approach, though not in content. Like Kant, Schopenhauer rests genuine morality on a *good will*. But whereas Kant defined the good will in terms of a stern and unfeeling sense of *duty*, Schopenhauer defines it in terms of the feeling of compassion. This creates an immense divergence between the two philosophies, however similar their original approach. Schopenhauer's ethics could be unmisleadingly described as a philosophical elaboration of the Christian idea of an unreserved love, whereas Kant's can be thought of as a Christian ethic in which duty to superhuman authority – in this case, the authority of reason – has replaced the sentiment of love.

Schopenhauer thought that people act from three basic incentives, which are egoism, compassion and malice. These he defined in terms of the weal or woe of either the agent, or others. Thus, egoism is described as the concern for one's own wellbeing, compassion as the unselfish concern for the wellbeing of other living things, and malice as the desire to injure others without expectation of any reward to oneself.

The first of these, egoism, is deemed the incentive from which virtually all persons act virtually all of the time. That is, almost all human actions, including those that are entirely proper and just, are self-regarding, having as their purpose nothing more noble nor base than the wellbeing of their agents. Schopenhauer was convinced, however, that genuinely unselfish actions are possible, and that such unselfishness can take the form either of compassion, or of malice. And it is, he thought, upon this puzzling fact that all genuinely moral good and evil rest.

There is, for example, nothing surprising, nor inspiring, nor repellent, in the fact that most people think of their own wellbeing most of the time. Much of the action that springs from this incentive is perfectly harmless, as in the case, for example, of earning for oneself an honest living through work that neither significantly benefits nor damages others. Sometimes this same incentive is positively beneficial in its fruits, as in the case of a politican who, seeking nothing but glory for himself, thereby saves his country from disaster. And again, the same incentive is sometimes, and indeed very often, pernicious in its fruits, as in the case of one who, in his pursuit of power, spreads misery around him. All such egoistically motivated action, Schopenhauer thought, is devoid of significance for ethics, though not necessarily without significance to the concept of justice. That is, when someone acts selfishly, then his incentive is the same, regardless of whether his actions are hurtful, beneficial, or neither. No one merits moral esteem for helping his fellows if all he was really concerned for was helping himself, nor does he merit moral condemnation for injuring others if his concern was only to help himself. We can indeed describe the results of such selfishness as good or as bad; but ethics, as distinguished from law, is concerned with the incentives of actions, not with their effects. In this Schopenhauer was in entire agreement with Kant, but differed with him in respect to what incentive is truly noble. Kant said it was the incentive of duty, and Schopenhauer, that it was loving kindness.

The virtue of loving kindness is in Schopenhauer's philosophy the incentive of compassion. Compassion, it must be clearly understood, is not merely the desire to help others, for that desire might arise from a purely selfish motive – for instance, from the wish to be thought well of, by oneself or others. No doubt much human kindness does in fact arise from incentives no nobler than this. But genuine compassion must, by definition, be an utterly unselfish interest in another's wellbeing; or in other words, one who acts from compassion must, if his motive is pure, seek no reward whatever for himself in so acting, not even the inner feeling of self-approbation.

Many persons doubt that such a genuinely selfless incentive can even exist, that beneath the appearance of it there must be some self-interest; or in other words, that compassion is only a disguised form of egoism. And indeed, Schopenhauer thought, it is quite impossible for this incentive to make itself felt except in the presence of suffering. No one can feel compassion for someone enjoying nothing but good fortune, and apparent expressions of love in such circumstances are apparent only. Behind the helping hand and the expressions of brotherly love is only a tender regard for oneself. In the presence of suffering, however, an agent can sometimes forget his dear self and his own concerns and, in an act of pure unselfishness, actually seek the good of another. Under these circumstances, Schopenhauer claimed, borrowing the expression from Indian philosophy, the 'veil of Maya' that normally separates a person from other living things is sundered, and he perceives his own identity with the sufferer. Not only does he then set aside his normal concern for himself, but his *self* or ego, as a separate thing, ceases to exist. It was this experience of oneself in others, aroused by the sight of suffering, that Schopenhauer thought was expressed in the Sanskrit expression, found in the *Upanishads*, 'Tat twam asi', which means, 'That thou art', and conveys the underlying identity of all living things. The phrase is often repeated in Schopenhauer's writings.

There is, on the other hand, another expression of unselfish motivation, and that is in genuine malice. For here, too, the agent ceases to think of himself and his own concerns, and is instead selflessly concerned with another living being that is capable of suffering, the difference being that here, instead of seeking to relieve it, he seeks to increase it. This is, of course, utterly puzzling, why anyone would want to go out of his way to cause suffering in another being, and one naturally wants to interpret it as just another form of disguised selfishness. People sometimes cause suffering, to be sure, but, it is usually thought, that cannot be their sole purpose. Beneath it they are, however perversely, really seeking something good for themselves.

Schopenhauer maintained, however, that pure malice, though rare, like compassion, is no less real, and that a person can, with no ulterior motive whatever, and in fact at some cost to himself, actually seek the woe of another being, just for its own sake. Of course there is no way of proving that this is true, but it is important to see that there is also no way of proving that it is not, and Schopenhauer claimed, plausibly, that our actual experience of the cruelty of which people are capable tends to confirm his claim, however unflattering to mankind this claim might be. People are not, to be sure, normally malicious, nor are they normally compassionate. They are normally just self-regarding. But they are, sometimes, capable of compassion, and sometimes, if rarely, of genuine malice. Or at least, our actual experience certainly suggests this.

What, then, have these incentives to do with ethics? And what relevance have they to the religious aspect of Schopenhauer's philosophy?

With respect to the first question, Schopenhauer claimed that compassion was the only genuinely moral incentive, and malice the only genuinely anti-moral incentive. That is to say, the first is that, and that alone, which stirs in the beholder a deep moral approbation, and the latter is what uniquely inspires profound moral revulsion. Benefits to others that accidentally spring from selfishness often rouse in us feelings of gratitude and thankfulness, and injuries resulting from the same incentive rouse feelings of fear and sometimes of hatred, but neither of these is the expression of a genuinely moral judgment. Only compassion and malice, he thought, can evoke this. Schopenhauer's quite convincing defense of that claim takes the form of presenting examples, wherein can be seen the absurdities that are implied by other ethical theories, and the clear truth of his own.

And with respect to religion, Schopenhauer found in Buddhism and in the *Upanishads* insights into metaphysics and ethics identical with his own. The monastic orders of Buddhism are older than any in Christendom, and the fact that a tradition as rich, profound and durable as this one should rest upon an ethic of compassion, so like his own, and that he should nevertheless have arrived at his own ethic independently of this tradition, was thought by Schopenhauer to be a confirmation of his philosophy. Buddhism denies the ultimate reality of the self or ego, as did Schopenhauer, and teaches the underlying identity of all living things. It was on the basis of the same claim that Schopenhauer explained, metaphysically, how genuine compassion for others is possible. In the presence of suffering, he claimed, the barrier of appearance that separates oneself from others drops away, and one discovers his identity with the sufferer. In no other way, he thought, could compassion be explained; and that explanation was disclosed no less in Buddhism than in his own metaphysical presuppositions.

The other respect in which Schopenhauer's ethics is virtually mirrored by Buddhism is, of course, the deep pessimism common to both. The doctrine of suffering, and its unavoidability, is the very foundation of Buddhism, and the path to overcoming it is its central theme. It is no wonder, then, that Schopenhauer should have become absorbed in this tradition, which was, prior to him, almost entirely ignored in European philosophy.

Schopenhauer's assessment of Christian ethics, on the other hand, was less sympathetic.[30] Although he sometimes declared the *agape* or *caritas* of the New Testament to correspond to his own idea of compassion, Christianity, he quite rightly pointed out, has always limited men's ethical consideration to their fellow men, removing the entire remainder of creation beyond the pale of ethics. Indeed, the Bible makes this quite explicit, declaring man, alone, to have been created in the image of God, and bidding us, in its very first book, to subdue all living things and, in effect, treat them as having been created for our own convenience and use. And that tradition has been upheld by the Church. One can search in vain through volumes of theology and theological ethics for the slightest suggestion that we have any obligations to animals, or to the relief of their suffering. They are in all such writings treated as mere things. We are, indeed, bidden to refrain from cruelty; not from any compassion for animals themselves, however, but rather, from a concern for our own characters, that these may not be rendered hard and unfeeling and thereby cloud our perception of our duties towards men. Schopenhauer, on the other hand, consistently and unabashedly included all living things within the scope of his ethics, thereby setting his thought quite apart, not only from the Christian tradition, but from virtually all of the ethical philosophies of the western tradition.

Schopenhauerian ethics, though profound, moving and unique, has never won widespread adherence among philosophers, largely because of the obstacle posed by Kantian ethics. This, with its emphasis on reason and law, bewitches thinkers whose whole acculturation has instilled in them a veritable reverence for both. The reverence for reason, so clearly exhibited in Kantian ethics, is the legacy of our philosophical tradition, derived from ancient Greece, and the value placed upon law and commands is the heritage of the whole Judeo-Christian tradition. Anyone able to see beyond these traditions, however, can hardly fail to be moved by the beauty and sensitivity of this part of Schopenhauer's philosophy.

The way of salvation

Schopenhauer's philosophy shared with Buddhism an unrelieved pessimism with respect to the world, both maintaining that suffering is inherent in existence. Most western philosophy and religion have taken the opposite view, that suffering, though common, is an accidental accompaniment to life that we can hope to avoid. Philosophical ethics began, among the Greeks, not as a search for the meaning of right and wrong, but for the nature of happiness and the means to its attainment; and Christianity, while emphasizing the sufferings of mankind and the illusory character of earthly happiness, has nevertheless held out the hope of happiness for the elect.

This hope for happiness, of whatever kind, was deemed by Schopenhauer, as well as by Gotama Buddha, to be an inborn error. We think of happiness as the fulfilment of our desires, that is to say, of our wills. But this is precisely what is impossible. No sooner is any satisfaction attained than the pleasure that is supposed to accompany it flees, and a new want replaces the old one, destined for precisely the same frustration. It is the very nature of the will to continue willing, so through no attainment of any end can it cease willing. From this it follows, according to Schopenhauer's analysis, that through no attainment can happiness be reached, or in other words, that happiness is, in the very nature of things, unattainable.[31]

Those who complete their lives without any insight into the vanity of their existence, or in other words, into the illusory character of its successive goals, are destined ultimately to the enforced cessation of their willing by death.

But this is no real salvation; indeed, death, and the final frustration that it represents, is everywhere deemed the profoundest catastrophe that can befall one. There must, therefore, be another way, and the one declared by Schopenhauer appears to have been lifted directly from Buddhism. In what are certainly the most puzzling declarations of his entire philosophy, he declared that the will to live must overcome itself, so that one achieves a kind of existence divested of will, evidently coinciding exactly with the *nirvana* sought by the Buddhist. Sometimes Schopenhauer describes this ultimate step to salvation as the will turning against and overcoming itself, and in other similarly metaphorical terms.[32]

Of course the fundamental idea here is not hard to grasp. If suffering is the product of willing, or of what in Buddhist literature is sometimes referred to as 'grasping', then release from suffering will have to be the overcoming of such willing. But the difficulty in Schopenhauer's philosophy is that he has declared the will to be reality itself, everything else being essentially illusory; and it is far from clear how reality can overcome and abolish itself, much less how any person, limited as he is, can by his own will achieve a kind of salvation this way. Gotama Buddha taught that such salvation is achieved through a hard-won enlightenment, but that solution is not open to Schopenhauer, whose voluntarism precludes any kind of salvation resting upon understanding, however this might be attained. This is, without doubt, the strangest part of Schopenhauer's entire system, and certainly its most puzzling. Yet most religions, by their very nature, culminate in mystery, and it is hardly fatal to Schopenhauer's concept of salvation that it does the same, salvation being everywhere as difficult to understand as it is to attain.

The general significance of Schopenhauer's thought

There is probably much truth in Schopenhauer's insistence that no part of his philosophy can be understood without understanding it all. Each part is like a piece to a jigsaw puzzle, the significance of which can be seen only when one sees how it fits in with the rest. It is therefore probably misguided to isolate this or that Schopenhauerian idea for criticism.

There are several quite different ways of looking at the world and at life; the way of materialism, for example, or the scientific way, as contrasted with a religious way. And it is quite impossible to show that any of these is false, except in relation to the assumed truth of another. Yet a philosophical system such as Schopenhauer's does lend itself to evaluation, in two ways. One can ask in the first place whether that system is coherent, or in other words, whether all its parts do hang together. And in the second place one can ask whether such a philosophy illuminates our actual experience of the world and life.

With respect to the first question, it is doubtful whether one could find in all of western philosophy a system more coherent. Platonism, for example, is rightly considered a system of great depth and power, and yet Plato was himself forced – in the *Parmenides*, for example – to concede that certain of his ideas appeared positively repugnant to each other, which is hardly a mark of coherence. Kantianism, similarly, was carried by its very originator into rational 'antinomies', as he called them; or in other words, into metaphysical claims and counter-claims, both of which could be proved. This, too, is hardly a mark of coherence.

But Schopenhauer's philosophy is beset with no such problem, unless, perhaps, in his conception of salvation, which certainly seems wildly incompatible with the totally voluntaristic character of his metaphysics. But apart from this – which could almost be considered an epilogue to his philosophy anyway – his system not only coheres in all its parts, in the sense that it is free from internal conflicts, the various parts in addition strengthen and illuminate each other. The system is indeed like a completed puzzle, and when we see that each part fits, then we can say with confidence that the individual parts are right. Thus the ethics, the metaphysical theory of the will, the concept of the person, the analysis of good and evil, each of these aspects of Schopenhauer's philosophy is precisely what it should be, given what each of the others is.

And with respect to the second question, whether this philosophy in fact sheds light upon our perception of the world and life, this must, of course, be a matter of individual judgment. Yet an observant person can hardly dismiss the Schopenhauerian claims that, for example, religion, as it is conveyed to the people by priests, is simply a substitute for the metaphysics that is beyond their ken; or that evil, however negative in value, is nevertheless what positively exists; or that genuine good will, and ill will, are to be construed as the irrational incentives of compassion and malice. This last claim is particularly illustrative, for both Kant and Schopenhauer supposed that they were, in their very different ways, expressing the truth of the Christian ideal of love, considered as the expression of a good will. Both philosophies are internally consistent with respect to this, but they result in totally opposed interpretations of the moral life. For Kant true love is something that springs from the mind, or reason, while Schopenhauer insisted that it is a matter of the heart, or feeling. Yet it was the latter who actually bade the reader to look at life and experience through his analysis of this idea, and see for himself which idea illuminates that experience, and which casts darkness upon it.[33] And here he was on sure ground. Viewed through Kant's analysis, and in fact through the conceptions of virtue worked out by virtually all modern moralists, human goodness turns out to be somewhat absurd and puppet-like, more a philosophical invention than a discovery. But viewed as an expression of the virtue of loving kindness, as Schopenhauer called it, we are able to see in a new light the love to which we are called by the Gospels, and the *caritas* or *agape* exalted by St Paul.

Notes

1 See 'On Man's Need for Metaphysics', in *The World as Will and Idea*, transl. R. B. Haldane and J. Kemp (London, 1948), vol. II. All references to this work are to this edition.
2 See, e.g., *On the Basis of Morality*, transl. E. F. J. Payne (Indianapolis, 1965), part III, sec. 7. All references to this work are to this edition.
3 References to Hindu and Buddhist literature appear in Schopenhauer's *World as Will and Idea*, published in 1819, and references to both primary and secondary sources of this literature become increasingly numerous in his later writings. See, e.g., his essay 'On Death and its Relation to the Indestructibility of our True Nature', in the third volume of *The World as Will and Idea*, and *On the Basis of Morality*, part V.
4 For an excellent biography, see *Life of Arthur Schopenhauer*, by W. Wallace (London, 1890).
5 This is most beautifully expressed in 'The Sufferings of the World', in *The Will to Live: Selected Writings of Arthur Schopenhauer*, ed. Richard Taylor (New York, 1967).
6 *The World as Will and Idea*, vol. I, p. 527, and 'The Sufferings of the World', *op. cit.*, p. 226.
7 E.g., *The World as Will and Idea*, vol. II, p. 372, vol. III, pp. 397, 437, 462.
8 E.g., *On the Basis of Morality*, part III, sec. 7.
9 E.g., in 'Transcendent Considerations Concerning the Will as Thing in Itself', in *The World as Will and Idea*, vol. III.
10 See 'Characterisation of the Will to Live', in *The World as Will and Idea*, vol. III.
11 *The World as Will and Idea*, vol. I, book 2. See also 'Transcendent Considerations Concerning the Will as Thing in Itself', *op. cit.*
12 *Ibid.*
13 Schopenhauer was fond of this analogy. See, e.g., 'On Death and its Relation to the Indestructibility of our True Nature', *op. cit.*, p. 274.
14 The clearest statement of this is in *The Basis of Morality*, part IV.
15 *The World as Will and Idea*, book II. Also *The Basis of Morality*, part IV.
16 'On Death and its Relation to the Indestructibility of our True Nature', *op. cit.*, p. 268.
17 *Ibid.*
18 *On the Basis of Morality*, part III, sec. 7.
19 'On Man's Need for Metaphysics', *op. cit.*
20 'On Death and its Relation to the Indestructibility of our True Nature', *op. cit.*
21 Plato, *Phaedo*.
22 Schopenhauer's pessimism pervades all his philosophy, beginning with *The World as Will and Idea*, but is most forcefully expressed in 'On the Sufferings of the World', in *The Will to Live*, and in 'The Vanity and Suffering of Life', *The World as Will and Idea*, vol. III.
23 *The World as Will and Idea*, vol. I, p. 419.

24 'The Sufferings of the World', *op. cit.*, p. 215.
25 'Characterisation of the Will to Live', *op. cit.*
26 *Ibid.*
27 *The World as Will and Idea*, vol. I, p. 403.
28 'On the Sufferings of the World', in *The Will to Live*, p. 226.
29 On the Basis of Morality. See also 'Human Nature', in *The Will to Live*.
30 See, e.g., 'The Christian System', in *The Will to Live*.
31 See 'The Vanity and Suffering of Life', in *The World as Will and Idea*, vol. III. This theme often recurs in Schopenhauer's popular essays.
32 *The World as Will and Idea*, vol. I, book 4. See also 'The Way of Salvation', in *The World as Will and Idea*, vol. III.
33 *On the Basis of Morality*, part III, sec. 8.

Bibliographical Essay

Primary sources

The original German works of Schopenhauer can be found in three collected editions. The oldest edition is *Schopenhauers sämtliche Werke*, ed. Paul Deussen in 13 volumes (Munich, 1911–42). The newer and now standard edition is *Schopenhauers sämtliche Werke* edited by Arthur Hübscher in 7 volumes (Wiesbaden, 1946–50). To this collection Hübscher has added *Schopenhauers handschriftlicher Nachlass* edited by Arthur Hübscher, 5 volumes (Frankfurt am Main, 1966–75).

There is no standard English edition of Schopenhauer's works. Individual volumes have been translated as follows: *On the Fourfold Root of the Principle of Sufficient Reason*, translated by E. F. J. Payne with an Introduction by Richard Taylor (La Salle, Illinois, 1974); *On the Will in Nature*, translated by Madame K. Hillebrand (London, 1897); *The World as Will and Representation*, translated by E. F. J. Payne (New York, 1966); *The World as Will and Idea*, translated by R. B. Haldane and J. Kemp (London, 1948); *On the Freedom of the Will*, translated by Konstantin Kolenda (New York, 1960); *On the Basis of Morality*, translated by E. F. J. Payne with an Introduction by Richard Taylor (New York, 1965); *Selected Essays of Arthur Schopenhauer* translated by Ernest Belfort Bax (London, 1891); *The Pessimist's Handbook: A Collection of Popular Essays* translated by T. Bailey Saunders, edited by Hazel Barnes, Bison Books (Lincoln, University of Nebraska Press, 1964); *Parerga and Paralipomena* translated by E. F. J. Payne (Oxford, 1974).

Secondary studies

The secondary literature on Schopenhauer is relatively small. Among older works one should mention Margrieta Beer, *Schopenhauer* (London, 1914). Though not a great work of scholarship it is still a useful summary. Four other older works also deserve attention. To begin with there is Helen Zimmern's *Arthur Schopenhauer: His Life and His Philosophy* (London, 1876). One of the first works on Schopenhauer in English it still retains some value for students seeking an introduction to the philosopher. Unfortunately, it is not of high philosophical merit by contemporary standards. Secondly, there is Edgar Saltus' *The Philosophy of Disenchantment* (New York, 1885). This work is still of considerable philosophical interest. Though not easy reading it repays study. Thomas Whittaker's *Schopenhauer* (London, 1920) has stayed the test of time less well. Finally among pre-War studies, K. Pfeiffer's *Arthur Schopenhauer: Persönlichkeit und Werk* (Leipzig, 1925) is notable. A work of considerable learning, though also containing a great deal of Germanic pedantry, it is still an essential monograph.

There are a number of valuable studies that have been produced since 1945. The two oldest of these are W. O. Döring's *Schopenhauer* (Hamburg, 1947) and Frederick Copleston's *Arthur Schopenhauer: Philosopher of Pessimism* (London, 1947). Döring's work is not of major consequence. Copleston's work, on the other hand, after more than a quarter of a century remains one of the standard works in English on Schopenhauer's philosophical outlook. It also has the considerable merit of being clearly written and well argued. Students might well be directed to begin their secondary reading with this work. Copleston has also provided a useful introduction to Schopenhauer's thought in his *History of Philosophy*, volume 7 (New York, 1965). This volume also includes additional bibliographical suggestions not included in this review.

Among German monographic treatments the studies of Hans Zint, *Schopenhauer als Erlebnis* (Munich, 1954), K. O. Schmidt, *Das Erwachen aus dem Lebens-Traum* (Pfullingen, 1957) and the four works of the indefatigible Arthur Hübscher, *Arthur Schopenhauer: Mensch und Philosoph in seinen Briefen* (Wiesbaden, 1960), *Schopenhauer: Biographie eines Weltbildes* (Stuttgart, 1967), *Schopenhauer-Bildnisse: Eine Ikonographie* (Frankfurt am Main, 1968) and *Schopenhauer Bibliographie* (Stuttgart, 1981), are notable. Zint's *Schopenhauer* is a careful, if somewhat idiosyncratic study. Though all its conclusions cannot be endorsed its value is certain. Schmidt's book is still more idiosyncratic. While important for serious students of the subject more casual readers can pass it by without significant loss. Hübscher's three works, by comparison, are 'must' reading. The leading Schopenhauer scholar-historian, these volumes sum up the result of his vast editorial and archival labors and give an exhaustive picture of Schopenhauer the man as well as Schopenhauer the philosopher. In addition, the bibliographical volume is an indispensible guide to the literature on Schopenhauer. However, it is important to recognize that Hübscher is more of a historian than an original philosopher and his studies are therefore stronger on the biographical and historical sides than on the technical philosophical front.

In English there are three additional interesting treatments of note. The first is my own *The Will to Live* (New York, 1962) which I will pass over without further comment. The second is by Patrick Gardiner, *Schopenhauer* (Harmondsworth, 1963). Gardiner's book is lucidly written and admirably cogent in its exposition of Schopenhauer's philosopher outlook. Though not an exhaustive study it retains considerable value as an 'Introduction' to Schopenhauer's thought. Finally there is D. W. Hamlyn's volume on *Schopenhauer* in the 'Arguments of the Philosophers' Series (London, 1980). This volume is intelligently and carefully done and adds considerably to the literature in English. It is, in particular, especially valuable as a philosophical work *per se*.

As in the past, the more recent issues of the *Schopenhauer Jahrbuch* (Frankfurt A.M.) continue to contain important essays relating to Schopenhauer's views on religion and related matters. Spatial limitations forbid the discussion here of individual essays; readers are urged to consult the volumes for themselves. However, special attention is called to the 1979 volume which contains several essays dealing with issues relating to Schopenhauer's understanding of religion. In the journal literature two articles are also relevant. Russell Goodman has published an interesting essay on 'Schopenhauer and Wittgenstein on ethics' in the *Journal of the History of Philosophy*, 17 (1979), 437–47 explicating Wittgenstein's views via Schopenhauer's Idealism. Georges Cottier has likewise done a useful essay on 'Schopenhauer et le proces de la raison' in *Revue Thomiste* (1979), 424–42. A recent collection, *Schopenhauer: his Philosophical Achievement*, ed. Michael Fox (Harvester Press, Sussex, 1980) gathers together essays on various aspects of Schopenhauer's thought, many of them published previously.

6

Søren Kierkegaard

ALASTAIR McKINNON

I

Kierkegaard's life and interpretation contains many more real paradoxes than his own thought. His writings are clearly rooted in his own personal experience but are obviously of universal significance. His thought is often virtually identified with the doctrine of the stages whereas this is merely the framework of his early authorship rather than something which he really believed or took seriously. He explicitly disclaimed the views expressed in his pseudonymous works but many commentators have focused upon these to the virtual neglect of the more central works which he signed in his own name. He is widely regarded as an irrationalist primarily because, like Socrates, he was honestly concerned to become clear about what could and what could not be known. In certain circles he is denigrated for having discredited theology by treating the Incarnation as a paradox whereas the truth would seem to be that in so doing he both described an ancient tradition and set theology upon a new and more promising path. He is often dismissed as an individualist and elitist whereas in fact he represents the most decisive break with nineteenth-century individualism and the elitism of traditional European culture. He is frequently described as 'sick' or 'psychiatric' whereas he was actually fairly normal and, further, laid the foundations of a psychiatric theory some of whose basic insights surpass even those of Freud. Finally, he is often referred to as 'the melancholy Dane' whereas at least much of his life was informed by that knowledge which is the source of man's only real and abiding happiness, *viz.*, the certainty that he is loved and cherished by God. In this brief study I shall try to resolve some of these strange paradoxes.

Unfortunately, current opinion concerning Kierkegaard in the English-speaking world is sharply and deeply divided. The division is, however, instructive and interesting. The relatively small group of Kierkegaard scholars who have done serious and detailed work on his writings may disagree among themselves on minor points of interpretation but virtually all are agreed that he is a major figure who has brought new and vital insight to our understanding of philosophy, religion and, indeed, life itself. Unfortunately, however, popular opinion has been formed by the writings of people like Laird, Paton, Blanshard, Murphy, Edwards, MacIntyre, Kaufmann, etc., who, though perhaps respected scholars in their own fields, are hardly serious students of Kierkegaard. Indeed, they appear to see their task as that of warning their colleagues and the public at large of the dangers of this anti-philosophical and perhaps deranged irrationalist. Unfortunately, this view is now so widespread that one must begin by showing how and why it is wrong. This is tedious but it does at least provide an opportunity to show the reader how not to approach Kierkegaard.

Though Kierkegaard's thought was deeply rooted in the nineteenth century he is essentially a creature of our own time. He is a man 'out of time' or, better, one whose time has just come. He understood his relation to the future and explained it very simply: the sickness of Europe, he said, was deeply rooted in his own soul and he was able to forecast its course and prescribe its remedy by overcoming it in his own life.[1] He had a profound grasp of the social forces of his time and foresaw the shape of the future with a terrible and searching clarity. He saw that modern man would deny his destiny as a spiritual being, retreat from individual responsibility, and forsake the riches of his cultural heritage. He saw that he would take refuge in the mass or crowd, conceive himself in essentially economic terms and, abandoning all thought for the common good, join in a ceaseless and self-defeating class war for what he imagines to be his own immediate and selfish advantage. In fact, in the middle of the last century he predicted the idiocies, crimes, and perversions which have become common in our age and the accuracy of his description suggests that we should at least give some thought to his proposed diagnosis and cure.

There is a close connection between Kierkegaard's life and thought, and a knowledge of the former can often illuminate some remark which might otherwise remain puzzling and obscure. On the other hand, and as experience has shown, such knowledge can be used in an attempt to explain away and thus avoid the necessity of coming to terms with his views. Kierkegaard recognized this latter possibility, made fun of those who fastened upon the details of his own personal life, and deliberately referred to certain of his own experiences as the 'occasions' of his writings. He meant that these were the circumstances prompting him to write but that they did not in any way diminish the validity or significance of what he had written.

The first and most important of these 'occasions' is his complex and life long relationship with his father.

Søren Kierkegaard was born in Copenhagen 5 May 1813, the seventh and last child of a prosperous merchant of that city. He was physically frail but the brightness of his mind more than compensated for this fact. His lively wit, his sharp tongue, and his indomitable pugnaciousness earned him the family nickname 'the Fork'. His mother, his father's second wife, hardly counted and the family seems to have been completely dominated by his father, a man of great native intelligence, profound melancholy, and a strongly religious temperament. His influence upon Søren was particularly strong; in fact, he was the boy's chief companion during his early years, the one who shaped his character, sharpened his imagination, trained his mind and introduced him to the world of current thought. His household was one of the chief intellectual centres of the city, a place where professors, clerics, and writers gathered to discuss the thought of the time and, especially, the reigning Hegelianism against which so much of Søren's later thought was to be directed.

But his relation with his father had another and darker side. Søren marked this by describing his religious upbringing as absolutely insane. The fact is that his father was haunted by the belief that he had committed the unpardonable sin and apparently intended to make atonement by giving his favourite son to the priesthood. To this end he supported him handsomely through ten years at the university and, by bequest, during the remainder of his life. From Søren's early youth until the death of his father, indeed until Søren's own death, their relations were complicated by the twin questions of the father's financial support and his son's relation to the church. Søren recognized this and on his father's death resolved that he must now 'take his side' and promptly proceeded to prepare for his theological examinations. He completed these but other circumstances intervened and he became an author using his considerable patrimony to support himself and his literary productions. The prospect of becoming a pastor became more and more remote and the last two years of his life were spent in a bitter attack upon the church and the established order which it represented. In fact, he exhausted himself in this struggle and at the end of his life only a tiny fraction of his very substantial fortune remained.

Of course, there were also other factors in this relationship. There is, for example, their shared melancholy, Søren's angry departure from his father's house, the 'great earthquake', their subsequent reconciliation and the son's return. There is also the father's morbid religiosity, his preoccupation with the figure of the crucified Christ, his conception of sex as essentially sinful, all of which left their mark on Søren's mind. But the bond between father and son remained strong and deep. For example, many of his edifying works are explicitly and touchingly dedicated to his late father. On the other hand, Søren was apparently unable to launch his long-prepared attack upon the church until after the death of Mynster, his father's friend and bishop. Clearly the relationship was both ambiguous and profound.

The second important occasion in Kierkegaard's life was his betrothal to the young and beautiful Regine Olsen. That engagement was only a few days old when he saw, or thought he saw, that it had been a tragic error and that he was completely unfitted for marriage. The next year was one of torment during which he tried almost everything in the hope of persuading her to break the engagement. But she was not deceived and finally he broke it off over her vain and sobbing protests.

Kierkegaard began what he called his 'authorship' immediately after this event. The connection is a real and important one; in fact, his writing grew out of his relations with Regine. Indeed, it was an attempt to lead her from what he called an aesthetic to a truly religious mode of life. In fact, all of the early pseudonymous works are more or less addressed to her: she is the first 'that individual whom with joy and gratitude I call my reader'. But of course these works have a much wider interest; their themes are universal and anyone seriously concerned about the ends of human life may himself become that reader.

The next notable occasion is generally known as 'the affair of the *Corsair*'. This journal was a weekly scandal sheet which, in the name of liberalism and democracy, satirized all the distinguished figures of Copenhagen and Denmark to the discomfort of its victims, the delight of its readers, and the profit of its owners. Kierkegaard alone remained unscathed, perhaps partly because its real but anonymous editor Nicholas Goldschmidt had borrowed money from the Kierkegaard family with which to start the paper and partly because of his own personal respect for Kierkegaard as a writer. In any event, Kierkegaard found the situation intolerable and publicly demanded that he should be treated like all his friends. Eventually Goldschmidt obliged and for approximately a year and a half the *Corsair* ridiculed and caricatured Kierkegaard and his writings. Rightly or not, Kierkegaard believed that this attack destroyed his bond with the common man and that those on whose behalf he had acted had failed to support him in what he took to be a noble cause. Goldschmidt was driven from Denmark and the *Corsair* virtually destroyed but Kierkegaard never forgot this incident. He felt isolated and rejected and until the end of his life held the view that journalists were the scum of the earth.

The fourth and final occasion is the struggle with the state church ordinarily dated 1854–55. There is no doubt that this struggle reached its climax in these years but neither is there any doubt that it had been brewing for a long time. For example, the term *Christendom*, which is central to this attack, occurs in *Concluding Unscientific Postscript* from 1845. *Two Ages*, from 1846, is a critique of the society which corresponds to and is an inseparable part of this Christendom. *Training in Christianity*, written in 1848, includes a sustained attack upon what is there identified as 'the established order'. In fact, there are many signs that Kierkegaard had been preparing this attack for a long time and that it was postponed only because of his loyalty to his father and, later, his scrupulousness concerning the election of Mynster's successor. No doubt this helps to explain why this attack, when it came, was so bitter, acrimonious, and violent.

Depending upon how one counts, Kierkegaard wrote thirty-four different books which together constitute an extremely complex authorship. He was much concerned about the question of their relationship but virtually all of his remarks on this matter are from 1848 or earlier, are mainly concerned with the relationship between the aesthetic and the religious writings, naturally do not refer to the later works, and take no account of those which antedate the authorship proper. It seems therefore worthwhile to attempt to divide this very rich corpus into its main groups. We do not claim that our division is wholly satisfactory but believe that it is one for which there is a considerable and growing body of evidence. Incidentally, it is this division which is assumed in the vocabulary distribution list. (See Table I, p. 214.)

Kierkegaard's first two works are *From the Papers of One Still Living* and his doctoral thesis *On the Concept of Irony with Constant Reference to Socrates*. Both are significantly different from any other work in the corpus and, as they antedate the authorship proper, I refer to them as the 'pre-authorship' works.

Kierkegaard's most famous works, indeed the only ones about which certain scholars seem to know, are the aesthetic or, in my terminology, the early pseudonymous works. These include *Either/Or*, vols. I and II, *Fear and Trembling*, *Repetition*, the untranslated *Forord* (*Prefaces*), *Philosophical Fragments*, *The Concept of Dread*, *Stages on Life's Way*, *Concluding Unscientific Postscript*, and *Crisis and the Crisis in the Life of an Actress*. As the reader will see from Table I, these works contain a very high proportion of all occurrences of those words commonly regarded as characteristic of Kierkegaard's 'existentialism'.

The third group contains a variety of writings but for our present purpose it is perhaps sufficient to describe them as the religious or acknowledged works. These include *Edifying Discourses*, *Thoughts on Crucial Situations in Human Life*, *Edifying Discourses in Various Veins* (in English, *Purity of Heart* and *The Gospel of Suffering*), *Works of Love*, *Christian Discourses*, 'The Lilies of the Field and the Birds of the Air', 'The High Priest' – 'The Publican' – 'The Woman that was a Sinner', 'An Edifying Discourse', 'The Unchangeableness of God', and 'Two Discourses at the Communion on Fridays'. Of course these could be further subdivided but all reflect Kierkegaard's conception of religion and, specifically, of Christianity. As such they are crucial for the interpretation of his thought and those who fail to take these works seriously can hardly expect to understand him and, still less, to secure a serious hearing for their views. In this connection, it is perhaps worth noting the relative absence of the so-called existentialist terminology from these works.

The fourth group, the late pseudonyms, consist of *Two Minor Ethico-Religious Discourses*, *The Sickness Unto Death*, and *Training in Christianity*. Of course, it may be objected that Kierkegaard had great difficulty in completing and publishing this last work and that he overcame his scruples only by assigning it to a pseudonym. It may also be argued that these works are not pseudonymous in precisely the same sense as the earlier ones. On the other hand, Kierkegaard makes it plain that Anti-Climacus, the author of the last two, is a real pseudonym; unlike Climacus, or Kierkegaard himself for that matter, he is 'a Christian to an extreme degree'. Further, these works mark the reappearance of much of the 'existentialist' terminology of the earlier pseudonymous pieces. It therefore seems useful to identify these works as a separate group.

As already indicated, Kierkegaard was much concerned about the relation of his works to one another and devoted three 'books' to this question. Leaving aside the important 'A First and Last Declaration',[2] these are *The Point of View for my Work as an Author*, *On My work as an Author*, and the thus far untranslated *Bladartikler, der staar i Forhold til Forfatterskabet* (*Newspaper Articles related to 'the Authorship'*). These deal with the internal relations, structure, and purpose of the authorship and I therefore describe them as the meta-works.

The sixth and final group I describe as 'the attack literature'. These include *Two Ages* (in the original translation, *The Present Age*), 'For Self-Examination', 'Judge for Yourselves!', the twenty-one newspaper articles, the ten instalments of 'The Instant', and the sermon 'What Christ Thinks about Official Christianity', the last three of which all appeared in English in *Attack upon 'Christendom': 1854–55*. I grant that there are problems involved in assigning *Two Ages* to this group; it does not even employ the telltale term *Christenhed* (Christendom) nor does it appeal to New Testament Christianity as its standard of reference. On the other hand, it is a work of perceptive social criticism which implicitly shares many of the assumptions of the rest of this group. I also recognize that the second and third of these works antedate the official attack but believe that they are an integral if veiled part of that attack and fit here better than elsewhere.

In his final writings Kierkegaard condemned the church as a betrayal of New Testament Christianity and accused its leaders and priests of dishonesty and hypocrisy. The tone of these works is bitter and virulent and they contain much which is repugnant and disturbing even to those prepared to grant their substantial truth. This has prompted some to suggest that we should set these works aside as the aberrations of a failing mind and, presumably, disregard their charges. I am therefore bound to report that a number of my own recent studies concerning the relative status of the various works tends to show that these are more or less central to Kierkegaard's authorship as a whole; certainly they show that these works represent a return to the 'style' and vocabulary patterns of the earlier writings.[3] It would therefore seem that we are not free to dismiss these works but must instead consider them seriously and attempt to decide concerning the truth of the charges which they urge.

One should perhaps also note the existence and importance of the *Journals*, substantial portions of which have recently become available in English.[3a] These include entries on a variety of subjects but consist mainly of his own personal reflections (Group A), writing in progress (Group B), and comments on his own reading and studies (Group C). They are therefore important for the understanding of his thought but are not part of his 'authorship' and hence naturally not part of any of the six groups mentioned above.

As already noted, Kierkegaard ascribed many of his works to one or other of his various pseudonyms. At least according to his first understanding, this was closely connected with his conception of himself as a 'corrective' to his age, his belief that his contemporaries lived in 'aesthetic or, at most, in aesthetic–ethical categories', his conviction that they were so trapped in these categories that they could be liberated only by an 'indirect communication', and his resolve to lead them from the aesthetic, through the ethical, to what he called the religious stage. Briefly, the pseudonyms are spokesmen giving idealized expressions of these alternative life views. It follows of course that, as Kierkegaard repeatedly insisted, they are not to be identified in any way with him. It is worth noting that this appears to be particularly true of the early pseudonyms.

Though he knew that he would be famous and widely read after his death, Kierkegaard thought of himself quite simply and humbly as a 'corrective' to his age. Hence if we are to grasp his thought we must first note those things which he was primarily concerned to correct. Chiefly, these are the following: the Hegelian transformation of Christianity from an *existence-communication* into a doctrine which asks only to be understood; the spiritual and social disintegration of his society; and, connected with this, the fact that, as he believed, his contemporaries had forgotten what it means to exist as truly human beings. These three points are all closely connected both with one another and with the questions we shall be discussing in the course of this chapter.

Kierkegaard made many important contributions to religious thought in both the narrow and the broad sense of this term. In this account, I shall concentrate upon one which is both crucially important and widely discussed and two others which I believe will become increasingly important in the future. These are, respectively, his account of the relation of faith and reason with special reference to belief in the Incarnation, his social and political views, and what, lacking a better term, I shall call his psychiatric theory.

II

I believe that Kierkegaard has given us a radically new view of the relation of faith and reason but confess at the outset that he appears to be an irrationalist and that our contemporary dons[4] seem to have most of the obvious evidence on their side. For example, his pseudonymous works applaud belief (and action) 'by virtue of the absurd' and contain such notorious phrases as 'subjectivity is truth', 'the crucifixion of the understanding' and 'the martyrdom of faith'. They also repeatedly insist that belief is possible only by virtue of the absurd and that in order to become a believer one must first accept the paradox. It is then not surprising that some have concluded that Kierkegaard conceives faith as irrational and belief in the Incarnation as equivalent to claiming both that it happened and that it was not even possible. I believe however that these plausible interpretations arise from a failure to see his writings in their historical and, perhaps particularly, their literary context and shall now attempt to make good this deficiency. I begin with the doctrine of the stages because of its apparent importance in the minds of those who know that Kierkegaard is an irrationalist, i.e., that he held that one can actually believe both that x happened and that it was not even possible. I shall however confine myself to the more formal aspects of this doctrine since it is these which are most relevant to this question.

Briefly, there are two main elements in what I shall describe as the traditional account of the stages. The first is that there are three separate stages, the aesthetic, the ethical, and the religious with, be it noted, irony and humour as intermediate border points. The second is that the individual passes successively from one to the next by a series of arbitrary and irrational choices. Given these assumptions it follows that Christian faith is conceived as the result of a series of such choices, and, connected with this, as narrow, inhuman, and cut off from most of normal human life.

There is no doubt that this account accords well with Kierkegaard's stated aim of leading his reader from the aesthetic through the ethical and, finally, to the religious. It does however fail to do justice to two distinct but related elements in his own account. Though he subsequently distinguished between religiousness A (the Socratic) and religiousness B (Christianity), his own final position was that there are but two stages and hence but one either/or: *either* the aesthetic on its own terms *or* religiousness B including within it, as dethroned or subsumed stages, religiousness A, the ethical and the aesthetic.[5] Secondly, and connected with the foregoing, he sees these not primarily as successive stages but rather as alternative life-views both of which may be present and expressed in the life of the individual at one and the same time. In brief, Christianity, rightly understood, includes normal human experience and is not an irrational alternative to it.

My own position in this matter can be stated very briefly. The traditional account of the stages does not represent Kierkegaard's own final position and reflects a serious misunderstanding of the nature and relation of the stages. Further, as we shall see, this doctrine is at best the rough framework of the pseudonymous authorship and plays no role whatsoever in his own acknowledged works. I conclude therefore that this doctrine cannot be cited as evidence that he conceived belief or faith as irrational in the sense with which we are here concerned.

As already indicated, there is no doubt that many of the early pseudonymous works appear to provide evidence of Kierkegaard's irrationalism. It is however a serious mistake to assume that they necessarily reflect Kierkegaard's own position. In fact his own position is quite the opposite. In the 'Declaration' which he appended to the *Postscript*,[6] Kierkegaard roundly and unequivocally declared that each of the pseudonyms was a distinct literary personality, that each had its own distinct point of view, that they contradicted one another, that anyone could make him look like a fool simply by quoting one pseudonymous work against another, that anyone who quoted from a pseudonym should kindly do him the favour of citing the name of the pseudonym in question, etc., etc. Indeed, he even went so far as to declare that he was not responsible for one single word in the pseudonymous works whereas he was, by contrast, responsible for every single word in his own acknowledged writings.[7] Such claims may be surprising but they are hardly open to question or dispute. In addition to his own clear and repeated declarations there is the fact that the pseudonyms express distinct and even contradictory life-views. It is then not simply that Kierkegaard explicitly disowns these views; in fact, given their disagreement, he could not possibly have held all of them. Further, his account of these matters is entirely consistent with the declared aims of the authorship. In short, there is clear evidence that these apparently implausible claims are quite serious and entirely justified.

In this connection I should perhaps add that some years ago I attempted to establish a hierarchy of eight of the pseudonyms and implicitly to examine Kierkegaard's claim that their writings were significantly different from one another and from his own. Because of a small mistake in applying the method I no longer accept all the results of that investigation but still believe that it clearly supports Kierkegaard's basic position. Specifically, it showed that each of the pseudonyms has such a large number of distinctive vocabulary items that he must be regarded as a distinct literary personality and that the pseudonyms as a group repeatedly employ a number of key terms which Kierkegaard, as we shall see, scarcely uses. In short, it proved that Kierkegaard's own claims must be taken absolutely seriously.[8] Of course it is ridiculous to spend years of one's life, thousands of dollars, and vast amounts of computer time proving that a literary genius understood the nature of his own work but, unfortunately, that still appears to be necessary.

The relevance of these points can be stated briefly with reference to *Fear and Trembling*. This book commends Abraham for his willingness to sacrifice Isaac, asserts that he believed 'by virtue of the absurd', and declares that therein he became 'the father of faith'. In fact, it presupposes a conception of the ethical (essentially a combination of the Kantian and the Hegelian) which Kierkegaard himself explicitly rejects and assumes an opposition between the ethical and the religious which, in the final analysis, he will not allow. Indeed, Kierkegaard's own later remark 'Had I had faith, I should have remained with Regine', is a confession that he had made a tragic mistake in renouncing her and, indeed, that he even rejected the opposition upon which this work is based. Further, this work is written not by Kierkegaard but by his pseudonym Johannes de Silentio who, incidentally, insists that he admires Abraham but cannot understand him. Hence, however we may read this particular book, we cannot cite it as evidence of Kierkegaard's irrationalism. This, of course, is also true of the other early works which presuppose the traditional account of the stages and are themselves pseudonymous. Of course this is not to deny that these works play a vital part in the strategy of the authorship but it does mean that their views cannot be ascribed to the man who conceived that authorship and articulated its conflicting life-views. Indeed, these works are only separate dialectical moves within a very much larger strategy.

It is perhaps worth pausing to point out that whatever various pseudonyms may actually say about the transition to Christian belief, the fact remains that the authorship as a whole treats such belief as a rational, valid, and defensible option. Indeed, the early pseudonymous works can be seen as a carefully orchestrated justification of Christian belief which, taken together, show that it is only Christianity which properly accentuates existence and guards against the 'forgetfulness' of philosophy. Similarly, the acknowledged works can be seen as exposing the confusions of merely human conceptions and articulating the inner logic or structure of Christian belief. But about all this more later.

There is further and decisive evidence against the irrationalist interpretation in the distribution of certain key terms shown in Table 1. For example, the word *absurd* appears only in the early and late pseudonyms while *paradox* is effectively restricted to these two groups, two of the remaining three occurrences being irrelevant to our considerations. In fact, he frequently refers to Christianity in other groups of his works without, however, using either of these terms. Granted the radical nature of his vocabulary partitioning we must assume that this is a matter of deliberate policy and that, for whatever reason, and with the single exception noted above, he was apparently unable to bring himself to describe Christian belief as absurd or paradoxical; indeed, this was a task which he seems deliberately to have left to the pseudonyms. In short, at least in this respect, we seem to have two quite different accounts of Christianity within the authorship. In this connection it is perhaps worth noting that *religiousness* does not appear in the acknowledged works and that *orthodoxy* appears only in the early and late pseudonyms, about which more later.

There are other interesting details in this Table. Note that the words *to exist*, *existence*, *existence-communication*, *stages*, and *subjectivity* are all absent from the acknowledged works but, *existence-communication* apart, all present in both the early and late pseudonyms. Note too that the word *the leap* is concentrated in the early pseudonyms and, though this is not shown in our

Table, that nowhere in Kierkegaard's published works is there any phrase which could even possibly be translated as 'the leap of faith'. Indeed, the early pseudonymous works contain no instance of this frequently cited 'evidence' of Kierkegaard's irrationalism. So much for the power of prejudice to generate support on its own behalf.

Our distribution table shows that whereas the pseudonyms repeatedly use the terms *absurd* and *paradox*, Kierkegaard himself can write about Christian belief at length without even using these terms. This seems puzzling but in fact has an obvious and important explanation. Very briefly, the pseud-onyms are not believers; they look at Christianity from the outside and are concerned with *the process of coming to believe*, with *the transition to belief*, or in the words of Climacus, of 'becoming a Christian'. They find Christianity absurd or paradoxical primarily because they are not yet themselves Christians. By the same token Kierkegaard has no use for these terms because in some sense he writes from within Christianity. In short, the use of these terms appears to be a function of their authors' position vis-à-vis Christianity. But about this too more later.

Thus far we have sought to counter the assumptions of those who believe that Kierkegaard is an irrationalist by discussing the stages, the pseudonyms, and the distribution of certain of his allegedly key terms. We now turn to examine the various main senses in which he or, more correctly, his pseudonyms use the term *paradox*.

Kierkegaard's most distinctive and characteristic use of this word can perhaps best be described as existential because of its connection with the fact that the knower is, in Climacus' language, 'an existing individual'. This is clear from the case of Socrates who, in his view, provides the proper introduction to Christianity precisely because of his emphasis upon the fact that the knower is an existing being. This appears to be the basic reason why he describes the truth as a paradox. As he writes in the *Postscript*, '. . . the fact that the truth becomes a paradox is rooted precisely in its having a relationship to an existing subject'.[9] Apparently, then, paradox in this sense results from the conjunction of the realms of existence and truth in the life of an existing individual. I am therefore inclined to the view that this sense of the word is fundamental in this work and that the others are in some way subordinate.

It is worth noting that, according to Climacus, Christianity is paradoxical in precisely this same sense. More correctly, it is yet more strictly so since it accentuates existence yet more strongly than the Socratic view. Further, unlike this latter view, it is also paradoxical in the various logical senses in which he uses that term.

When we turn to these logical senses the situation is somewhat more complicated. Here there are at least five distinct senses: the dialectical, the systematically incomprehensible, the *Self*-contradictory, the historically dependent, and the apparently contradictory.

The first, or dialectical sense, appears in the following journal entry: 'The paradox is really the *pathos* of intellectual life . . . it is only the great thinker who is exposed to what I call paradoxes which are nothing else than grandiose thoughts in embryo'.[10] While the closing words fail to do full justice to the complexity of Kierkegaard's conception, the sense intended is quite clear: a paradox is a thought containing a contradiction which can and should be untied, and it is precisely the business of great thinkers to untie them.

The second, or systematically incomprehensible sense, appears in another journal entry, which reads in part as follows:

. . . the inexplicable, the paradox, is a category of its own . . . it is the duty of the human understanding to understand that there are things which it cannot understand, and what those things are. Human understanding has vulgarly occupied itself with nothing but understanding, but if it would only take the trouble to understand itself at the same time it would simply have to posit the paradox . . .[11]

Kierkegaard's point is of course about the nature and operation of the human understanding as such. He is asserting that any coherent understanding rests and must rest upon something which cannot itself be expressed in terms of that understanding. He is claiming that any system of thought rests ultimately upon something which cannot be understood in terms of that system, upon something which is systematically incomprehensible. Anyone who doubts this point has only to reflect for a moment upon contemporary views about the place of primitive postulates in a deductive system.

The third, or *Self*-contradictory sense, is more closely associated with Christianity and particularly with Kierkegaard's assumption that there is an implacable opposition between its goals and those of natural man, especially when, as in the Hegelian philosophy, the latter are identified and bound up with human reason. Whether these goals are in any sense rational is really beside the point. For Kierkegaard Christianity is unalterably opposed to them and hence can only be experienced and accepted as paradoxical in the sense of *Self*-contradiction.

The historically dependent sense is constantly linked with the preceding but is concerned more with the form than the content of Christianity. In particular, it is connected with the fact that it is an historical religion and that the believer must base his faith upon what is in some sense a merely historical fact. Kierkegaard has Hegel particularly in mind but his point can perhaps be best understood with reference to Hume. Against Hegel's claim that the historical facts of Christianity are merely helpful illustrations of timeless and eternal truths, Kierkegaard insists that these facts are vital since without them we are incapable of imagining or conceiving these truths. Like Hume he wants to point out that our beliefs are dependent upon the facts of experience, but with one very important difference: we may well be annoyed that our knowledge of the properties of bread is apparently derived from experience but we are bound to be offended that even our salvation is similarly based on historical fact. This is *one* of the reasons why, particularly in the *Fragments*, paradox is so closely linked with offence. We are offended because Christianity proposes to base our salvation upon some merely historical fact.

The apparently contradictory sense is much more familiar, straight-forward, and closer to common use. Apart from the existential sense, it is also the one which figures most largely in Kierkegaard's authorship. When he declares Christianity to be a paradox in this sense he is simply saying that it, or any other new view for that matter, *appears* and must appear to the would be believer as a contradiction. His point here is simply that as a new view it necessarily conflicts with the would be believer's earlier conceptions and that one can *become* a believer only by first accepting a claim which is, or at least appears to be, logically self-contradictory. The emphasis upon *becoming* a Christian is fundamental to the *Postscript* and many of the claims that Christianity must be *accepted* as a paradox in that work are, I believe, to be understood at least partly in this way. I put the matter deliberately thus because of course many of the uses of this term actually involve more than one of the senses which I have identified.

It is perhaps worth noting that this use of *paradox* seems very close to Kierkegaard's concept of 'the absurd'. That the Eternal has come into being in time, that God has existed in human form, that the eternal is the historical – all these are described as both paradoxical and absurd. Further, Kierkegaard's presentation of the absurd suggests that it is somehow essentially self-contradictory. For example, in the *Postscript* he speaks of 'the contradiction that something which can become historical only in direct opposition to all human reason, has become historical . . . It is this contradiction which constitutes the absurd, and which can only be believed.'[12] This might prompt one to think that such claims are really unthinkable and genuinely self-contradictory but that impression stems, I shall argue, from the very peculiar focus and concern of the authorship.

Indeed, as I hope to show, Kierkegaard's position is that even those claims which appear to unbelief as absurd or contradictory are not essentially, permanently, and incorrigibly so. But this is a view whose foundations have yet to be laid.

It is clear that there is no evidence for the irrationalist interpretation of Kierkegaard in any of these uses of the word *paradox*. Certainly there is none in what we have called the existential sense. *Paradox* in this sense is simply Kierkegaard's way of describing the relationship of the truth, which belongs to one realm or sphere, to the existing individual, which belongs to another. The truth becomes a paradox in such cases simply because, as already stated, the two realms are essentially distinct. *Paradox* may be a peculiar name for the result, but neither the use of this term nor the point it is intended to convey constitutes evidence of irrationalism of the kind with which we are here concerned.

The charge is equally implausible in connection with the first of our five logical senses. Real intellectual life does have a pathos in Kierkegaard's sense and those who are intellectually alive are constantly attempting to iron out the contradictions in their thought. These are the facts of life and their admission can hardly be an offence, intellectual or otherwise. The important thing is the confidence that, with reflection, these contradictions can be removed. This sense assumes that they can and, to that extent, reflects Kierkegaard's view that our beliefs can be made internally consistent. Hence, this sense of *paradox* is really evidence against rather than for the irrationalist charge.

At first glance it might seem that the systematically incomprehensible sense is tinged with a kind of irrationalism, but this reflects what is at best surely a pious rationalist hope. We now know that any deductive system is based upon postulates which cannot be defined in terms of that particular system. Kierkegaard is making or rather recognizing the same point in connection with belief. He sees that any coherent belief system rests upon certain fundamental assumptions and that it cannot therefore ever be fully justified or explained. This concession may be disappointing to some but it is a properly logical point and scarcely open to doubt or dispute.

The same general conclusion appears to hold with respect to the *Self-*contradictory sense. In the course of human history the reason may have become identified with the values of natural man but this association is merely accidental. Kierkegaard does not for a moment suppose that there might be a clash respecting values between Christianity and the reason as such. Indeed, as Swenson[13] long ago pointed out, his conception of reason renders such a conflict quite inconceivable. In fact, reason does not have any values and can enter this particular fray only by aligning herself with values not in any sense her own.

The significance of the historically dependent sense seems equally clear. The point of this sense is simply that even in matters of Christian belief we are dependent upon the facts of history. But this is simply to grant one of Hume's points and certainly does not constitute any endorsement of self-contradiction.

The case of the apparently contradictory sense is admittedly less clear. Indeed it might seem an obvious instance of the very irrationalism we have been attempting to deny. That it is actually not so follows from one peculiar but important feature of the 'authorship'.

As already mentioned, and as Kierkegaard repeatedly insisted, the pseudonyms are specifically concerned with the process of coming to believe and this as something distinct from the state of belief. This is especially true of the works of Johannes Climacus with which this last sense is particularly linked. But Kierkegaard, or rather Climacus, does not use it to claim that Christianity is in itself logically contradictory. His point is rather that, in the process of coming to believe, the unbeliever must necessarily experience it as contradicting his former conceptions. But, again, this is simply a function of the process of coming to believe; it is something necessarily involved in moving from one life view to another. Kierkegaard made his point with special reference to Christianity but it seems clear that he saw it as an instance of the general point that the adoption of a new outlook necessarily involves accepting something which, at the moment and in the process of transition, seems paradoxical or absurd.

This crucial point is borne out by a relatively late journal entry in the midst of which we are given a rare glimpse of the real Kierkegaard, the hidden figure who stood behind the authorship and its sometimes deliberate contortions. The entry is a long one and it begins in a familiar way. It insists that for the unbeliever the content of belief is absurd and that in order 'to become a believer everyone must be alone with the absurd'.[14] But suddenly, and in the very midst of these claims, we find this single sentence: 'While naturally it is a matter of course that for him who believes it is not the absurd.'[15] Now, obviously, the fact of belief cannot alter or dissolve the second, third, or fourth of the logical senses of *paradox*; these are permanent and inescapable features of Christian belief as such. But the fact of belief can change the situation regarding this last sense. This is because it is possible to revise our conceptions in the light of our claims; because real belief is, by its very nature, internally consistent and logically coherent. Kierkegaard recognized this and the present aside is simply an obvious consequence; that, indeed, is why he says 'naturally it is a matter of course'. This is because the claim follows from the very nature of belief. The claims of Christianity do seem absurd in the light of our natural conceptions but it is possible to take these claims seriously and to revise our conceptions in their light. It is possible to render belief internally consistent. In short, at least so far as this is a purely intellectual matter, we can move beyond paradox in this particular sense.

In fact, there are a number of other passages in Kierkegaard's writings which clearly suggest that he himself believed and even assumed that there can be a resolution of the paradox within faith or belief. I now note some of these briefly.

Shortly after the appearance of the *Postscript*, Kierkegaard was attacked by the theologian Magnus Eiriksson writing under the pseudonym Theophilus Nicolaus. In his unpublished reply Kierkegaard makes his position quite clear. The object of faith is the absurd or paradox but only for one who sees it from the outside, for one who does not yet have faith. For the man of faith it is no longer absurd or paradoxical. This view is expressed in the following journal entry: 'When the believer has faith, the absurd is not the absurd – faith transforms it, but in every weak moment it is again more or less absurd to him. The passion of faith is the only thing which masters the absurd – . . . Therefore, rightly understood there is nothing at all frightening in the category of the absurd . . .'[16] Kierkegaard's underlying point is quite clear: Nicolaus has misinterpreted the pseudonyms because, unskilled in dialectics, he has failed to note the fundamental point that their role is simply to illuminate faith negatively or from the side of unbelief. That indeed is why he can write '. . . true faith breathes healthfully and blessedly in the absurd'.[17]

In this connection, it is interesting to note another journal entry quoted by Fabro concerning the 'recognizability' of Christ. This, he writes 'implies that he is recognizable by his divine authority, even though it requires faith to resolve the paradox'.[18] Hence apparently there is, for faith at least, something which can be called a resolution of the paradox.

It would be possible to provide other similar examples from the journals but it is, I think, much more important simply to make the point that these writings are quite privileged because in them Kierkegaard no longer feels constrained to look at faith from the side of unbelief. Now he does not need to worry about possibly misleading his reader, and his only concern is to get these matters as straight as possible for himself. We are then, I think, allowed and even obliged to attach special importance to passages such as those we have been considering.

Earlier in this account we discussed the occurrence and meaning of the words *absurd* and *paradox* in the early pseudonymous works. Before proceeding it is therefore important to pause and comment upon one notable and, perhaps by design, almost hidden feature of the *Works of Love*, a book which follows closely upon these works and which, as Swenson says, represents the centre of gravity of his thought. In fact, it is the fullest and most perfect expression of his Christianity and, though dwelling at length upon faith or belief, makes no reference to the absurd or to the paradox. Instead it contains twenty-eight occurrences of several variants of what is obviously a deliberately formulaic utterance, all of which can be roughly translated as 'Christianly understood'. The meaning is, I think, unmistakable and clear. There is a Christian understanding of things and Christian perfection involves attaining that understanding. Of course it is not surprising to find this phrase in the *Works of Love* which deals with the state of belief but the fact that it appears for the first time in the *Postscript* suggests that Kierkegaard clearly understood the inseparability of belief and understanding as early as 1845.

In this same general connection it is perhaps worth noting that Kierkegaard frequently and repeatedly distinguishes between a Godly (*gudeligt*) and a worldly (*verdsligt*) understanding. The constant repetition of this contrast is clear evidence that he opposed the two and that he thought that belief or faith could and must become internally coherent.

I believe the foregoing to be an accurate account of Kierkegaard's position but must report at least briefly that his typical use of the word *belief* (and *faith*) is significantly different from that which we have been considering. Specifically, we have been treating belief as it relates to a doctrine whereas, as already indicated, Kierkegaard insists that Christianity is instead an existence-communication. Hence belief in the relevant sense is not something more or less continuous with knowledge but is instead, as Kierkegaard insists, a passion or resolution, a decision by which we move from fathomless uncertainty to absolute certainty. It is action as, for example, in the case of Abraham. It is what one does when one actually trusts in the forgiveness of his sins i.e., when one actually believes that his sins have been forgiven. This is why Kierkegaard later links belief with obedience and why he has an almost pathological fear that belief might somehow be transformed into understanding, a fear which makes no sense if they are indeed part of a continuum but which is entirely justified if they are instead of entirely different orders. Of course, this also explains his repeated insistence that faith is a sphere of its own and that there is an absolute heterogeneity between it and reason. It is, of course, by this belief or faith that one apprehends Christianity as an existence–communication but of course it does not follow from this that the content of that communication, once given, need remain incorrigibly unintelligible.

Though Kierkegaard recognizes the necessary coherence of the content of faith he has relatively little to say about the Incarnation as such. Most of his references occur in the writings of Anti-Climacus and reflect the orthodox view of the Incarnation as a scandal and an offence but there is reason to believe that for Kierkegaard even this paradox is resolved in the life of faith. He puts Christ at the centre of his life and thought to the almost total exclusion of natural theology. He constantly emphasizes the Teacher at the expense of the teaching. He places great stress upon consistency and 'consequences' and frequently rejects positions on the grounds that their implications are nonsense or absurd. In general he assumes that those who have had an experience will find it intelligible and that those who have not, will not. Though he prefers the existential sense of *belief* he clearly understands the more familiar one according to which to believe p is also to believe the propositions implied by p. Because of his reading of the times he chose to emphasize the transition to belief rather than the state of belief, the necessity of accepting the paradox rather than assimilation of its consequences, but there can be no doubt that he knows that the latter is no less important than the former. Indeed, with Anti-Climacus, he knows that there is a true resolution of even the existential paradox in the imitation of Christ in which one achieves true contemporaneity with him. He also knows that in faith the absurd is no longer absurd, that in it one can 'resolve' the paradox, that, as we shall see in a moment, there can be a Christian understanding of such things. Indeed, and apparently against all the claims of Climacus, he allows Anti-Climacus to speak of the likeness (*Ligheden*) and kinship (*Slaegtskabet*) between God and man.[19]

But there is another piece of evidence in *Training* which, in its own way, is as conclusive as all of the above. It does not even mention the Incarnation but its relevance to our discussion is plain and obvious. Reflecting Kierkegaard's notion of 'human conceptions as embodying our rebellion against God', Anti-Climacus writes

Christ never desired to conquer in the world; He came to the world to suffer, *that* is what He called conquering. But when human impatience and the impudent forwardness which ascribes to Christianity its own thoughts and conceptions, instead of letting its thoughts and conceptions be transformed by Christianity – when this got the upper hand, then, in the old human way, to conquer meant to conquer in this world, and thus Christianity is done away with.[20]

Apparently then even Anti-Climacus believes that human thoughts and conceptions can be transformed and that, if this is not done, 'Christianity is done away with'. If this interpretation is correct, and if as I believe Kierkegaard shares this view, it follows that he does not see even the Incarnation as incorrigibly self-contradictory; indeed, given the focus of his work and the first logical sense of *paradox* already identified, we must surely understand him as saying that it is the responsibility and duty of the serious Christian to reshape his conceptions of God and man in the light of this event.

I conclude this section with two brief but related comments. In the *Postscript* Climacus repeatedly insists that Christianity can be accepted 'only as a paradox'. But Climacus is much too astute himself to confuse 'believing x' with 'believing x regarded as a paradox'. Indeed, given the many and quite atypical references to orthodoxy in this work, I see this claim as, among other things, reporting the fact that orthodox Christianity has traditionally presented the Incarnation as a paradox. At the very least it reflects its real but unstated assumption that one can believe in this event in this way. In short, Climacus' claim is really an historical one and certainly no evidence that Kierkegaard himself held that belief in the Incarnation must involve the believer in continued and incorrigible self-contradiction. Indeed, his own evident and obvious aversion even to the use of the word *orthodoxy*, together with some of the uses of *paradox* already noted, seems to suggest rather the opposite.

The second point is closely connected with this. In the *Fragments* Johannes Climacus speaks of Reason as 'capable at the most of saying "yes" and "no" to the same thing, which is not good divinity'.[21] Again, I think there is good reason to interpret this as a comment upon orthodoxy's traditional treatment of the doctrine of the Incarnation. If this is correct it surely follows that Kierkegaard himself proposes to treat that doctrine in another and quite different way. Briefly, he sees that the orthodox approach will not work and that the true Christian must accept the Incarnation as a coherent and intelligible event or claim. Many of Kierkegaard's remarks concerning the Incarnation are no doubt primarily about the past but it seems clear that, put in context, they also hold real promise for the future.

III

The majority of modern political and social philosophers conceive their subject almost entirely in terms of structure and forms of organization. For Kierkegaard politics in this sense represented an abbreviated or foreshortened perspective on life. He believed that the so-called political problems of his time were essentially religious and could be solved only in a religious way; that, indeed, they had already been solved by Christianity long ago.[22] This makes him virtually unintelligible to many of our contemporaries and prompts others to dismiss him as totally irrelevant. In the brief available space I shall argue that it is rather the source of his interest and value.

Kierkegaard's social views are connected with his understanding of history and his central concept of 'the individual', a thought in which, as he said, 'is contained an entire philosophy of life and of the world'. I shall therefore attempt to state these views in terms of these two notions.

Kierkegaard repeatedly compares antiquity favourably to the modern age but he was by no means blind to the shortcomings of the societies of the ancient past. He recognized that the tyrant ruled by fear and that the life of the society was ordered solely for his benefit. He knew that the individual had no real life of his own and that he existed only in and through the life of his ruler. He knew that the ethos of such societies was aesthetic and worldly and that the eminence of its rulers depended therefore upon the subjection of its members. There is then no question of Kierkegaard approving these archaic social structures; for him, they are simply the best available in the absence of a religious conception of the individual. On the other hand, he believed that such societies have much to commend them. The will of the tyrant provides a coherent, rational, integrated state and his undoubted eminence meets many of the deep psychic and social needs of his subjects. The great leader, whether tyrant or king, provided a vicarious life for his people; he was someone they could admire and through whom they could find meaning and purpose for their life. He was a point of reference through whom they could identify with the society as a whole. Sophisticated moderns who have difficulty grasping this relationship might well try to understand the attachment of the London char to the Queen.

By comparison Kierkegaard finds his own age seriously deficient. The reformers have come to the fore demanding equality in respect of worldly rights and privileges. At the same time, the press and the public, inspired by the philosophers, have brought into disrepute the traditional values of ethics and religion and replaced them by worldly and aesthetic ones. Thus we have the curious paradox of an age which is at one and the same time revolutionary and 'passionless and reflective'. The result is what Kierkegaard calls a 'levelling' of both classes and values.

Kierkegaard is profoundly suspicious of the political leaders and reformers of his time. He fears that the former will exploit the masses, use the 'bread-uprisings' for their own advantage, neglect the education of the population, disregard questions of right and wrong, and, instead of providing leadership, will seek rather to run to the front of the masses to secure their own election. In short, he anticipated all the abuses associated with the modern forms of democracy. His assessment of the reforms is equally critical. He understood perfectly well the mentality of the socially privileged who, discerning the signs of the times, exploit the new political situation as cleverly as their ancestors once exploited the economic.

But these concern only particular classes and Kierkegaard's criticisms go much deeper. He believed that the older societies of Christendom had been possible because they had a Christian foundation, because everyone understood that they were essentially equal before God. Now, however, politicians and reformers have destroyed this foundation and taught the masses to demand equality in this world. Kierkegaard is not opposed to such equality in principle; indeed, he grants that association in respect of material interest may be legitimate and even necessary. But he is deeply troubled by this shift of interest to the worldly which he regards as the sphere of the differential and the invidious. He thinks that it will be impossible to attain equality in this area or to convince people that they have been justly treated. Further, he believes that this demand is bound to further class interest, to destroy the rational, integral state, and to create an order in which no one any longer cares for the society as such, or identifies with it in any meaningful way.

Kierkegaard's account of the psychic changes of his age is much less easy to understand but the following account may provide a useful point of departure.

A passionate tumultuous age will *overthrow everything, pull everything down*; but a revolutionary age, that is at the same time reflective and passionless, transforms that expression of strength into *a feat of dialectics: it leaves everything standing but cunningly empties it of significance. Instead of culminating in a rebellion it reduces the inward reality of all relationships to a reflective tension which leaves everything standing but makes the whole of life ambiguous: so that everything continues to exist factually whilst by a dialectical deceit*, privatissime, *it supplies a secret interpretation – that it does not exist.*[23]

This is very similar to his criticism that Hegel, without denying Christianity outright, had instead emptied it of any real significance simply by transforming all its fundamental concepts. In precisely the same way, he believed, his followers had emptied the social forms and values of their time.

His argument here is extremely compact but can perhaps be summarized as follows.

Morality or character has been replaced by reflection and the whole of life has become ambiguous. The traditional hierarchical relations no longer exist and have become instead objects of reflection. 'More and more people renounce the quiet and modest tasks of life, that are so important and pleasing to God, in order to achieve something greater; in order to think over the relationships of life in a higher relationship . . .'[24] The traditional human relations which characterize a healthy society have been replaced by a state of exhausted tension rendering these relations ambiguous and 'almost meaningless'. Hence the established order continues to exist but in an ambiguous and meaningless way. Everyone is prepared to keep the king provided only that it is understood that his power is purely fictitious. Similarly, everyone is prepared to keep Christianity on the understanding that its concepts have no really fixed meaning. Given this reflective tension, envy becomes the negative unifying principle of the society, reflection within the individual prevents him from acting and, even if he succeeds in throwing off his yoke, he is imprisoned by the reflection of those around him. As Kierkegaard says 'With every means in its power reflection and the age are thus imprisoned, not imprisoned by tyrants or priests or nobles or the secret police, but by reflection itself, and it does so by maintaining the flattering and conceited notion that the *possibility* of reflection is far superior to a mere *decision*.'[25] Envy therefore becomes a kind of social poison neutralizing all that is best in men and fostering all that is despicable. Man is no longer capable of 'the happy love of admiration' but knows only 'the unhappy love of envy'.[26] As reflection gains the upper hand envy becomes more and more dangerous, a kind of negative principle of character refusing to recognize that there can be any distinction either now or in the future. This envy therefore results in a process of levelling which '*hinders* and *stifles* all action'[27] and represents the victory of abstraction over the individual. Such is this power that no one dares any longer to have an individual opinion or to do something on his own. The individual is no longer his own man but belongs 'in all things to an abstraction to which he is subjected by reflection, just as a serf belongs to an estate'.[28] This levelling process is not the work of an individual but rather of reflection and scepticism in the hands of an abstract power. It cannot therefore be halted by any worldly leader, outstanding individual or any society or association since these are themselves 'in the service of the levelling process'. It cannot even be halted by the individuality of the different nationalities, for this process is itself a 'negative representation of *humanity pure and unalloyed*'.[29]

While Kierkegaard insists that the general tendency of modern times has been toward levelling, certain changes have not truly fostered this end because they were not sufficiently abstract. In order to have true levelling one must first have those 'phantoms' and 'monstrous abstractions' known as 'the public' and 'the Press'.[30] In times of passion and tumult, when people strive for ideas, the press has a certain concrete character but in a passionless, reflective age it loses this character and fosters 'the public' which is in fact the real Levelling Master, though in reality it is nothing but 'a monstrous nothing' which nevertheless 'becomes everything and is supposed to include everything'.

It is important to realize that Kierkegaard's concept of the mass has nothing to do with numbers, has absolutely no aristocratic overtones, and is defined by the mere absence of responsible opinion. This can be seen by comparing it with groups such as the majority and minority which consist of real people whose lives are made up of the relative, concrete, and particular. To identify oneself with such a group is to take a stand and therefore to risk being found wrong. The public, by contrast, is an abstraction which consists only of individuals in their abstractness and can therefore remain the public even after it has reversed itself completely. There is therefore no question of the public ever being wrong and hence the person who identifies himself with it need never take a stand.

I have attempted to summarize Kierkegaard's analysis of his time but confess that this summary seems altogether inadequate. This is perhaps partly due to the density of Kierkegaard's thought and the brevity of our account but I believe the real difficulty is that most of us are afflicted with the disease in question. What he regards as abnormal and reprehensible is now the more or less general and accepted state of affairs. No one any longer wants to take a stand in case he should be proven wrong. Except in the worldly and aesthetic sense, no one even aspires to be anything but a nobody. Kierkegaard's description has become true and that, as I have suggested, is at once the source of its unintelligibility and interest.

No doubt many would agree with Kierkegaard's analysis of what has happened during the past hundred years. Marcuse, for example, regarded him as one of the most perceptive social critics of his time.[31] Many would however disagree entirely with his evaluation of these processes. For example, the Marxists celebrate the birth of the public or the mass society because they know it means the eventual triumph of the party over the individual. They applaud this event because they realize it represents the passing of the only effective opposition to their truly totalitarian state. And, granted their terms, they are no doubt correct in doing so. It is, however, only fair to add that Kierkegaard believes that the levelling process will make individual life intolerable and organized social life finally impossible and that he is implacably opposed to it on both these grounds.

One might gather from the preceding that Kierkegaard's view was entirely negative and pessimistic but nothing could be further from the truth. His account of the age contains many references to 'the individual' and he seems to believe that some such persons will appear even during the preliminary catastrophes of his own time. More importantly, he believes that the very goal of history is nothing less than the emergence of 'the individual' in the religious as opposed to the worldly sense and that the levelling process, at least when it has reached its final development, must, in its own demonic way, foster that emergence. Of course, he knows it will be a time of terrible suffering. Individual life will become intolerable and organized social life will simply break down. There will be many, many casualties and, as the hopeless forest fire of abstraction burns across the plain, no one can any longer be of assistance even to his beloved. But it is a time for hope rather than fear. The levelling process, particularly in its final stages, will be a marvellous education, particularly for the young. Liberated from worldly and aesthetic values, confronted with the abyss of eternity, many will escape the deluge by leaping over the sharp scythe of the Leveller – into the waiting arms of God. This is the goal of history. He who makes this leap 'becomes a man and nothing else, in the complete equalitarian sense. That is the idea of religion.'[32] But this is something which anyone, absolutely anyone, can do if he only wills it. 'The *taedium vitae* so constant in antiquity was due to the fact that the outstanding individual was what others *could not be*; the inspiration of modern times will be that any man who finds himself, religiously speaking, has only achieved what *every one can achieve*.'[33]

Toward the end of *On Authority and Revelation* Kierkegaard expresses the hope that the reader will get 'the impression that it is ethico-religious and has nothing to do with politics, that it investigates ethico-religiously how it comes about that a new point of departure is created in relation to the established order'.[34] But even this account reveals that he assumes the closest connection between religion and politics. This is obvious at many points in his work. He writes of the people of Europe as having 'lost themselves in problems which can be solved only in a godly way, which only Christianity can solve, and *has* solved long ago'.[35] He suggests that the Reformation appeared to be religious but was really political whereas the present situation appears to be political but will prove eventually to be religious.[36] He looks to the day when 'the *political* ministers are gone' and 'this thing of eternity might get permission at least to be taken into consideration'.[37] He knows that religion is the true humanity and believes that the restoration of ethical and religious values will restore health and sanity to Europe. As he writes '. . . the religious is the transfigured rendering of that which the politician has thought of in his happiest moment . . .'[38]

One of the problems of social philosophy is to bind men together into some real or integral whole. To the modern secular mind society is an arrangement of mutual interest between persons of competing and sometimes complementary interests. Kierkegaard has a much more radical goal and will settle for nothing less than true human community. Briefly, and in contradistinction to modern thought, he believes that the individual must first have a real relationship with God and with himself; only then, he holds, can there be any question of his entering into real relationships with other persons. Only then can there be any truly human community. Much of the authorship is concerned with the conditions for and nature of such a relationship. For example, *Fear and Trembling* shows, among other things, the necessity of a religious foundation for human society. *Purity of Heart* is designed to cure its reader of all moral self-deception by bringing him into a right relationship with God and himself. *Works of Love* explores what is involved in treating the other as a neighbour rather than merely as a rival or fellow-citizen.

The political theorist also wants to know how the society is to be governed. Kierkegaard's answer to this question may seem less convincing but I believe that it is no less true and appropriate. He foresees the day when modern secular man will become ungovernable by any worldly means and knows that in such a time society can be ruled only by the blood of its martyrs. Of course this is not government in any ordinary sense but it is perhaps the only one which has any hope of success. In fact, it is government by example imposed by those true reformers who are able to understand that historical categories change and that it is now their duty to oppose the masses.

IV

People find it strange to speak of Kierkegaard's psychiatric theory for a number of reasons, all of them quite mistaken. They assume that psychiatry began with Freud, that Kierkegaard is concerned only with man's eternal salvation, and that Christianity has no contribution to make to psychiatric theory. Now it is true that Kierkegaard insists upon the necessary limits of psychology (as he calls it) and that he formulates his thoughts in this area in specifically religious rather than merely secular terms. Indeed, he does so quite deliberately adding that it will do no harm if we make a little reference to theology. In fact, his position here is very similar to that which we have already seen with respect to politics, *viz.*, that only Christianity can solve these problems and that it has done so long ago. Of course, his psychiatric theory is extremely detailed, rich and complex but limitations of space prevent us from giving more than its broadest outline.

It may be useful to begin by recalling two points already mentioned. We have noted Kierkegaard's description of his age as reflective and passionless. In fact, he believed that the majority of his contemporaries had completely neglected the eternal aspect of their natures and had therefore forgotten what it means to exist as truly human beings. They were entirely content to act out the roles laid down by the society without ever thinking of exploring or testing the limits and possibilities of their own natures. They were content if they got through life escaping disgrace and disaster and showed no trace of that passionate concern for self-understanding which, for Kierkegaard at least, was a condition of being truly human. In a word, they were Philistines whose lives were inane and trivial. Kierkegaard was concerned about this as a human tragedy and particularly distressed that this lifestyle was accepted as the properly Christian one. In fact, in his view Christianity involved a constant probing of the limits of the human condition.

Kierkegaard's first account of the pseudonyms links them with his doctrine of indirect communication and in fact makes these two sides of the same coin. His later view however presents them as possibilities within his own psyche and the authorship as his own 'education' provided by a beneficent Providence. In fact, it is possible to interpret most of the pseudonyms and at least many of their creations as ideal psychological types and the authorship as a kind of autotherapy. It must, however, be added that they are also 'reader-therapy'. Kierkegaard constantly speaks of himself as practising the maieutic art, as deceiving the reader into the truth. This is usually taken to mean Christianity, but the truth in question is often the truth about ourselves as opposed to the lies with which, as we believe, we make our lives tolerable.

Kierkegaard's writings contain two distinct types of psychiatric material. The first are the ideal types already mentioned. These include figures such as Abraham, Nero, Napoleon, the Seducer, etc., all of whom are described in rich and perceptive detail. The second are the specifically psychological or psychiatric works themselves. These include *Repetition* (1843), *The Concept of Dread* (*Anxiety*) (1844), and *The Sickness Unto Death* (1849). Considerations of space require that we confine our attention to the last two.

The Concept of Dread insists that the only real and final explanation of original sin is the Christian dogmatic one that 'sin came into the world through sin'. It also insists that every man is his own Adam and that Adam's sin and disobedience is essentially identical with that of every other man. At the same time it holds that, psychologically speaking, sin is due to dread or anxiety. Briefly, man begins his life in immediate unity with the world around him and therefore in a state of innocence and ignorance. However, even as a merely psycho-somatic being, he rises above nature and discerns a future of possibilities, a realm of nothingness, by which he is at once attracted and repelled. This in turn engenders anxiety which is a mark of his freedom and which moves him toward knowledge and guilt. In short, his disobedience is due to anxiety regarding the future and hence to something which differentiates him from the merely animal creation. Anxiety is at once man's misery and glory.

Kierkegaard provides a very similar account in a journal entry from 1842.

The nature of original sin has often been explained, and still a primary category has been lacking – it is anxiety [*Angst*]; this is the essential determinant. Anxiety is a desire for what one fears, a sympathetic antipathy; anxiety is an alien power which grips the individual, and yet one cannot tear himself free from it and does not want to, for one fears, but what he fears he desires.[39]

In fact, this concept of anxiety plays an important role in Kierkegaard's psychiatric theory.

The Sickness Unto Death deals with despair of the Spirit or the Self which it declares to be universal and recovery from which is a condition of man's psychic health and salvation. This condition arises from the fact that 'The Self is a relation which relates itself to its own self . . .' and is intimately connected with the fact that 'Man is a synthesis of the infinite and the finite, of the temporal and the eternal, of freedom and necessity . . .'[40] Despair is sometimes unconscious of itself and may be due to a lack of finitude or infinitude or of necessity or possibility in the life of the individual. Alternatively, despair may become conscious through awareness of the fact that the Self is a synthesis of both the temporal and the eternal self in which case one may either weakly will not to be oneself or defiantly will to be oneself. In fact, Anti-Climacus argues that despair is sin and that health and salvation come only when man forsakes earthly goals and accepts God's forgiveness of his sins.

Obviously the foregoing is a ridiculously brief account of these two great works and does not begin to do justice to their complexity and sophistication. Equally obviously, it is impossible to do anything like justice to Kierkegaard's psychiatric theory in the space remaining at our disposal. We can however perhaps briefly note some of his more important and notable insights.

Kierkegaard's basic position is that man is a synthesis of the temporal and the eternal, that this ambiguous mixture generates anxiety and dread, and that his basic problem is to achieve a proper balance or synthesis between these elements of his nature. However, man is unable to face his ambiguousness and, particularly, the prospect of his own death which is implicit in his temporal body and the curse reported in the Adamic legend. In order to mask this terror he resorts to a variety of defense mechanisms which are really lies or self-deceptions about his own nature. These mechanisms enable him to function automatically within his society but for that very reason they prevent his development in the direction of true freedom. They are the product of that 'half-obscurity' or 'shut-upness'[41] about which Kierkegaard speaks and which we today connect with repression.

One of the commonest of these defense mechanisms is the denial of our creatureliness and, specifically, of the limited nature of our values and insights. In fact, we absolutize these in order to repress our feelings of anxiety. But this merely imprisons us within our own finitude and shields us from that ultimate education which we can experience by honestly facing up to our anxiety about our own creatureliness.

Kierkegaard provides an extensive catalogue of the various forms of illness resulting from the failure to accept our ambiguous status. The individual who affirms possibility and denies necessity becomes schizophrenic while he who affirms necessity and denies possibility becomes depressed. Between these two extreme psychotic states there is the 'normal neurosis' which Kierkegaard calls Philistinism and which is characterized by the fact that the individual tranquilizes himself with the trivial in order, as he believes, to shut out anxiety and dread. In addition, Kierkegaard also distinguishes 'the immediate man', the introvert, and the self-creator. The first is unaware of anxiety or dread and experiences these states only unconsciously. The second plays with the idea of his own difference and superiority but is frightened to express this in his lifestyle; in fact, he conforms to social norms and his secret conviction is transformed into a veiled hostility toward those around him. The third is fully conscious of his anxiety and dread and seeks to quell these by losing himself in great tasks and undertakings. This begins as defiant self-creation but may develop into conscious rebellion against the character of human existence itself. This is he 'who in Despair wills to be oneself'.

Of course, Kierkegaard is not content simply to record the various forms of human illness; in fact, his real aim is to point his reader toward true mental health and salvation. Very briefly, this involves a full and free acceptance of

209

one's ambiguous status, a conscious embracing of anxiety and dread, an abandonment of all defense mechanisms and finite aims, a dying to the natural or worldly self and an opening up to God to whom 'all things are possible'. In short, salvation requires faith or belief that one's life has meaning in the eye of the Creator. Such faith can be learned only through anxiety and dread and only such faith can lead man to the freedom which is his true destiny.

V

We have sketched Kierkegaard's position in respect of three quite fundamental issues in religious thought and it now remains to indicate the extent of his originality by placing these contributions in their broad historical setting.

Many contemporary orthodox theologians blame Kierkegaard for, as they imagine, first introducing paradox into theology. The fact is however that, especially with respect to the Incarnation, the orthodox have themselves always followed 'the way of paradox' and been guilty of the irrationalism which they all too readily ascribe to Kierkegaard. Indeed, Kierkegaard's role in this connection has been a very positive one. By introducing the word *paradox* into theology he has made us conscious of the irrationalism of the tradition and, as we have attempted to show, has at the same time pointed the way to a theology which is 'beyond paradox'. In this connection it is perhaps worth noting that his treatment of the Incarnation anticipated that of the later Barth by almost one hundred years, that many of his other numerous and valuable contributions to contemporary theology have also gone unnoted, and that, indeed, he must be one of the most 'under-footnoted' authors in all of modern thought.

Kierkegaard's originality as a social thinker can be gauged by contrasting his thought with that of most contemporary Marxists. Almost without exception, the latter are still caught up in the snares of nineteenth-century individualism; they do not question the value of worldly goods but simply demand that these should be shared more evenly. Kierkegaard explicitly celebrated 'the individual' but this is a truly religious category and one which, as he shows, contains the foundation of a truly just and lasting social order. Marcuse may have dismissed Kierkegaard's answers as 'religious' but, as the latter has argued, the truth is that the problems of society are themselves ultimately religious and can be solved only in a religious way.

Kierkegaard's accomplishments in psychiatry are equally remarkable. As Becker and others have shown, he has provided an account of human nature in terms of which it is possible to locate and understand the major psychiatric illnesses of modern man. Further, he did so prior to Freud and without benefit of either medical training or actual counselling experience. Indeed, this accomplishment, like the others we have noted, clearly entitles him to recognition as a major figure of the nineteenth or, perhaps better, the twentieth century.

I conclude with two brief comments. Kierkegaard is an incredibly rich and 'complete' thinker having something of interest to say on most questions of philosophy and religion. I hope and trust that the focus of the present account does not obscure or hide the richness and variety of his thought.

Every successful study of a major author should of course send the reader back to the original sources. This is particularly true in the case of Kierkegaard; indeed, no study of his thought can possibly substitute for the actual reading of his works. I shall be more than satisfied if my remarks prompt some to read Kierkegaard and help them to avoid some of the more obvious pitfalls in doing so.

Notes

1   Cf. *The Journals of Søren Kierkegaard*, tr. Alexander Dru (Oxford, 1951), § 680.
2   This brief piece was appended as an afterthought to *Concluding Unscientific Postscript* (Oxford, 1945).
3   Cf., e.g., Alastair McKinnon, 'Aberrant frequencies as a basis for clustering the works of a corpus', *Revue CIRPHO Review*, 3, no. 1 (1975–76) and Alastair McKinnon, 'Most frequent words and the clustering of Kierkegaard's works', *Style*, 12, no. 3 (Summer 1978).
3a *Søren Kierkegaard's Journals and Papers*, tr. Howard V. Hong and Edna H. Hong (Bloomington, Indiana, 1967–78).
4   I mean, of course, persons such as those mentioned on p. 182.
5   Cf. *Postscript*, p. 261.
6   'A First and Last Declaration', *Postscript*, pp. 551–4.
7   *Ibid.*
8   Cf., e.g., Alastair McKinnon, 'Kierkegaard's pseudonyms: a new hierarchy', *American Philosophical Quarterly*, 6, no. 2 (April 1969).
9   *Postscript*, p. 176. The material used in the following few pages is based on my 'Paradox and faith in Kierkegaard', in *The Challenge of Religion Today*, ed. J. King-Farlow (New York, 1976). I wish to make due acknowledgement to the publisher, Neale Watson.
10 *Journals*, tr. Alexander Dru, § 206.
11 *Ibid.*, § 633.
12 *Postscript*, pp. 189ff.
13 See especially D. F. Swenson, *Something About Kierkegaard* (Minneapolis, 1945), pp. 220f.
14 *Journals*, tr. Alexander Dru, § 1084.
15 *Ibid.*
16 *Kierkegaard's Journals and Papers*, tr. Howard V. Hong and Edna H. Hong, vol. 1, § 10.
17 *Ibid.*

18 *Papirer*, IV A 103, quoted in Cornelio Fabro, 'Faith and reason in Kierkegaard's dialectic', *A Kierkegaard Critique* (New York, 1962), ed. Howard A. Johnson and Niels Thulstrup, p. 176.

19 *The Sickness Unto Death* (New York, 1954), p. 253.

20 *Training in Christianity* (Oxford, 1946), p. 218.

21 *Philosophical Fragments* (Princeton, 1976), p. 66.

22 *On Authority and Revelation* (New York, 1966), p. lvii.

23 *The Present Age* (New York, 1962), pp. 42f.

24 *Ibid.*, p. 45.

25 *Ibid.*, p. 48.

26 *Ibid.*, p. 50.

27 *Ibid.*, p. 51.

28 *Ibid.*, p. 53.

29 *Ibid.*, p. 55.

30 *Ibid.*, pp. 59–67.

31 Cf., e.g., Herbert Marcuse, *Reason and Revolution* (Boston, 1968), pp. 262–7.

32 *The Present Age*, p. 57.

33 *Ibid.*, p. 62.

34 *On Authority and Revelation*, p. 192.

35 *Ibid.*, p. lvii.

36 *Ibid.*, p. lix.

37 *Ibid.*

38 'That individual', *The Point of View* (Oxford, 1950), p. 109.

39 *Papirer*, III A 233, quoted in Gregor Malantschuk, *Kierkegaard's Thought* (Princeton, 1971), p. 34.

40 *The Sickness Unto Death*, p. 146.

41 *The Concept of Dread* (Oxford, 1946), pp. 110–16, 124 and *The Sickness Unto Death*, p. 181.

Bibliographical essay

A general bibliography of Kierkegaard's works and the secondary literature may be found in Jens Himmelstrup, *Søren Kierkegaard International Bibliography* (Copenhagen, 1962) and in François H. Lapointe, *Søren Kierkegaard and his Critics: an International Bibliography of Criticism* (Westport, Ct. 1980). The question of Kierkegaard's pseudonymous authorship and the different phases of his work is discussed in G. B. and G. E. Arbaugh, *Kierkegaard's Authorship* (London, 1968).

Of Kierkegaard's own *oeuvre* the following books are most relevant to the issues discussed in this essay: *Fear and Trembling* (New York, 1954); *Philosophical Fragments* (Princeton, 1967); *Concluding Unscientific Postscript* (Oxford, 1945); *Training in Christianity* (Oxford, 1946); *The Present Age* (New York, 1962); *On Authority and Revelation* (New York, 1966); *The Concept of Dread* (Oxford, 1946); *The Sickness Unto Death* (New York, 1962); *The Journals* (Oxford, 1951); and *Journals and Papers*, (Bloomington, Indiana, 1967–78) tr, Howard V. Hong and Edna H. Hong.

The following works in English are useful accounts of Kierkegaard's general thought: J. Collins, *The Mind of Kierkegaard* (Chicago, 1953); E. Geismar, *Lectures on the Religious Thought of Kierkegaard* (Minneapolis, 1937); J. H. Gill (ed.), *Essays on Kierkegaard* (Minneapolis, 1969); T. Haecker, *Søren Kierkegaard* (Oxford, 1937); H. A. Johnson and N. Thulstrup (eds.), *Kierkegaard Critique* (New York, 1962); W. Lowrie, *Kierkegaard*

(Oxford, 1938); G. Malantschuk, *Kierkegaard's Thought* (Princeton, 1971); D. F. Swenson, *Something About Kierkegaard* (Minneapolis, 1945).

For further discussions of the issues treated in the foregoing essay, the reader is referred to more specialized studies. First, for helpful treatments of *Faith, Reason and Paradox* see: E. H. Duncan, 'Kierkegaard's Uses of "Paradox" – Yet Once More', *Journal of Existentialism* VII, no. 27, 1967; C. Fabro, 'Faith and Reason in Kierkegaard's Dialectic', in *A Kierkegaard Critique* (New York, 1962), and 'The "Subjectivity of Truth" in the Interpretation of Kierkegaard', *Kierkegaard-Studiet* I. (Osaka, 1964); R. Herbert, 'Two of Kierkegaard's Uses of "Paradox"', *Philosophical Review*, LXX (1961); E. D. Klemke, *Studies in the Philosophy of Kierkegaard* (The Hague, 1976); W. Lindstrom, 'The Problem of Objectivity and Subjectivity in Kierkegaard', in *A Kierkegaard Critique* (New York, 1962); A. McKinnon, 'Kierkegaard: "Paradox" and Irrationalism', *Journal of Existentialism*, VII, no. 27 (1967); 'Believing the Paradox: a Contradiction in Kierkegaard?' *Harvard Theological Review* LXI, 1968; 'Kierkegaard's Irrationalism Revisited', *International Philosophical Quarterly* IX, no. 3 (1969); P. Sponheim, *Kierkegaard on Christ and Christian Coherence* (New York, 1967); N. H. Søe, 'Kierkegaard's Doctrine of the Paradox', in *A Kierkegaard Critique* (New York, 1962); J. H. Thomas, *Subjectivity and Paradox* (Oxford, 1957).

Secondly, regarding Kierkegaard's *Social Theory* see especially the following: E. L. Allen, 'Kierkegaard and Karl Marx', *Theology* XL (1940); M. Carignan, *Individu et Société chez Kierkegaard* (Halifax, 1977); H. A. Johnson, 'Kierkegaard and Politics', in *A Kierkegaard Critique* (New York, 1962); B. H. Kirmmse, *Kierkegaard's Politics: the Social Thought of Soren Kierkegaard in its Historical Context* (California, 1977); G. Malantschuk, 'Kierkegaard and the Totalitarians', *American Scandinavian Review* XXXIV (1946); *The Controversial Kierkegaard* (Waterloo, 1980); S. Moore, 'Religion as the True Humanism – Reflections on Kierkegaard's Social Philosophy', *Journal of the American Academy of Religion* XV (1969); J. W. Petras, 'God, Man and Society, the Perspectives of Buber and Kerkegaard', *Journal of Religious Thought* XXIII (1966–67); and L. Richter, 'Kierkegaard's Position in his Religio-Sociological Situation', in *A Kierkegaard Critique* (New York, 1962).

Thirdly, *Psychiatric Theory* is dealt with in the following studies: E. Becker, *The Denial of Death* (New York, 1973); J. P. Cole, *The Problematic Self in Kierkegaard and Freud* (New Haven, 1971); C. P. Malmquist, 'A Comparison of Orthodox and Existential Psychoanalytic Concepts of Anxiety', in *Journal of Nervous and Mental Diseases* CXXXI (1960); L. L. Miller, *In Search of the Self: The Individual in the Thought of Kierkegaard* (Philadelphia, 1962); K. Nordentoft, *Kierkegaards Psykologi* (Copenhagen, 1972); and Ib Ostenfeld, *Soren Kierkegaard's Psychology* (Waterloo, 1978); and F. Sontag, 'Kierkegaard and the Search for a Self', *Journal of Existentialism* VII (1967).

The relationship between Kierkegaard and Hegel has been an area of wide interest in recent years. See especially: M. Taylor, *Journeys to Selfhood* (California, 1981) and N. Thulstrup, *Kierkegaard's Relation to Hegel* (Princeton, 1980).

Table I. *Distribution of key terms in main groups of the authorship*

number of word-tokens percentage of corpus	'Pre-authorship' 121,600 6.26	Early pseudonyms 865,174 44.55	Acknowledged works 566,932 29.19	Late pseudonyms 143,628 7.40	Meta-works 55,773 2.87	'Attack' literature 188,925 9.73
absurd						
Absurde, -s		86		3		
Christendom						
Christenhed, -en, -ens	8	17	56	163	48	112
Christianity						
Christendom, -men, -mens		624	371	297	89	1025
contemporaneity						
Samtidighed, -en, -ens		37	2	48	1	34
exist, to						
existere	1	274		6	4	
existence						
Existents	46	371		13	2	7
existence-communication						
Existents-Meddelelse		21				
inwardness						
Inderlighed, -en, -ens	8	472	91	42	17	65
leap (the)						
Springet	1	62	1	1	1	5
orthodoxy						
Orthodoxi, -ie, -ien		23		5		
paradox						
Paradox, -et	2	357		23		1
religiousness						
Religieusitet, -en, -ens		222		2	18	23
scandal						
Forargelse, -en, -ens	1	101	45	268	1	21
stages						
Stadier, -ne	7	108		1	3	1
Stadium, -s						
subjectivity						
Subjectivitet, -en, -ens	62	173				
Subjektivitet, -en, -ens				6		2

7

David Friedrich Strauss

HANS FREI

I. Faith and knowledge before Strauss

The opening of the nineteenth century's fourth decade in intellectual Germany was a time of extraordinary brilliance. One need only rehearse a few of the dazzling array of names that still graced the scene: Goethe, Hegel, Schleiermacher, Schelling. Friedrich Schlegel had only just died. The previous six decades had witnessed an astonishing explosion of literary and literary-critical, philosophical and theological talent, made all the more impressive for the interweaving of these three (and other) topics by the leading writers. But by now the classic statements of this brilliant period had been set down and the major systems frozen into place, so that the name tags so dear to intellectual historians were ready for application: there were Rationalist, Romantic and Idealistic systems. Within a few years the greatest writers (except Schelling) were dead. Not that there were no important new historical developments now. On the contrary; social, economic and political historians have found the subsequent era a fertile field. But in theology and philosophy the day of the epigones had come. (F. C. Baur in Tübingen is a partial exception to that generalization.)

But disciples need not be confined to small matters and they can show independence. Even if they lack originality and synthesizing ability they can raise powerful issues. And none did so with greater skill and impact than David Friedrich Strauss. Better than anyone in his day or for the most part since, he managed to clarify the issues posed by the previous generation's ways of relating theology and philosophy to each other and historical criticism of the Gospels to both. Theology in his day and for several decades previously was very much an academic discipline taught as a *Fachwissenschaft* by the appropriate university faculty. At the same time it was intrinsically related to a positive faith which was embodied in another state-related institution, the church. Theologians and ministers knew that they had to come to terms both with *Glaube*, a faith to be preached and lived and with *Wissenschaft*, i.e., orderly and systematic procedure which is open to general inspection and can be pursued at least to some extent without adherence to religious convictions. *Wissenschaft* was not only 'science' in the sense of the study of physical data, systems and theories but coherent method and system applied to any topic, including cultural subjects and the humanities. In addition, *Wissenschaft* was used in a special sense by Hegel and his followers, who equated it with his own logic and dialectical method in philosophy. Other contemporaries adopted this usage only half-heartedly, if at all.

At a more general level the relation between *Glaube* and *Wissenschaft* was preeminently a matter of basic conviction, deeply influenced by emotional, intellectual and communal loyalties. But given the German universities' penchant for concentration in depth on specific *Fachwissenschaften* and on the 'methods' appropriate to them – a habit reinforced by philosophy from Kant onward – it was almost inevitable that this issue in basic life stance would be converted into a technical subject matter. And so, during the first half of the nineteenth century several schools of thought came to be formed among the more prominent Protestant theological faculties over various ways of relating *Glaube* to *Wissenschaft*, each replete with its own house organ.

The conflict of voices was all the more cacophonous because, as usual in the conversion of concepts from broad and contextual use to technical status, their definition was sometimes loose or ambiguous, more often arbitrary or philosophically loaded. *Glaube* could describe either a religiously committed disposition of trust or personal devoutness, or else a set of Christian beliefs or propositional claims, or finally various combinations of the two. *Wissenschaft*, when related to *Glaube*, could have the limited meaning of untrammeled critical inquiry into the natural and historical data of Christian origins and development, free from dogma and based solely on evidence and natural canons of probability. Or it could refer to a theory about the meaning and truth of Christianity relying on non-extraneous criteria such as internal coherence and rational plausibility. Finally, it could broaden out from the latter and refer sweepingly to the exercise of Reason as a universal speculative capacity, applicable to Christianity as to all other areas of reflection because it is of the essence of human nature and of reality. It could also signify the passage from one of these uses to the other.

Sweeping philosophical points of view and the penchant for *Fachwissenschaft* united somewhat incongruously to turn the relation of *Glaube* and *Wissenschaft* into a formal theological topic for specialized study which generated vigorous argument over a period of time lasting from the latter part of the eighteenth through the first half of the nineteenth century.

Conservatives, largely of Pietist persuasion, held that in matters Christian a 'living faith' governs and sets bounds to all rational reflection and evidential analysis. In taking this position they used both *Glaube* and *Wissenschaft* in their various meanings. They therefore resisted any independent, free and critical inquiry into the origin and meaning of biblical writings, except for a limited use of philological analysis. And they rejected all suggestions that Christian beliefs could possibly undergo development in meaning or change in interpretation. Some of them were even suspicious of conservative endeavors to argue from general canons of rationality and evidence to the possibility or rationality of 'supernatural' Christian doctrine. They would settle for nothing less than faith in the Bible's inspiration as the sole source of all belief. And if this authoritative stance brought them in conflict with science and philosophy – so be it. Let the faith reign. As for their opponents who denied such a self-effecting authority of the Bible and, by derivation, of dogmatic confession – they stood accused not only of wrong-headed intellectualism but at least by inference of a hard and perverse heart.

Among those on the opposite side, some still held the Rationalist or Enlightenment views that had been most influential toward the end of the previous century. Others followed Idealist views on religion, especially those of Hegel. They had in common a persuasion that 'Reason' is a single capacity, uniformly applicable to all areas of inquiry, including religion. To Idealists *Glaube* was finally a more lowly, not yet truly self-conscious form of universal Reason (*Vernunft*). To radical Rationalists, by contrast, the traditional *Glaube*, both in its authoritarian credulity and in the supernatural propositions to which it held, especially about a direct divine revelation in history, was on a collision course with reason (*Verstand*, which they used in a more restrictively logical and mathematical and a less historical and dialectical fashion than the Idealist *Vernunft*).

Some few of these radicals – if that is the right term for them – fought traditional Protestant Christianity as the enemy who deliberately holds a species of superstitious and dangerous nonsense. Others, by far the greater number not only among the Idealists but even among the 'Enlightened', believed that Christianity could be freed by the reinterpretative power of Reason from its literalistic biblical shackles and from faith as blind assent to authoritarian biblical and ecclesiastical dogma. Specifically and centrally, they rejected or rather reinterpreted in radical fashion the doctrine of Jesus as the unique, final and absolute revelation of God.

Between conservatives and radicals stood a group of thinkers who came to be called 'mediating' theologians, although the position antedated the name by decades. Adopting the methods of modern critical investigation and philosophy, they agreed that faith and autonomous modern thought could and should live in peace and harmony. Philosophically and in their use of historical-biblical criticism they went all the way from quite conservative (e.g., 'rational Supernaturalism') to quite progressive (e.g., 'Neology'), and their philosophical outlooks varied considerably. By the fourth decade of the nineteenth century mediating attempts using Rationalist methods were definitely old hat, although representatives of that outlook were present in abundance. But in places like Berlin and Heidelberg and finally now in Tübingen, Schelling and then increasingly Hegel or else Schleiermacher set the agenda for mediation between *Glaube* and *Wissenschaft*. For Hegel and his mediating (or right-wing) followers the harmony of the two was a matter of generic connection, since faith is a lower form of reason (and therefore amenable to interpretation by *Wissenschaft*). For Schleiermacher and his mediating disciples, *Glaube* and *Wissenschaft* were of equal valency but so heterogeneous in character that when properly understood they should not come in conflict. (Unlike Hegel, Schleiermacher tended to see *Wissenschaft* as a rather limited enterprise, chiefly as the formal method(s) of a variety of specific fields of physical-natural and cultural inquiry.)

The older Rationalist theologians, mediating and otherwise, tended to identify religion or *Glaube* with assertions of true or false beliefs. The followers of Schleiermacher and Hegel saw *Glaube* or religion more nearly as a general qualification of human nature or consciousness, its specific doctrinal and other expressions varying with the particular cultures in which it lived. (The modern study of religion, though indebted to both views, owes more to the latter than the former.) But most striking is the fact that even though philosophical and methodological ways of thinking about religion and reason, *Glaube* and *Wissenschaft*, changed quite drastically over the decades for those on the left, right and centre alike, there was an astonishing consensus over what constituted the chief test case for conflict, mediation, defense or reinterpretation.

It was, in a word, the claim to the absolutely unique status of Jesus of Nazareth as embodiment of salvation and ultimate religious truth. G. E. Lessing, for example, had already stated the issue, and his opponents had picked up the challenge on his very terms. Some sixty years later D. F. Strauss restated Lessing's views on the same subject, albeit with different conceptual means, and forced the mediating theologians of his day to meet him on his own terms. Like Lessing he was a radical, able to dictate the terms of the argument because in conceptual form as well as doctrinal content he started from a consensus shared with his chief mediating opponents. And both Lessing and Strauss were most antagonistic toward their mediating and not their conservative opponents. Just what was the point of agreement over three generations and a broad spectrum of conflict?

In the course of the eighteenth century preceding Lessing's theological investigations, a subtle change in the apprehension of the Bible had taken place among both defenders and foes of its claim to privileged religious status. Hitherto it had been seen as a text containing doctrines and edifying writing, and possessed of the power to move the affections. Its truth or inspiration was guaranteed and implemented by the same Holy Spirit's suffusing the words on the printed page and enlivening the reader's mind and heart. The truth of the Bible's *historical* content was entailed by these other functions and was not the subject of a special argument. But now, with the rise of Empiricist philosophy, Deism and historical criticism, Scripture turned instead into a cognitive source, a book of (true or false) *information* ('revelation') about a specific sequence of past history – information which was at once of supernatural-doctrinal and miraculous-factual character. (The combination came to be called 'positive religion'.) Friend and foe now began to argue over the historical likelihood or accuracy, the logical conceivability and the real possibility of this dual revelation. While the argument was focused on a number of points in the biblical sequence, e.g., the 'Mosaic' creation account, the crucial test case by general agreement came to be the status of Jesus of Nazareth. Were the writings about him accurate, and did their factual truth or falsity constitute decisive evidence for or against the other, viz., doctrinal information about him?

Lessing, like David Hume before him, denied that testimony to a past miracle, no matter how voluminously or even well certified, was sufficient to make the event credible if it contravened our own direct and uniform experience. But secondly, even if a supernatural miracle should turn out to be likely, Lessing challenged the idea of the *conjunction* of the two types of information, which such a revelatory event was supposed to provide – factual-historical on the one hand, doctrinal-metaphysical on the other. 'Accidental truths of history', he said in his single most famous theological statement, can never become the demonstration of necessary truths of reason.'[1] Necessary truths of reason, metaphysical truths, in contrast to truths of fact, were proved only by their internal and mutual coherence, by the impossibility of their not being what they are or of being thought to be contrary to what they are. In Lessing's view Christian theologians erred fatally in trying to combine the two things. In effect, he denied both the logical or conceptual and the real or metaphysical possibility of joining together the historical and doctrinal claims derived from the New Testament about Jesus of Nazareth. He clearly implied that he regarded the notion of divine revelation in the shape of a single individual member of human history as both inconceivable and impossible. Kant, in parallel fashion, said that the notion that the idea of absolute perfection – the moral or religious content of revelation – had been supernaturally begotten and hypostatized in (or as) a particular individual is morally and religiously meaningless[2] besides being inconceivable.[3] No human being is eternal truth or the full revelation of eternal truth. Logically, metaphysically, morally and religiously it is a meaningless doctrine.

It is *arguable* that such historical and conceptual questions about revelation and Jesus remained at the centre of academic Protestant theology until the middle of the twentieth century; it is *certain* that they did so in the view of all parties to the argument until the middle of the nineteenth. By the time Strauss began to publish, they formed the focus of the attempt to articulate both historically and in principle the 'essence' of Christian *Glaube*, its specifying difference within the universal phenomenon of human consciousness called religion. The modern – Idealist or Romantic – mediating theologians of Strauss's day conceptualized rather differently from their Rationalist predecessors, but the same content was still recognizable: could and did the divine eternal 'Idea' or 'Archetype' find full realization in one particular and fully human individual, Jesus of Nazareth?

The most consistently rationalistic and idealistic thinkers both denied it, but with rather different interests at heart. Rationalists were interested in the purely human, exemplary quality of Jesus's being and character, and the natural explicability of his effect on human life and character. His relation to the eternal 'Archetype', moral character of the Deity – or whatever it was that he embodied in the same way as other good people except to a greater extent – did not concern them greatly, provided it was understood to be of the same character as everyone else's. Idealists likewise stressed that Jesus was a purely human and exemplary person who did not embody the eternal 'Idea' or 'Archetype' in a qualitatively different or absolute way, but their interest was focused on the eternal Idea (or Archetype) and its relation to all of humanity, which Jesus mirrored in individual symbolic form. As an individual person in his own right they (unlike the Rationalists) did not have much interest in him.

But by the beginning of the nineteenth century's fourth decade, Idealist and Romantic philosophers had worked out a *modus vivendi* with theology for which the full realization of the eternal 'Idea' in the one particular individual, Jesus of Nazareth, appeared to make a good deal of sense. In contrast to the pietistic conservatives who affirmed it (simply on grounds of faith and biblical inspiration) and to the radicals who denied it (and consequently urged a complete reinterpretation of christological doctrine), the mediating theologians of both Hegelian and Schleiermacherian stamp not only affirmed this christological *Glaube* as crucial but asserted either that it is a demonstrable part of *Wissenschaft* (the Hegelians) or that it demonstrably does not run counter to it (Schleiermacher and his followers). Mediation between faith and *Wissenschaft* seemed triumphant, the credibility of the doctrine of particular incarnation, historical revelation or positive religion seemed assured.

Interestingly enough, it was not the historical but the other argument in its favor, call it conceptual, philosophical or religious, that prevailed. Lessing's second objection, which, like Kant's rejection, had amounted to a plea for the radical revision of the meaning of the doctrine of Christ because its traditional, orthodox version was meaningless and impossible, had been turned back. Hegel rightly or wrongly seemed to his followers to have said that far from being meaningless the traditional doctrine was the very essence of true rationality; and far from being impossible its truth was actually a necessity. Schleiermacher not only apparently but clearly did say that being Christian meant being in a new, redeemed state of consciousness which could not be accounted for by anything less than one who, far from being merely an occasion for the vision of religious perfection, had to be that perfection itself in fully human shape in order to be able to accomplish the change in the rest of us.

It was people like Strauss and Ludwig Feuerbach who turned their backs on this harmonious state of affairs between theology and philosophy, *Glaube* and *Wissenschaft*, and said that warfare was the natural state between them. But even Strauss said so only after considerable hesitation. First, he was well aware that he was thereby terminating an armistice that had been negotiated over several decades and had seemed a welcome relief from the abrasive and often arid arguments over religion in the Enlightenment period. But second, it took him considerable time to come to the reluctant conclusion that traditional Christianity, 'ecclesiastical faith' he called it, was not only inconceivable in its native form but also could not be interpreted into any other mode of thought or faith, and that it was therefore totally anachronistic in an age that could no longer believe in miracles or authoritatively imposed dogma.

II. *Strauss and his* cause célèbre

When his *The Life of Jesus, Critically Examined* came out in 1835 (the second volume appeared in 1836),[4] Strauss was a twenty-seven-year old tutor at the Tübingen *Stift*, the Protestant seminary in the university. The work's utterly negative conclusions concerning historical support for Christian claims about the unique, divine status of Jesus Christ galvanized not only theological but ecclesiastical and wider cultural opinion throughout the land, indeed throughout the Western world. Seldom has a book on a theological topic had so powerful an effect. It made Strauss the most famous theologian in the land overnight. The all but universal revulsion against it cost him his academic career and turned him into a homeless wanderer among his peers.

Commentators have never been able to pinpoint precisely why the book produced such a furor. The veracity of the New Testament miracles had long been under severe attack. Even the category of 'myth', which Strauss appropriated tellingly to his own critical analysis of the Gospels' miracle stories, had already been applied at least to the birth stories about Jesus. And, as he freely admitted, some of his critical instruments had been taken from his predecessors' tool chest.

Perhaps the reason for Strauss's cause célèbre was that he explained the supposedly miraculous incidents of Jesus's life as 'myths' with a hitherto unheard-of skeptical consistency and elegance. The architectonic of Strauss's argument is graceful; each miraculous incident in the Gospel story is examined by means of the mutually contradictory explanatory procedures of Supernaturalists who defended its historical veracity as it stood, and Rationalists who reduced it to a non-miraculous factual kernel erroneously clothed by the authors in miraculous form. Supernaturalists are loyal to the text and hence make unbelievable historical claims. Rationalists give natural, credible explanations for miracles but as a result abandon the meaning of the biblical text. Having uncovered the contrary difficulties and common absurdities of the two positions, Strauss proceeds to show that under the explanatory hypothesis of myth these difficulties vanish, together with the assumption of any historical residue whatever: each miracle story is simply typical of the folklore inhabiting the spiritual climate of the area and era, given the Old Testament tradition and the common anticipation then and there of the advent of the Messiah. If Jesus, an obviously charismatic figure, was taken to be that Messiah, mythical tales and Old Testament themes were bound to be applied to him. There is therefore no need to resort to any factual explanations whatever for the origin of the miracle stories about Jesus. Their full explanation lies in the working of the religious mind or spirit, the structure of which is manifestly mythical, even when a residue of historical fact adheres to them.

The consistency and elegant simplicity of the book help account for its unprecedented impact and for the virtually unanimous howl of condemnation with which it was received by the theological profession. In addition, and more subtly, the book offended by its pervasively cool and detached tone, even when Strauss analysed material he thought historically reliable – a tone that rose to acid ridicule of some modern biblical commentators. Many critics took it to be *prima facie* evidence of the author's ironic detachment – if not worse – from the terrifying religious havoc he had wrought. *The Life of Jesus* was virtually the first inquiry into this topic – hitherto conceded by members of *all* theological parties to be of the loftiest import – that was quite consciously written without the slightest stylistic echo of the topic's 'elevated' status or of emotional involvement with it. Strauss brilliantly explained and defended the tone of his book against outraged attacks from all sides, arguing that it was appropriate for a *wissenschaftliche* undertaking and implied no disrespect either for the person of Jesus or the New Testament and its writers, and indeed even allowed for a variety of separate but correlative religious or aesthetic moods.

Beyond that, as Marilyn Chapin Massey has shown,[5] by its realistic and ironic literary structure the book became grist for the mill of a section of the public who had become culturally (and in some cases politically) radicalized, and who were ready to attack every aspect of the dominant system as part and parcel of the same reactionary state of affairs in Restoration Germany. In this sense irony refers not to the book's tone but to its controlling literary strategy; it moves by a variety of formal tactics to exhibit effectively the regnant romanticization of the past and at the same time to confront a present, stagnant situation through a kind of doubt that dissolves the positive religious (and by implication the social and political) 'givens' of the age. In view of Strauss's anything but radical political and cultural outlook, the book's form or strategy outstripped his own intention, which confined radicalism to religion. And even the content may have been in conflict with the form, for the overt philosophy of the book is not its ironic or realistic thrust but wavers between Idealism and empirical Positivism. It is the sort of tension in modern writing, partly between form and content, partly internal to both, that is thoroughly familiar to Marxist literary critics.

While Strauss rightly never claimed to be an original thinker, it is not enough to regard his *Life of Jesus* merely as a climactic and cold-blooded synthesis of preexisting scholarly skepticism. Original or not, it represented a 'paradigm shift' (to use Thomas S. Kuhn's widely cited term) in theological analysis. With enormous skill Strauss not only sorted out the various contemporary theological options for relating the categories *faith* and *Wissenschaft* but breathed life into their bloodless methodological subsistence by making their very meaning virtually dependent on the ways they were deployed in connection with the answer to the single overriding theological issue of christology. Do the meaning and truth of the dogma of Christ, the heart of the Christian religion in Strauss's view, depend on the historical reliability of the Gospel reports about the life of Jesus and his miraculous uniqueness? Are the Jesus of history and the Christ of faith identical? If the Christian response to these two interconnected questions was 'yes', he thought he could demonstrate the collapse of the Christian case. In retrospect then, the 'high culture' category juxtaposition of *Glaube* and *Wissenschaft* took on concrete force by Strauss's riveting it to the relation between christology and the critical investigation of the life of Jesus. It was fated to be a contribution of long-range significance. Not only did he give sharp focus and substance to a contemporary theological discussion and thereby climax a debate that had been leading up to it. In addition he shifted the terms in which it would be carried on thereafter: he assured the priority of the historical over the conceptual argument in the attack on traditional christology.

Not a profound thinker, either in originality or constructive synthesis, and therefore always overshadowed by his teacher F. C. Baur in the estimates of professional theologians and historians of religious ideas, Strauss was nonetheless a brilliant critic and intellectual narrator who was able, in his *Life of Jesus* as well as his slightly later *Dogmatics* or *Christliche Glaubenslehre*,[6] to pursue a systematic thesis single-mindedly, clear-headedly and persuasively through an immense thicket of historical literature. Quickwitted, sensitive and moody, of Rationalist inclination despite early flirtations with Mysticism and Romanticism, he proved himself a formidable controversialist who bloodied many a mediocre theological opponent by his sheer argumentative and analytical skills and his determined honesty. Increasingly radical in his anti-theology, he quickly became conservative and provincial in his politics. His correspondence with Ernest Renan at the time of the Franco-Prussian War of 1870 furnished a typical demonstration of his blinkered pro-Prussian German nationalism. The literary and historical writing to which he had turned in theological exile was happily not nearly so stunted by the same blight.

In the early 1860s he returned to the discussion of theology, in a series of works including a new life of Jesus[7] and a devastating critique of

Schleiermacher's lectures on the same subject.[8] His late summary confession, *The Old Faith and the New*[9] (1872), caught him at a disadvantage: in his theology (or anti-theology) he had always previously argued a normative case by critical depiction of a historical sequence; the history of dogma, he had tried to show in his *Glaubenslehre*, is itself the critique if not the destruction of dogma. But now he tried his hand at a systematic and constructive synthesis, and the result was flat and uninspired. The remnants of his old Hegelianism long since gone, he had turned under Darwinist tutelage into a straight-out mechanistic materialist, for whom religion was simply a matter of gladly acknowledging one's place in a vaguely supportive universe, and of ordering one's life in good, bourgeois decency. Even his analysis of Christianity – the old miracle faith – was now flat-footed in a way it had never been before. Nonetheless, even with or perhaps precisely because of its two-dimensional literalism, the book can still serve as an enduring warning to the 'hermeneutical' arts of those theologians who invariably find a modern 'understanding' ready to hand, with which to 'interpret' Christianity so that it is guaranteed *a priori* against every threat that it might be an anachronistic, superannuated outlook. Even in this, perhaps his most unsuccessful book, Strauss displays that stubborn and courageous honesty which had been his life-long hallmark and had made him in his day – ideologically much more narrow-minded than our own – a lonely and restless exile from his academic home.

III. The centrality of Christ in Christian theology

Strauss first laid the plans for *The Life of Jesus Critically Examined* in the flush of the youthful enthusiasm that had taken him, a budding Hegelian, to Berlin in 1831. The plan for the book was originally part of a more ambitious scheme. He was first going to set down the traditional Christian view of Christ, i.e., the Gospel portrait as well as the impression it left in the piety of Christian people, and the junction of the two in the great Christian creeds. The second, critical or negative part was to consist of testing the historical trustworthiness of the original reports and their portrait. Out of their destruction, like a Hegelian phoenix 'negating his negation', would arise the third, affirmative section, the eternal, i.e., philosophically reconstructed dogma of Christ. It would raise the eternal idea of Christ above its tie to the life and destiny of Jesus, the historical occurrence that had occasioned it, and thus beyond the inferior literal status to which it had to be assigned in the scheme's first section, the depiction of the traditional faith of the church in Jesus as the Christ.

Strauss dropped the first part of this plan and reduced the third to a brief constructive sketch appended to a concluding philosophical and theological critique of christological doctrine. It is the second, historically negative or critical section that forms the bulk of the published work. He did not abandon the even larger plan of which this original scheme had been only one ingredient: he had planned to trace the whole history of dogma in its dialectical development from the Bible by way of mutually opposed heretical positions into ecclesiastical dogma, and then its dissolution through Enlightenment criticism down to its reestablishment in independent philosophical fashion.[10] His *Glaubenslehre* came as close as he could to fulfilling the larger plan, though the philosophical transfiguration attempt fades away.

But with some interruptions, it was really the topic of *The Life of Jesus* that remained Strauss's theological preoccupation for the rest of his life. Whenever he returned to theology, it was with the dogma of Christ and its relation to Jesus of Nazareth in view, even though he changed his mind about the way faith and *Wissenschaft* should be deployed in respect of it. Not that other Christian doctrines were unimportant to him, but he tended, especially as long as Hegel had any influence on him, to see them in relation to the distinguishing essence of Christianity, the 'Idea' of absolute-finite or divine-human unity. In the late 1830s he sketched out a general history of religious outlooks in the West, the built-in thrust of which was a broadly Hegelian conception of the divine relation to the world.[11] In antiquity a transcendently real world was posited by the then prevalent cultural consciousness above and over against our own finite world, the abyss between them conceived as greater and greater as time went on so that commerce between them depended on mediating powers or notions. The novel contribution of Christianity was the unification of these two realms, in which their abiding distinction remained, however, so that the unity was confined strictly to a single person or focus. In the long history of Christian theology, its critical dissolution and reconstruction into speculative philosophy, the notion of the divine-human or transcendence-immanence relation finally passed through a complete Materialist reduction of 'transcendence' on the one hand and the countering Idealistic sacrifice of materiality to the realm of 'consciousness' (a form of 'transcendence') on the other. In both cases the two-realms-but-single-individual-unification view of Christianity had first been extended instead into a *general* conception of the transcendence-immanence unity, and then into the denial of one *relatum* in favor of the other. The tide against such one-sidedness began to turn with Spinoza.

For him not only spirit and matter but God and nature became co-extensive, and yet he refused to call the one side more basic than the other.

Like other commentators then and since, Strauss considered Spinoza's monistic metaphysics of overpowering significance for the formation of nineteenth-century Idealist ontology. It set the stage for universalizing divine-human unity, rather than either confining it to one historical occasion or individual, or allowing one side of this unity to swallow the other. This metaphysics initiated the common modern philosophical denial of a personal Deity, self-enclosed, singular and extrinsically related to the world which He had created at a specific moment of time – the Deity that corresponded logically to the single-individual notion of divine-human unity. The subsequent philosophical tide, awash with the mutual immanence of God and world, crested with Hegel for whom the two realms came together not substantively after the fashion of Spinoza's thought, but in and as consciousness or spirit, in such a manner that each realm is an abstraction without the other. Yet their unity is not an undifferentiated mergence (as in pure pantheism) but a full coinherence of both in one. And so the doctrines of God and incarnation, theology in the narrower sense and Christology, become one and the same in different perspectives, each a function of the other. And since under this description the God-world relation is a single, general and eternal act (if that is the correct word to use), the doctrine of creation may be added: it is the eternal expression of the same relation of which incarnation is the indefinitely continuing temporal embodiment.[12] Both as historical expositor and constructive thinker Strauss moves steadily toward Pantheism. But the chief focus in this systematically unitary complex is for him always the idea of divine-human unity, in other words the christocentricity of the whole scheme. Christology rather than theology was his preoccupation. And whether as theologian or later as anti-theologian he wanted the representatives of the ecclesiastical tradition also to admit that christocentricity was the essence of Christianity. He continued to demand it of them even long after he had abandoned this Hegelian account of divine-human unity.

Notable is the general, schematic character of this christocentricity. Its focus is a pure 'Ideal', gradually to be realized in the history of human consciousness. The context in which this Idea or Ideal becomes meaningful is not so much a religious need for redemption from beyond ourselves as the search for a conceptual strategy to supply coherence to a cultural and metaphysical quest. In these ways Strauss was (temporarily) a Hegelian without Hegel's combinatory subtlety and ambiguity. (Hegel always tried to unite and balance the ideas of incarnation and redemption, to preserve the affectively religious within the conceptual aspect of consciousness, and of course to balance the idea of divine-human unity with its individual representation in Jesus of Nazareth.) Strauss's outlook was fit for an era of cultural confidence and Strauss, though personally pessimistic, moody and self-confessedly without much *joie de vivre*, was nothing if not a cultural optimist.

Right from the beginning his quest was theological rather than historical. As he wrote to a friend in 1846: 'I am not a historian. Everything for me started from my dogmatic (resp. anti-dogmatic) interest.'[13] From his later university days until the early 1840s Hegel's philosophy played a heavy role in that interest.

IV. Christology and the Hegelian connection

Hegel's vision was one of several that started out from Kant's Copernican revolution in philosophy, the so-called 'turn to the subject'. Kant had separated the self (subject, consciousness) out from the panorama of all other things and made it a distinctive, unique perspective upon them all. It is irreducible to any of them in being, and therefore cannot be known as they are. The true self does not belong into the same series with the purely objective world, not even as the highest member in a common metaphysical or epistemological scale. This, at any rate, seemed to Kant's Idealist successors to be implied by his thoughts. They believed that he had not managed to reintegrate what he had put asunder – the tough, intractable order of natural and cultural reality, including human institutions, and the perspective of human consciousness upon this order which is 'other' to it. The quest for that reintegration at an absolute rather than merely human level of consciousness became the order of business for the post-Kantian Idealists.

The climax of the philosophical development after Kant, so far as it bore on Christian theology, came with Hegel, in the form of the most nearly complete compact of peace between subjective and objective reality, and between *Glaube* and *Wissenschaft* (speculative philosophy). His basic philosophical stance he signalled in the powerfully climactic announcement: 'In my view, which can only be justified through the presentation of the system itself, everything depends on grasping and expressing truth not so much merely as substance but rather as subject.'[14] It was the triumphant announcement of the complete reintegration of subject and object, the two sides of experience, knowledge and truth which Kant had – in discovering them – torn asunder. Unlike his Idealistic precursors and colleagues, especially Schelling, Hegel claimed this union both in being and in thought not as an intuition or immediate divine gift but as the climactic and therefore genuinely achieved, concrete product of the long mediating effort of logic, phenomenology and ontology – of the joint dialectical process of thought and reality.

On this road Christianity, which Hegel calls the absolute or revealed religion, is the penultimate stage, in the sense that absolute Spirit, absolute truth is already fully itself or fully present in it, but not yet in fully fitting form. The heart of Christianity is Christ and the dogma about him, his incarnation and the infinite-finite reconciliation in him. This has first to appear in its literal, sensuous, historical form, i.e., as a spatio-temporal occurrence and the story of an individual. Hegel calls this the 'representational' stage or form of the absolute truth. But from there one must go on to see the same content, the Idea of absolute-finite unity, first as collective consciousness and then in its absolute and thus fully appropriate form – as philosophical truth and therefore set forth in the form of 'concept', in contrast to 'representation'. At this, the ultimate stage, form and content are completely one, as they were not at the representational, imaginative level. But Hegel always insisted that despite this difference in the two forms, the content is one and the same in both and, concomitantly, that the representational form is at once overcome and yet preserved in the conceptual stage. (That ambiguity is the meaning of *aufheben*.)

'In philosophy', Hegel said, 'religion receives its justification from the point of view of thinking consciousness.'[15] More boldly yet, one can assert that the identity of absolute religion, (i.e., Christianity) and speculative philosophy is accessible only to those who have the special knowledge vouchsafed to philosophy, not available at the lower level where its form is faith: 'The esoteric view of God and of identity as well as of knowledge and concepts is philosophy itself.'[16]

As for those who cannot reach so high, just how severe is their loss for having to remain at the exoteric or representational level of faith? In a modern, increasingly secular age, which has abandoned miracle and particular, supernatural providence, is the Christian tradition an anachronism if taken at face value, as the exoteric faithful do? Or does the crucial hinge of Christian doctrine on which all the others hang and which is the expression of Christianity's religious uniqueness, viz., the literal, factual, historical incarnation of Godmanhood as this individual, Jesus of Nazareth, remain a permanent aspect of its essence for exoteric and esoteric alike, even if the latter have to go on from there to grasp this event as an element in a higher speculative synthesis?

It was just at this point that Strauss pressed Hegel for answers. He was far more concerned than Hegel with the relation of religious truth to the actual ecclesiastical belief and practice of the day, in parish life as well as theological party strife. For that and other reasons he, unlike Hegel, had the profoundest stake in the bearing which the philosophical system's claims concerning the truth of the Christian religion had on the practices and results of a rational-empirical historical inquiry into the fact claims of the Gospel reports about Jesus, especially those testifying to his absolute religious uniqueness. It seemed to him that only by straightening out this religious-historical issue could he also get clear guidance on the other matters. He became a historian in order to clarify his religious or dogmatic problems.

Saying that he could not get decisive answers from Hegel, he made up the Master's mind for him posthumously, much to the outrage of the philosophers of Hegel's 'school'. The difference between representation and concept, which distinguished between them as forms while affirming the identity of their content, was – in the early view of Strauss and his friends – Hegel's most important contribution to theology (though it may be doubted that Hegel himself would have accorded this relation the same high significance or, for that matter, have distinguished them quite as sharply as Strauss did). It mediated and brought harmony, as no one else had done, between Bible and dogma on the one hand and free *Wissenschaft* on the other. But true mediation required clarity of distinction and not only positive correlation.[17]

The most important question in this connection for us soon became this, what the relation of the historical elements of the Bible, particularly those of the Gospels, is to the concept; whether the historical character is part of the content which, the same for representation and concept, requires acknowledgement from the latter also; or whether it is to be assigned merely to the form, so that conceptual thought is not bound to it.[17]

It was of course possible that Hegel meant to affirm not the necessity for the appearance of the individual God-man in history, but only that of the temporary, representational, believing consciousness taking this representational shape. In that case the main issue was moot, and we can proceed to the concept while leaving empirical history to go on its trivial though independent course.

On the other hand, right-wing followers of Hegel insisted indignantly that this is not Hegel at all but a fall-back to a Kantian position, for which the real – in this case objective history – remains intractable to the rational – in this case the Idea of incarnation as a universal need and rational truth. The rational would in that case be forced to abide outside the real at a level of subjective consciousness or ideality. But Hegel's advance, they said, was precisely that the objectively real and the rational are joined, without subjectivity or particularity being submerged or lost in that union, i.e., without surrendering the Kantian subjectivity to a Spinozistic notion of all-encompassing, objective substance in which all particularity and subjectivity is dissolved.

In this interpretation of Hegel, which is doubtless the better one, the Idea has to be *actually* realized and not only *believed* to have been realized. However, the following issues still remain.

First, does the Idea, including the necessity of its external appearance, also include the necessity of its being realized as one specific individual? Or is this individual its realization only in reciprocal interaction with all its other manifestation – so to speak as *primus inter pares*?[18] In espousing the latter view, Strauss consciously departed from the Hegelian school and from Hegel's own explicit position. Nevertheless, this did not keep him from claiming that he was doing so on grounds that were basically compatible with Hegelian philosophy.

Second, and most important for Strauss, is the further question: even if it is granted that the Idea must necessarily manifest itself externally in *a* qualitatively unique individual, is the factual claim that he is *this* particular person settled by speculative philosophy? Yes, said Hegel's theological followers. At this point, and it was decisive for him, Strauss simply demurred. It is tempting to say that he broke completely with Hegel over this matter for, said Strauss, speculative philosophy simply does not have the resources to answer questions of historical fact. But even here he was quite uncertain whether he had actually broken with Hegel.[19] For it seemed to him that Hegel was quite ambiguous on this point. Sometimes he claimed that the system of speculative philosophy demonstrated the necessity at least of the broad outlines of the particular history of Jesus as the absolute individual self-manifestation of the Idea: there had to be such an individual, and the account of his being, outlook and destiny *had* to be what in fact it was in this specific instance. In that case the historical facts belonged to the religious and philosophical content and thus to the conceptual form of Christianity. At other times Hegel consigned the purported facts about Jesus to the role of purely external appearance or representation: they may or may not have happened; in any event the matter is neither crucial for the meaning contained in them nor definitely ascertainable, as philosophical truths must be. In that case of course the history and the story (the two are often run together for Hegel, who could comprehend both factual history and mythical story under the single category of 'representation') remain at the level of the representational form which, not belonging to the content, is stripped away by the conceptual form. The further consequence, most important for Strauss, was that in that case Hegel leaves all judgment about the historical facts, as a matter of philosophical indifference, entirely to the free inquiry of the historical critics. Empirical, critical-historical inquiry alone can then determine whether a particular individual was the full embodiment of the Idea.

Strauss claimed that he was still a follower of Hegel in adopting this latter or 'left Hegelian' position, for which all philosophical contact between philosophical or religious meaning and historical fact judgments has been broken, so that the historical facts and the spiritual meaning of the Gospel story have no philosophical, necessary bearing on each other. This was the position he had struggled toward and finally attained as a student, and from it he wrote the *Life of Jesus*. While he did not want to lose the connection between critical-historical *Wissenschaft*, and *Wissen* or *Wissenschaft* in the loftier, speculative sense, his stance was now firmly fixed: Critical-historical analysis and judgments were independent of speculative philosophy and therefore only disjunctively or externally related to it.

As a result one may now see their relation from two perspectives. From the vantage point of historical criticism it meant to him that the latter stands on its own feet; it is 'presuppositionless'. It requires no grounding in a prescriptive and universal theory of reason or of the nature of reality. It need find no rational 'Ideas' that would be bound to shape events. It simply generalizes for all times and eras our present uniform experience of the natural cause-effect connections between natural events. They are not miraculous; they do not exhibit, as Supernaturalists claim, the interruption by immediate divine intervention of the secondary cause-effect sequence. This uniform experience may be so far generalized and called a law of nature that by invoking it we may regard as unhistorical any narrative that claims to violate it (*LJ* § 14). From the perspective of the dialectic of speculative philosophy on the other hand, this independent historical-critical world view meant that historical-critical science has to be regarded as a negative even though necessary moment in the process of the dialectic's raising of the contents of religious truth to the level of philosophical truth.

Strauss was fully prepared to say both things together, since he did not at that time see any contradiction between his free and 'presuppositionless' historical science and his Hegelian philosophy. But it is fair to say that by one of those pre-reflective, pre-rational orderings that we all undertake in our basic outlooks, he had made a priority choice even if it took him some years to discover the fact. As he wrote *The Life of Jesus*, the empirical inquiry into the historical factuality or non-factuality of the Gospel narratives, independent of their interpretation by speculative philosophy, became at least as important to him as the philosophical, trans-historical reconstruction of their meaning and truth, even though he still held to the latter. And historical-critical inquiry was to him in its own right as damaging to traditional Christological claims as were the deliveries of modern philosophical *Wissenschaft*, i.e., Hegelian philosophy.

In *The Life of Jesus* Strauss had just begun to travel this road. He had only covered the first lap – but it was vital. He had arrived at the position that while historical-critical reconstruction of the figure of Jesus in the Gospels had no bearing on the truth of the 'Idea' and its relation to the course of history in general, perhaps not even on the relation of the 'Idea' to the necessity of some particular, full historical embodiment of itself, historical argument could and did invalidate the claim that *this* particular individual was the full embodiment of the 'Idea', i.e., the Messiah. The potential significance of this conclusion was great, even if it took Strauss considerable time to realize it. He was in effect even then asserting the priority of the historical over the conceptual or philosophical argument in the battle against all mediating christology. More than that, while not eliminating the conceptual argument he made it dependent on the historical argument to a degree that his equally radical forebears Lessing and Kant had not done.

V. The Life of Jesus

Strauss's critical aims in *The Life of Jesus* were simple: to distinguish fact from fiction in the Gospel records concerning Jesus; to establish the most likely shape of those events that fell on the historical side of this obscure boundary, and to account for the writing of the non-historical stories.

Of these three tasks, the first and the third went together and were the easiest. The first because it simply involved putting forth a credible set of general criteria, the third because the non-historical accounts fitted nicely under them. The second was and remained far more difficult, because there were no *general* criteria for distinguishing with any great degree of probability what was more and what was less likely in any given case whose historical possibility had been admitted in the first place. In such situations, it was a matter of every individual example having to fend for itself. The burden of argument always rested on the affirmation and actual reconstruction rather than on the denial of a historical core, once allowance had been made for clearly unhistorical embellishments. No wonder then that for general as well as certain narrower, technical reasons Strauss's critical procedure and results were deemed 'negative'. And yet, it is actually surprising how much positive historical content he claimed for the first three Gospels. (The Gospel of John was another story.)

To establish fact from fiction Strauss employed two concentric sets of criteria, one negative, the other positive. The first tells us negatively the general sort of thing, i.e., miracle, that does not happen, the other identifies positively the marks of the particular type of miracle we confront in the Gospels, i.e., myths.

First, then, we know we are dealing with non-factual material whenever the known and universal laws which govern the course of events, laws of causality, succession and psychology, are being violated by a story. Miracles, internal inconsistency and contradiction with other events are signs that we are in the presence of the unhistorical. Positive indications of myth, and therefore of the unhistorical, can be formal, e.g., conversation in more elevated strains than the education of the participants warrants or conversation carried on by means of hymns, etc. They may also be more substantive, e.g., 'if the contents of a narrative strikingly accords with certain ideas existing and prevailing within the circle from which the narrative proceeded' and if these ideas are themselves 'the products of preconceived opinions rather than of practical experience'. Thus, 'knowing . . . that the Jews saw predictions everywhere in the writings of their prophets and poets, and discovered types of the Messiah in all the lives of holy men recorded in their Scriptures', we are bound to suspect myth in descriptions of incidents in Jesus's life which dovetail precisely with such genres (*LJ*, pp. 88f).

The 'positive' criteria of 'evangelical' myth connected with Jesus may be further subdivided, so as to make the category a more precise analytical instrument: there are pure myths, in which preexistent stories were simply identified with him, or else new or modified stories evolved as the result of the impression he had made. Historical myths are those in which historical facts have been transmuted into marvels (e.g., Jesus's baptism). Distinct from all these, which contain 'ideas' in representational or imaginative form, there is the final written produce of relatively unfocused and variously transmitted oral tradition which we call legend. And finally, there is also the deliberate editorial work of the author.

Strauss's consistent and drastic use of the category of myth earned him the greatest obloquy at the time of the publication of *The Life of Jesus* and led to painful misinterpretations of the book, because it was thought that he had declared the whole of the Gospels' account to be fiction – which was of course nonsense. But there is no doubt that, having evolved the criteria for miracle and myth, he obviously found it easiest to apply them to those episodes in the Gospels which they fitted most completely. Broadly speaking these were stories in which Jesus's thoughts and proclamations were least in evidence, and most to the fore were miracles done by him and, even more, those performed on and in connection with him.

In other words, Strauss used 'myth' chiefly to explain purely super-natural accounts, rather than those borderline episodes in which natural and supernatural, historical and unhistorical elements were intermixed, and which were therefore the most difficult to account for. Myths, he said, are not deliberate inventions but rather unconscious folk poetizing, the manifestations of a culture's rather than an individual consciousness. They express in imaginative, i.e., story form the religious ideas – the origin and destiny of the universe and the soul, the idea and means of salvation, etc. – of 'pre-scientific' cultures that have not yet risen to the level of conceptualization or rational reflection. The crucial assumption making Strauss's notion of 'myth' operative was the intelligibility and coherence of the idea of 'cultural consciousness', and of course of the drastic difference in cultural consciousness, especially religious ideas, between antiquity and modernity. As such, the category was by Strauss's day the common property of Romantic and Idealistic thinkers, as well as of a good many biblical critics who had little affinity with either of these philosophical views. Among the critics in particular it already had a fairly long history, on which Strauss confessedly depended.[20] It is obvious that 'myth' could serve nicely as a critical category for determining the historical or fictional character of a given Gospel *pericope*. Equally evident is its usefulness as a hermeneutical instrument. With the aid of the definition of myth as 'idea' in imaginative or 'representational' form, or – the same thing – as immediate or sensuous embodiment of group consciousness, Strauss was able to render a (Hegelian) philosophical interpretation of myth as an early stage of the self-development of 'spirit' or 'Idea' through its own history.

Strauss used 'myth' in both ways, never confusing the two. Critically (our present context), in the analysis of purely supernatural stories he proceeded, as F. C. Baur said, dialectically and negatively. Natural and supernatural explanations always present mutually cancelling sides of the same dilemma. Each explanation argues persuasively against one aspect or the other. The supernatural explanation is loyal to the text and as a result demands adherence to fact claims that are unbelievable: the natural explanation by contrast distorts the text beyond belief in the interest of positing a factually credible occurrence as its origin. As he sums up the procedure in one instance, the story of the transfiguration (*LJ*, pp. 540f, 545):

Thus . . . after having run through the circle of natural explanations we are led back to the supernatural; in which, however, we are precluded from resting by difficulties equally decisive. Since then the text forbids a natural interpretation, while it is impossible to maintain as historical the supernatural interpretation which it sanctions, we must apply ourselves to a critical examination of its statements . . . we have here a mythus, the tendency of which is twofold; first to exhibit in the life of Jesus an enhanced repetition of the glorification of Moses; and secondly, to bring Jesus as the Messiah into contact with his two forerunners, – by this appearance of the lawgiver and the prophet . . . to represent Jesus as the perfecter of the Kingdom of God, and the fulfilment of the law and the prophets; and besides this, to show a confirmation of his messianic dignity by a heavenly voice.

Apply the category of myth, eliminating the need to explain the text as a factual report at all, but also the suspicion that the writer was a deliberate fabricator whether for moral or immoral reasons, and you get rid of the conflict between supernatural and natural readings by eliminating both. The origin of the text has been explained from the cultural consciousness out of which it arose, and with it its factual or rather non-factual status. With this conclusion Strauss rests his case – in this kind of story. As Baur says of him, he really has no interest in the character, shape or 'tendency' of the Gospels as writings except as they bear immediately on the 'fact' question. 'The absolute certainty of the purely negative result of the criticism of the history eliminates every further question in respect of the writings.'[21]

The upshot of this analysis is to explain to Strauss's satisfaction such stories as the birth accounts of both John the Baptist and Jesus, the accounts of Jesus's infancy and childhood, the circumstances attending his baptism, the stories of his temptation and transfiguration, Jesus's performance of miracles in the strictest sense, where neither psychological impact nor extrapolatively extended natural explanation can be argued, e.g., his command over the wind and the sea (*LJ* § 63, p. 101), many of the stories embellishing the passion, and finally of course – and above all – Jesus's resurrection and ascension.

Nonetheless, Strauss believed that there are real historical foundations for major parts of the synoptic Gospels' accounts of Jesus's public ministry and his death. Individual accounts individually examined yield positive results, in which historical facts can be relatively well established and distinguished from myth. True, we cannot reconstruct a reliable chronological sequence of his ministry from them, and the so-called harmonies of the Gospels, trying to iron out verbal, chronological and other discrepancies among the four accounts, cannot be considered as anything more than 'a tissue of historical conjectures' or worse (*LJ*, p. 279). Moreover, on individual incidents and sayings and on groups of sayings such as the Sermon on the Mount, Strauss remains curiously vague and indeterminate. He neither suggests definite reconstructions for their formation and meaning nor does he place them within a unified view of Jesus's outlook and teaching. Albert Schweitzer is right that 'each separate problem is indeed considered, and light is thrown upon it from various quarters with much critical skill. But he will not venture on a solution of any of them.'[22]

But on one crucial matter Strauss was clear. There was a development in Jesus's view of his own mission, especially of the relation of his person to it, and of this knowledge we can be confident. This, from first to last, was of great interest to Strauss, since for him it is at all times the *person* of Christ and his vocation that is the centre of The New Testament and of Christianity. His message concerned Strauss only in that context. As for the long-range religious effect of Jesus's personality, it always fascinated Strauss but played a subordinate part in his reflections. At first Jesus, like John the Baptist whose disciple and successor he considered himself, thought of himself as a preacher of repentance and forerunner of the Kingdom of Heaven, and from the beginning he taught a spiritual version of the Mosaic law. But later he 'held and expressed the conviction that he was the Messiah; this is an indisputable fact' (*LJ*, pp. 287, 284). Further, Strauss believed that the synoptic texts warrant the conclusion that Jesus thought of his messianic mission as temporal rather than purely spiritual. However, he did not plan (as H. S. Reimarus had argued) a political Messiah's revolution. The only option left is that his was a hope whose fulfilment was to be brought about by supernatural miraculous intervention in the external affairs of the nation: he would himself come down in a second advent in the clouds as the heavenly Son of Man, speedily following upon the destruction of Jerusalem (*LJ*, pp. 589f). And yet Strauss was at times hesitant to claim that this realistic eschatological conclusion is a complete description of Jesus, for his attitude toward Jesus was always ambivalent in one respect or another. And so he could also say of Jesus's view of his own person and mission: '. . . it was the national, theocratic hope, spiritualized and ennobled by his own peculiar moral and religious views' (*LJ*, p. 296; cf. pp. 293–6). The idea of a suffering Messiah was not part of the Jewish tradition. Still, as Jesus's ministry drew to its close it is likely that he came to adopt it (*LJ*, pp. 572f); indeed, Strauss apparently assumed that Jesus finally came to believe that his messianic Kingdom would be brought in by the Father only after his death, when he himself would return in glory.[23]

In sum, Strauss was confident that by means of historical-critical method we can and indeed do attain reliable historical knowledge about the indispensable and theologically essential element in the Gospels: Jesus did in fact believe that he was the Messiah, the Son of Man, and he believed it in a certain way, which was neither that of political revolution nor that of spiritual regeneration. It was the result of a resurrection of the dead, to be effected speedily and through the Messiah's agency, and it would usher in the messianic times. He expected to restore the throne of David and rule a liberated people with his disciples on the still hidden, sudden signal of his Father. All the nations would bow before the Son of Man in his glory, surrounded by angels, and would present themselves together with the awakened dead before his judgment seat (*LJ*, p. 296).

They who shrink from this view, merely because they conceive that it makes Jesus an enthusiast, will do well to reflect how closely such hopes corresponded with the long cherished messianic idea of the Jews, and how easily, in that day of supernaturalism, and in a nation segregated by the peculiarities of its faith, an idea, in itself extravagant, if only it were consistent and had, in some of its aspects, truth and dignity, might allure even a reasonable man beneath its influence.

Commentators rightly remark on the similarity between this conclusion and that of Reimarus, that Jesus died a deluded fanatic. He did not return after his death, and the fall of Jerusalem went by without ushering in the end times. Strauss denied the only other possible alternative, that all these predictions had actually been retroactively attributed to Jesus by the early Church. Such was the upshot of Strauss's exploratory journey along the historical side of the obscure boundary between history and myth. If his mythical analysis had resulted in a complete *historical* negation of the supernatural aspect of traditional Christology, his historical reconstruction culminated in total *theological* negation of the same phenomenon. The two together added up to the complete denial of ecclesiastical christology, of any possible positive correlation or conjunction between judgments of historical *Wissenschaft* and the affirmations of traditional *Glaube*.

The essence of Christianity in its traditional ecclesiastical version, said Strauss, was that salvation depended on the identification of the Christ, the divine Son, with the individual Jesus of Nazareth. The truth or falsity of this claim, he continued, depended on how well it stood up in a close critical reconstruction of the outlook and destiny of Jesus. It would have to show him at once as a credible human being and yet absolutely unique. We have seen the result. Jesus thought himself the Messiah in a way that is meaningless or, rather, absurd in a modern age. Many years later, when his views had changed considerably, Strauss said that 'the critical examination of the life of Jesus is the test of the dogma of the person of Christ', a position which as a left-wing Hegelian he had been at pains to avoid in 1835, when he severed the Idea of Christ completely from the historical person of Jesus in the concluding section of his book. But because historical criticism had for him even then already achieved its autonomy from speculative philosophy as well as traditional dogma, the saying holds for his view of the *ecclesiastical version* of the dogma even in *The Life of Jesus*: the Christ *of the tradition* stood or fell with the independent critical inquiry into the life of Jesus. And the outcome of the examination was that the dogma failed the test.

That result simply left Strauss as an apostle of the failure of all mediation between historical-critical *Wissenschaft* and traditional *Glaube*. As a 'modern man' he could now turn in one of two directions. He could either declare that in the upshot faith simply collapses or he could make the plea that faith can and must be completely reinterpreted by cutting the christological Idea loose from the claim that it can be and has been fully embodied in a particular historical individual. In *The Life of Jesus* Strauss, still adhering to the Hegelian scheme for which the notion of divine-human immanence as incarnation and reconciliation was the goal of truth marching to its own apogee, adopted the latter course. After all, the vindication of the Idea by means of the radical revision of traditional christology had been the aim of the book right from its inception in 1832. And so he now had to follow up the *historical* critique of the historical Jesus and of traditional christology depending on him, with a *philosophical* critique of the christological Idea and of its history. Its positive speculative transformation would come naturally in the wake of this two-fold critical negation. But first he would show that just as historical criticism had demonstrated that *this* particular individual was not the full embodiment of the christological Idea, so the history of the Idea itself demonstrated the collapse of its conceptual tie to *any* particular historical person.

And so the concluding dissertation of *The Life of Jesus* is the dogmatic or philosophical criticism which readies faith for final reinterpretation. It is a faith no longer mediated by the 'positivity' of necessary and specific historical facts, or rather it is a faith 'truly mediated' by being turned into '*Wissenschaft*'.[24] From the very beginning of the orthodox system the idea of two full but undivided natures, divine and human, constituted as one particular person, contained irresolvable tensions which modern thought has gradually articulated. The same was true of the corollary, viz., that this person's act, at once divinely judging and forgiving and humanly sinless and propitiating, had substituted itself for all human guilt and sin. The more explicit the qualities, divine and human, in the exchange of which the personal unity of Christ is constituted (e.g., divine eternity on the one hand, human mortality and temporal limitedness on the other), the more one recognizes that the exchange is purely verbal. It is actually inconceivable and therefore the particularized personal unity likewise. Again, moral transgressions simply cannot be conceived after the fashion of 'transmissible obligations' that would allow one person to stand in and make payments for another (*LJ* § 146, pp. 764, 766). And so on.

One may resolve the contradiction in modern Rationalist fashion by cutting the Gordian knot and turning Christ simply into an ambassador from God, a most distinguished man. But then, while one has indeed removed the stumbling block for modern *Wissenschaft*, one has also *forsaken* rather than *reinterpreted* the *Glaube* whose very essence it is to have Christ as its object. By contrast, the most serious attempt at mediation has been the 'eclectic' christology of Schleiermacher who tried to transcend Rationalist and rational Supernaturalist views at the same time. Schleiermacher claimed that being Christian involves a uniquely *religious* grasp of Jesus, rather than the kind of propositional and historical knowledge of him on which Rationalists and Supernaturalists alike had insisted. To this distinctive religious awareness, Jesus is present as a fully natural individual and yet one whose God-consciousness is so pure and unimpeded as to be absolutely unique and to constitute a veritable being of God in him – the full, unsurpassable particularization of the divine-human Archetype. Schleiermacher has to look for that particularized unity in the inmost centre of Jesus's consciousness. But, says Strauss, what we find in Jesus's as in any other person's hidden core is in fact the same ideal of humanity which we discover whenever we go past the outward manifestations of any individual that actually constitute his true historicity and move to his supposed hidden centre: it is universal, not particular. There is therefore no reason why the Christian community's experience of the Archetype which Schleiermacher postulated should not be adequately accounted for by Jesus's particularity having *occasioned* rather than fully *embodied* it. Schleiermacher to the contrary, the religious awareness of Christians does not presuppose the necessity of the full particular embodiment of the Archetype. Despite himself, Schleiermacher's portrayal of Jesus remains an ideal construction. His Christ is an ideal and universal and not an historical Christ.

If Schleiermacher's is a failure in traditional restatement, Kant's is one in modern reinterpretation. To him, the idea of particular incarnation serves simply as a symbol for the perpetual challenge of a moral faith, in which individuals seek to order their lives in accord with an eternal rational-moral idea or archetype. This theory deliberately adopts what Schleiermacher would seek unsuccessfully to avoid – an ongoing dichotomy and tension between the moral 'ought' and the real human 'is'. For Kant, perpetual non-incarnation is at once the rejoinder to and the reinterpretation of the traditional *Glaube*'s particular incarnation. It may be the former, but it cannot be the latter for the Hegelian Strauss, for whom ideality and historical reality are, on the contrary, one and reconciled, and for whom this Hegelian message is at once the very heart of philosophical *Wissenschaft* and of Christian *Glaube*. He agrees with Kant's plea for a radical reinterpretation rather than mediating restatement of traditional Christology, but he is bound to reject Kant's particular proposal for it. But even though the unity of ideality and reality must be affirmed against the Kantian's enduring dichotomy, it cannot of course be turned back into the Church's traditional 'unscientific' unity in one individual, not even in the modern garb Schleiermacher supplied. The only option left that will do justice to both *Glaube* and historical and philosophical *Wissenschaft* is that *all* of human history in the cumulative interaction of all its particulars – in effect Hegel's 'concrete universal' – is the incarnate Christ. The Idea, not wont to pour its fullness into one exemplar, spreads its riches only in the full manifold of mutually positing and transcending individual examples. Whether or not Hegel himself would have had to endorse this result, announced in his name, is a matter which has been debated ever since. Certain it is that he would never have stated it so flat-footedly.

For the residue that Strauss had salvaged from what he considered all but total historical and philosophical wreckage is by common consent a feeble affair, the paltry yield of identifying the idea of the genus *homo sapiens* as the actual, demythologized subject 'Christ'. It is to Strauss's honor that he did not stay long with this proposal. His genius was the criticism, not the construction of theology.

Small wonder that by 1844 Karl Marx, surveying the condition of the religious superstructure of German culture with the impact of this book and Feuerbach's works in mind, could say: 'For Germany, the criticism of religion is in the main complete, and the criticism of religion is the premise of all criticism.'[25] Whether or not the story of humankind is one of enslavement and subsequent delivery or of alienation and reconciliation, the Christian version of it, viz., that the person and fate of Jesus of Nazareth are indispensable to the redeeming sequence, had received a powerful, perhaps lethal blow at the hands of a new naturalistic or realistic historical outlook.

As for the book's theological impact, Albert Schweitzer, writing at the turn of the century, summed it up in two stages, each deeply disturbing in its own day:

> Strauss's *Life of Jesus* has a different significance for modern theology from that which it had for his contemporaries. For them it was the work which made an end of miracle as a matter of historical belief, and gave the mythological explanation its due.
>
> We, however, find in it also an historical aspect of a positive character, inasmuch as the historic personality which emerges from the mist of myth is a Jewish claimant of the Messiahship, whose world of thought is purely eschatological.[26]

Schweitzer was right, but that also was not the end of the story. For the history of modern theology, at once moving on and yet doubling back on itself, went on to a third topic, more nearly akin to the first than the second on the agenda Strauss set.

In regard to the first stage, the mythical point of view has done its negative work. The supernaturalist view of miracle, in which the truth of the dogma of Christ is tied to the factuality of the 'absolute' miracles of the New Testament, has all but disappeared from the arsenal of explanatory tools used by all but the most conservative students of the Bible. On the other hand, 'myth' has played an increasingly important and in many respects un-Straussian part in the interpretation of religious phenomena across a spectrum of literary, anthropological and theological commentaries. In the welter of opinions which place myth all the way from covertly existential language to the disclosure of worlds of metaphor, to permanent sets of narrative functions, to a binary linguistic code for cultural kinship rules, the only sure thing is that Strauss's positive Hegelian understanding of the concept as a lower-level, undeveloped idea is out of fashion. Strauss had largely confined his actual, critical use of 'myth' to the distinction between fact and fiction, and he was – probably for historical reasons – not in a position to exploit it as a potentially rich hermeneutical device. Had he done so, some critics claim, he might have developed a more profound appreciation of the Gospels as literary products, and this in turn would have given far richer texture to his understanding of the relation between the historical criticism and the interpretative penetration of the texts. In any event, there is agreement that as a pioneer he used the concept too broadly, unrefinedly, and indiscriminately. But as a critical instrument against the Supernaturalist or 'absolute' view of miracle, 'myth' remains a decisive weapon which no one used more effectively than Strauss. As such it also remains a powerful challenge to every endeavor to restate a christology relying on the unique, final and unsurpassable religious status of Jesus of Nazareth.

Concerning Schweitzer's second or eschatological challenge in *The Life of Jesus*, historians have not only long since come to doubt that Jesus himself claimed to be the Messiah or that he identified himself with the future Son of Man, but even when they have said that he did so they either cast suspicion on picturing his views fully in terms of 'consistent eschatology', or else believed that this picture in its time-conditionedness is capable of interpretation into other modes, without losing its eschatological force. With the exception of a few devoted souls like Martin Werner, the consistent eschatological view set forth by Reimarus, Strauss and Schweitzer, the view of Jesus as a great deluded man has found a smaller latter-day echo than one might have expected.

And yet its influence has not been negligible – at least indirectly. For one thing, Strauss's rejection of the Gospel of John as historical source for Jesus's life and outlook came to be the majority opinion of critics after him, sustained as it was by the far more careful and incisive literary and historical investigations that F. C. Baur undertook independently about the same time and published a few years later.[27] This at one stroke robbed historians and theologians of the one source which some of them – e.g., Schleiermacher, Karl Hase – had regarded as the most nearly continuous, complete and historically reliable portrait of Jesus, the picture apparently allowing the most intimate inside knowledge of him, the smallest degree of crude, miraculous and eschatological supernaturalism and the most spiritual interpretation of Jesus's identity and mission. The emergence of a New Testament portrait of Jesus as a radically futuristic, supernatural Messiah could never be banished with complete effectiveness once the mystical, incarnate Word of the Fourth Gospel was no longer available for strongly countervailing historical pressure.

In addition to this, the resemblance of successive critics' portraits of Jesus to their own or their era's ideal personality has become notorious. This feature was enhanced by the fact that, as Peter Hodgson rightly observes,[28] the ironic result of Strauss's negative christological yield from his historical labours was that the subsequent commentators, who had to engage in the same quest in order to contradict his historical portrait, found themselves forced to locate the hinge between historical claims and a theological christology in Jesus's teaching and outlook rather than in his acts or his (doubtless unreconstructable) life sequence. As long as that remains the case, the picture of an eschatological hero and a genius strange to ordinary expectations will always remain a powerful antidote to a reading which finally posits Jesus's identity in a thin and hypothetical conjunction between his winnowed-out, supposedly authentic sayings and his 'self- and world-understanding'. The eschatological reconstruction will doubtless have at least as much impact on religiously or even morally and aesthetically inclined imaginations as this and similar options, which then often go on to identify Jesus first with his message, then with the 'kerygma' in which he is proclaimed and finally with the reception of the message – all of this in a farrago of magnificent terminology, at once highly technical and loftily rhetorical.

But whatever the negative or positive outcome of the consistent eschatological view, Strauss's persistent presence on the theological scene has led to a third issue or stage, parallel to the argument about myth rather than that about eschatology. Revivified by powerful early-twentieth-century voices like that of Ernst Troeltsch, Strauss's *Life of Jesus* and his subsequent writings have forced to the forefront once again the relation between *Wissenschaft* and *Glaube*, specifically between 'the Jesus of history and the Christ of faith' – an expression he was among the first, if not the first, to use. It is a general methodological reconsideration of the powerful paradigmatic case Strauss had introduced with the category of myth in christology.

After the first world war, 'crisis' or 'dialectical' theology broke radically with liberal theology and its confident sense of affinity with historical scholarship. Now the issue of a theological method claiming a distinctive path to Christian 'truth' was reopened with a vengeance: Was it the case that a christocentric faith was simply totally external to and in that sense neither negatively nor positively related to the results of historical labour? Or was it, rather, that under the impact of a more open-textured method, historical investigation could find hermeneutical instruments to help it turn from its 'positivistic' path to a view of our relation to the past in which faith and historical method would supplement each other in a kind of kinship relation? Or was it, finally, that the judgments of faith and those of historical investigation were on a collision course, because it was impossible both to claim a basis for faith in historical fact and at the same time disallow the testing of its truth or falsity by historical science? In the latter view the problem was made all the worse by the covert reappearance of miracle as the fact claim, and also by the strange character of the sources which almost seem intended to yield no reliable factual information at all, and therefore no basis for the requisite confirmation of historical claims as astonishing as those of traditional christology.[29] But this set of issues and options is identical or at least very close to those that were at issue between Strauss and

Schleiermacher, once Strauss had decided to concentrate on testing the issues between faith and reason by focusing them on the direct contact between 'presuppositionless' historical *Wissenschaft* and Schleiermacher's mediating transformation of ecclesiastical *Glaube*. Van A. Harvey describes the results of the encounter of Troeltsch's views about historical method with Karl Barth's and Rudolf Bultmann's theology in the early 1920s as follows: they agreed with him that all events have to be explained in terms of their causal nexus, so that supernaturalistic modes of explanation have to be rejected. But they denied the implication Troeltsch (like Strauss before him) drew from this, 'that no event could fully manifest divine life'.[30] It was Schleiermacher's desire to say what Barth and Bultmann were in this view to say later (supposedly in utter rejection of Schleiermacher) that finally made Schleiermacher more important than Hegel for Strauss, once he had gained his basic historical-critical position, which was identical to that of Troeltsch.[31]

VI. Strauss and Schleiermacher

No later work by Strauss had the impact of *The Life of Jesus*. In 1840 and 1841 he published his *Glaubenslehre*, the last gasp of his Hegelianism. Unwilling to dissociate reason and religion completely, Strauss nevertheless now rejected their essential identification by Hegel. Under the influence of Feuerbach he moved in Schleiermacher's direction (as he was to acknowledge later) and said that 'representation', i.e., feeling and imagination as well as their conceptual embodiment in traditional ecclesiastical doctrines, constituted the content and not merely the external form of Christianity.[32] Increasingly, Schleiermacher stood out as the thinker who had posed the right issues, whereas Hegel and his school had simply invented an instrument for evading them from the outset. Schleiermacher thought that *Glaube* and *Wissenschaft* were heterogeneous but nevertheless in direct contact, so that they could be related in one of two and only two ways: either there would be warfare between them, which would turn faith into an anachronism, or they would reach an 'eternal accord' between them.[33] For Hegel, by contrast, their relation was always mediated by the common embrace of the speculative scheme which absorbed and neutralized all such sharp alternatives.

Between *The Life of Jesus* and the *Glaubenslehre* Strauss, under attack from every side, made some telling concessions to Schleiermacher and his school in the third edition of *The Life of Jesus*. He granted them the possibility that the Fourth Gospel might contain authentic material about the life, discourses and (therefore) the character of Jesus. He toned down his criticism of Schleiermacher's views on miracles. And while he never conceded that Jesus or any individual was the Archetype, he did now describe Jesus in those terms of unexcelled religious genius or perfect intensity of God-consciousness that Schleiermacher had applied to him. He drew the consequence that as a result Jesus's influence might indeed be universal and unsurpassed – in fact though of course not in principle.[34] He thus toned down the first edition's argument that Jesus's historical particularity was one with his outward manifestation and not with a supposedly unique, individual, inner core. And thereby he cautiously made room for a 'subjective' or individual historical etiology that ran counter to the first edition's historical (and to some extent Hegelian) emphasis on an 'objective' or cultural explanation of all historical connections.

By the time the fourth edition appeared, Strauss had returned to his previous, tougher stance. Nonetheless, the concessions had been a straw in the wind. After this he moved with increasingly greater ease – albeit for purposes of dissent – in an intellectual atmosphere that had affinities with Schleiermacher more than Hegel. After 1841, Hegelian thought form disappears together with its content.

Strauss was always persuaded that Schleiermacher had compromised both modern culture and Christian faith in his effort to relate them directly and harmoniously and thus provide a modern restatement rather than a radical revision of the latter. And yet Schleiermacher's restatement was sufficiently traditional that if one criticized it effectively one would also do away with the traditional christology. Schleiermacher's task had been to show the distinctiveness of each, *Wissenschaft* and *Glaube*, as well as their mutual correlation or reciprocity.[35]

In this connection *Wissenschaft* meant three things to Schleiermacher: (1) a semi-empiricist, semi-speculative theory of development in nature and culture, in which each novel stage is partially explicable as a synthesis of what precedes it and yet, being new, is partially unique and inexplicable; (2) philosophy, i.e. ideas ranged into conceptual order and connected by the procedure of dialectic, the result being in part genuine knowledge and in part speculation outstripping knowledge; (3) empirical and historical-critical procedure. In relation to the origins of Christianity this meant to Schleiermacher – just as it did to Strauss – the independent testing of the likelihood of specific religious and factual claims under the ordinary rules of evidence, viz., the uniformity of natural experience and the causal connections governing it.

In each of these three instances, both autonomy and reciprocity governed the relation between faith and *Wissenschaft*, but the balance between them was different in each case. In the first, reciprocity was most to the fore. Schleiermacher was persuaded that 'miracle' was an indispensable ingredient in Christian faith, especially in christology. If 'redemption by Jesus' – which constitutes the very essence of Christianity – is to be meaningful, Jesus must be an absolutely unique figure, one in whom God-consciousness is so unimpeded and sinless that it constitutes a 'veritable being of God in him'. He is therefore no mere prototype, distinguished from sinful humankind by degrees; instead he is differentiated from us in kind as the divine-human Archetype in unsurpassable historical-individual shape.[36] Yet Schleiermacher was equally persuaded that because the Redeemer is a fully historical individual, his being and presence are not to be explained as an exception to or rupture of the 'system of nature'.[37] He is not, as the Supernaturalists would have it, a direct divine interference in the causal nexus, but a genuinely new development within it. In order to affirm both claims at once, Schleiermacher proposed a notion of 'relative' in contrast to 'absolute' miracle.[38] In a famous throw-away line he said: 'If science must admit the possibility that even now matter conglomerates and begins to rotate in infinite space, then it can also concede a manifestation in the realm of spiritual life which we can similarly explain only as a new creation, as the pure beginning of a higher spiritual life development.'[39] In other words, 'relative' miracle was a way of conceiving Christ as a partially unaccountable and novel development in a cosmic process, in analogy to other natural facts as 'science' observes them. Such is the positive correlation which leaves faith not only 'unentangled' with science but creates conceptual reciprocity (or was it perhaps identity?) between the two. 'Relative' miracle in this context obviously refers not to specific reported events in the Gospels but to the conception of the person of Jesus as such. Faith is autonomous because Jesus is unique, yet uniqueness is itself a category establishing reciprocity. Clearly, the latter is the more important explanatory device for this sense of *Wissenschaft* in relation to faith.

In regard to philosophy, the autonomy of faith is more significant than reciprocity. Here theology as 'science' is actually simply the second-order conceptual ordering of the non- or pre-conceptual contents of immediate self-consciousness, 'feeling' or faith. It is sharply distinguished from the knowledge in which we grasp empirical data and ideas – the province of the ordering activity of philosophy. The complete heterogeneity of the two capacities guarantees their mutual autonomy. Still, reciprocity or correlation between them is not completely lacking. Not only does theology make formal (though not material) use of philosophy, but Schleiermacher, who participated in the general Idealist 'turn to the subject', was persuaded of the harmony of the unitary self within which faith and knowledge are distinguished. He said that his dogmatics and his philosophy always 'temper and more and more approach one another . . . understanding and feeling . . . touch one another and form one galvanic column'.[40]

Strauss addressed himself to these two uses of *Wissenschaft* in relation to *faith* in *The Life of Jesus* and the *Glaubenslehre*, leaving the third (empirical) sense for discussion until the 1860s, when he returned to theology with the strong conviction that the empirical or historical-critical sense of *Wissenschaft* was the most important, and that Schleiermacher's endeavour to reconcile it with faith demonstrated the hopelessness of the project. Broadly speaking, he criticized Schleiermacher's christology conceptually in his earlier writings and historically in his later work, after he had rid himself of the Hegelian incubus – a process in which Schleiermacher's thought played a large part.

In the earlier writings Strauss analysed Schleiermacher's 'relative' miracle as a conceptual means for interpreting the person and religious significance of Jesus. He argued that Schleiermacher really claims an absolute rather than a relative miracle, for everywhere else except in his Christ 'we find the ideal realized . . . only in an entire cycle of appearances, which reciprocally complete each other'.[41] Such analogies as that of the conglomeration of new matter in space are totally misleading, not only because all such developments are completely natural once we are past an absolute beginning point, but also because they never posit the perfection of the development at the beginning, as ecclesiastical christology does. Even one miracle, that of Christ's immediate divine origin, goes counter to the laws of nature and rationality – even if it does not involve the instrumentality of a virgin birth for Schleiermacher. Moreover, it goes counter to uniform experience even if immediately thereafter Christ is subject to an entirely natural development. But in fact, though Schleiermacher claims natural development for him he describes the opposite. At every point Christ's God-consciousness is pure and unimpeded, which is to say his lower or sensate consciousness is perfectly receptive to it. But where there is no struggle and no imperfection, where duty and inclination coincide completely, we have the Ideal or Archetypal – and not a human individual. The idea of the archetypal individual is inconceivable or impossible on philosophical grounds, whether derived from speculation or experience.

Not only is the idea *impossible* but the appeal to the *necessity* of a reality corresponding to it is specious. For the requirement of faith, viz., that we account for our experience of the change from consciousness of sin to consciousness of redemption, does not need the appeal to the full individual existence of archetypal God-consciousness. It is not true, as Schleiermacher held, that because of its sinfulness humanity could not conceive an ideal of absolute perfection which it would then project onto the historical Christ, whose relative excellence had occasioned it in the first place. The very possibility of the conception of imperfection or sin necessitates a general conception of its opposite, and while the concrete image of the perfect projected by any individual or age cannot be without blemish, it is serviceable for the purpose even for later generations as long as they can modify it in their own best light.[42] No such miracle as Schleiermacher posited, even if *per impossible* it was relative rather than absolute, is necessary to account for the state of affairs for which he thought it was needed.

Strauss had already come to this conviction in his student days, under the influence of his teacher F. C. Baur who had employed his own version of the argument against possibility against Schleiermacher, saying that on his own grounds he could be convicted of trying to combine the uncombinable. Baur argued that Schleiermacher was philosophically inconsistent in trying to unite a Christ who is 'an idea which forms a stage of development belonging properly to the human consciousness' with the real, historical Christ. The ideal or archetypal Christ was appropriate to the basic form of theological propositions which, for Schleiermacher, describes inner human states. The historical Christ could be introduced properly only if propositions describing the constitution of the world (including any historical instance within it such as the historical Jesus external to religious consciousness) were independent of the previous form. But Schleiermacher makes this kind of proposition a function of the first, and the result for christology is that the historicity of Christ is left either meaningless or else disconnected from his identity.[43] As late as 1865 Strauss approvingly quotes Baur in the same vein, repeating the argument both of them had reiterated over and over again.[44]

But by the 1860s the emphasis of Strauss's criticism of Schleiermacher had actually shifted drastically. He now addressed himself to the third sense in which Schleiermacher used *Wissenschaft*, viz., as empirical or critical-historical procedure. The concept of the archetypal individual, its possibility or conceivability are no longer examined in their own right but only for their (negative) bearing on a critical use of the sources.[45] In regard to this third sense of 'science' also Schleiermacher wanted to maintain both autonomy and reciprocity between faith and science. Autonomy in this case means two things: first, that the ground of faith in Christ is not the claims of the written sources to historical reliability but the religiously inescapable, necessary relation of the believer's consciousness of redemption to Christ as the founder of the Church, the community of redemption; second, that the religious view of Christ, viz., of his archetypal and sinless God-consciousness, may be applied to interpret the New Testament portrait of Jesus.

But if a scientifically honest critical and reconstructive reading of the Gospels – especially of the Fourth Gospel, to Schleiermacher the most trustworthy of our four sources – does not give at least some degree of independent support to the deliverances of religious consciousness, the latter stand in mid-air. If it seems likely that Jesus was not the kind of person who can be regarded as the perfect embodiment of the Archetype, or if the record seems altogether unreliable in reporting his external deeds and manifestations, then our faith may be autonomous and certain but it cannot be a faith in Jesus. Here precisely, and here more than anywhere else, the 'reciprocity condition' has to be met. 'Scientific' exegesis of the New Testament may not be able to unveil for us the mysterious innermost kernel of the archetypal individual; it certainly cannot awaken faith in him. But if such a reading, using the sources for the most credible reconstruction, reveals only an ordinary, perhaps exemplary but in any case time-conditioned individual, or if it indicates that the confession of Jesus's redeeming power is a fantasy of the succeeding generations which has no factual basis in his person and deeds and in the faith of those who knew him, then the attachment of autonomous religious consciousness to this figure is simply an error. It would then be a projection based on 'nothing' rather than fact, as Schleiermacher put it.[46]

In this connection Schleiermacher tries to bolster reciprocity by reintroducing 'relative' miracle, this time not as principle of novelty but as an argument for the credibility of specific, contingent events of an unusual sort connected with the unique Redeemer's appearance. Schleiermacher proposed an extended view of what may be regarded as 'natural' and therefore possible. He argued that we do not as yet have in hand a general explanation of the way spiritual activities connect with natural phenomena. And yet such connections or influences of the former on the latter are well known, especially in moments of drastic spiritual intensity. While they are unusual, they do not constitute a break with the principle of natural uniformity and explanation.[47] It was Schleiermacher's way of safeguarding the historicity of at least some of the healing miracles and providing backing for his claims to the authenticity of the Fourth Gospel.

In Strauss's view, Schleiermacher's direct, mediating efforts between christological *Glaube* and *Wissenschaft* were virtually bound to make Schleiermacher lecture on the life of Jesus. And the result was bound to be what it was: he had to substantiate a modified supernaturalist faith with the results of a rationalist historical reading. So far as Strauss was concerned, it was the worst of both worlds – the conjunction of reduced christology with hobbled scientific exegesis. In his earlier years he had asserted the failure of Schleiermacher's correlation of christological faith with modern science by arguing against Schleiermacher's claims to the conceptual and real *possibility* and the religious *necessity* of the doctrine. Now Strauss adds Schleiermacher's argument from historical *actuality* to the list of his failures. The demand for *compatibility* between faith and science governs (and has to govern) Schleiermacher's reading of the personal description of Jesus and the events of his life fully as much as the *independence* of science from faith. But if it governs as much, it in fact governs completely. And then all the features of the dogmatic conception of Christ, based on the supposed need of Christian experience, come floating in as hermeneutical tools for interpreting the data of the Gospel portrait. Schleiermacher discovers the 'relatively miraculous' individual congenial to modern faith in the New Testament. On the one hand he must be able to exclude – as something not held either by the writers or Jesus himself – the absolutely miraculous, supernaturalist view of him. On the other, he must also be able to show the historical credibility of the qualitative uniqueness of Jesus, and therefore its compatibility with natural development. Strauss points out that

Statements that this or that 'is not harmonizable with our presuppositions about Christ,' or that 'he could be what he is in our faith only if . . .' and so on . . . are repeated endlessly as reasons why this or that passage is to be interpreted in a certain way, or why this relation or this action of Jesus is to be understood in this way.[48]

First, Schleiermacher's christology governs his evaluation of the authenticity of the sources. It is most compatible with the theological portrait of Christ in the Fourth Gospel, and it rather than the synoptic gospels seems to him the most authentic eyewitness source.[49] Strauss, in agreement with earlier work by K. G. Bretschneider, came to the exactly opposite conclusion and it had formed an important ingredient in his argument about the mythical character of the Gospels. He showed that the evangelist had put his own language in the mouths of John the Baptist and Jesus, and that the utter contrast between the farewell discourses in John and the synoptic Gospels' description of the scene in the Garden of Gethsemane clearly point to a further advanced and more deliberate formation of legend in John.[50]

Second, Schleiermacher's dogmatic assumption controls not only his view of the authenticity of the sources but his exegesis of their contents. At point after point Strauss shows the connection and its fruits. Two examples must suffice. Schleiermacher's Christ is sinless and his God-consciousness, while developing naturally, is in unhindered accord with the perfection appropriate to each stage of his career. And so when Schleiermacher, who had no theological qualms about being indifferent to the factual or fictional status of the birth and infancy stories, comes to the story of the twelve year old Jesus in the Temple (Luke 2:41ff) 'all doubts must suddenly cease' and it becomes the 'naive expression of a scene which is highly probable', whereas to Strauss of course it is typical of all hero-stories, for which 'the rose is fragrant already in the bud'.[51] Again, the Fourth Gospel's self-description of Jesus is closest to Schleiermacher's archetypal person who does nothing of himself but everything from his Father, i.e., from his perfect God-consciousness. To Schleiermacher, Jesus's speeches in this Gospel are his authentic discourses. However, it is religiously and historically credible only if its view of Jesus remains at the 'relatively' miraculous level of the archetypal individual, not to be turned into the absolutely miraculous, supernatural (and docetic) Christ anathema to modern *Wissenschaft*. But the prologue of the Gospel seems to imply the latter, with its apparent imputation to Jesus not only of pre-existence but of conscious remembrance of it in his earthly life. That interpretation is bolstered by such sayings as, 'And now, O Father, glorify thou me with thine own self with the glory which I had with thee before the world was made' (John 17:5). So in order to guard the authenticity of the Gospel and its congruence with his own theology, Schleiermacher has to resort to the disciples' silence about Jesus's pre-existence as evidence that he never mentioned it to them and therefore did not hold it. Says Strauss:

the silence is quite natural if we see the Evangelist as the author of Christ's discourses, for to him only this was dogmatically certain – that there must have *been* such a pre-existence . . . If one does not want to give up the Fourth Gospel, and at the same time does not accept its fundamental doctrine, one must distort it.[52]

In this manner Schleiermacher pursues his exegetical path until he comes to the end of Jesus's life. Religiously and dogmatically, it does not matter to him whether Jesus died and whether he rose again. But it is clearly important, if the trustworthiness of the narratives counts at all. And if they are totally false here, what else in them can be regarded as historical fact? So the matter, directly not important for religion, becomes immediately if indirectly significant again, for Schleiermacher has agreed that it is religiously important that faith in Christ originated in his having been an historical, reliably describable fact. And if there is a correlation between faith and fact here – if the character of what happened or did not happen here counts for or against the faith, then there must also be (to a modern thinker like

Schleiermacher) compatibility between faith and a scientific-historical perspective on the facts. However, to apply the 'extended' view of the natural to these final events of Jesus's life (unlike the case of some of the healing miracles) would be to stretch it beyond the breaking point. Recourse to 'relative miracle' will not do at this point: Schleiermacher has to choose between absolute miracle and natural explanation if he wishes to maintain the correlation between faith and the factual basis of the accounts. But if he wishes to preserve the natural assumptions underlying scientific study of history, he has to choose between a natural occurrence and illusion on the part of Jesus's followers to account for the belief in Jesus's resurrection and ascension. From among these three options he chooses a natural occurrence for explanation: a deep coma followed by withdrawal and natural death.

The factual basis of the accounts has been saved; the contact between Jesus and his disciples after the crucifixion is no fable. But here the Rationalist character of Schleiermacher's exegesis is most evident in Strauss's view of the matter, and so – at least by implication – is the artificiality, the untenability of his whole exegetical procedure and of the claim to independent scientific inquiry into the sources. For the sake of this supposedly historical basis of the accounts and the supposedly relatively supernatural character of the portrait of Jesus in them (especially the Fourth Gospel), Schleiermacher has been forced into a Rationalist exegesis of clearly absolutely supernatural texts.

From both sides the pressure against the coherence of Schleiermacher's position is overwhelming. The *texts*, indeed especially the Fourth Gospel, clearly imply in Strauss's reading of them not only an Archetype but much more, a supernatural Redeemer who is more nearly divine than human. Schleiermacher's exegesis constantly struggles against this clear implication, but he carries little conviction. His own Christ, having paid tribute to modernity, has none of the powerfully miraculous redemptive character of the traditional figure of the Gospels and Church history; and yet, having paid tribute to orthodoxy, he retains the docetic quality of the latter's Christ and cannot meet modernity's demand for a natural man, Jesus of Nazareth, emerging from the sources, whose actions and outlook have a natural explanation.

The pressure from the side of the character of *historical inquiry* is obviously equally great: Schleiermacher has neither taken the texts unvarnished, nor has he done the opposite, i.e., estimate their possible truth value on a completely natural historical basis. The hybrid that is relative miracle or the relatively supernatural closes both paths and forces him to adopt a course that is critically-historically really non-existent.

Schleiermacher in his argument from actuality had once again posed the right issue in Strauss's eyes: a direct, philosophically unmediated encounter or reciprocity between the ecclesiastical faith in Christ and the modern, autonomous scientific inquiry into the reliability of the accounts about him. His answer in this instance fared no better in Strauss's view than when he correlated this faith with science in its other senses. Indeed, in this instance the case was worse, because response to it involved not speculative argument but appeal to consistency in agreed-upon empirical procedure.[53] Strauss did not have to resort to his own far simpler and more consistent mythical explanation of the supernatural texts to show the difficulties in Schleiermacher's views.

Starting from Schleiermacher's formulation of the issue and his failure to provide a satisfactory answer, Strauss stated a negative answer to it in exactly the same way as Ernst Troeltsch would two generations later: a person cannot at one and the same time be an absolutely unique manifestation of the divine life and fully a part of the nexus of history as are other human beings.

Schleiermacher's *The Christian Faith* has really but a single dogma, that concerning the person of Christ . . . Schleiermacher's Christology is a last attempt to make the churchly Christ acceptable to the modern world . . . The illusion, which is supported primarily by Schleiermacher's explanations, that Jesus could have been a man in the full sense and still as a single person stand above the whole of humanity, is the chain which still blocks the harbor of Christian theology against the open sea of rational science.[54]

The dilemma is at least as old as the fourth- and fifth-century endeavor to describe both the indivisible unity of the person of Christ and the presence of two unabridged natures, divine and human, in him. The modern shift in categories from those of substantialist personhood to self-conscious, inward and at the same time historical personality gave the problem a new urgency and changed its expression. By general agreement it became most urgent when christocentric faith was to be reconciled with the assumptions and judgments of modern historical inquiry. The rise of a metaphysics of divine-human immanence; the displacement of metaphysical by a functional christology, for which 'Christ' need not have a divine *nature* ascribed to him but only something like the archetypal status of his human God-consciousness sufficient to allow him to function divinely toward the rest of us; the all but universal nineteenth- and twentieth-century agreement in the West that religious discourse is a distinct mode that does not brook identification with 'ordinary' or 'objectifying' talk – all of these changes have made for a reconceptualization of the problem, but they have neither eliminated it nor turned it into a recognizably different issue.

The real difference between the ancient and the modern christological problem seems to emerge in another way: what was for the ancient theologians basically an endeavour to provide as good a conceptual description as possible of their faith has become in modern days an endeavour to argue not only its internal coherence but its conceivability – its very possibility. This is not necessarily to fault what has happened but to point out a difference that is doubtless largely due to a perceived difference in the basic nature of the theological task required in that day and this. And no doubt phrases like 'the challenge of modern secularity' will be invoked to explain this recent, more strenuous demand placed on the shoulders of theologians to explain what is involved in belief in God and Christ. But in that case it is all-important to point out that if Schleiermacher was the progenitor of most recent attempts to state as well as meet that challenge from within the theological guild, Strauss and Troeltsch bear witness that the agenda he set or that the times set for him remains unfinished, because at the very least the issue has received no resolution that is satisfactory either from a theological or a secular point of view.

Perhaps Schleiermacher set forth the wrong issue and he – and therefore much of theological modernity – conceived the theological task wrongly and started a misplaced argument. Perhaps the issue was right but the description (by all parties to the debate) of 'modern thought', 'science', 'historicity', 'factuality', etc., was all too slavishly obedient to a nineteenth-century current of thought that confused itself with eternal verity on these and related large and difficult ideas. Perhaps the issue was right but such drastic, almost exclusive theological concentration on christology was wrong, for perhaps to identify the fate of theology with that of a full, unreduced or unrevised christology is only to doom them both together. Perhaps the argument was – and is – a matter of continuing 'belatedness' on a minor scale – a tempest in a bourgeois and increasingly shrinking academic teapot. But short of that option, one has to say that something like Schleiermacher's posing of the issue between theological method and *Wissenschaft* – and Strauss's and Troeltsch's iconoclastic answer to it – keeps emerging.

Notes

1 'On the Proof from Spirit and Power', in *Lessing's Theological Writings*, transl. Henry Chadwick (Stanford, 1967), p. 53.
2 Kant, *Religion Within the Limits of Reason Alone*, transl. Theodore M. Greene and Hoyt H. Hudson (New York, 1960), pp. 56f.
3 Kant, *The Critique of Pure Reason*, transl. Norman Kemp Smith (London, 1963), pp. 486f.

4 *Das Leben Jesu kritisch bearbeitet*. All quotations are from George Eliot's translation of the fourth edition, edited by Peter C. Hodgson (Philadelphia, 1972), and will be given in parentheses in the text with the abbreviation *LJ*.

5 Marilyn Chapin Massey, 'The literature of Young Germany and D. F. Strauss's *Life of Jesus*', *The Journal of Religion* 59, no. 3 (July 1979), 298–323.

6 *Die christliche Glaubenslehre in ihrer geschichtlichen Entwicklung und im Kampfe mit der modernen Wissenschaft* (2 vols., Tübingen & Stuttgart, 1840 and 1841). Hereafter cited as *Glaubenslehre*.

7 *Das Leben Jesu für das deutsche Volk bearbeitet* (Leipzig, 1864).

8 *Der Christus des Glaubens und der Jesus der Geschichte. Eine Kritik des Schleiermacher'schen Lebens Jesu*. All quotations from this book are from *The Christ of Faith and the Jesus of History. A Critique of Schleiermacher's Life of Jesus*, transl. Leander E. Keck (Philadelphia, 1977) and will be abbreviated *CFJH*.

9 *Der alte und der neue Glaube, Ein Bekenntnis* (Leipzig, 1872).

10 See *Ausgewählte Briefe von David Friedrich Strauss*, ed. Eduard Zeller (Bonn, 1895), pp. 12–14. The sketch of a plan for *The Life of Jesus* is contained in a letter which Strauss sent to his friend Christian Märklin on 6 February 1832. The letter is reprinted in full in Jörg F. Sandberger, *David Friedrich Strauss als theologischer Hegelianer* (Göttingen, 1972), pp. 192–9. For a sketch of the larger plan for a Hegelian dogmatics see *Briefe von David Friedrich Strauss an L. Georgii*, ed. H. Maier (Tübingen, 1912), p. 4; cf. also Strauss, *Streitschriften zur Vertheidigung meiner Schrift über das Leben Jesu und zur Charakteristik der gegenwärtigen Theologie* (Tübingen, 1837), 3 Heft, p. 59. This work will be cited hereafter as *Streitschriften*.

11 Cf. *Glaubenslehre* 1, §§ 3–5; *Zwei friedliche Blätter* (Altona, 1839), pp. xv–xxxiii.

12 *Glaubenslehre* 1, § 48, pp. 656ff.

13 *Ausgewählte Briefe*, p. 183, letter to Märklin, 22 July 1846.

14 *Phänomenologie des Geistes*, ed. J. Hoffmeister (Hamburg, 1952), p. 19.

15 *Vorlesungen über die Philosophie der Religion*, vol. 2, *Sämtliche Werke*, Jubiläumsausgabe, ed. H. Glockner (Stuttgart, 1959), vol. 16, p. 353; cf. *The Christian Religion* (Pt. III of *Lectures on the Philosophy of Religion*), transl. Peter C. Hodgson (Missoula, Montana, 1979), p. 292: 'Sustained by philosophy, religion receives its justification from thinking consciousness.'

16 *Enzyklopädie der philosophischen Wissenschaften im Grandrisse*, ed. F. Nicolin and O. Pöggeler (Hamburg, 1959), § 573, p. 461.

17 *Streitschriften*, 3, p. 58.

18 *Ibid.*, pp. 58, 68ff.

19 *Ibid.*, pp. 76–94; cf. C. Hartlich and W. Sachs, *Der Ursprung des Mythosbegriffes in der modernen Bibelwissenschaft* (Tübingen, 1952), pp. 122–34.

20 Hartlich and Sachs, *Der Ursprung*, ch. III *passim*; *LJ*, §§ 8–12.

21 F. C. Baur, *Kritische Untersuchungen über die kanonischen Evangelien, ihr Verhältniss zu einander, ihren Charakter und Ursprung* (Tübingen, 1847) p. 43.

22 A. Schweitzer, *The Quest of the Historical Jesus. A Critical Study of its Progress from Reimarus to Wrede*, transl. W. Montgomery (New York, 1956), p. 90.

23 See *LJ*, p. 656. Peter Hodgson believes that Strauss was firm in this assumption (editor's introduction to *LJ*, p. xxxiii and editorial note, p. 794), but Schweitzer (*Quest of the Historical Jesus*, pp. 93ff) thinks that Strauss only claimed that it was likely. Strauss was a very cautious radical.

24 *LJ*, p. 758. I have revised the translation.

25 Introduction to 'Contribution to the Critique of Hegel's Philosophy of Right', in *Marx and Engels on Religion*, introd. by Reinhold Niebuhr (New York, 1964), p. 41.

26 Schweitzer, *op. cit.* p. 95.

27 Baur, *op. cit.* pp. 77–389.

28 Editor's introduction to *LJ*, pp. xxxiif.

29 See Van A. Harvey, *The Historian and the Believer. The Morality of Historical Knowledge and Christian Belief* (New York, 1966), p. 18, ch. V *passim*. In highly oversimplified fashion, the first of these positions is that of Rudolf Bultmann; the second is that of the 'new quest' or 'word event' school in hermeneutics, history and christology, most characteristically set forth in J. M. Robinson, *A New Quest of the Historical Jesus* (Naperville, Ill., 1959); the third is that of Van A. Harvey, *The Historian and the Believer*, which is also the most incisive analysis of the *status quaestionis* of the topic.

30 Harvey, *op. cit.* p. 30.

31 For a typical expression of Troeltsch's frequently repeated views on this matter, see 'Über historische und dogmatische Methode in der Theologie', *Gesammelte Schriften*, vol. 2 (Tübingen, 1913), pp. 729–53.

32 See *Glaubenslehre* 1, § 2, p. 22; cf. 'Die Halben and die Ganzen' (1865), *Gesammelte Schriften*, vol. 5 (Bonn, 1877), pp. 176f, 181f.

33 *2. Sendschreiben an Dr. Lücke, Schleiermacher's sämmtliche Werke*, 1. Abtheilung, 2. Band (Berlin, 1836), pp. 612ff, 617f. Hereafter cited as *2. Sendschreiben*.

34 See *LJ*, pp. 798–802, concluding section of the third edition; cf. *Charakteristiken und Kritiken* (Leipzig, 1839), esp. p. 201; *Zwei friedliche Blätter passim*.

35 For a carefully reasoned description of this type of mediating theology, see John P. Clayton, *The Concept of Correlation: Paul Tillich and the Possibility of a Mediating Theology* (Berlin and New York, 1980), p. 42.

36 F. Schleiermacher, *The Christian Faith*, transl. H. R. Mackintosh and J. S. Stewart (Edinburgh, 1956), §§ 11, 93, 94, 98. Hereafter cited as *The Christian Faith*.

37 *Ibid.*, §§ 14, 47.

38 *Ibid.*, p. 72.

39 *2. Sendschreiben*, pp. 618f.

40 See W. Dilthey and L. Jonas, *Aus Schleiermachers Leben in Briefen* (2 vols., Berlin, 1858), vol. 2, pp. 343ff.

41 *LJ*, p. 770.

42 *LJ*, pp. 772f.

43 F. C. Baur, 'Anzeige der beiden academischen Schriften', *Tübinger Zeitschrift für Theologie*, I, 1828, pp. 220–64 (esp. 244–47); cf. *Die christliche Gnosis oder die christliche Religions-Philosophie in ihrer geschichtlichen Entwicklung* (Tübingen, 1835) pp. 637–56, esp. pp. 646–52, fn. 22.

44 *CFJH*, pp. 27f.

45 *CFJH*, ch. 2.

46 *2. Sendschreiben*, p. 613; Schleiermacher, *Das Leben Jesu. Vorlesungen an der Universität Berlin im Jahr 1832, Sämmtliche Werke*, 1. Abtheilung, 6. Band, ed. K. A. Rütenik (Berlin, 1864), pp. 23f.

47 *The Christian Faith*, § 47.3, pp. 183f.

48 *CFJH*, pp. 35f.

49 Schleiermacher, *Einleitung ins neue Testament, Sämmtliche Werke*, 1. Abtheilung, 8. Band, ed. G. Wolde (Berlin, 1845), §§ 80–4, pp. 315–44.

50 *LJ*, § 126, pp. 640–9; cf. W. G. Kümmel, *Das Neue Testament. Geschichte der Erforschung seiner Probleme* (Munich, 1970), pp. 147–55, for a summary report of Strauss's place in the development of New Testament study.

51 *CFJH*, pp. 56f.

52 *Ibid.*, pp. 61f.

53 *Ibid.*, pp. 159–69.

54 *Ibid.*, pp. 4f.

Bibliographical essay

1. The primary sources

There is no complete edition of Strauss's works. The reader who turns to the *Gesammelte Schriften von David Friedrich Strauss* (12 vols., Bonn, 1876–8), edited by Strauss's friend and literary executor Eduard Zeller, quickly discovers that it lacks not only most of Strauss's major works on theological topics but many important fugitive essays and reminiscences. A new edition of Strauss's works under the editorship of Walter Sachs is on the drawing board, but neither scope nor schedule has so far been announced.

The original editions of Strauss's two most important theological works have been reprinted by the Wissenschaftliche Buchgesellschaft, Darmstadt: *Das Leben Jesu, kritisch bearbeitet* (1st edition 1835 and 36, reprinted 1969) and *Die christliche Glaubenslehre in ihrer geschichtlichen Entwicklung und im Kampf mit der modernen Wissenschaft* (1st edition 1840 and 1841, reprinted 1973). In addition, *Der Christus des Glaubens und der Jesus der Geschichte. Eine Kritik des Schleiermacher'schen Lebens Jesu* was edited by Hans-Jürgen Geischer and reprinted as *Texte zur Kirchen-und Theologiegeschichte* No. 14 (Gütersloh, 1971).

For all other works the reader has to go back to the nineteenth century editions. It would be especially useful to collect together the essays Strauss wrote just before and after the publication of the more or less abortive third edition of *Das Leben Jesu* (1838–9), including large selections from *Streitschriften zur Verteidigung meiner Schrift über das Leben Jesu und zur Charakteristik der gegenwärtigen Theolgkogie* (3 parts Tübingen, 1837), *Zwei friedliche Blätter* (Altona, 1839), and *Charakteristiken und Kritiken* (Leipzig, 1839). Strauss's later reminiscences of his early thought may be found in *Christian Märklin. Ein Lebens-und Charakterbild aus der Gegenwart* (*Gesammelte Schriften*, vol. 10), and *Literarische Denk-würdigkeiten, Kleine Schriften*, ed. Eduard Zeller (Bonn, 1895).

Strauss was a superb letter writer and it would be of great importance for the history of nineteenth century theology to draw his widely scattered correspondence – some of it still unpublished in the Schiller National Museum in Marbach am Neckar – into a single edition. The best overview at present remains the very imperfect and all too discretely edited selection by Eduard Zeller, *Ausgewählte Briefe von David Friedrich Strauss* (Bonn, 1895). A complete list of his published correspondence may be found in Jörg Sandberger, *David Friedrich Strauss als theologischer Hegelianer* (Göttingen, 1972), pp. 235–7, and in Horton Harris, *David Friedrich Strauss and his Theology* (Cambridge, 1973), pp. 285–7, who for good measure adds a list of the locations of the most important manuscript letters.

2. Translations of Strauss's works into English

Strauss's major impact on the English-speaking public came through George Eliot's magnificent translation of the fourth edition of *The Life of Jesus, Critically Examined*. It was reissued in a major editing feat by Peter C. Hodgson (*Lives of Jesus Series*, Philadelphia, 1972). Hodgson's otherwise informative and skilfully drawn introductory essay is marred only by an uncritical reliance on the controversial views of Gotthold Müller, *Identität und Immanenz. Zur Genese der Theologie von David Friedrich Strauss* (Zurich, 1968, see below under (3)). *The Christ of Faith and the Jesus of History. A Critique of Schleiermacher's 'Life of Jesus'* has been translated and edited by Leander E. Keck, who also provided the volume with a skilful and broad-gauged introduction, (*Lives of Jesus Series*, Philadelphia, 1977). Marilyn Chapin Massey has translated and edited Strauss's crucial explicative commentary on the genesis and purpose of his *Life of Jesus*, part 3 of the *Streitschriften*, under the title *In Defence of my 'Life of Jesus' Against the Hegelians* (Hamden, Ct., 1983) and given it an able explanatory introduction. Two of Strauss's other major works (in addition to one or two shorter essays) were put into English in the nineteenth century: *A New Life of Jesus* (2 vols., London, 1865), the authorized translation of *Das Leben Jesu, für das deutsche Volk bearbeitet* (1864), and *The Old Faith and the New*, transl. by Mathilde Binder (London, 1874).

3. Secondary works in German

Among the many older standard works Theobald Ziegler, *David Friedrich Strauss* (Strassburg, 1908), continues to be the most valuable. No major works were written about Strauss from the middle of the first until well after the Second World War. It has been suggested that Karl Barth and his school (see his not wholly felicitous essay, 'David Friedrich Strauss als Theologe, 1839–1939' *Theologische Studien*, No. 6, Zurich, 1939), may have served to inhibit Strauss scholarship. After the war, the vexed relation between Strauss and his teacher F. C. Baur stimulated renewed interest in both men. Adolf Rapp and Ernst Barnikol wrote essays on both, the latter also publishing the rediscovered remaining correspondence between Baur and Strauss. But it is Strauss's understanding or misunderstanding of Hegel that has subsequently become the focus of interpretation of Strauss, both in works on Strauss himself and on Hegel and his school. Only the former can be considered here, and of these Gotthold Müller's (see above, section 2) is the pioneering work. It is valuable in many respects, particularly in his rediscovery of and commentary on Strauss's doctoral dissertation. However, his wholly genetic procedure, his omission of Strauss's profoundly Hegelian writing between 1831 and 1835, and his dubious assimilation of Strauss to the monistic-mystical Swabian tradition, are serious flaws in this focal work. In the wake of Müller's work it is often claimed that Strauss reduced monistically a whole series of crucial and paired Hegelian concepts: form/content; representation/concept; theology/philosophy; theism/pantheism. In each case, so it is supposed, Strauss converted the Hegelian dialectic of *aufheben*, i.e., the preservation of the first even as it is overcome in the second of the pair, into a pure dissolution or destruction of the first. The further implication is that the problem in this situation is Strauss's and not Hegel's, and that if only Strauss had been able to see the consistency and appropriateness of Hegel's dialectical balance, he would have realized that the central or right-wing interpretation of Hegel is not only the correct one but philosophically perfectly sound and feasible. In other words, Müller's thesis opened the door to a utilization of Strauss as a foil for Hegel interpretation, rather than as a thinker who posed a set of powerful theological problems in his own right. Strauss in this procedure becomes a means for the rehabilitation or repristination of that right-wing Hegelianism which, one would have thought, had mercifully disappeared for good beneath the waves in the wake of left-wing Hegelian and historicist critique.

A thorough and much more balanced estimate of Strauss's complex relation to Hegel during the crucial period between 1830 and 1837 is Jörg F. Sandberger, *David Friedrich Strauss als theologischer Hegelianer* (*Studien zur Theologie und Geistesgeschichte des neunzehnten Jahrhunderts*, No. 5, Göttingen, 1972). He rightly insists that Strauss did not succeed in combining historical criticism with speculative philosophy into one cohesive structure, and that, in the process, he laid (from a Hegelian point of view inordinate) stress on the dialectic between representation and concept, and gave a one-sided interpretation to 'representation'. He finally found Hegel's dialectical way of ordering these two categories through the movement of *Aufhebung* simply unpersuasive – although it took him considerable time to admit his disagreement in principle with Hegel over this matter and over the larger issue of the 'Idea' related to history. But all this is a long way from Müller's and the twentieth century Hegelians' simplistic reduction of Strauss's view to a 'monistic reduction' of Hegel.

A painstakingly careful recent study of Strauss in a broader context is Dietz Lange, *Historischer Jesus oder mythischer Christus. Untersuchungen zu dem Gegensatz zwischen Friedrich Schleiermacher und David Friedrich Strauss* (Gütersloh, 1975). In addition to its remarkable investigative energy and precision, it has two important merits: first, Lange demonstrates that Strauss's basic skepticism about relating the 'Jesus of history' positively to the 'Christ of faith' still remains an important, unsolved issue today. Second, he goes a long way toward demonstrating that by virtue of concern precisely for this problem Strauss's attitude toward Schleiermacher is in the long run intrinsically more important than the question of his relation to Hegel. Lange's dramatic thesis is that *The Life of Jesus* was in fact primarily written against Schleiermacher, and he mounts an admirably powerful argument in favour of the claim. My own view, implied in the present study, is that this specific claim is exaggerated, but that Lange moves in the right direction: Schleiermacher becomes more important than Hegel to Strauss, beginning about 1837.

The latest and very large work, Friedrich W. Graf, *Kritik und Pseudo-Spekulation. David Friedrich Strauss als Dogmatiker im Kontext der positionellen Theologie seiner Zeit* (Munich, 1982), argues that Strauss's theological intention was constructive rather than destructive from the beginning, but that his climactic endeavour in this respect, the *Glaubenslehre*, was a failure in positive theological, especially Christological speculation.

4. Secondary works in English

For an introduction to Strauss that takes account of twentieth century developments in scholarship as well as theological discussion, the reader will do well to combine readings of the introductions cited above (section 2) by Leander Keck, Marilyn Chapin Massey and Peter Hodgson (bearing in mind the important *caveat* about the accuracy of Hodgson's views resulting from his Hegelian tilt on Strauss in the wake of G. Müller's work). For generations, students – other than those who have nodded briefly in Strauss's direction on their journey from Hegel to Marx – have made Strauss's acquaintance through Albert Schweitzer, *The Quest of the Historical Jesus* (London, 1910; English transl. of *Von Reimarus zu Wrede. Geschichte der Leben-Jesu-Forschung*). The work remains interesting, but Strauss is skewed by Schweitzer's engrossment in realistic eschatology and his lack of speculative interest.

Relatively recent essays on Strauss may be found in Claude Welch, *Protestant Thought in the Nineteenth Century* (New Haven, 1972); William J. Brazill, *The Young Hegelians* (New Haven, 1970); Hans J. Hillerbrand, *A Fellowship of Discontent* (New York, 1967); Hans W. Frei, *The Eclipse of Biblical Narrative* (New Haven, 1974); and John Edward Toews, *Hegelianism. The Path Toward Dialectical Humanism, 1805–1841* (Cambridge, 1980). An appreciation of Strauss as historian and a critique of him for lacking a hermeneutical stance is Van A. Harvey, 'D. F. Strauss's *Life of Jesus* Revisited', *Church History*, 30 (1961), pp. 191–211. Marilyn Chapin Massey, 'David Friedrich Strauss and his Hegelian Critics', *The Journal of Religion* 57:4 (October 1977), is a vigorous defence of the authenticity of Strauss's Hegelianism in the 1830's, against his twentieth century Hegelian detractors. Epoch-making is Massey's later article, 'The Literature of Young Germany and D. F. Strauss's *Life of Jesus*', *The Journal of Religion* 59, no. 3 (July 1979), which for the first time attempts a textual analysis of *The Life of Jesus* from a socio-historical and literary perspective. This pioneering work, which may well be a landmark not only in the study of this but other nineteenth century theological texts, has now been expanded to book length as *Christ Unmasked. The Meaning of 'The Life of Jesus' in German Politics* (Chapel Hill and London, 1983).

Two recent, thoroughly researched if pedestrian, biographies in English are Richard S. Cromwell, *David Friedrich Strauss and his Place in Modern Thought* (Fair Lawn, New Jersey, 1974) and Horton Harris, *David Friedrich Strauss and his Theology* (Cambridge, 1973). Of these two, the latter work contains more useful intellectual as well as bibliographical information.

Finally, three unpublished Ph.D. dissertations are well worth mentioning: Stephen T. Crites, 'The problem of the positivity of the Gospel in the Hegelian dialectic of alienation and reconciliation' (Yale University, 1961); Carl E. Hester, III, 'Schleiermacher in Tübingen: a study in reaction' (Columbia University, 1970); Marilyn Chapin Massey, 'David Friedrich Strauss's christological thought: the influence of Friedrich Schleiermacher' (University of Chicago, 1973).

8

Ferdinand Christian Baur

ROBERT MORGAN

I

The inscription on the grave of Ferdinand Christian Baur (1792–1860) describes him in a single word: *Theologe*. The once bitterly attacked founder of the Protestant Tübingen school of radical historical criticism was indeed a *theologian*, in Dilthey's and Hirsch's view second only to Schleiermacher, convinced that the Christian tradition witnessed to divine truth and seeking to make this apparent in an intellectual milieu dominated by German idealist philosophy and the new discipline of critical history. He not only set the critical study of Christian origins on a sound methodological basis from which subsequent research could advance, but also integrated the science and philosophy of his time and place into his own understanding of Christianity. That the resulting restatement of Christian faith was cast in the form of theologically interpreted historical investigations, including critical assessments of the contemporary scene, is what is meant by the *historical theology* which he pioneered. As this phrase of Schleiermacher[1] suggests, it is 'part of the modern study of history', but is theology, not 'unintelligent empiricism'; it includes exegetical theology (in effect, New Testament), church history, and 'historical knowledge of the present condition of Christianity'.

After two years preparatory study in philosophy Baur received his theological training (1811–14) in the old Tübingen supernaturalist school of G. C. Storr (d. 1805), Süskind, the Flatts and above all E. G. Bengel, in which the independence of biblical revelation was asserted but harmonized with and supported by Kant's philosophy.[2] He had perhaps read Schelling as a student, but his break with the theology of his teachers was gradual, and only the publication of Schleiermacher's *Glaubenslehre* in 1821 finally convinced him that following the Enlightenment criticism of divinely guaranteed tradition any future theology would have to be based upon human self-consciousness.

But Baur's enthusiasm for Schleiermacher's achievement was from the outset tempered by criticisms. He had little understanding for Schleiermacher's assertion of the independence of theology and philosophy and thought that the strong philosophical element in the work should have been made more explicit.[3] He also found the christological section 'the hardest to grasp' (p. 242), on account of its conflation of the historical and the ideal or archetypal perspectives on Jesus. He shortly afterwards, in his inaugural dissertation (1827),[4] developed this objection through a comparison of Schleiermacher's system with second-century gnosticism.

Between 1817 and 1826 Baur had taught classics at the Blaubeuren seminary and become familiar with the new source critical methods of B. G. Niebuhr's *Römische Geschichte* (1811–12). His study of ancient religion, stimulated by Creuzer's *Symbolik und Mythologie der alten Völker* (2nd ed. 1819–23), bore fruit in the three volumes of his own *Symbolik und Mythologie* (1824–5).[5] The foreword contained the often quoted statement that 'for me history without philosophy is eternally dead and dumb' (p. viii). This does not imply that history should be forced into a philosophical mould, but that its meaning cannot be made plain without the help of metaphysics. Here it is Schelling who provides the interpretation necessary to grasp the theological meaning of this research in the history of religions. Thus a decade before he found in Hegel the most helpful metaphysical handmaid for a contemporary theology Baur already saw the need of a philosophical conceptuality which would allow him to speak of God in and through his critical historical work.

It was a prior theological commitment and interest in exposing the truth of the Christian tradition which drove Baur to modern philosophy and to critical history. This could never warrant violence to the historical data; Baur believed that his freedom from traditional dogmatic presuppositions enabled his historical work to function as a control against subjectivism. But just as 'since Kant every philosophy that understands its task must adopt the idealist standpoint for which all that exists is only true and real for consciousness' (*KG*, p. 349), so modern theology is bound to follow Schleiermacher in this respect and take the form of *Religionsphilosophie*.

That conviction received its clearest statement in *Die christliche Gnosis* (1835).[6] This account of 'Christian *Religionsphilosophie* in its historical development' (subtitle) turns in the final Part IV from 'the old gnosticism' and its ecclesiastical opponents, to the modern religious thought of Boehme, Schelling, Schleiermacher and especially Hegel. Just as the situation of religious pluralism out of which Christianity emerged once gave rise to the various systems of Christian gnosticism, so the new recognition of other religions which naturally follows the collapse of the traditional view of revelation was bound to lead intellectuals into modern equivalents of these systems.

Baur does not endorse any of the syntheses he describes, though he sees in the latest of them an intellectual and spiritual advance upon its predecessors. His own attempts to restate Christian faith in the light of modern knowledge would have to build on this, but would also be based upon the latest advances of the human mind to which he was already contributing by his own historical research, and which were about to explode upon the Christian world by the hand of his friend and former pupil, D. F. Strauss.

Neither historical questioning nor rationalistic criticism of the gospels were new. The *Wolfenbüttel Fragments* of Reimarus (d. 1768), published anonymously by Lessing in 1774–8, had caused a stir. But Strauss's *Life of Jesus* (1835) marked an epoch. Baur later praised it for clarifying the situation, destroying what had to be destroyed and forcing the age to face the destruction of its false supports. 'Strauss was hated because the spirit of the age could not endure its own image which he held up before it in a sharply profiled form.'[7]

Baur must have recognized at once how effectively Strauss had demolished the citadel of supernaturalism and the compromises of rationalism. However, he never fully identified with Strauss's direct confrontation with orthodoxy – to the chagrin of the pupil who knew the extent of their agreement. Whatever the full reasons for this ambivalence,[8] Baur's subsequent explanation was that he 'had not yet himself done the necessary (exegetical) spade-work' (*KG*, p. 397) for forming his own conclusions, and this is supported by some rather general private comments made at the time on Strauss's 'far too negative criticism' and lack of a 'constructive criticism' which would estimate the historical data more 'positively' and say more about 'the impression of Jesus' personality and his whole significance'.[9] When he later did his own Gospel criticism, Baur was to emphasize Strauss's methodological flaw in criticizing the Gospel history without first providing a critical evaluation of the sources.[10]

Presumably, too, Baur sensed that for all the book's critical merits, Strauss's solution to the christological problem in his 'Concluding Dissertation' broke with the New Testament and Christian tradition in a drastic and unacceptable way by its denial of the significance of (the man) Jesus for Christian faith. Unlike Schleiermacher, Strauss had correctly distinguished between the critical historical and the speculative philosophical viewpoints. But he did not even try to hold the two sides together as Christian consciousness seemed to require. How to do this was a problem for Baur and that perhaps explains his important exploratory monograph comparing the place of Jesus in Christianity with the place of Socrates in Platonism,[11] and also his quite unStraussian use of Hegel in the studies in the history of doctrine which immediately followed,[12] and even his subsequent insistence upon the theological importance of 'the founder of Christianity' (see below, p. 279). Theological and ecclesiastical responsibility is at least as good an explanation of his reservations as professorial ambition.

Before Baur could reach his own conclusions he was in 1836 compelled to defend himself against conservative attack. His 'Abgenötigte Erklärung' or 'Necessitated Explanation' against an article in the Protestant Church Magazine, edited by Dr E. W. Hengstenberg, Professor of Theology in the University of Berlin,[13] was written in haste (eight days), and contains an unfortunate argument relating canonicity to authenticity. It disappointed Strauss by stressing the differences between their work rather than what they had in common, though Baur comments on the reaction to Strauss that there is something wrong with the foundations of a faith which could be thrown into such a panic by the first book of a young scholar (p. 297). More especially it defends the harmony of reason and faith, and the legitimacy of using historical criticism to destroy untenable and irrational theological positions. Historical investigation performed a service for faith by destroying illusions and providing a reduced but reliable foundation for Christian belief. What matters is not how much one believes but how, and whether it is securely based, making possible a joyful confidence (pp. 301ff). Baur can appeal to Luther's theological criticism of the ecclesiastical tradition, and even the canon itself, in defence of his own critical procedure. Critical theology, which for Baur means Protestant theology, subjects all tradition, including Scripture, to rational scrutiny (p. 305).

Although he had not yet tackled the johannine question and resented Hengstenberg's premature accusations (pp. 288–90), Baur's 'positive' reconstruction of early Christian history was as far distant as Strauss from the older Protestant theology and the supernaturalism repristinated by Hengstenberg. But quite apart from actual conclusions (p. 294), and methods ('laborious study of the sources', p. 295), Baur felt that his denial of the authenticity of the Pastoral Epistles in 1835, which had occasioned the attack, did not throw into question 'the whole objective basis of Christianity' (*ibid.*). Rather, it recovered the course which history, under God's providence, had actually taken.

Baur's disagreement with his former pupil on the grounds that Strauss engaged in historical criticism solely to destroy the tradition, and thus represents the Enlightenment standpoint, was confirmed by the latter's *Die Christliche Glaubenslehre* (1840–1), with its claim that 'the true criticism of dogma is its history' (vol. 1, p. 71). Baur thought that this anti-dogmatic approach to the history of dogma fails to do justice to the *history* because it is more interested in destroying than in understanding.[14] 'Rationalism can only adopt a negative stance towards the history of dogma' (*ibid.*). His own aim in tracing the course of dogma through history was to interpret it rather than annihilate it, and he believed that this more sympathetic hermeneutical approach to the data provided a more 'objective' (because responsive to the object) history-writing. He also thought it better theology; he considered his own work 'positive', not only because it provided a credible reconstruction of the history, but also because this reconstruction enshrined a new theological interpretation of the tradition. Out of the rubble left by the Enlightenment's demolition of the Christian tradition he rebuilt a new account of Christianity which would withstand the critical scrutiny of the day. The old materials of the tradition were rearranged in what was now perceived to be their historical order and were held together by a new metaphysical cement to replace the decayed foundations and fallen buttresses of belief in supernatural interventions.

Baur 'had begun [his] critical investigations [of Christian origins] long before Strauss, and had set out from a quite different point', (*KG*, p. 395) namely, the history of the primitive Church. He responded to Strauss's critical demolition of the Gospel history with a critical evaluation of the sources for a life of Jesus – which involved an assessment of their position within the development of early Christianity. And he responded to Strauss's Enlightenment type of critical dissolution of the history of dogma with his own speculative interpretation of this history, in which the 'concept' of dogma attained a truly scientific expression, as the latest stage of a process grounded in the nature of Spirit itself (*Lehrbuch*, p. 58). For what is history but 'the eternally clear mirror in which the Spirit contemplates itself, considers its own picture, in order to be for itself, for its own consciousness, what it is in itself; and to know itself as the moving force behind what has come to pass in history' (*ibid.*, p. 59)?

In other words, Hegel's metaphysics of history provided Baur with a doctrine of God which enabled him to articulate the theological subject-matter of the Christian tradition in and through his critical reconstruction of its history. This interpretation can be tested at the historical level. One must ask, as Baur challenged his opponents to do,[15] whether it illuminates the development in ordinary historical terms. Baur was convinced that his presentations were rational, as those of the supernaturalists were not, because they could be tested by reference to the evidence. He also thought them superior to the positivist (or, as he would say, 'pragmatic') accounts of the development because these failed to make clear the inner powers propelling it forward and thus reduced history to a mere succession of events: 'Even if we take the best and most accepted works on the history of primitive Christianity, and examine them with a view to seeing how far they succeed in combining the historical materials which are of so heterogeneous a nature, and have to be collected from such different quarters, to the unity of a whole, – how isolated and fragmentary, how destitute of inner principle and motive, how vague and dim do they appear in many respects.'[16]

But in addition to evaluating the history as history, it is necessary to consider the 'divine truth' which the interpreter is claiming to show that the tradition contains. Is the theology which the interpreter finds in the tradition recognizably continuous with previous theological interpretations of the tradition, and so Christian? But this is not the sole criterion by which a theological position is judged. Its claim to truth should also be tested by asking logical, moral and even aesthetic questions, and exploring its relation to Christian praxis.[17]

II

In 1826 Baur was appointed to the Tübingen Protestant chair for New Testament, church history and history of dogma (including symbolics) which he occupied until his death in 1860. He was already then suspect for his advanced philosophico-theological views, but from 1835 onwards the growing hostility was directed at his novel historical and literary conclusions which evidently destroyed traditional views of the Bible and appeared to deny the supernatural origin of Christianity.[18] Since the reasoned conservative reply was to challenge his conclusions and accuse him of forcing the New Testament evidence into a predetermined philosophical mould, it will be necessary to examine (this small proportion of) his scholarship in some detail before enquiring whether his christology does not indeed justify the orthodox opposition.[19] Even if the 'Bible question' is in principle settled, and even Roman Catholic theology come to share Baur's historical methods (and some of his results), it is still possible that as 'the first person to make the historical critical method the basis of a theological system in a consistent and comprehensive way' Baur is to be credited (or debited) with 'the decisive false step in the history of modern theology'.[20]

In retrospect, the decision to study Christianity by a historical method which refuses to see the web of history disrupted by supernatural interventions appears the only realistic option for a theology committed to relating Christian faith to the knowledge of the day. Even if the possibility of miracles is not rejected *a priori*, the historian who evaluates evidence by analogy with his own experience is unlikely to be persuaded by these reports, familiar as the genre is from other religious sources. A 'purely historical' account of Christianity was bound to conflict with traditional super-naturalism.[21]

For the traditional believer, 'the fact which lies at the root of Christianity [is] that the only-begotten Son of God descended from the eternal throne of the Godhead to the earth, and became man in the womb of the Virgin' (*Ch. Hist.*, p. 1). Baur's theology would allow him to interpret constructively such mythical expressions of the post-resurrection Church's faith. But here his concern is with the fundamental choice between a modern historical and a miraculous account of Christian origins: 'He who regards this [the Incarnation] as simply and absolutely a miracle steps at once outside of all historical connexion' (*ibid.*). Rejecting this dogmatic presupposition, the modern historian will seek 'to show how the miracle of the absolute beginning may itself be regarded as a link of the chain of history, and to resolve it, so far as the case admits, into its natural elements' (*ibid.*). He will seek to understand Christian origins in their historical context (p. 2).

The debate concerning the compatibility of historical and theological accounts of Christian origins has in recent years centred upon the resurrection of Jesus. In language very similar to that of contemporary critical scholarship,[22] Baur insists that

The nature and the reality of the resurrection lies outside the sphere of historical enquiry. History must be content with the simple fact, that in the faith of the disciples the resurrection of Jesus came to be regarded as a solid and unquestionable fact. It was in this faith that Christianity acquired a firm basis for its historical development. What history requires as the necessary antecedent of all that is to follow is not so much the fact of the resurrection of Jesus, as the belief that it was a fact. The view we take of the resurrection is of minor importance for the history . . . (*Ch. Hist.*, pp. 42f)

But while Baur denies that an act of God could be established by historical research, he himself affirms the early Christians' faith and speaks in his own way of the resurrection: After the death of Jesus, faith in him had either to die with him, or it had to 'break through the barrier of death itself, and force its way from death to life. Nothing but the miracle of the resurrection' could disperse the doubts which seemed bound to drive faith itself away into the eternal night of death (*Ch. Hist.*, p. 42).

For Baur himself and for his opponents the issues were clearest in his criticism of the Fourth Gospel.[23] He observed in his *Church History* (pp. 24f) that the decision for or against its historicity was a decision for or against incarnational christology. In retrospect this is plainly wrong, but neither side had yet learned to distinguish the christological dogma from untenable assumptions about the historicity of its presentation by John. When these were challenged the dogma seemed to collapse.

By confirming the critical judgment of Strauss on the Fourth Gospel and siding with his pupil against Schleiermacher, Baur provided the basis for subsequent liberal Protestant christology. A purely historical method yields a purely historical Jesus. By this time he had learned from Hegel how the Jesus of history and the Christ of faith could be both distinguished critically and integrated theologically (see below, p. 279).

Understanding the Fourth Gospel as essentially a source for the theology of the not-so-early Church, rather than for the ministry of Jesus, was consequently no loss to Baur. Theologically, a historical knowledge of the early Church was important for him, and 'the less we can consider the authors of the four Gospels mere reporters, the more they gain significance as composers whose writings are themselves again a source for New Testament theology'.[24] A critical judgment both increases our knowledge of post-resurrection belief and also opens the way to a more secure historical knowledge of Jesus, based on the Synoptics: 'In proportion as the historical value of John drops, that of the Synoptics rises . . . This does not mean that the Synoptics give a purely historical account [Baur looked also for their theological tendency – cf. n. 10], – but we do have here a quite different historical basis' (*KG*, p. 397). Criticism of the Fourth Gospel removed from consideration as a source for Jesus' teaching an account which 'brought down the historical credibility of the other three to so low a level that they virtually forfeit their position as historical sources' (*Ch. Hist.*, p. 25).

Baur's criticism of the Gospel sources (1844–7) thus made possible the historical account of Jesus' teaching first published at the beginning of the *Church History* (pp. 23–42) and included in the *Lectures on New Testament Theology* (pp. 45–121, cf. n. 24). Modern historical methods applied to the Gospels yield a human figure and provide no direct support for the orthodox belief that this man is God incarnate. Strauss and Baur were free to pursue their historical research without fear of theological consequences because they had in quite different ways learned from Hegel to separate their Christian evaluation of Jesus from the historical reality of the man from Nazareth. The reason for the orthodox reaction was a sense that the very structure of incarnational christology was broken by such a separation, and Christianity was again being developed along lines which had been rejected in the second century. But before Baur's christology is evaluated it is necessary to consider how far the repudiation of his *historical* conclusions

268

was justified, and in particular whether the charge of fitting the history to a predetermined philosophical framework can be maintained.

In vindicating the authenticity of the seven authentic Ignatian epistles J. B. Lightfoot knew that he had destroyed Baur's chronology of second-century Christianity, in particular his late dating of the Gospels.[25] Again, most specialists would now agree with Baur's early admirer Hilgenfeld that in restricting himself to the 'big four' pauline epistles he rejected (albeit cautiously[26]) the authenticity of Philippians, 1 Thessalonians and Philemon on insufficient grounds. His epoch-making work on Acts[27] was also substantially corrected, by Overbeck in 1870. There was no consensus on the 'Synoptic problem' until after Baur's death,[28] and his acceptance of the priority of Matthew was almost certainly mistaken,[29] as was his preference for Marcion's Luke.[30] His liberal successors observed that he over-emphasized the general at the expense of the particular; that he under-emphasized (as they over-emphasized!) the importance of world-historical personalities; that he was concerned with intellectual at the expense of social history. But they adopted his methods and many of his results, thus vindicating his insistence that even if his pioneering conclusions should prove mistaken, nevertheless 'the basic axioms and basic views of the school are still thereby not refuted; it would simply be a case of carrying them through more strictly and precisely'.[31]

Granted the importance of German idealist philosophy for Baur's theological interpretation of religious and Christian history generally, and the history of doctrine[32] and pauline theology[33] in particular, it is necessary to ask whether this has distorted his historical judgments, as conservative polemic has ever asserted.[34]

It is striking that the philosophical conceptuality employed to interpret gnosticism, the history of doctrine and pauline *theology* is almost entirely absent from Baur's literary and historical critical essays and monographs, such as *Die sogennanten Pastoralbriefe des Apostels Paulus* (1835), or the first two parts of his *Paulus* (1845) on the historicity of Acts and the authenticity of the epistles. The theological diversity and conflict at Corinth, by recognizing which Baur in 1831 destroyed the myth of apostolic harmony and laid the foundations for his critical reconstruction of Christian history, was read out of, not into, the evidence.[35] His basic model of an original antithesis between Jewish and Gentile Christianity being gradually softened on both sides, leading to the catholic unity visible at the end of the period of origins, rests on his insight that the historical question of Christian origins must be posed as 'the question how Christianity, which was at one time so closely interwoven with Judaism, broke loose from it and entered on its sphere of world-wide historical importance' (*Paul*, vol. 1, p. 3), and his correct historical judgment that Paul was the key figure in this development.

The weakness of this model, based though it was on exegetical observations, is that it is over-simple and over-schematic. Baur conceived the historical development in too linear a fashion and gave insufficient consideration to the possibility of a variety of parallel developments in early Christianity. This led him to underestimate the speed of the development, and was a factor in his mistaken chronology. Because his framework was dominated by one – admittedly central – issue, his search for the 'tendency' of each document was too narrowly conceived. The opposition of Jewish and Gentile Christianity over the law can be seen from the synoptic tradition as well as from Paul to have been a burning issue, at an early stage. But it is not the only grid to apply to the documents. The response at both the doctrinal and the ethical level to the delay of the parousia also helps place and date the documents and reconstruct the history.

Was Baur's failure to correct his framework (which is only ever a working hypothesis) in the light of other indications in the evidence, influenced by its supposed correspondence to a Hegelian (or Fichtean) pattern? Possibly. The fault can also be explained as the inevitable one-sidedness of the pioneer. But Baur was clearly right to look for the theological 'tendency' of each source. If this *Tendenzkritik* was a factor in such mistaken judgments as the late dating of Mark, that was the result of its one-sided application.

Baur also over-emphasized the significance of the Clementine Homilies and the Paschal controversy in looking for support for his conflict hypothesis. But it was natural for the pioneer, breaking with a great weight of traditional opinion, to over-value Jewish–Christian and heretical writings generally as he struggled to overcome the bias against them and achieve freedom for objective judgments. Church history has generally been written by the opponents of heretics and most of their literary remains have been destroyed. One of the first tasks of critical historiography was to recover a sense for the significance of those whose influence on the total development has either been underestimated or has been primarily a negative one.

Baur's conservative critics have traded on the fact that Baur's historical theology has two rational foci, history and metaphysics, and have asserted without argument that the (soon dated) metaphysics influenced his historical judgments – which are thus discredited and require no further refutation. The critics have not sought to establish a pattern in Baur's eccentric judgments all leading support to the frame, or shown that he resisted counter-evidence which threatened it. His irritation with students who like Ritschl deserted the Tübingen construction is explained by his (in the case of Ritschl, justified) suspicion that a return to more conservative judgments involved a nostalgia for the supernaturalism which was incompatible with his critical method.

The questionable word 'opposition' (*Gegensatz* – implying opposites or antitheses), with which Baur describes the relationships of Christianity and Judaism, Jewish and Gentile Christianity, Catholicism and Protestantism,[36] may have derived from his philosophical background, whether from Hegel, Fichte or Schelling. But the concept perhaps owes more to Baur's Lutheranism, kept in the forefront of his mind by his lectures on Symbolics[37] and his controversy with Möhler.[38] His view of Paul's antithetical relationship to Jewish Christianity derives some of its colour from Luther's opposition to Catholicism – which was itself shaped primarily by a reading of Galatians and Romans.

The relationship between Lutheran theology and German idealism which surfaces especially in the letter-spirit antithesis cannot be explored here. The main question about the concept of *Gegensatz* is not its origin but whether it led to distortions in Baur's interpretation of the history. Did it lead him to exaggerate the element of conflict in early Christianity, or to neglect other aspects of the evidence? Did it foreclose certain options in the interpretation of the evidence, or tip the scales in favour of certain sorts of judgments? Or did it help Baur to achieve sharp profiles in his presentation of the history and to resist the temptation to blur necessary distinctions? Did it stimulate, or over-stimulate the historian's imagination which necessarily comes into play where the perspective is long and the available evidence short? Historical method combines a sense for the whole development with close attention to individual pieces of evidence. If Hegelian philosophy of history strengthened Baur's sense of historical movement and also sharpened his eye for detail by teaching him to expect conflicts and their resolution; if it encouraged him to ask about the character and tendency of each piece of evidence when scholars expecting apostolic harmony were overlooking this – then its effect was beneficial. Subsequent research has vindicated Baur the historian; biblical scholarship today is more or less knowingly the heir of its nineteenth-century pioneers. Whether this longer perspective has vindicated Baur's theology as faithful to the tradition it intended to interpret, is another question.

III

Baur's doctrine of God, and therefore his christology, depends upon German idealist metaphysics of history. But his respect for the meaning and integrity of historical research led him beyond the christologies of his masters in *Religionsphilosophie*. This is where he had parted company with Schleiermacher, and while Hegel's speculative christology was the best so far available, Baur realized that the 'big question of the day' (*Vers.*, p. 737; cf. *Gn.*, pp. 734f), the relationship between this and the historical Jesus, was not yet solved. The big question about his own theology is whether it could be solved when posed in these terms.[39]

Schleiermacher had set modern theology on the right lines by developing everything from human self-consciousness. He had also (in Baur's opinion) travelled further along this road than he cared to admit. But Kant's copernican revolution had to be carried through in theology more consistently. Schleiermacher's attempt to unite the historical and the archetypal Christ was a compromise with orthodoxy. Within a year or two of the publication of Hegel's posthumous *Lectures on the Philosophy of Religion* in 1832, in the decade of Hegel's greatest influence in Germany, Baur found there a solution to the problems which Schelling and Schleiermacher had failed to answer. Hegel had opened the door to a reconciliation between Christian faith and modern knowledge by making sense of the history of religion in a way that showed Christianity to be the absolute religion. Finding God in this history overcame the dualism of Schelling's, and the empty abstractness of Schleiermacher's, concept of God (*Gn.*, pp. 621–6, 668; *Drei.*, p. 843). The objective knowledge of God provided by an authoritative tradition had been destroyed in the eighteenth century by a newly free human reason, and this advance had reduced theology to speaking subjectively. But Hegel seemed to offer theology objective knowledge by advancing to a standpoint in which both the subjective freedom of man and objective reality itself are respected.

The supposed objectivity of the Hegelian standpoint soon looked the height of subjectivism and Baur's confidence in the irresistible advance of science (*Abg. Erk.*, p. 299) naïve. There is nothing about the history of research which guarantees Baur's objectivity, and history gives no obvious support for metaphysical beliefs. Yet for Baur this 'eternally clear mirror in which the Spirit regards itself' revealed the truth of religion and Christianity.

If theology must employ metaphysics in constructing a doctrine of God, Hegel's looks promising for as long as people believe it. Its speculative interpretation of the doctrine of the Trinity was certainly a radical innovation, but an innovation which conserved an admittedly central doctrine might be preferable to the liberal alternative of discarding it – or relegating it to an appendix. The alternative of developing one's doctrine of God out of a starting-point in revelation rather than reason, christology rather than a modern philosophy, was not systematically explored in comparable depth for another century. Whether Hegel, Schleiermacher or Barth is the best modern guide to theologians in search of a doctrine of God is an open question. Process theology and also Pannenberg, indicate that the Hegelian type of solution is still viable.

It was his theological quest for objective knowledge of God which initially attracted Baur to Hegel's religious philosophy. Once he had integrated this into his theology it impelled him to historical research, because only the combination of this philosophy of history with an empirically based history of religion could overcome the danger of subjectivism in one's theological judgments. Prior to his conversion to Hegel, Baur had been in no hurry to advance along the historical bridgehead he had established in 1831. But Hegel provided a philosophy of history which took historical development seriously. Baur drew the conclusion that the objective study of the development could confirm the objective truth of his theological judgments, and avoid the subjectivism of Schleiermacher's appeal to the Christian consciousness as the criterion by which the value of all cases of religious life is determined. Like its second-century equivalent, Marcionitism,[40] Schleiermacher's subjective form of *Religionsphilosophie* also involved a huge devaluation of the Old Testament and Judaism. With their concept of development, Hegel and Baur could say how the Old Testament religion is both superseded and confirmed by Christianity.

Far from Baur's philosophical theology tempting him consciously to distort the history for the sake of his theory, it motivated him to make his research as objective as possible. Since it is in the real course of history that the Spirit comes to himself, it is imperative that the perceiving historian resolutely sets aside all personal prejudices and surrenders himself entirely to the subject-matter (*Abg. Erk.*, pp. 275, 295). What this ideal led to in terms of a working day that began at 4 a.m. summer and winter, without central heating,[41] has been repeated often enough. More relevant is the consideration that as a practising historian Baur stands closer to his successor Troeltsch than to Hegel. They both knew that historical research must be done inductively, not deduced *a priori*, before it can carry, by means of a philosophy of history, theological weight. And because they did their historical work with impartiality and integrity they knew that they could

appeal to it for controls which would protect their contemporary restate-
ments of Christianity (which Troeltsch knew better than Baur contained a
strong subjective element[42]) against the dangers of subjectivism.

Important as Baur's dissatisfaction with Schleiermacher's doctrine of
God undoubtedly was, it looms less largely than his dissatisfaction with his
christology. The main objection to this attempt to unite the historical and the
archetypal Christ was that like the Fourth Gospel it swallowed up the
historical reality of Jesus. Hegel was not interested in the historical Jesus, but
at least his Christology indicated its place – if only to leave it behind and
progress from history to the standpoint of faith, and then to knowledge of the
union of the human and divine spirit. Baur compares Hegel's transition from
traditional Christian faith to philosophical knowledge of God with the
transition from unbelief's merely historical evaluation of Jesus, to orthodox
faith (*Gn.*, pp. 714f). For the Christian philosopher neither the historical
Jesus nor orthodox faith's relation to the Risen Christ is strictly necessary,
though without these stages the philosophical standpoint of knowledge of
God could not have been attained.

In the 'Concluding Dissertation' to *The Life of Jesus* Strauss had clarified
the unimportance of the historical Jesus for the Hegelian standpoint which
he had adopted, by insisting that the idea of the unity of the divine and
human natures cannot be concentrated in a single individual. Baur evidently
agreed about this impossibility – though he saw it as a problem for
contemporary theology (*Gn.*, pp. 717, 734, *Vers.*, p. 730) rather than an
occasion boldly to abandon the tradition in favour of a consistent development of Hegelian philosophy. But he did insist that Schleiermacher's
criticism of the orthodox two natures doctrine in *The Christian Faith*
must be taken further, and the confession of the divinity of Christ
freed from its reference to the historical Jesus. The price of a theology
based upon consciousness was a clear distinction between the Jesus of
history and the Christ of faith, and the attribution of divinity to the latter
only. All attempts (thus far) to predicate divinity of the historical Jesus, had
(in his view) fallen into the inevitable docetism of the orthodox christology.
Baur had no sympathy at all for the attempts of the right-wing Hegelian
theologians Marheineke, Daub, Göschel and Conradi to combine Hegel's
speculative Godman with their orthodox christology, as though Hegel's idea
could simply be pinned to the reality which they possessed (*Vers.*, p. 735,
KG, p. 358). Since the philosophical and historical criticism of the
Enlightenment, the only thing that could be pinned to the orthodox
christology was an obituary. Hegel's great merit was to have distinguished
clearly between the Jesus of history and the Christ of faith, and Baur

followed him in this. They have been followed by subsequent liberal theology, even though the strong internal connexion provided by Hegelian thought was soon lost.

The distinction is inevitable and right. There is indeed an external, historical view of Jesus which sees in him a martyr for the truth, like Socrates. This is not Christian faith, and must be distinguished from what Hegel calls the second 'moment', that of faith, which no longer views Jesus as an ordinary man, but as the Godman in whom the divine nature is revealed. For Hegel the transition to this second moment, from unbelief to faith, is mediated by the pouring out of the Spirit in the death and resurrection of Jesus.

Christ is only Godman in that he has overcome death, done death to death, negated the negation, and so annihilated finitude and evil as something alien to him, and so reconciled the world to God. Everything depends upon how this death is understood; it is the criterion by which faith must be tested; the Spirit could not therefore come until after Christ was removed from the flesh and his direct material presence had ceased. (*Gn.*, p. 712 cf. pp. 693–8)

Nothing could sound more orthodox. Hegel gives constitutive significance to the death of Jesus as a historical fact and the emergence of resurrection faith. In this respect he is more traditional than the gnostics or Schleiermacher. Because they thought of Jesus as already Godman in his earthly appearance the former had little to say about his death and the latter little about his resurrection (*Gn.*, p. 713). What Christ is as Godman, he is only for the believing community, since it is faith which unites the divine and human in Christ by mediating between them. After the death of Jesus, faith transfigures what was material into something spiritual. The strength of Hegel's position is that faith presupposes only the historical Jesus, not a figure recognizable as God incarnate. The supernatural traits in the Gospels' presentations of Jesus stem from their having been written from the standpoint of faith (*Gn.*, p. 714).

This is now a commonplace of Gospel criticism – which does not mean that it is a satisfactory basis from which to construct a christology. But before discussing that it is necessary to follow Hegel and Baur further.

Baur adopted Hegel's speculative interpretation of christology. Though Christianity is in the first place a matter of external authority, and can never dispense with this if it is to remain a religion; and though consciousness of the new principle has to be mediated through a historical figure before it is available for humanity generally; and though this happens through a death which proves to be a transition to life; nevertheless its content must finally correspond to 'the absolute authority of reason', if Christianity is to be acknowledged as 'the religion of thinking reason' and therefore absolute religion (*Gn.*, p. 734).

One might object that this rationalist theology knows in advance what it is looking for and therefore has no place for revelation. But Baur could reply that it is only through the event of Jesus that this highest truth of reason is attained. Further, he understands the unity of God and man not as an abstract philosophical theory, but religiously, as an experienced relationship – union with God, the Christian experience of reconciliation. It is related so tightly to the person of Christ that Hodgson can call Baur 'a Christocentric theologian'.[43]

Christianity can be essentially nothing other than that which Christian consciousness of all times, in whatever form it may occur, has perceived in the person of Christ – the unity of God and man. However else one may conceive the essence of Christianity – as everything it ought to be to man according to various connections, such as revelation of absolute truth, the establishment of redemption, reconciliation, blessedness – it has its absolute conception and expression in the unity of God and man, and it is perceived in the person of Christ and in this perception becomes a fact of Christian consciousness . . .[44]

Once distinguished from the historical Jesus, the Christ of faith can be interpreted in a remarkably orthodox sounding way which avoids all the compromises involved in Schleiermacher's attempted accommodation to orthodoxy at this point by identifying the Christ of faith, i.e. his archetypal Christ, with the historical figure. Schleiermacher's redeemer has to be as far as possible like other men in history. As a man of his time he believed in angels and demons; and the virgin birth, Jesus' miracles, his resurrection, ascension and second coming are not allowed into this bloodless christology. But when historical criticism is given such free reign over the contents of christology, Christianity can be protected from a damaging loss of substance only by the status of the redeemer being secured in an area independent of historical research. Schleiermacher's attempt to combine two essentially different ways of looking at Christ thus leads to bad history as well as to bad theology (*Gn.*, pp. 639f).

Hegel, Strauss and Baur avoid these difficulties by assigning the christological predicates to the Christ of faith only. Strauss took the denial that the 'idea' of Christ could be fulfilled in any single individual further and offered a positive solution to the christological problem. His 'key to the whole of christology' was to replace the individual Jesus by the idea of the race, humanity, 'as subject of the predicate which the Church assigns to Christ'. Baur agreed that 'If we think of human nature from the point of view of the idea which is realizing itself, it lies in the nature of the case that idea and reality cannot completely coincide at an individual point, because

276

whereas the idea is infinite, the real is only finite and temporally conditioned' (*KG*, p. 201). If, following the Enlightenment criticism of traditional Christian belief, one adopts the standpoint of German idealism in order to vindicate Christianity as the absolute religion, it is necessary to distinguish the absolute idea which through Jesus enters into the consciousness of humanity, from the claim that it is perfectly realized in the historical man from Nazareth (*Gn.*, p. 711). God in his fulness, as understood in this panentheistic philosophy, cannot be realized in a single individual (*Vers.*, p. 729).

But Baur did not go on to make Strauss's complete disjunction between the Jesus of history and the Christ of faith by identifying the latter with the idea of humanity. The orthodox christology refers to Jesus of Nazareth; Strauss, on the other hand, is fundamentally uninterested in the man from Nazareth. Baur's position between Strauss and orthodoxy can be plotted by asking how important Jesus of Nazareth is for him, and how closely he relates what he followed Hegel (and Strauss) in distinguishing.

What Baur said about Schleiermacher's christology makes it plain that for him the ground rules of this type of theology based on consciousness precluded the possibility of an absolute identity between the Jesus of history and the Christ of faith. Only dogmatic orthodoxy could assert that – and it was docetic. There is a fundamental incompatibility between the orthodox christology and a theology based upon German idealism. What the Spirit is and does is not history; the Incarnation is not an historical fact but an eternal determination of the essence of God. The reconciliation achieved by Christ is not a temporal act; God is eternally reconciling himself with himself (*Gn.*, p. 715; cf. p. 696). Like Lessing, and unlike orthodox dogmatics, Baur is aware of a big ugly ditch between truths of history and truths of reason (and Christian faith). He could not identify the historical Jesus and the Christ of faith by a sheer, philosophically ungrounded assertion, as Daub and Marheineke had done (*Vers.*, p. 735).

Hegel's transition to the third 'moment' in which faith in the individual Godman passes over into philosophical knowledge of the essential unity of God and man, involves abandoning the standpoint of faith in the Godman. The spiritual content of orthodox Christian faith is internalized by faith being raised to speculative thought, for which the Incarnation is not an event in history. Hegel thought that his system replaced orthodox theology and it is natural to assume that Baur followed its logic and transcended faith in Christ – especially in view of his inability to identify the Christ with the individual Jesus.

But this would be a mistake. Strauss followed Hegel in making the transition from faith to knowledge, from religion to philosophy, and kicked away behind him the ladder by which he reached the absolute standpoint. The historical Jesus and orthodox faith were necessary for getting there, but having arrived Hegel and Strauss never looked back. They were not interested in the historical Jesus because for them he stood in no integral relationship to their speculative christologies. The orthodox standpoint of faith in Jesus Christ was also superseded; it only reflected the speculative christology in the inferior form of *Vorstellung*, in contrast to its form as *Begriff* (cf. n. 12). The orthodox theologians were therefore justified in repudiating Strauss, not for his radical Gospel criticism, but for his lack of interest in the historical Jesus and faith in Jesus Christ.

Baur, on the other hand, remained a theologian and a preacher. *Religionsphilosophie*, which had found its most developed expression to date in Hegel's work, replaced the traditional dogmatic theology for Baur. But it did not replace the standpoint of faith. Baur's Hegelianism was a matter of 'faith seeking understanding', as the Anselmic echoes of the sentences of the '*Abgenötigte Erklärung*' quoted above (p. 264) suggest. (See also *Lehrbuch*, p. 18.) *Religionsphilosophie* remains for him a form of theology, which is why we have translated it 'philosophical theology', whereas Hegel's lectures are more properly translated 'Philosophy of Religion'. Baur the theologian pressed on for philosophical knowledge of the identity of the divine and human spirit which would vindicate his faith and give him joy in believing. Like the *Religionsphilosophie* or Christian gnosticism of Clement and Origen, which was also orthodox in intention, it did not involve abandoning the standpoint of faith in the Christ.

Nevertheless, this Christ of faith could not be simply identified with the historical Jesus, and at this point a tension is evident between Baur's Hegelian theology and his intention to remain an orthodox Christian theologian – not in the sense of one who accepted the old dogmatics, but as one who remained loyal to the biblical faith out of which this developed. He could not repeat the traditional formulae and mean by them what the fourth- and fifth-century Fathers had meant. In order to stand with them he went behind them and attempted to be true to their intention. Hence the importance of New Testament theology within his historical theology.

Baur's orthodox intention and his standpoint of faith in Jesus Christ become clear in his recognition of the importance of the historical Jesus for Christian faith and theology. He could not identify him with the Christ of faith, but he said as much as he could say without denying his philosophical position: that is, the historical Jesus and the Christ of faith are integrally related, and the former absolutely indispensable. Without denying the speculative 'christology' in which he found the most satisfying expression of his own understanding of faith, (the unity of the human and the divine spirit), he attempted to link this with the historical figure, and so produce the only kind of christology tolerated in the Christian Church thus far: i.e. a theological interpretation of Jesus of Nazareth.

This christology is summed up in the phrase 'the founder of Christianity' and Baur insists that while avoiding the old orthodoxy's docetism he is not himself falling into ebionitism. This functional christology in which Jesus is defined by what he does rather than by who he is 'vindicates for Jesus a value and eminence which specifically distinguishes him from all other men, and places him far above them' (*Vers.*, p. 735). The link between this and the speculative christology depends upon finding in Jesus' teaching or behaviour the presupposition of subsequent Christian faith. Even then, without Hegel's vision of the onward march of Spirit in history the two sides, Jesus of history and Christ of faith and theology, are likely to fall apart.

Baur thought the 'merit of Hegel's philosophy of religion was to have distinguished the objective and the subjective sides of the truth in question and to have seen the Christian revelation as providing the necessary means by which the idea of the Godman, or the self-subsisting unity of the divine and the human got across into the consciousness of humanity' (*Vers.*, p. 736). But he was also aware of the inadequacies of the Hegelian Christology 'in the form it has been given so far' (*ibid.*). It did not fully satisfy the Christian consciousness – presumably because it was not interested in the historical Jesus. For Hegel,

The historically factual objective reality which lies behind faith and made it possible for a merely external historical view to become faith, remains veiled in a mystery into which we should not penetrate, because the question is not whether Christ in himself was the Godman in his objective historical appearance. All that matters is that he became the Godman for faith. Faith did at one time arise, and the object of faith can only be the Godman . . . [and] all that Christ is as Godman he is only in faith and through faith. (*Gn.*, pp. 712f)

But whereas Hegel did not go behind the Christ of faith, Baur did. Though he could not assert the absolute identity of the Jesus of history and the Christ of faith he comes so close to this criterion of orthodoxy, as sometimes to touch it: 'How could faith in him as Godman arise unless he was in some way also objectively what faith took him to be? The necessary presupposition is in every case that the self-subsisting truth, the unity of the divine and human nature, first became in Christ a concrete truth, a self-conscious knowledge, and was expressed and taught by him as truth' (*Gn.*, p. 717). This reflects what I have called the 'integral relation' which Baur maintains between the historical Jesus and the Christ of faith. They are 'integrally' related because neither would be what it is without the other. This comes as close as can be imagined to the traditional identification of them.

The same combination of distinction yet inseparability of the historical Jesus and Christ of faith is implied a little later by the word *zugleich*: 'But this single individual is *at the same* time man as such, the general, ideal man, the Godman' (*Gn.*, p. 734, my italics). For Baur as a philosophical theologian the individual Christ is 'not an incidental and external form, but an absolute one'. It 'recedes' before the Hegelian truth in itself (*ibid.*), but does not disappear. W. Geiger therefore misses the nuances of Baur's christology, when he describes his account of the relation between the historical and ideal Christ quite simply as one of 'non-identity'.[45] The evidence quoted in support of this assertion comes from Baur's account of Hegel. But it is a mistake to identify Baur's own view with that of Hegel, on the grounds that he defends Hegel against certain criticisms.[46] Baur used Hegel critically, for his own theological purposes, and rightly resented being called a Hegelian without qualification (*Abg. Erk.*, p. 313). The main problem about Hegel's christology is (arguably) not his distinction between the historical Jesus and the Christ of faith, nor even his refusal to identify them. It is rather that in the last resort for him as for Strauss the heart of Christianity is found not in a person, but in an idea – the idea of the unity of the human and the divine. This is the point at which German idealism and orthodox Christianity part company, and it perhaps provides justification for Barth's massive repudiation of neo-Protestantism. Baur quite rightly considered that his doctrine of God must be constructed within the framework of contemporary understandings of reality reflected in modern philosophy. He also thought, again rightly, that his whole theology should be coherent in terms of contemporary rationality. He also thought, over-optimistically, as it now appears, that the latest philosophy would vindicate his faith by showing its reasonableness (*Gn.*, pp. 696–700). But at the crucial point Baur insists that Christianity is all that it is on account of a person. The 'idea' is a specialist concern of philosophical theologians like himself, and there is no avoiding the advance from what is essentially a matter of the heart to the understanding of the mind. But he thought it necessary to return continually to that religious standpoint, lest one's speculative theories became like the aprioristic deductions of the scholastics (*Vers.*, p. 288).

Baur's move in relation to Hegel and Strauss is analogous to the move taken by some of Bultmann's pupils. The heart of the controversy between Käsemann and Bultmann was whether Christianity is ultimately about a person or an idea. Of course Bultmann and Braun insist that essentially Christianity is not an idea but an event. But the question may be posed whether for them the kerygma is the happening of an idea or of a person. Is Christianity essentially a matter of new self-understanding, in which case the historical Jesus was at most necessary to launch it, or is it essentially a matter of a living Lord, whom faith identifies as the man from Nazareth, and from obedience to whom a new self-understanding derives?

Like Käsemann and Ebeling, Baur realized that the continuity between the Jesus of history and the Christ of faith has theological significance as well as historical interest. His account of Jesus, the founder of Christianity is integral to his theology.[47] Although he could not write this until his Gospel criticism was complete, and although his Jesus is remarkably Kantian, his theological interest in Jesus was not a late return to Kant as the star of Hegel waned, as Geiger asserts.[48] He had discussed the matter in his own way during the controversy over Strauss, with whose Hegelian presuppositions he was in broad agreement; the dependence of Christianity upon the person of its founder is as strongly emphasized in 'Das christliche des Platonismus' (pp. 90, 123, 128) as in the *Church History* (p. 23) sixteen years later.

The relationship between Hegel's speculative christology and the historical Jesus (*Gn.*, pp. 716f) was the point at which the philosophical theology which seemed to Baur the only way forward for Christian thought at that time, conflicted with the traditional faith of the Christian Church. Baur's main contribution was to explore further the continuity which he saw must exist between the Jesus of history and the Christ of faith. This was where his chief interest lay, and in this he differed from Hegel and Strauss who were far more concerned with the next step, from faith to philosophy. The link which he forged emphasized the historical connexion between Jesus' attitude to the Jewish law, and the controversy about the Jewish law which played such an important role in the first generation of the Christian Church. He saw a material connexion between Jesus' ethical teaching and Christianity. Subsequent research has shown that his account of the connexion requires correction, though opinions vary on how much. The eschatology of Jesus, and with it his whole relationship to Judaism, requires more attention than Baur devoted to it, and this in turn affects the account given of Jesus' moral teaching. These corrections then threaten Baur's account of the relationship between Jesus and the early Church, which also requires correction in similar ways.

Baur claimed that the Jewish Christians took over one aspect of Jesus' teaching – his messianic self-consciousness – and the Gentile Christians his universalism and ethical idealism. This account of their material relationship, especially that between Jesus and Paul, is inadequate. But the statement of the problem and the historical approach to its solution have been broadly accepted. Whether rightly, is another matter; modern New Testament theology is arguably the heir of the unresolved dualism in Baur's christology reflected in the overworked antithesis 'Jesus of history – Christ of faith'.

The same combination of accepting both his statement of the problem and his historical methods for solving it while rejecting his own proposals on exegetical and philosophical grounds may be observed in the reception of Baur's interpretation of pauline theology by his critical admirer Bultmann.[49] Both these exegetes have drawn their own philosophical commitments, their understanding of religion and Christianity, their doctrine of God and of reconciliation into their historical presentations of New Testament theology. Some would deny the propriety of this. But if talk of God is necessarily self-involving it is difficult to see how this recourse to one's own pre-understanding can be avoided in theological interpretation. Without it New Testament studies and church history cannot properly be called historical *theology*; they cannot be said to speak of *God*.

Every pre-understanding is open to criticism in the light of the texts. There may be a final incompatibility between idealist panentheism (or existentialist anti-theism) and biblical faith in the personal God who creates from nothing, justifies the ungodly and raises the dead. Baur evidently thought not, since although his doctrine of God is panentheistic he could insist that 'The God of the Old Testament is also the God of the New, and everything taught by the Old Testament with respect to the essential distinction of God from the world, and the absolute holiness of his nature is also an essential part of Christian doctrine' (*Ch. Hist.*, pp. 17f). Whether he was right or merely inconsistent depends upon whether he was able to span the gulf by means of his theological interpretation of the Christian tradition.

Theological interpretation takes up whatever truth the contemporary intellectual scene can offer. German idealism's debt to the Christian tradition and its notion of the unity of God and man allow it to appear initially promising for articulating the reconciliation and union with God of which the Gospel speaks. It also offers a modern theological anthropology such as must surely form the basis of any doctrine of God today. And the difficulty about this new handmaid for theology, expressed in Kant's dictum that the historical serves only for illustration and Fichte's dictum that only the metaphysical, never the historical, brings bliss (*Vers.*, pp. 706–8), is partly overcome by Hegel's metaphysics of history. It makes the historical process central to theology and even gives to the contingent historical event of Jesus an irreplaceable significance.

Theological interpretations must also be tested at the exegetical level; they cannot ever be proved correct (because recognition of truth in a theological context implies that the addressee is illuminated) – but they can be discredited if they do violence to the author's intention.[50] Judgments will vary about how wrong Baur was at the exegetical level, but on some points there is a consensus. Thus Baur's interpretation of Paul's key concept of 'spirit' was falsified when its Jewish and hellenistic background was recognized, even though his use of classical and modern philosophy to interpret the term was in principle unexceptionable. Baur is sometimes closer to Paul's gnostic opponents echoed in 1 Cor. 1–4 than to the apostle – assuming that the somewhat Lutheran Paul of modern study is broadly true to the historical Paul.

Baur is amongst those who have found in the authentic epistles 'the clearest gospel of all'. But similar critical questions may be laid against his interpretation of Jesus, the Fourth Gospel, and all the Christian tradition. Such criticism in the light of subsequent historical research confirms what Baur and Strauss themselves demonstrated most clearly: that historical study has a negative function in criticizing theological interpretations.[51] It does not of itself generate these (though it makes a positive contribution to this also) since theologically speaking 'history without philosophy (metaphysics) is for ever dead and dumb'. And this is as true in Church history and history of doctrine, which form the vast bulk of Baur's massive (20,000 pages) output, as in New Testament theology, which constitutes the first chapter of this.

Historical research is a cumulative process, and it would be strange if many of the pioneer's conclusions had not been modified, and some of his hypotheses rejected. But even without these corrections Baur's interpretations would by now belong to the history of interpretation – worth attending to, often illuminating, but not expecting repristination. Theological interpretation of key Christian witnesses, like the doctrinal theology of which it is a part, is developed at a particular time and place for that generation and culture. Baur's intellectual milieu is not ours. But his *method* of doing theology in a historically conscious age provides a model for the late twentieth century. In place of the deductive 'dogmatic method' (cf. n. 21) of traditional supernaturalism, he gave flesh and blood to the ideal of historical theology sketched by Schleiermacher in the *Brief Outline*. The programme must be fulfilled rather differently today, with the social dimensions of history receiving more attention. But critical history and philosophical reflexion will remain central in that 'living complex of conditions and factors – of philosophic thought, critical acumen, historical insight, and religious feeling – without which no deep theology is possible'.[52]

Notes

1 *Brief Outline on the Study of Theology* (1811; 1830). Eng. tr. T. N. Tice, John Knox Press (Richmond, 1966); quoting §§ 69, 256, and the three subdivisions of Part 2 'On Historical Theology'.

2 Baur discusses the school in his *Kirchengeschichte des neunzehnten Jahrhunderts* (1862), reprinted as vol. IV of *Ausgewählte Werke in Einzelausgaben*, ed. K. Scholder, with an introduction by H. Liebing (Stuttgart – Bad Cannstatt, 1970), p. 98. Cited as *KG*. See also Baur's contribution to K. Klüpfel (ed.), *Geschichte und Beschreibung der Universität Tübingen* (Tübingen, 1849), pp. 216–47.

3 See H. Liebing, 'Ferdinand Christian Baurs Kritik an Schleiermachers Glaubenslehre', *Zeitschrift für Theologie und Kirche*, 54 (1957), 225–43, reproducing Baur's letter to his brother (July 1823) discussing the work.

4 See 'Anzeige der beiden academischen Schriften von Dr F. C. Baur' (Part II), *Tübinger Zeitschrift für Theologie*, 1 (1828), and the discussion by C. E. Hester, *F. D. E. Schleiermacher in Tübingen: A Study in Reaction*, Diss., Columbia, 1970.

5 On this period of Baur's career see G. Müller, *Identität und Immanenz. Zur Genese der Theologie von D. F. Strauss* (Zurich, 1968), pp. 174ff.

6 Reprinted Darmstadt, 1967. Cited as *Gn*.

7 *Kritische Untersuchungen über die kanonischen Evangelien* (Tübingen, 1847), p. 48. Cited as *Kan. Ev.* Cf. p. 380. (The saying echoes what Schelling had said about the treatment Fichte received, quoted at *KG*, p. 76.)

8 Horton Harris, *The Tübingen School* (Oxford, 1975), emphasizes Baur's interest in securing a chair at Halle, while quoting from his letter to Tholuck that he contentedly left this to the Guide of his life (p. 35). On the ecclesiastico-political background see also R. Bigler, *The Politics of German Protestantism* (University of California Press, 1972).

9 See his letter to Heyd (Feb. 1836), translated by Harris, *David Friedrich Strauss and his Theology* (Cambridge, 1973), pp. 86–8.

10 *Kan. Ev.*, pp. 40f. See also 'Der Ursprung und Charakter des Lukas–Evangeliums', *Theologische Jahrbücher*, 5 (1846), p. 453.

11 'Das christliche des Platonismus oder Sokrates und Christus', *Tübinger Zeitschrift für Theologie*, 10 (1837).

12 J. F. Sandberger, *David Friedrich Strauss als theologischer Hegelianer* (Göttingen, 1972), p. 152 makes clear the difference between Strauss and Baur on this point.

13 'Abgenötigte Erklärung . . .', *Tübinger Zeitschrift für Theologie*, 9 (1836). Reprinted in *Ausgewählte Werke*, vol. I, with an introduction by Ernst Käsemann, 1963, pp. 267–320. Cited from there as *Abg. Erk.*

14 *Lehrbuch der christlichen Dogmengeschichte* (1847), reprinted Darmstadt, 1968, p. 44. Cited as *Lehrbuch*.

15 E.g. most impressively in *An Herrn Dr Karl Hase, Beantwortung des Sendschreibens 'Die Tübinger Schule'* (Tübingen, 1855). Reprinted in vol. V of *Ausgewählte Werke*.

16 *The Church History of the First Three Centuries* (1853) Eng. tr. Williams and Norgate (London, 1878), vol. I, p. xi. Cited as *Ch. Hist.*

17 This cannot be attempted in the space available here.

18 The conservative Scottish theologian A. B. Bruce, for example, wrote of 'a theory which makes of Christianity a thing of purely natural origin, calls in question the authenticity of all but a few of the New Testament books, and makes the whole collection contain not a harmonious system of Divine truth but a confused mass of merely human and contradictory opinions as to the nature of the Christian religion'. 'F. C. Baur and his Theory of the Origin of Christianity and of the New Testament Writings', *Present day Tracts*, 38 (1885), p. 5.

19 I have discussed this question in 'Non angli sed angeli: Some Anglican reactions to Tübingen gospel criticism' in S. W. Sykes and D. Holmes (eds.), *New Studies in Theology*, 1 (London, 1980).

20 Quoting K. Scholder's question in his foreword to vol. 1 of the *Ausgewählte Werke*, p. vi.

21 Troeltsch learned much from Baur. See 'Über historische und dogmatische Methode in der Theologie' (1898), *Gesammelte Schriften* II, pp. 729–53, Eng. tr. forthcoming. Also his article 'Historiography', in Hastings' *Encyclopedia of Religion and Ethics*, vol. 6 (Edinburgh, 1913).

22 E.g. G. Bornkamm, *Jesus of Nazareth* (London, 1960), p. 180.

23 'Über die Composition und den Charakter des johanneischen Evangeliums', *Theologische Jahrbücher* 3 (1844), summarized in *Kan. Ev.* (1847).

24 *Vorlesungen über neutestamentliche Theologie*, ed. F. F. Baur, (Leipzig, 1864), reprinted Darmstadt, 1973, p. 24. Cited as *NTT*.

25 *The Apostolic Fathers*, Part II, vol. 1 (London, 1885), pp. xv, 283. Whether an earlier date makes a significant difference on the question of historicity is another matter.

26 *Paulus, der Apostel Jesu Christi. Sein Leben und Wirken, seine Briefe und seine Lehre. Ein Beitrag zu einer kritischen Geschichte des Urchristenthums* (Stuttgart, 1845). Eng. tr. of second edition, 2 vols., Williams and Norgate, 1875. Cited as *Paul*. See vol. 1, pp. 246, 287.

27 Part I of *Paul*. I have discussed this in 'Biblical Classics: II'. F. C. Baur: *Paul*, *Expository Times*, 90 (1978), pp. 4–10. For its (in his view, malign) influence, see W. Gasque, *A History of the Criticism of the Acts of the Apostles* (Tübingen, 1974), passim.

28 Although C. G. Wilke and C. H. Weisse had argued for Marcan priority in 1838, H. J. Holtzmann, *Die Synoptische Evangelien* (Leipzig, 1863), established the consensus. Baur appreciated the merits of Weisse's *Evangelische Geschichte* (*KG*, pp. 373f) but showed little interest in the issue.

29 Despite W. R. Farmer, *The Synoptic Problem* (New York, 1964), who revives the order of Griesbach and Baur.

30 Following his pupil Ritschl (who, however, changed his mind) *Das Evangelium Marcions und das kanonische Evangelium des Lucas* (Tübingen, 1846).

31 *Die Tübinger Schule und ihre Stellung zur Gegenwart* (Tübingen, 1859), p. 58, quoted by Horton Harris, *The Tübingen School* (OUP, 1975), p. 242. This claim is impressively vindicated by W. G. Kümmel, *The New Testament: The History of the Investigation of its Problems* (SCM Press, 1973) p. 143: 'Since Baur's time, scientific work on the New Testament has been possible only when the fundamental methodological principles he indicated have been followed and his overall historical view has been superseded or improved.'

32 Especially *Die christliche Lehre von der Versöhnung in ihrer geschichtlichen Entwicklung von der ältesten Zeit bis auf die neueste* (Tübingen, 1838). Cited as *Vers.* And *Die christliche Lehre von der Dreieinigkeit und Menschwerdung Gottes in ihrer geschichtlichen Entwicklung* (3 vols., Tübingen, 1841–3). Vol. III is cited as *Drei*.

33 Part III of *Paul*, and (rather different) *NTT*, pp. 122–207. I have discussed the latter in 'F. C. Baur's lectures on New Testament theology', *Expository Times* 88 (1977), pp. 202–6.

34 The crude form of this theory, associating Baur's account of 'the opposition of petrine and pauline Christianity in the early church' (1831) with a supposedly Hegelian dialectic, was

criticized by Peter Hodgson, *The Formation of Historical Theology*, (New York, 1966). However, conflict theories of history were in the air, and Baur could have been influenced by them.

35 Cf. 1 Cor. 1.12 and Käsemann's introduction to vol. 1 of the Scholder edition, *Ausgewählte Werke in Einzelausgaben*. Käsemann also shows how Baur's hypothesis has been superannuated by subsequent history of religions research.

36 I.e. 'Die Christuspartei in der korinthischen Gemeinde, der Gegensatz des petrinischen und paulinischen Christenthums in der ältesten Kirche, der Apostel Petrus in Rom', *Tübinger Zeitschrift für Theologie* v:4 (1831), 61–206. Reprinted in *Ausgewählte Werke* 1 (1963), introduction by E. Käsemann. *Der Gegensatz des Katholicismus und Protestantismus nach den Principien und Hauptdogmen der beiden Lehrbegriffe. Mit besonderer Rücksicht auf Herrn Dr Möhler's Symbolik* (Tübingen, 1834).

37 Peter Friedrich, *Ferdinand Christian Baur als Symboliker* (Göttingen, 1975), quotes extracts from Baur's earliest lectures on Christian Symbolics (1828/9), and discusses the dialectical structure of his 'Gegensatzlehre', pp. 111–13.

38 On this see also J. Fitzer, *Moehler and Baur in Controversy, 1832–8: Romantic-idealist assessment of the Reformation and Counter-Reformation*, AAR Studies in Religion 7 (American Academy of Religion, Florida, 1974).

39 Hans Frei, *The Eclipse of the Biblical Narrative* (Yale University Press, 1974), has probed this question most profoundly.

40 According to Baur's typology, *Gn.*, pp. 660, 667.

41 See E. Zeller, 'Ferdinand Christian Baur', in *Vorträge und Abhandlungen geschichtlichen Inhalts* (Leipzig, 1865), p. 363, on the ink freezing in its pot, etc.

42 *Abg. Erk.*, pp. 295, 299. See Ernst Troeltsch, *Writings on Theology and Religion* (London, 1977), pp. 166–9.

43 *Formation of Historical Theology*, p. 122.

44 Quoted by Hodgson, *op. cit.*, p. 125 from *Die Epochen der kirchlichen Geschichtsschreibung* (Tübingen, 1852), p. 251. See Hodgson's (slightly altered) English translation in *Ferdinand Christian Baur on the Writing of Church History* (OUP, 1968), p. 244.

45 *Spekulation und Kritik* (Munich, 1964), p. 71.

46 This point, first made by Zeller against Ritschl, is repeated by Hodgson (*op. cit.*, p. 62, n. 92) and wrongly disputed by Harris (*Tübingen School*, p. 158, n. 40). Geiger also claims that in his interpretation of Hegel Baur is expressing his own position (*op. cit.* p. 71).

47 In practice the decision whether or not to include a section on the 'historical Jesus' in one's New Testament theology turns on whether one considers this theologically important. Baur included the teaching of Jesus, but insisted that it is not a part but 'the basis and presupposition' of New Testament theology; religion rather than theology (p. 45).

48 *Op. cit.* pp. 77–95. Geiger simply disputes Baur's denial of this suggestion (p. 81) and admits he cannot explain the change (p. 85). Confidence in his interpretation is undermined by his failure to understand Baur's conception of Paul (p. 94). However, a shift of emphasis in the *Church History* should be conceded. (See p. 84) D. Jodock, *F. C. Baur & Albrecht Ritschl on Historical Theology*, Diss. Yale, 1969, p. 107.

49 'Zur Geschichte der Paulus – Forschung', *Theologische Rundschau*, n.f. 1, 1929. See pp. 29–33.

50 Cf. E. D. Hirsch, *Validity in Interpretation* (Yale UP 1967), p. 206.

51 This is my argument in 'A Straussian question to New Testament theology', *New Testament Studies*, 22 (1976) 243–65; and in 'Expansion and criticism in the Christian tradition', in *The Cardinal Meaning: Buddhism & Christianity in comparative hermeneutics*, ed. M. Pye and R. Morgan (The Hague, 1973).

52 A. Schweitzer, *The Quest of the Historical Jesus* (London, 1910), p. 1.

Ferdinand Christian Baur

Bibliographical essay

For English readers the basic resource remains Peter C. Hodgson's monograph, *The Formation of Historical Theology. A Study of Ferdinand Christian Baur* (New York, 1966). It contains a classified list of Baur's books, more important journal articles, other published writings, and unpublished manuscripts in the Tübingen University Library. It also lists a judicious selection from the secondary literature on Baur. This monograph partly redeems the generally inadequate treatment of Baur in English. The more typical negative evaluation survives in Horton Harris, *The Tübingen School* (Oxford, 1975), though as this author is candid about the dogmatic premises which guide his historical judgment, it is possible to benefit from the letters and other material made available here, without being seriously misled by his *Tendenz*. Harris lists all the available letters to and from Baur, and his bibliography provides a fuller account of Baur's review articles than Hodgson's.

A surprisingly large number of Baur's voluminous works were reprinted in the 1960s and 70s, reflecting the conviction of the 1960s that 'a generation which has undeniably run into a general crisis over historical understanding must turn back to the beginnings of historical criticism and reflect on its necessity and the problems it contains . . .' (E. Käsemann). That quotation is from the introduction to the first of the five volumes of *Ferdinand Christian Baur: Ausgewählte Werke in Einzelausgaben* (Stuttgart – Bad Cannstadt, 1963–7), edited by Klaus Scholder. The first volume contains three early NT monographs (See n. 36; also on the purpose of Romans and the origins of episcopacy) and the reply to Hengstenberg (n. 13); the second contains *Die Epochen der kirchlichen Geschichtsschreibung* (n. 44); the third reprints volume I (n. 16: *Das Christenthum und die christliche Kirche der drei ersten Jahrhunderte*) and the fourth the posthumous volume V (n. 2) of Baur's *Church History*; and the fifth reprints contemporary attacks by Hase, Uhlhorn and Ritschl, together with Baur's defences of the Tübingen School against the first two (nn. 15, 31), and Zeller's against the third.

The Darmstadt Wissenschaftliche Buchgesellschaft reprinted *Die christliche Gnosis* (n. 6) in 1967, Baur's summary of the history of Christian doctrine (n. 14) in 1968, and his posthumous lectures on NT theology (n. 24) in 1973. Its *Wege der Forschung* volume *Gnosis und Gnostizismus* (ed. K. Rudolph, 1972) begins with an excerpt from the *Church History*. In addition, Zeller's second (1866–7) edition of Baur's *Paulus* (n. 26) was reprinted by Otto Zeller Verlag, Osnabrück, in 1968, as was the second edition (1836) of his 694-page reply to Möhler (n. 36), in 1978. Further back, the monograph on Manichaeism was reprinted by Vandenhoeck & Ruprecht, Göttingen, in 1928.

Only two of Baur's works were translated into English in the nineteenth century: *Paul* in 1875 and vol. I. of his *Church History* in 1878–9. More recently Peter Hodgson translated *The Epochs of Church Historiography* (1852) and the Introduction to the posthumous *Lectures on the History of Christian Dogma* (1865) in a volume entitled *Ferdinand Christian Baur on the Writing of Church History* (OUP, 1968).

Of the older secondary literature special mention must be made of two long essays by Baur's friend and son-in-law E. Zeller: 'Ferdinand Christian Baur' (1861, n. 41); and 'Die Tübinger historische Schule' (1860), both reprinted in his *Vorträge und Abhandlungen* I (Leipzig, 1865; 2nd edn 1875). The enthusiastic essay by Dilthey (1865) reprinted in vol. IV of his *Gesammelte Schriften*, 2nd edn (Leipzig, 1925) also deserves singling out. Other contemporary and near-contemporary accounts still worth reading include the criticisms of Karl von Hase, *Die Tübinger Schule* (1855), and G. Uhlhorn 'Die älteste Kirchengeschichte in der Darstellung der Tübinger Schule' (1858) (both in the Scholder edition, vol. 5), and J. Köstlin's review of Baur's lectures on NT theology in *Theologische Studien und Kritiken* (1866). Sympathetic assessments from the British side were made by Mark Pattison on 'The Present State of Theology in Germany' (*Westminster Review*, 1857; reprinted in vol. II of his collected *Essays*, edited by H. Nettleship, Oxford, 1889), and by R. W. Mackay, *The Tübingen School and its*

Antecedents (London, 1863). But the best way of seeing Baur in context remains his own posthumous *Church History of the Nineteenth-Century* (vol. IV of the Scholder edition).

During the period of Ritschlian ascendency (1870–1920) Baur was under-appreciated. Adolf Hilgenfeld wrote sympathetically in his *Zeitschrift für wissenschaftliche Theologie*, vol. 36 (1893), and O. Pfleiderer even more so in his *Development of Protestant Theology since Kant* (London and New York, 1890). Two monographs were written in this period, the better by G. Fraedrich and the less useful by E. Schneider, both published in 1909. In the post-First War period E. Hirsch's unqualified admiration in vol. v of his *Geschichte der neueren evangelischen Theologie* (Gütersloh, 1960²) Gerd Mohn (pp. 518–52) is amongst the best written on Baur, and Karl Barth's qualified admiration in his *Protestant Theology in The Nineteenth Century*, pp. 499–502 (Zürich, 1952; ET SCM Press, 1972) is one of the best parts of that book. Another excellent long essay is found in Christoph Senft *Wahrhaftigkeit und Wahrheit: Die Theologie des 19 Jahrhunderts zwischen Orthodoxie und Aufklärung* (Tübingen, 1956), pp. 47–86. Since histories of theology and exegesis have not usually done justice to Baur it is worth noting that W. G. Kümmel (n. 31) and C. Welch *Protestant Thought in the Nineteenth Century*, vol. 1 (Yale University Press, 1972) fully appreciate his significance.

In recent scholarship discussion has concentrated on theological biography, especially Baur's relationship to Strauss; his enormous significance for NT history and theology; his wrestling with the christological problem; and his contribution to ecumenics: E. Barnikol published an annotated edition of the Strauss–Baur correspondence in *Zeitschrift für Kirchengeschichte*, vol. 73 (1962), pp. 74–125. Their relationship was discussed by W. Lang in *Preussischer Jahrbücher*, vols. 160–1 (1915), by A. Rapp in *Blätter für Württembergische Kirchengeschichte*, vols. 52–4 (1952–4), and by H. Harris (with a bias against Baur) in his *David Friedrich Strauss and his Theology* (CUP, 1973), pp. 85–116. Barnikol's two other essays are also relevant: 'Das ideengeschichtliche Erbe Hegels bei und seit Strauss und Baur im 19. Jahrhundert' in the *Wissenschaftliche Zeitschrift der Martin-Luther-Universität Halle-Wittenberg* (1961), pp. 281–328 contains valuable information, and the more hostile evaluation in *Ferdinand Christian Baur als rationalistisch-kirchlicher Theologe* (Evangelische Verlagsanstalt GMBH, Berlin, 1970) deserves the respect due to an honest opponent.

Of Baur's other letters, the most important one discussing Schleiermacher's *Glaubenslehre* was edited by Liebing (n. 3; see also n. 4 on the Baur–Schleiermacher debate). H. Pölcher's Erlangen dissertation on Hilgenfeld (1962) contains all or part of nineteen letters by Baur; and Harris published Baur's letter to Tholuck concerning his candidature for Halle and Berlin in 1836 (*Zeitschrift für Kirchengeschichte*, vol. 84, 1973). The same issue of that journal contains two letters of Baur to L. A. Bauer, edited by Carl Hester. K. Schuffels has published oddments of Baur's correspondence in *Blätter für Württembergischer Kirchengeschichte* (1968–9) and an account of the Baur *Nachlass* in *Zeitschrift für Kirchengeschichte*, vol. 79 (1968). G. Müller's monograph (n. 5), contains a detailed account of Baur's intellectual development while he was teaching Strauss at Blaubeuren in the early 1820s, and claims that Schelling was the dominant philosophical influence upon him.

Baur's significance for contemporary NT research has a wider interest. Rudolf Bultmann gave him pride of place in his article on the history of pauline research (n. 49, reprinted in *Das Paulusbild in der neueren deutschen Forschung*, ed. K. H. Rengstorf (Darmstadt, 1964). He also insisted upon Baur's importance for New Testament theology in the 'Epilogue' to *The Theology of the New Testament*, vol. II (1953; ET SCM Press, 1955). Baur's influence is even more pervasive in Käsemann's work, whether in substantial agreement (on John, and even in some respects on Jesus) or admiring disagreement (on Paul). O. Merk, *Biblische Theologie des Neuen Testaments in ihrer Anfangszeit* (Marburg, 1972) recognizes Baur's key position in the development of this discipline, as does W. G. Kümmel in his foreword to the Darmstadt edition of the lectures on NT theology. F. Regner, *'Paulus und Jesus' im 19. Jahrhundert* (Göttingen, 1977) rightly gives prominence to Baur's place in this structurally central issue in NT theology, as does V. Furnish, 'The Jesus–Paul debate: from Baur to Bultmann' (*Bulletin of the John Rylands Library*, vol. 47, 1965). The influence of Baur on subsequent Acts research, highlighted by Ward Gasque, was noted at n. 27.

Baur's NT conclusions and the importance of these for his christology are presented as well by W. Geiger, *Spekulation und Kritik: Die Geschichtstheologie Ferdinand Christian Baurs* (Munich, 1964), as by Hodgson. Their contrasting conclusions are discussed by K. Penzel in the *Journal of Religion*, vol. 48 (1968). There is also a lucid discussion of Baur's christology in E. Teselle *Christ in Context* (Philadelphia, 1976).

The controversy with Moehler has been lightly and usefully presented by J. Fitzer, *Moehler and Baur in Controversy, 1832–38: Romantic-Idealist Assessment of the Reformation and Counter-Reformation*, (American Academy of Religion, 1974). Peter Friedrich *Ferdinand Christian Baur als Symboliker* (Göttingen, 1975) offers a more comprehensive account from Baur's side, including extracts (pp. 62–97) from his earlier (1828/9) lectures on Symbolics.

The conclusions of the pioneer historian have naturally dated more quickly than literary, philosophical and doctrinal classics. This, coupled with the sheer bulk of Baur's writing, partly accounts for the relatively small quantity of major secondary literature. Nevertheless, a book such as B. A. Gerrish, *Tradition in the Modern World* (Chicago, 1978) shows what possibilities the kind of 'historical theology' which Baur represents may contain. There is scope for further research here, along the lines of D. Jodock's dissertation, *F. C. Baur and Albrecht Ritschl on Church History* (Philadelphia, 1978). Baur's understanding of Protestantism, of the essence of Christianity, of the necessity of historical methods in theology, of the place of philosophy of history in historical theology will prove instructive for theologians and students of religion alike. Issues much discussed with reference to Troeltsch and to Bultmann need testing by reference to Baur who influenced them both deeply and was in some respects their master.

9

Ludwig Feuerbach and Karl Marx

VAN A. HARVEY

Most discussions of the relationship between Karl Marx (1818–83) and Ludwig Feuerbach (1804–72) focus on the brief period between 1841 and 1844 when the young Marx was profoundly influenced by Feuerbach's criticism of Hegel, his theory of religion as the projection of human attributes, and his new humanism. Because Marx was ultimately to emerge as the more influential thinker of the two – although at the time it was Feuerbach who was famous and Marx almost unknown – such discussions tend to interpret Feuerbach as a minor, transitional figure in the larger movement of intellectual history from Hegel to Marx. They concentrate, therefore, on Feuerbach's writings around 1841 and ignore the subsequent development of his ideas, especially those concerning religion. From the standpoint of religious thought, however, this interpretation underestimates the significance of Feuerbach's life-long attempt to develop what Paul Ricoeur has called a 'hermeneutics of suspicion', that is, a systematic interpretation of religion based on atheistic principles.

If the conventional interpretation of Feuerbach and Marx tends to be unfair to Feuerbach, a discussion of the two figures that focuses primarily on their criticisms of religion will seem unjust to Marx. Not only did he not write a great deal about religion as such but he believed that any attempt to develop an abstract theory of religion was itself a serious error. Religion, he argued, is not an autonomous sphere of human behavior and belief but reflects a more fundamental social alienation; hence, the only way to deal with it is by means of a critical theory of society as a whole.

It is precisely this difference between the two interpretations of religion that is worth exploring, however, because it reflects a more basic disagreement regarding human nature and its relationship to culture. In an oversimplified way we might say that Feuerbach tended, like Freud after him, to see religion rooted in universal psychic structures that underlie all

291

culture, whereas Marx tended to view psychic structures as themselves products of social and economic conditions. When viewed in this light, the contrast between the two thinkers illustrates a basic cleavage that runs through much contemporary scholarship in the disciplines of psychology, sociology, history, and philosophy, On the one side of this cleavage are those who, like Feuerbach, postulate a universal human nature while, on the other, are those who, like Marx, stress the historical and social determinants of human nature. A comparison and assessment of the views of Feuerbach and Marx on religion may, therefore, cast some light on this contemporary issue.

The early Feuerbach

The young Feuerbach and Marx, like so many other mid-nineteenth-century intellectuals – Strauss, Bruno Bauer, Schelling, and Kierkegaard, to mention a few – were preoccupied with the significance of Hegel, whose shadow so dominated the intellectual horizon of the time that it was necessary to rebel against him if they hoped to cast shadows of their own. In the case of the Young Hegelians, a loosely knit group of brilliant young thinkers centered in Berlin and which included Bruno and Edgar Bauer, August von Cieszkowzski, Marx, Engels, Max Stirner, Moses Hess, and Arnold Ruge, the relationship to Hegel had the emotional ambivalence associated with father-rejection. Hegel was a god-like figure whose magnificent philosophical vision had liberated them from provincial political and religious views and taught them to think critically, or, as they would have said, universally.[1] He taught them that the advance of Spirit into freedom was only made possible by ruthless criticism of everything static and irrational in cultural life. They aspired, like him, to become professors. And yet, when they did criticize the religious and political irrationalities of German culture, they were censored by governmental authorities. This censorship radicalized them still more until, within a few months, they were mounting wholesale attacks on the alliance of Christianity and German culture of which Hegel, ironically, was often seen as the legitimating symbol. Moreover, not only were their writings censored but they were denied those prestigious academic appointments for which they had been trained and to which they aspired. Consequently, as Karl Löwith has pointed out, an entire generation that had been nurtured by and for the university found itself alienated and driven to create a new type of intellectual vocation: the pamphleteer, journalist, and solitary writer dependent on publishers, patrons, readers, and censors.[2] It is not surprising that the professorship, which was once their ideal, became an object of scorn and ridicule.

These controversies had their intellectual roots in certain ambiguities in Hegel's own philosophy that can only be touched on here: his conception of the relationship between the real and the rational, philosophy and religion, Church and State. For Hegel had conceived philosophy to be nothing less than the systematic exhibition of reality taken as a whole and conceived as a dialectical process in which the Absolute manifests itself in nature and history and comes to self-consciousness (as Subject) in and through human self-consciousness. The Infinite perpetually pours out (objectifies) its life in the finite (creation), struggles with the resulting externality (self-alienation) until finally overcoming it in self-knowledge (freedom). Because this process is the logical unfolding of the eternal Idea, the real may be said to be the rational. And since the Spirit comes to self-knowledge in and through the expressions of finite spirits, which is to say, through human cultural expression, all of these human expressions are manifestations of the life of the Absolute and are necessary to its progressive self-realization. Thus, one can say that the same truth implicit in the highest manifestations of the life of the Spirit, for example, in Christianity, will be found as well in the highest manifestations of speculative philosophy; which is to say, in Hegelian philosophy. One may even say that the same spiritual content will be found also in the ideal form of the State. Consequently, the morality of the Church and of the State should mutually guarantee each other; so much so that the ideal State should provide aid to the Church to the extent of demanding that citizens participate in it.

It is clear that Hegel's philosophy could be interpreted either as an endorsement of the status quo (what is *real* is rational) or as a charter for radical, even revolutionary, criticism (only what is *rational* is real). Theologically, it could be used to endorse Christian theism or, on the other hand, a form of atheism (Christianity is a mythical version of the metaphysical process by means of which the Absolute comes to self-consciousness). The Young Hegelians interpreted Hegel in the radical sense and they accounted for the more conservative reading of him by distinguishing between an esoteric and an exoteric Hegelianism. However much his philosophy of the Spirit might appear to justify Christian belief, they argued, it was really irreconcilable with it. D. F. Strauss's *Life of Jesus* argued that the Christian doctrine of the Incarnation could not be logically true on Hegelian principles; and an anonymous pamphlet by Bruno Bauer (*Die Posaune des Jüngsten Gerichts über Hegel den Atheisten und Antichristen*) cleverly exhibits how atheistic Hegel's doctrines must appear to a naive but devout Christian.[3]

The literary review, the *Hallische Jahrbücher für deutsche Wissenschaft und Kunst*, and its successor, the *Deutsche Jahrbücher*, were the organs through which the Young Hegelians addressed the public. At first, the *Hallische Jahrbücher* was intended to be a journal of independent criticism, dealing with contemporary literary, artistic, and theological issues. Its political tone was to be liberal rather than radical. In a few months, however, a controversy over official policy on mixed marriages among Catholics escalated into a wholesale attack on Christian orthodoxy and the very idea of a Christian State. The tightening of censorship that followed pushed the editorial policy still further to the Left until by the early 1840s the *Jahrbücher* emerged as the spokesman for revolutionary politics. It was forced by pressures of censorship to move its editorial offices to Saxony and then again to Paris where under the new title, *Deutsch-französische Jahrbücher*, it expired in 1844 after one issue under the joint editorship of Karl Marx and Arnold Ruge.

It was Feuerbach who formulated a way (the 'transformative method') of interpreting Hegel that enabled the Young Hegelians, especially Marx, to articulate their intellectual ambivalence toward the great philosopher, to understand why his work was at once so profoundly illuminating and a source of mystification. That this should have been Feuerbach's contribution is surprising because he had begun his career as a disciple of Hegel, ready and eager to defend him against all critics. By 1839, however, Feuerbach was expressing many of the same criticisms of Hegel he had once combatted. By 1841, he had come to regard Hegel as the last philosopher of an epoch from which it was necessary to make a complete break. Feuerbach's method of interpreting Hegel is most explicit in his philosophical works published in 1843: *Vorlaüfige Thesen zur Reformation der Philosophie*, and *Principles of the Philosophy of the Future*;[4] and it is implicit in *The Essence of Christianity*, the book for which he is best known. Indeed, its publication in 1841 created a sensation – Strauss hailed it as the 'truth for our age' and Engels later reminisced that it had made all of them Feuerbachians.[5]

The critique of religion this book embodies, while self-contained, can best be understood when taken together with Feuerbach's other works. When placed in this context we can observe five essential components: (1) a more or less straightforward philosophical criticism of theism; (2) an interpretation of the significance of Hegel for the development of Western philosophy; (3) a method – the 'transformative method' – by means of which one can abstract what is legitimate in Hegel's philosophy of Spirit; (4) a new anthropology and a correlative view of the future task of philosophy; (5) an account of the origins and function of religion as the objectification of the attributes of the human spirit.

Because Feuerbach's theory of religion relies so heavily on the Hegelian concept of objectification (*Vergegenständlichung*), which George Eliot rendered as 'projection' in her influential English translation, commentators frequently overlook the importance of Feuerbach's more or less straightforward criticism of theism. His argument is that the Christian idea of God is a hopeless melange of metaphysical attributes, on the one hand, and personal attributes on the other. The God of the theologians is an unchangeable, impassible, omniscient spirit while the God of the naive believer is a personal being that loves, grieves, suffers, and answers prayer. The pathos of Christian theology, Feuerbach argues in anticipation of the similar criticism made by contemporary process theologians, is that it cannot reconcile these antithetical predicates. But whereas contemporary process theologians criticize the classical metaphysical idea of God in order to develop a more coherent notion of God as personal, Feuerbach rejects all such attempted modifications of the idea in favor of atheism; partly because he thinks a personal God would have to be corporeal, even sexual,[6] and partly because he thinks the anthropomorphic predicates can best be explained as projections of the essential qualities of human nature. Although this criticism of theism is a part of Feuerbach's overall argumentative strategy, one could argue that it stands independent of that strategy.

Feuerbach's criticism of theism is related to his interpretation of Hegel and of Hegel's relationship to Christianity. In order for Hegel to claim that Christianity holds the same truth in figurative form which the philosopher holds conceptually, Hegel had to demythologize (to use a contemporary expression) the traditional doctrine of an already perfectly actualized deity who freely creates the cosmos out of nothing. Hegel interpreted this doctrine to mean that the Infinite necessarily and perpetually pours out its life into the finite in the process of coming to its own self-realization as Spirit (Subject). The implication of Hegel's view, Feuerbach claimed, is that matter is not, as in orthodox Christianity, something external to the divine life; rather, matter is the self-objectification of Spirit, a 'moment' in the life of the Absolute. Feuerbach concluded that this could only mean that matter itself is divine, a view that is indistinguishable from pantheism and, finally, atheism.[7] Hegel, however, obscures this conclusion by means of his dialectic in which the negation itself is annulled as the Spirit comes to self-consciousness in and through human self-consciousness. The Absolute 'negates the negation'. God, in short, only becomes God because He negates matter. For Feuerbach, this dialectical move reveals that Hegel is the 'last magnificent attempt to restore Christianity, which was lost and wrecked, through philosophy and, indeed, to restore Christianity . . . by identifying it with the negation of Christianity'.[8]

Throughout his polemic, Feuerbach regards Hegel's error to be the latter's inveterate tendency to treat abstract predicates as entities, especially the predicates of self-consciousness and reason. In this respect, Hegel is the culmination of Western philosophy since Plato, which always thinks of Ultimate Reality in terms of some human attribute like reason. Having construed some such attribute to be the essence of human existence, it then transforms this predicate into an individual being. It converts an idea into a subject. Since the clue to understanding Hegel is this inversion of predicates (universals), it follows that whatever is valid in Hegel can be extracted simply by inverting the subject and the predicate once again and restoring them to their proper relationship. For example, instead of construing the predicate 'thinking' as an entity, one simple transforms the equation and asserts that thinking is the activity of existing individuals. Thought comes out of being, not being out of thought. If Hegel argues that the world is the self-objectification of the Absolute, the truth is that the idea of the Absolute is the objectification of the predicates of human nature. In short, the secret of both speculative philosophy and theology is anthropology properly conceived.

The fourth element in Feuerbach's *Religionskritik* is a new anthropology that eschews all abstractions in favor of thinking concretely and in harmony with the senses. The existing individual, Feuerbach argues in a way anticipatory of later existentialists, is a temporal, suffering, needy, passionate being limited by space and time and by other objects and organisms. The real world is not some hidden metaphysical reality behind given objects we experience but, it is rather, whatever offers external resistance to our own self-activity.[9] The real is whatever is given in and through our senses, by which Feuerbach means not only those organs receptive to what contemporary philosophers call 'sense data' but the internal feelings as well. The ego, or the I, is also an object of the senses for Feuerbach, as is the ego (Thou) of others. There is, in fact, no awareness of an I except as mediated through the encounter with a Thou. The human self is a communal or social self. Consequently, 'Love is objectively as well as subjectively the criterion of being, of truth, and of reality.'[10] Only that which is an object of love or passion exists. 'Thus, love is the true ontological proof of the existence of an object apart from our mind; there is no other proof of being but love and feeling in general.'[11]

It is, of course, the theory that the idea of God is nothing but the objectification of human attributes with which Feuerbach's name is primarily associated. The central argument is simply an application of the transformative method to Hegel's philosophy of Spirit, and many of its complexities derive from this fact. If Hegel presented creation and history as the self-alienation of the Absolute, Feuerbach regards the idea of God as a self-alienating 'moment' in the process of the human spirit coming to self-consciousness. In Feuerbach's view, consciousness is what distinguishes the human from the animal species, and 'consciousness in the strictest sense is present only in a being to whom his species (*Gattung*), his essential nature (*Wesenheit*), is an object of thought'.[12] The human species is then characterized in two ways: as having certain attributes or capacities (reason, will, and affection) and as being essentially social. Since religion is unique to human beings, Feuerbach argues, it is rooted in consciousness; more strongly, it is identical with consciousness.[13] The idea of God, in short, is simply the idea of the species unconsciously and involuntarily made into an object of thought and treated as a separate, heavenly being. It follows that the knowledge of God is really knowledge of essential human attributes.

This deceptively simple argument is interwoven with a number of ancillary arguments that are sometimes both abstruse and doctrinaire. One of them, for example, is that since religion is consciousness of the infinite, it can be nothing less than mankind's awareness of its own infinite nature, by which Feuerbach presumably means the infinitude of consciousness itself.[14] Another argument is that consciousness necessarily experiences its own nature as absolute. Any given individual, it seems, feels its own essential attributes as perfections so that it cannot conceive of them as limited in any way. Mankind cannot get beyond its own true nature.[15] All of these arguments, as well as others, add up to the conclusion that religion is, so to speak, an acoustical illusion of the consciousness, the means by which the species gradually becomes aware of its own essential nature. Although the religious person is, of course, not aware of this, every advance in religious consciousness is an advance in self-knowledge, the culmination of which is, paradoxically, atheism.

Feuerbach, like Hegel, regarded Christianity as the most highly advanced (or absolute) religion. He therefore subjects the Christian idea of God to his transformative analysis and shows that the Christian idea of God simply expresses the most developed view of mankind's essential nature. The idea of God, first of all, represents the objectification of the human attribute of reason, hence the divine predicates of incorporeality, necessity, omniscience, self-subsistence and the like. A purely reasonable God, however, cannot satisfy the heart and since Feuerbach regards religion as basically a practical matter, the God of reason gives way to the God of morality, the objectification of the human attribute of will. But a fully moral deity does not fully satisfy the feelings either. It creates an 'unhappy consciousness' because a perfectly moral being inevitably stands as a reproach to mankind's moral imperfection. The heart is only satisfied by a God of compassion.

Consequently, love is the principle of reconciliation, the absolute perfection. 'Love is God himself, and apart from it there is no God. Love makes man God and God man.'[16]

All of the above arguments, here regrettably oversimplified, reflect Feuerbach's refusal to attribute predicates to a being that transcends finite beings. Indeed, his point is that the predicates of divinity are themselves felt perfections of human nature. It is only naive religion and speculative theology that postulate a subject to which the predicates are attached. How does this illusion arise? In speculative theology it comes about from the tendency to confuse generic concepts with individual things. In naive religion it comes about through the superstitious tendencies of the imagination (*Phantasie*) operating on human feeling. Religion is essentially a matter of feeling; and the imagination, casting aside all reality, lets wish and feeling run riot. To show that this is true, Feuerbach turns to the writings of Luther and his celebration of faith.[17] For Luther, Feuerbach claims, faith is nothing else than the unfettered feeling that God can and will do anything for human beatitude despite the laws of nature and reason. This is why faith demands miracles. Faith is the conviction that what humans wish for is actually true.

The closer religion remains to its naive origins in feeling and wish and imagination the more vital it is because the naive religious consciousness makes no qualitative distinction between humanity and the gods. As culture advances, however, and mankind begins to cogitate on the idea of God, the original and harmless distinction between God and the human becomes a sophisticated type of theology that overlays the personalistic conception with more abstract speculative attributes. It creates a deity that possesses all human perfections and that stands in sharp contrast to mankind's own impoverished condition. More strongly, the projection alienates mankind from its own perfections. 'To enrich God, man must become poor; that God may be all, man must be nothing.'[18] Just as Hegel's Absolute comes to full self-consciousness and freedom by overcoming its alienated objectifications, so Feuerbach's humanity can only come to self-conscious freedom by annulling the objectivity of God. 'In the religious systole man propels his own nature from himself (stösst der Mensch sein eignes Wesen von sich aus), he throws himself outward (er verstösst, virwirft sich selbst); in the religious diastole he receives the rejected nature into his heart again.'[19]

This ingenious inversion of Hegel's philosophy of Spirit enabled Feuerbach to do several important things. First, it enabled him to adopt a genuinely critical stance towards religion; that is, to affirm both its necessity and value while at the same time rejecting its truth claims. Unlike his eighteenth-century atheistic predecessors who simply dismissed religion as primitive superstition, Feuerbach argues that religion is a necessary stage in the development of human consciousness. More strongly, his position is that the development of human consciousness is a function of the development of religion, an extremely provocative suggestion. Secondly, this view enabled Feuerbach to follow Hegel in holding that Christianity is the highest form of religion and self-consciousness while at the same time claiming that its inner meaning is atheism. The basis for this paradoxical claim lies in his interpretation of the Christian doctrine of the Incarnation. In this doctrine, Feuerbach argues, is enshrined the insight that God is an altogether human being, that is, one who feels and loves. More important is the implicit (and atheistic) insight that God so values human happiness that He renounces his own divinity on humanity's behalf. The Christian admittedly loves God because God 'first loved us, indeed died for us'. But what is this but to confess that the worth of the divine being consist in its willing self-surrender on behalf of human well-being? Through the idea of God, mankind learns to estimate its own human nature. A fully matured self-consciousness will see through the doctrine and grasp its atheistic implications. 'As God has renounced himself out of love, so we, out of love, should renounce God; for if we do not sacrifice God to love, we sacrifice love to God, and, in spite of the predicate of love, we have the God – the evil being – of religious fanaticism.'[20] Feuerbach could thus claim to be the true friend of religion while being an atheist; he could argue that real (his) anthropology had more claim to the name of theology than theology itself.[21]

A third consequence of Feuerbach's method is that it enabled him to develop a powerful 'hermeneutics of suspicion', which is to say, a body of principles for the atheistic interpretation of specific Christian doctrines in contrast to sweeping negative generalizations about religion so characteristic of other atheistic criticisms. He uses these principles to explain why specific doctrines are at once so conceptually confused and so emotionally powerful. One must read his interpretations of the doctrines of creation, providence, miracles, the Trinity, and immortality to fully appreciate their brilliance. Especially noteworthy is the chapter on 'The Contradiction of Faith and Love' in which Feuerbach explains how a religion of love can so easily become a religion of fanaticism and hate. In his discussion of the doctrine of the Trinity, for example, he attempts to show why the idea of God must necessarily include elements of sociality (the relationship of an I to a Thou) and why this sociality, in turn, must be three-fold. The bond of love, he argues, must be taken as essential and this bond will inevitably take on the characteristics of the feminine. The doctrine, though unintelligible conceptually, is emotionally powerful because 'the disconsolate feeling of a void, of loneliness, needed a God in whom there is a society, a union of beings fervently loving each other'.[22] After having shown how each Christian doctrine can be interpreted according to his principles he then, in the last half of the book, demonstrates how contradictory they are if taken as theological claims. The entire book is controlled by the aim to exhibit the doctrines as profound insights into human nature but a mass of contradictions if taken as metaphysical truths.

It is by no means simple to discern the degree to which these five elements in Feuerbach's *Religionskritik* are logically interdependent. Would it be possible, for example, to accept his logical criticism of theism but reject his account of the origins of the idea of God? Feuerbach himself obviously did not think so because he argued that his own theory must be correct (theology is anthropology) because theism itself is obviously a mass of contradictions. But this conclusion is not valid, as contemporary process theologians have established, because it could be the case that classical theism is false but that some modified form of theism is not. Feuerbach, like many atheistic critics of religion, only had contempt, however, for any attempt to modify theism in order to make it more intellectually acceptable. He insisted that it was precisely the literal anthropomorphism of theism that reveals its true origins and that constitutes its appeal. This may, perhaps, be the case, but it is not self-evidently so and if accepted without any question puts the theologian in an unfair position: insofar as the theologian attempts to modify the idea of God, he or she is accused of not dealing with real religion; if, on the other hand, the theologian accepts anthropomorphism, he or she is ridiculed. The force of Feuerbach's approach is to force the option of literalism or atheism.

Another problem with his early *Religionskritik*, as he was aware, is that it is not a theory of religion generally but a theory of Christianity. This criticism is more serious than may initially appear because the entire argument rests on the premise that religion as such is the projection of human attributes. How then is one to account for non-theistic religions? One has only to ask this question to notice how effortlessly Feuerbach interchanges the concepts 'religion' and 'Christianity'. He was able to do this because he accepted the Hegelian assumption of the development of religion from lower to higher forms, of which Christianity is the highest. It is the same assumption that enables Feuerbach to regard Christian doctrine as the penultimate stage to atheism. But if one does not accept this Hegelian assumption, and if the projection theory does not illumine non-theistic religions, in what sense is this a convincing theory of religion? Feuerbach, to his credit, soon became aware of this problem and after the publication of his sensational book turned his attention to solving it.

The early Marx

Feuerbach's *Essence of Christianity* made him the most discussed philosopher of the decade in Germany, not surprisingly since it is such a *tour de force*, resting as it does on what still appear to be shocking paradoxes: Christianity is a religion proferring salvation but which alienates humanity; nevertheless, Christianity is instrumental to salvation because its doctrine of redemption expresses the truth that mankind is more important than deity; religion is the great educator of mankind but, like all educators, must be left behind in the interests of maturity.

To the author's Young Hegelian friends, the book was especially powerful because, as Sidney Hook has noted, it provided a theory of the 'natural fetishism' of human consciousness, a theory that could form the basis for criticism of all fetishism.[23] Among these friends, it was Karl Marx who saw most clearly the social significance of Feuerbach's work. For him, Feuerbach's writings constituted the first theoretical revolution since Hegel's *Phenomenology* and *Logic*.[24] He was especially impressed by the social conception of the self, but, above all, he saw in the transformative method a means by which he could appropriate Hegel's philosophy without accepting the latter's idealism. 'Feuerbach', Marx wrote, 'is the only person who has a *serious* and a *critical* attitude to the Hegelian dialectic and who has made real discoveries in this field. He is the true conqueror of the old philosophy.'[25]

Feuerbach made the greatest impact on Marx's thinking during a brief period in the early 1840s, although the extent of that influence was not appreciated until our own century when Marx's *Economic and Philosophic Manuscripts* and his *Critique of Hegel's 'Philosophy of Right'* were published for the first time. Before these manuscripts were discovered, one might have fairly regarded Feuerbach largely as a catalyst precipitating Marx's more radical social criticism of religion. This, for example, is the conclusion one can easily draw from an article Marx published in the *Deutsch-Französische Jahrbücher* in 1844 entitled 'Toward the Critique of Hegel's Philosophy of Right: Introduction'. There Marx does acknowledge Feuerbach's criticisms of religion to be the prerequisite of all criticism because Feuerbach established that man makes religion and worships his own heavenly projection. But Marx writes that this criticism fails to explore the further implications of the fact that the individual is not an abstract being 'squatting outside the world' but a being living within a world of social and political structures which it has created. The State and society produce religion, and if religion is the expression of an unfulfilled existence then the struggle against religion should become a struggle against that world of which religion is the 'inverted consciousness'. In short, Feuerbach's criticism of religion is merely the embryo of a more radical and social criticism of 'that vale of tears of which religion is the halo'. The aim of philosophy is to unmask all forms of alienation and to be effective must unite with revolutionary political action.[26]

The *Economic and Philosophic Manuscripts* reveal, however, that Feuerbach was more than a catalyst; Marx was engaged in a profound inner dialogue with him and, through him, with Hegel. This document contains a systematic criticism of the theorists of capitalism who take for granted the categories of 'land', 'labor', 'property', 'money', 'rent' and 'credit'. The text falls into three main sections: the first deals with the way in which labor is conceived in this system of thought; the second deals with private property and communism; and the third is concerned with Hegel's dialectic. The dominant theme Marx pursues is that the so-called science of political economy uncritically assumes that exchange and trade are the determinative relationships among human beings and, consequently, takes the resulting impoverishment of life as the norm. The two critical concepts in the text are 'alienation' (*Entfremdung*) and 'species-being' (*Gattungswesen*),[27] and the employment of these two concepts tell us a great deal about Marx's intellectual relationship to Feuerbach and to Hegel.

Marx uses the term 'species-being', as well as its synonyms 'species-character' (*Gattungscharakter*), 'species-life' (*Gattungsleben*), to refer to those distinctive human capacities the exercise of which constitutes self-realization. Like Feuerbach, who used the less technical terms 'species' and 'essential nature', Marx assumes (a) that human nature is intrinsically social and can only be fulfilled in community; (b) that consciousness permeates human activity and, therefore, how the person relates to the world is constitutive of its being; and (c) that the appropriation of sensuous objects is essential to human well-being. Unlike Feuerbach, however, Marx insists that productive activity (*produzierenden Tätigkeit*) constitutes the species-life of human beings. It is through the fashioning of the objective world that the species-being comes into existence, that 'nature appears as *his* work and his reality. The object of labour is therefore the *objectification of the species-life of man*' . . .[28] Since Marx knew this view to be similar to Hegel's, he was forced once more to rethink through his own relationship to the philosopher. Hegel, too, conceived of history as the self-creation of humankind, a dialectical process in which human activity manifests itself as objectification or loss of the object and the subsequent overcoming of this alienation.[29] Hegel also understood that the individual can only realize its distinctive species-life insofar as he actually brings forth all his species powers, and that this is made possible through the collective effort of mankind, which is to say, history. The one-sideness of Hegel, in Marx's opinion, is that he viewed human development solely in terms of abstract thought. Because he reduced alienation to the alienation of self-consciousness, the overcoming of alienation is also equated with an alteration of consciousness. Freedom is identified with Absolute Knowledge. Thus, the philosopher who lives in a world of abstract thought and is himself an abstract form of the alienated individual 'sets himself up as the *yardstick* of the alienated world'.[30] Consequently, Hegel's profound insight into the nature of human self-creation is spoiled by what Marx understands as a mystifying mode of thought that has not achieved clarity.

Marx understands Feuerbach's great contribution to be the transformative method that enables one to extract what is valid in Hegel's philosophy of Spirit without becoming entangled in his mystifications. Feuerbach showed, first of all, that concrete, existing beings can only exist in relation to external objects. These are objects of human need, and therefore a part of its 'species-life', indispensable to the exercise and confirmation of its essential capacities. Marx writes that 'A being which does not have its nature outside itself is not a natural being and plays no part in the system of nature . . . A non-objective being is a non-being.'[31] Further, human beings are not merely parts of nature but corporeal, sentient, suffering beings who must express themselves in sensible existence and activity as well as in thought. Since objectivity is a part of species-life, there is no necessity, as Hegel thought, to annul this objectivity. There is no need to negate thinghood. It was the genius of Feuerbach, Marx claims, to have seen that this negation of thinghood is the source of Hegel's mysticism and political conservativism, because after having interpreted the State and religion as the self-externalization of Spirit, Hegel then proposed that the Spirit recognize its own authentic nature *in* them.

Marx extends his criticism of Hegel further by making a sharp distinction between objectification as such and alienation, a distinction he accuses Hegel of obliterating with fatal consequences.[32] For Marx, not all objectification involves alienation. There are objectifications that are alienating, to be sure, but there are others that are not. An alienated objectification is a human product that takes on an independent existence such that it is no longer amenable to human control, and cannot be appropriated humanly. By virtue of this distinction, Marx escapes the tragic conception of human destiny so characteristic of Hegel. Whereas in Hegel alienation is an ontological feature of human existence, imbedded in the unfolding life of the Absolute Spirit, in Marx alienation is a product of specific social conditions. There is no ontological necessity about it. This more optimistic view of history helps to explain Marx's subsequent revolutionary and even utopian appeal.

This revision and appropriation of Hegel's philosophy of Spirit, it could be argued, not only underlies the early *Economic and Philosophic Manuscripts* but Marx's later socio-economic writings as well. The demonic nature of capitalism is that it imposes a structure on human relationships such that mankind's distinctive activity, labor, is no longer meaningful and free. It is not free because the person finds it necessary to work simply in order to survive, and the worker, therefore only feels like a human being when he or she is at leisure, that is, not engaged in the distinctive activity of the species-being. Since the distinctive species-life itself is meaningless, the objectification (product) of that life is also alien. It is not produced as a thing of beauty or interest. It is simply a part of a world of objects that the laborer does not appropriate and over which he or she has no control. The more objects produced in this alien fashion, the more impoverished the laborer feels (and is) inwardly, a phrase that, incidentally, almost literally echoes Feuerbach's indictment of the idea of God. Moreover, the pattern of relationships dictated by the economic structures of capitalism, with its various forms of specialized labor, also distorts social relationships. Persons are essentially related to one another through the system of ownership, property, and money. Individuals produce in order to own objects in contrast to expressing their own individuality through them or to satisfy the genuine needs of others.

Finally, Marx argues that this alienated pattern of labor distorts the human relationship to nature. There is, incidentally, no section of these manuscripts more dependent on the notion of species-being or that expresses an aspect of Marx's thought ignored by those critics who treat him as a crude materialist than this section dealing with nature. In almost Romantic terms, Marx argues that species-life is dependent upon a living relation with organic nature; that plants, animals and external objects constitute 'a part of human consciousness' because they are objects of art, sensuous enjoyment, and science. Alienated labor distorts this relationship with nature because the species-life becomes merely a means to the survival of individual life. But individual life is a mere abstraction because the person is a social being. 'The universality of man manifests itself in practice in that universality which makes the whole of nature his *inorganic* body, (1) as a direct means of life and (2) as the matter, the object and the tool of his life activity. Nature is man's *inorganic body*, that is to say, nature insofar as it is not the human body.'[33]

The later Marx

Throughout his entire intellectual life, Marx periodically engaged in disciplined self-clarification, and in 1845 and 1846 he devoted himself to a final settling of accounts with the Young Hegelians and with Feuerbach. The results of this self-clarification are found in two documents, both of which remained unpublished during his life. The first was a massive tome of over seven hundred pages, *The German Ideology*, written in collaboration with his new colleague and friend, Friedrich Engels, while the second, *Theses on Feuerbach*, consists of but eleven cryptic paragraphs. Considered together, these documents are profoundly revealing of the directions Marx's new insights were leading him. They also lead the reader to the ironic conclusion that although it was Feuerbach who enabled Marx to appropriate Hegel's view of Spirit as self-creative activity, this appropriation, in turn, was to provide the basis for Marx's final break with Feuerbach.

The most general criticism of the Young Hegelians is similar to that previously levelled at Feuerbach in the earlier article in the *Deutsch-französische Jahrbücher*; namely, that they simply take for granted the dominance of philosophy, theology, and religion in German life and do not understand that these abstract modes of thought are themselves nothing but reflections of the German society in which they are rooted. Consequently, the Young Hegelians mistakenly assume that erroneous ideas can be reformed simply by subjecting them to abstract criticism in the Hegelian mode. Having never left the domain of abstract thought, they simply perpetuate the fog of mystification spread by Hegel. As for Feuerbach, Marx concedes that his materialism is superior to previous materialisms insofar as he stresses that the person is an object of the senses. Nevertheless, Feuerbach remains within the realm of pure theory, viewing objects, persons, and things as mere objects of knowledge. He does not regard the sensuous world as the total living sensuous activity of the individuals that comprise it. He does not understand that the sensuous world is not something directly given to the mind but is organized by and filtered through the concepts and language that reflect practical human activity. Feuerbach writes abstractly about love and friendship but he has nothing to say about the existing social conditions that make persons what they are. He claims that happiness consists in the exercise of humankind's distinctive species-powers but he treats every exception to this as a mere abnormality. If Feuerbach knows that millions of workers are depressed, he accepts this unhappiness as a mere misfortune. He tries to resolve the religious projections into the human essence, to dissolve the holy family into the secular family, but he fails to see that the human essence is 'no abstraction inherent in each single individual' but is 'the ensemble of the social relations'.[34] He talks about the religious sentiment but does not grasp the notion that this sentiment is itself a social product. He proudly calls himself a communist but does not proffer any criticism of existing social conditions. He is, therefore, impotent to envisage the real liberation of humanity. The only truly rational solution to human practice, Marx concludes, consists in the comprehension of this practice, which is to say, a philosophy that aims to change the world and not merely to understand it.

These criticisms of Feuerbach rest on two interrelated ideas fundamental to the later Marx's anthropology: persons relate to nature and one another through their practical activity; and consciousness is radically conditioned by social existence. Both ideas are the basis for his repudiation of purely abstract (philosophical) discussions of human nature, in contrast to socio-historical analyses which consider the material conditions that concrete individuals produce and under which they live. It is a mistake, Marx argues, to attempt to understand human existence by appeal to some universal characteristics like consciousness, speech, or religion. The first premise of a valid materialism is that human beings distinguish themselves from animals as soon as they begin to produce their own means of subsistence. This production, in turn, depends on what any given group of people find already there in nature (which itself depends upon physical, climatic, geographical, and technological conditions) and what must be reproduced in order for the group to survive. So far as what has to be reproduced is concerned, Marx argues that any mode of reproduction will indirectly create forms of specialized labor, patterns of social organization and political authority, as well as forms of ownership, rules of conduct, and appropriate forms of social intercourse. As societies grow larger and more complex, for example, agriculture will be distinguished from commerce, towns from country, and among these spheres there will soon develop further divisions among the individuals who cooperate in various forms of labor. Indeed, 'How far the productive forces of a nation are developed is shown most manifestly by the degree to which the division of labour has been carried.'[35] Marx then briefly sketches the different stages of the division of labor that have been dictated by various patterns of ownership: tribal ownership, communal and state ownership, and feudal or estate ownership.

It is important to stress that Marx does not conceive of this historical process in materialist terms alone. What persons produce establish corresponding ways of life, and ideas and concepts are then also produced in order to deal with these ways of life. In short, the thinking process is conditioned by the development of productive forces and the social intercourse corresponding to them. The language of politics, law, morality, philosophy and religion are all forms of consciousness that should not be treated as though they had an autonomous history of their own. It is people who alter their thinking as they develop their material productions and mutual intercourse. 'Life is not determined by consciousness, but consciousness by life.' [36] It follows that since the means of production are relative to a given stage of historical development, so, too, are the legal, religious, and philosophical ideas that were formulated to deal with the practical activities of that stage. If Feuerbach thought that there was some general universal human nature, Marx states that 'The positive expression "human" corresponds to the definite conditions *predominant* at a certain stage of production and to the way of satisfying needs determined by them, just as the negative expression "inhuman" corresponds to the attempt, within the existing mode of production, to negate these predominant conditions the way of satisfying needs prevailing under them, an attempt that this stage of production daily engenders afresh.'[37]

Marx's claim that consciousness is determined by social existence has been labelled 'economic determinism'. This label is much too crude because it ignores the dialectical relationship Marx sees between practical activity, on the one hand, and the objectifications created by that activity, on the other. Persons create sociological structures out of their needs. These, in turn, take on the characteristics of given, objective existence which, in turn, modify and condition the consciousness of individuals born into that society. These objective structures, and the ideas and concepts which are created to deal with them, not only delimit and define possibilities of further thought and action but also create new needs, desires, and dissatisfactions that then stimulate new forms of creative activity. What Marx has envisaged, Sholomo Avineri observes, is a never-ending dialectical pursuit of creations and satisfactions. This pursuit is what constitutes historical development.[38]

Marx's view of the dialectical relationship between consciousness and society has had an enormous impact on modern intellectual inquiry generally – the sociology of knowledge is unintelligible apart from him – as well as on religious studies particularly. For Marx's view makes possible an interpretation of religious ideas that regards them as reflections of the social and economic conditions of a given society. Moreover, since Marx believed religion to be the peculiar expression of an alienated society, he saw it as the 'sigh of the oppressed creature', something destined to pass away just to the degree the species-life of humanity was realized.

Marx's view of the relation of ideas to the underlying social 'infrastructure' obviously raises the question of the truth not only of religious but of all ideas. As Robert Merton has pointed out, this view inevitably tends to relativize, secularize, and devaluate any claims to knowledge.[39] All beliefs may be seen as rationalizations, myths, and projections. Many Marxist philosophers have also noted this but argued that Marx's great contribution to philosophy consists in his challenge to the classical idea of truth in which the essentially receptive mind apprehends objective, essential structures of an external world. In contrast, it is claimed, Marx sees that how people organize, classify, differentiate, and evaluate reflects the needs and interests of specific historical communities. This view, incidentally, is what apparently lies behind one of Marx's own somewhat cryptic *Theses on Feuerbach*. 'The question whether objective truth can be attributed to human thinking is not a question of theory but is *a practical question*. Man must prove the truth, i.e., the reality and power, the this-sidedness of his thinking in practice.'[40]

It is scarcely possible to pursue here the complex epistemological issues this Marxist position raises except to point out that it still remains for those sociologists of knowledge who accept it to specify more precisely than they yet have what precise relationship obtains between ideas, knowledge, and beliefs and the social structures in which they are rooted. As Merton has pointed out, many different answers have been given to such questions as: (1) Where are we to locate the basis of mental productions: in social position? class? occupational role? ethnic affiliation? power structure? historical situation? (2) What mental productions are the objects of our sociological analysis: moral beliefs? ideologies? categories of thought? science? technology? (3) How is the social basis related to those ideas: causally? functionally? as necessary conditions? (4) What manifest or latent functions are imputed to these mental productions: to maintain power? to promote stability? to provide motivation or reassurance or control?

Marx's view that the religious sentiment itself is a product of an alienated social existence surely implies, as we have noted, a negative evaluation of it. But some recent interpreters of Marx have argued that there are good reasons for believing that his position does not require such a negative evaluation. Although it is the case, they concede, that Marx was personally hostile to religion, one may regard this hostility as an historical accident, a reflection of his own superficial encounter with reactionary forms of religion. In fact, they suggest, the logic of his criticisms of Feuerbach and Hegel opens up a new avenue for rapprochement with more authentic (non-alienating) types of religion. For example, although Marx accepted Feuerbach's early identification of religious objectification with alienation, he later made a sharp distinction between objectification and alienation. But if there are human objectifications that are not intrinsically alienating, why must one assume that all religious objectifications are? Why could there not be forms of religious expression in which human dignity, responsibility and freedom are affirmed, which is to say, religions that can be appropriated humanly? Moreover, it would seem possible to employ Marxist interpretative principles regarding the interpretation of religion without assuming religious ideas to be false. Thus, a sociologist of knowledge might operate on the assumption that religious symbols and ideas are projections without affirming them to be any more true or false than are other human projections like, say, mathematics or scientific theories. The sociologist is simply a methodological agnostic in the sense of suspending judgments about this issue.

There are other interpreters of Marx, however, who are suspicious of this attempt to soften his hostility to religion. They claim that his view dictates that religion be seen as the 'sigh of the oppressed creature', an illusory happiness that reflects an unfulfilled social existence. Moreover, all religions, however demythologized, posit either some inherent human defect not amenable to *praxis* or some transcendent reality over which human beings have no control. As such, religions are, by definition, alienating mystifications.

In order to speak intelligently to this controversy, it is necessary to distinguish among three separate though related issues: (1) Marx's own hostile posture towards religion; (2) his view that the religious sentiment is a social product and the expression of an unfulfilled existence; and (3) his view that religious ideas can best be interpreted in terms of the social function they serve in any given group. Having then made these distinctions, it seems clear that there are several ways one might reason. For example, one might concede that the religious sentiment is a social product but argue that since human existence is inherently social and all human sentiments reflect this sociality, nothing positive or negative about religion follows from this. Or, one might concede that religion is indeed the expression of an unfulfilled existence but argue that human existence is, in the nature of the case, unfulfilled. Neither claim as such entitles one to draw a negative conclusion regarding religion. A negative conclusion need be drawn only if it is assumed (a) that the religious sentiment is intrinsically alienating or expresses itself in forms that are alienating; or (b) that fulfilled existence is a genuine historical possibility and, hence, a moral imperative to realize; or (c) that insofar as human existence is unfulfilled, it is wrong to express one's longings in a religious form. A consideration of these issues leads us once more to Marx's conception of human nature and the related concept of alienation.

Unfortunately, Marx had very little interest in what he considered the abstract questions of philosophical anthropology and his views are, therefore, subject to various interpretations. In fact, even among Marxist philosophers who stress the historicity of human nature, there are significant differences. On the one hand, there are those who, like István Mészáros,[41] argue that Marx denied that there is any universal human essence. The human, it is claimed, is relative to any given stage of historical development. On the other hand, there are those who, like Adam Schaff[42] and Erich Fromm,[43] argue that although Marx may have abandoned the terminology of species-being, he never departed from the intrinsic content contained in that conception. They argue that he really distinguished between a fundamental universal nature and a relative nature conditioned by historical and social existence.

The historicist view claims that for Marx the instruments and forms of human interchange are inherently historical, changing, and socio-historically specific. He is alleged to have created an ontology that is dynamic and open since the historical process is a never-ending dialectic of activity issuing in alienating objectifications that are then superseded (*aufgehoben*) and that, in turn, create new needs and dissatisfactions which again are objectified, etc. The objection to religion in this view, an objection that applies equally to idealistic and existentialist philosophies, is that religion inevitably mystifies concrete social situations by assuming that alienation is rooted in human existence as such. It assumes that there is some ontological or psychological fault not amenable to human practice and change. In short, it assumes that alienation is a fundamental dimension of history (Heidegger).

This criticism of religion, although most obviously directed against Christianity, also applies to all those forms of religion (so often taken as paradigmatic, by Mircea Eliade, for example) that sacralize recurrent and non-historical patterns of nature like death and rebirth, just as it also applies to any alleged universal way of salvation. Any religion or *Weltanschauung* that rests on the assumption that humanity is suffering from some disease for which religion is the alleged cure is, by definition, alienating and mystifying.

One of the difficulties with this radically historicist criticism of religion, however, is that just because it conceives of history as a never-ending process in which various concrete forms of alienation are overcome it also seems to assume that alienation is, in some sense, a fundamental dimension of history. Consider, for example, the position of Mészáros in this regard. He argues that Marx not only historicized the concept of human nature but of alienation as well. Just as the concept 'human' is relative to the possibilities and needs of a given historical epoch, so also the concept 'alienation' does not derive its meaning in contrast to some universal human nature; rather, alienation is also defined relative to the possibilities and needs of a historically relative situation. It follows, Mészáros insists, that for Marx alienation is never completely annulled because in the process of *Aufhebung* there will be preserved certain 'moments' of the previous (though annulled) alienation. Thus, Mészáros concludes that there is no place in Marx's vision for any complete abolition of alienation. 'Such a golden age would be an end of history, and thus the end of man himself.'[44]

But if Marx held that alienation is never abolished, how does Mészáros avoid the conclusion that alienation, if not necessary, is, nevertheless, inevitable, to paraphrase the famous paradox of the Protestant theologian Reinhold Neibuhr? This is, in fact, the interpretation of Marx proposed by Jean Hyppolite and Martin Heidegger who, ironically, see the profundity of Marx to be his insight that alienation is constitutive of the historical process. Mészáros concedes that there is some grain of truth in these interpretations of Marx, 'otherwise they could hardly succeed in their mystificatory function',[45] but he argues that they are, nevertheless, exaggerations that succeed only because they suppress the dialectical connections and mistakenly identify 'alienating propensities', which are always present in any situation, with ontological necessities. Of course, Mészáros insists, there are dangers in the alienating potentialities of technologies, bureaucracies, and institutions; and, of course, there are no *a priori* assurances that can be given for the practical abolition of alienation; and, of course, no achievement of an unalienated state can be regarded as final. Nevertheless, these dangers can be controlled in principle and the real issue is the degree of alienation in any concrete situation. Idealists and existentialists who talk of alienation as if it were a fundamental dimension of history are simply projecting 'capitalistic alienation'.[46]

This reply of Mészáros is convincing only if (a) the idealist or existentialist or theologian really does confuse the basic, existential alienation with social injustice and uses it to obfuscate all attempts at social reform, and (b) if the historicist can successfully sustain the case that there is no ontological basis for alienation in human life, which is to say, that mankind has no nature but only a history. The formal issue is whether human existence as such is subject to limitation, crushed hopes, tragic choices, and death, all of which give rise to the questions to which religion attempts to give some answer. One might argue, as Freud did, that civilization as such requires the repression of some instincts and the creation of institutions that are never completely amenable to human control. Or it is possible to argue, as some existentialists and others have done, that the very structure of the human organism – a self-transcending consciousness in a decaying body – drives it to ask the question of the 'meaning of life'. If these are intelligible positions one might expect human beings always to seek solace for the sorrows endemic to human life, to look for some larger assurance than that promised by political change. The issue is whether the historicist view of Marx could acknowledge the legitimacy of the religious sentiment and of those symbolic forms that assuage these sorrows but that are not inimical to human responsibility for social reform. In short, could there be a humanistic religion within a Marxist perspective?

The interpretation of Marx that is less historicist, which views him as having distinguished between a basic (universal) and a relative (historically conditioned) human nature, poses the problem of religion in a slightly different form. Everything now depends on determining which instincts and needs are to be assigned to the basic and which to the relative nature. Insofar as it is characteristic of every human being to be a self-transcending consciousness in a physical body, it seems reasonable to say that everyone will be confronted by limitation, disease, crushed hopes, and death. If the religious sentiment is rooted in these endemic human crises, it will be unconvincing to explain religion away simply as a reflection of the contradictions in a given social situation. Here, also, the issue is whether the Marxist could concede that there might be a legitimate form of religion that attempts to thematize these perennial human dilemmas, legitimate in the sense that such a religion is not socially reactionary or corrosive of human responsibility for the world (*praxis*).

However passionately Marx was himself moved by the problem of injustice, he also seems to have had an unmusical ear so far as the existential sorrows that play such a role in human religion are concerned. On the whole he felt – perhaps justifiably – that the forms of religion with which he was acquainted privatized the self by stressing either personal salvation or cultic identity; or they legitimated social and economic privilege; or they diverted feelings of oppression into non-reformatory channels. In all of their forms, they weaken the sense that the person is basically a social being, that the powers of the individual are social powers and that these ought not to be separated from political power.[47] Consequently, they are all inimical to the truth that human beings create themselves through *praxis*.

The later Feuerbach

If Marx ignored the importance of existential problems like death for the interpretation of culture, Feuerbach believed such problems held the key to understanding it. He thought the religious sentiment to be innate in human nature,[48] and to understand why this was the case he returned again and again to just those issues of philosophical anthropology Marx eschewed. If, for Marx, the most important aspect of human nature is creative activity, for Feuerbach it is the existence of an ego in the grip of an insatiable urge to live and to be happy while mediated to the world through an organism fated to die. Feuerbach's later works are a series of attempts to formulate his anthropological insights in a convincing theory of religion.

In a small book published in 1845, *Das Wesen der Religion*, and then again in his *Lectures on the Essence of Religion* (1848), which he delivered at Heidelberg at the invitation of the students (to whom he was a cultural hero), he attempted to reformulate a new theory and to answer criticism made against *The Essence of Christianity*. The most important criticisms were that he had not developed a theory of religion generally in contrast to a theory of Christianity; that he had interpreted religion too much in anthropomorphic terms and had ignored religions of nature; and that his theory of projection could not account for the ordinary believer's sense of the external reality of God. To these criticisms Feuerbach even added an important one of his own: he had not done sufficient justice to the role of the senses in religion. In his *Lectures* he concedes that he had given too much attention to human nature in contrast to nature generally and he modifies his theory of projection, a modification that involves subtle but important shifts away from the Hegelian model of the Spirit that dominated *The Essence of Christianity*.

In the early sections of the *Lectures* Feuerbach expands on an idea he had introduced in *Das Wesen der Religion*, namely, that the foundation (*Grund*) of religion is the human feeling of dependence (*Abhängigkeitsgefühl*), the first object of which in the history of the species is obviously nature. This appeal to a feeling of dependence calls to mind the theology of Friedrich Schleiermacher, with whom Feuerbach had intended to study in Berlin before he transferred his allegiance to Hegel and philosophy. Feuerbach, however, takes pains to distance himself from Schleiermacher's use of this concept. Whereas the Protestant theologian had used the term to refer to the sense of being a part of an interrelated and lawful system of causes and effects, a 'universal nature system', Feuerbach refers to specific types of dependencies various cultures have on the animals, objects, and crops that sustain them physically. Archaic man, Feuerbach argues, does not have some vague general sense of being part of a universal nature system; rather, the primitive experiences sensible feelings of dependence on this or that specific animal or object essential to the group for its survival. These beings inspire, fear, hope, awe, love, and delight. Realizing that physical welfare depends upon them, the primitive cajoles, propitiates, and worships them. The first definition of a god, he notes, is simply 'what man requires for his existence, and specifically for his physical existence . . .'[49] This helps explain why primitive sacrifice is the key to the origins of religion, as in animal worship and polytheism.

The propitiation and worship of the beings upon which humans depend presupposes two closely related things: first, that the beings or objects are believed to be capable of giving and withholding favor, that they have, so to speak, hearts and minds; and, secondly, that people set supreme value upon their own survival and happiness. The former reveals the phenomenon of the projection of human attributes; the latter discloses that this projection really reflects humankind's love for itself. Since both presuppositions are consistent with the theory Feuerbach developed in *The Essence of Christianity*, he argues that he has merely enlarged his earlier view. If in the earlier work he had said that theology is anthropology, he now simply adds that it is 'anthropology plus physiology'. Even in nature worship, the human objectifies its own being. My formula, he writes, can be 'summed up in two words: *nature* and *man*'.[50]

As the argument proceeds, Feuerbach drops the term 'feeling of dependence' in favor of a considerably more flexible term, egoism (*Egoismus*). Egoism includes the feeling of dependence but encompasses much more: wishes, needs, instincts, and desires. Abstractly stated, it is not only the instinct for self-preservation but the self-love that spurs the person on 'to satisfy and develop all the impulses and tendencies without whose satisfaction and development he neither is nor can be a true, complete man'.[51] It is clear that egoism is not merely a psychological category but an ontological one in the sense that Nietzsche's Will-to-Power is. Since egoism underlies and encompasses the feeling of dependence, Feuerbach argues that it is the 'ultimate hidden ground' (*den letzten verborgenen Grund*) of religion.[52] It is hidden because the ego is unaware of it even though this drive determines whether an object will be religiously valued or not.

Although egoism is the subjective ground of religion, nature is the objective ground, at least at the beginnings of history. Nature is the first object of the senses and it is in nature that humanity lives and moves and has its being. As it is first encountered, nature is not, of course, an object of science or knowledge but an object of practical need. It is also filtered through ignorance and superstition, which is to say, through the imagination (*Phantasie*). It is the imagination that endows nature with anthropomorphic qualities, that projects upon it wishes, desires, and dependencies. In this sense, Feuerbach can say that the imagination is the 'theoretical cause of religion' (*die theoretische Ursache*) that creates the gods.[53]

If the problem of *The Essence of Christianity* was how Feuerbach accounts for nature religions, the problem of his lectures is how he explains the religions of spirit (theism) and their relationship to the religions of nature. To some extent, the lectures are ambiguous on this crucial point; partly because Feuerbach offers several not always consistent arguments and partly because he sometimes regards human nature as part of nature generally while at other times he takes pains to distinguish them.[54] Insofar as he writes as though there are two distinct types of religion with different objects, he tends to see no progression from nature religion to theism. In this vein, he can write that the two types of religion are to be understood as reflecting two different types of wishes. Paganism desires a sensuous object whereas the theist deifies the mind.[55] At other times, there seems to be a more unified concept at work. Thus, in an extended note to the fifth lecture, he proposes a theory that synthesizes the two views, a theory which, incidentally, is remarkable when read in the light of contemporary psychological theory. It is also much closer to Schleiermacher's view than his earlier disclaimers allow. Religion emerges, he writes, when everything external to the I, the conscious ego, is transformed into a being possessing subjectivity.

Man with his ego or consciousness stands at the brink of a bottomless abyss; that abyss is his own unconscious being, which seems alien to him and inspires him with a feeling which expresses itself in words of wonderment such as: What am I? Where have I come from? To what end? And this feeling that I am nothing without a *not-I* which is distinct from me yet intimately related to me, something *other*, which is at the same time my *own* being, is the religious feeling.[56]

Indeed, this fusion of I and not-I is the secret, the essence of individuality and the 'foundation of individuality is also the foundation of religion . . .'[57] If the person was a mere I, there would be no religion, for the person would be God. But there would also be no religion if the person was a not-I, or an I undifferentiated from the not-I, for then the person would be a plant or an animal. 'The ultimate secret of religion is the *relationship* between the *conscious* and *unconscious*, the *voluntary* and *involuntary in one and the same individual*.'[58]

Feuerbach then attempts to show that monotheism emerges when the not-I is envisaged as a unified whole and regarded by the imagination as a subjective being. All of objective nature is construed as a subject; the class of all beings (being itself) is transformed into an individual being. Because humans are dependent upon it, they also regard it as an absolutely unconditioned being. Monotheism, in short, is nothing more than a compendium of the most universal attributes abstracted from nature and transformed into an individual being.[59] Thus, Feuerbach can argue simultaneously that inversion is the secret of theology, that monotheism is a disease of language (the reification of a universal), that nature is the true object of religion, and that 'God' is the objectification of the human essence.

This brief rehearsal scarcely does justice to the complexity or the ambiguities of Feuerbach's argument but perhaps it suffices as a background for certain comments. First of all, the appeal to egoism and the encounter with nature involves something of a shift from the concept of projection in *The Essence of Christianity*, which is so heavily dependent on the Hegelian model of the development of Spirit coming to self-consciousness in and through its projections. To be sure, some continuity with this model still remains since the projections of religion are still regarded as objectifications of human attributes. But whereas in *The Essence of Christianity* the objectifications of spirit are a necessary aspect of the process of coming to self-consciousness, in the *Lectures*, they reflect the wishful thinking of the imagination at work and, consequently, religion is linked more closely with ignorance and superstition. Moreover, in the earlier work the objectivizing activity of consciousness is spontaneous and self-reflexive whereas in the *Lectures* the imagination reifies the qualities of external objects. It is, in fact, the actual externality of nature that accounts for the believer's (illusory) sense that there is an external deity. This stress on the reification of qualities given in nature leads Feuerbach, in turn, to suggest a somewhat different explanation for the attribution of certain predicates to deity than he did in *The Essence of Christianity*. There, it will be remembered, all of the attributes of God were regarded as the objectification of certain essential human predicates. In the *Lectures*, however, not only are the divine predicates of eternity, infinity, 'superhumanity', universality, and omnipotence to be explained as abstractions from nature but so, also, are the moral attributes of justice, wisdom, and goodness. 'God's goodness is merely abstracted from those beings and phenomena in nature which are useful, good, and helpful to man, which give him the feeling or consciousness that life, existence, is a good thing, a blessing.'[60]

One significant result of this shift away from the Hegelian model is reflected in Feuerbach's classification of religions and the correlative evaluation of them. In his earlier work, following Hegel, the religions of Spirit (especially Christianity) were regarded as higher stages in the development of self-consciousness. Indeed, as we have seen, the basic argument of *The Essence of Christianity* depends on this developmental scheme. Although remnants of this developmental model remain in the *Lectures*, he more characteristically argues that Christianity is not a higher form of religion but, on the contrary, is inferior to, perhaps even a retrogression from, nature worship.[61] His purpose, he claims, is to justify and defend paganism and nature religion against theism.[62] Nature religions are more in accord with the senses whereas Christianity puts too much emphasis upon the spirit and makes God a being distinct from nature. Christianity raises the fantastic hope that the individual spirit will live forever.

It should be noted that this altered view of the relation of theism to paganism tends to undercut Feuerbach's earlier claim that he is simply preserving what is valid in Christianity in an atheistic form. On the contrary, he now rejects what he claims is the major concern of Christianity, the deification of man. Pagan religion has the virtue, he argues, that its desires 'did not exceed the nature of man, the limits of this life, of this real sensuous world. And for this very reason, their gods were no such unlimited and supernatural beings as the Christian God.'[63] Thus if Feuerbach in *The Essence of Christianity* could regard God and Christ as mythological projections embodying the perfections of the species, in the *Lectures*, Christianity is the expression of a diseased eros. It 'tries to make more of man than he should be, and consequently makes less of him than he could be; it tries to make him into an angel and consequently, given the opportunity, makes him into a true devil'.[64]

Feuerbach had not yet finished his lectures at Heidelberg when he conceived and started working upon yet a third version of his critique of religion. The major parts of this third version were written between 1851 and 1856, and it appeared the following year under the title *Theogonie nach den Quellen des klassischen, hebräischen und christlichen Altertums*. A second, unchanged version under a slightly altered title appeared in 1866. In the *Theogonie*, Feuerbach once more concentrates upon the subjective ground of religion, this time not under the rubric of egoism but of the drive for happiness (*Glückseligkeitstrieb*). It is an undeiestimated book – although Feuerbach himself thought it was his best – despite its many limitations. One might call it a phenomenology of the wish because the discussion ranges imaginatively over the relationship between the fundamental wish for happiness and such cultural phenomena as systems of morality, law, conscience, the taking of oaths, dreams, miracles, pain, the desire for immortality, and, of course, the creation of the gods. He illustrates his arguments copiously from classical Greek, Hebraic, and early Christian sources. Indeed, one of the defects of the book, which probably accounts for its lack of public acceptance, is that the arguments tend to deteriorate into a mass of learned historical and philological discussions, a difficulty the Bolin and Jodl edition of Feuerbach's works (1907) tried to remedy by the dubious device of eliminating the illustrative materials – dubious because the book is scarcely intelligible without them.

The basic argument of the *Theogony* is that the gods do not spring out of the human feeling of dependence or from the encounter with nature but are, rather, the reified wishes of humankind. These wishes, in turn, are rooted in the fundamental human wish to be happy to the greatest possible degree. As a conscious being bent on its own fulfilment or happiness, the person has purposes, needs, and desires, the shadowside of which is the awareness that these may be frustrated and aborted. Hence, all wishes are accompanied by anxiety and fear, a pervading sense of the nothingness that clings to all human activity. With the wish that this nothingness might be removed, the conception of the gods arises because when one wishes and sees the many intermediate links in the chain between the wish and its realization, the imagination seizes upon the notion of a being that is not subject to limitation and failure, a being that can do what it wishes to do. The gods represent the unity of willing (*Wollen*) and being able to succeed (*Können*). Indeed, the essential difference between men and the gods is simply that a god can do what it wishes to do. A god is simply a being in which the distinction between wish and realization has been annulled. The gods are simply the supplements to our own defective being. A god is the unity of wish and reality. 'Where there are no wishes there are no gods.'[65]

By stressing the importance of wishing, we can see that Feuerbach is once more harkening back to the conception of religious faith he claims to find in Luther who regards faith as the conviction that the deepest wishes of the heart will be fulfilled. For Feuerbach, the gods are praiseworthy because they grant human wishes. People do not first believe and then wish; rather they believe because they wish.[66] The highest being is nothing but the personified propensity of people to intensify their wishes to the highest degree. The gods are the superlative of human wishes.

Although the basic wish of humankind is for happiness, this general wish naturally becomes manifest in a variety of specific wishes. Given the diversity of cultures and the vicissitudes and complexities of human existence, there is scarcely anything that has not at some time in history been the object of wishing. The variability of the gods reflects the variability of human wishes. But underneath these various wishes are more basic wishes: for evildoers to be punished, to be free from hunger and disease, the limitations of time and space and, above all, from death. Since all human wishes are contingent upon chance and luck and the strictures of necessity, human beings inevitably pray and sacrifice to the beings who can grant these wishes.

By defining the gods as human wishes freed from necessity, of which death is the symbol, Feuerbach is led to consider, in a very difficult passage, the relationships among the ideas of necessity, death, and immortality.[67] His problem is how to account for the fact that although necessity seems to be the limit and end of the gods, the idea of immortality is present in Greek as well as Christian religions. But if the wish 'congeals in the ice-coldness of impossibility', how then does one account for the strength of the wish for what seems impossible: immortality? His answer is that there are important differences between the Greek idea of immortality and that of the Christian. The Greek idea did not, he argues, express a positive wish because the Greeks wished for no other kind of life than this. They did not demand eternal life; they only wanted to postpone death. Moreover, death even had its benign aspects so far as they were concerned. The Christian, in contrast, regarded human happiness and fulfilment as possible only on the other side of the grave. Since what contradicts this hope for immortality is the apparently natural process of death itself (necessity), the Christian was forced to posit an omnipotent god who is creator of and sovereign over nature. The whole of Christian theology, Feuerbach argues, is a circle in which everything is calculated to undergird the hope for immortality: creation *ex nihilo*, the Incarnation, predestination, and eschatology.[68] As a consequence, Christianity inevitably devaluates everything natural in the interest of an unearthly fulfilment of fantastic desires.

This final version of Feuerbach's critique of religion in which wishing plays such a crucial role has certain theoretical advantages and disadvantages over his earlier theories. Its disadvantage is that as a theory of both the origins and the psychological function of religion, the appeal to wish is so flexible and thus can be invoked arbitrarily at any point that it has very little utility as an explanatory theory. The wishes of people are so various that to explain the origin of any given religion as nothing but the expression of a wish is about as explanatory as positing an instinct whenever one wishes to explain some otherwise unintelligible behavior of an organism. Moreover, since the appeal to some general wish for happiness is compatible with all human activity, it can hardly be invoked to explain any single activity. The advantage of his analysis is, however, that it is not bound up with a speculative and developmental theory of consciousness like Hegel's but is rooted in a philosophical anthropology that helps account for the emotional power of religion quite apart from its validity as a theory of the origins of religion. Religion, Feuerbach claims, is best understood in terms of the conscious, narcissistic ego aware of the vulnerability of its body. In this sense, Feuerbach is not so much a Hegelian as a precursor of Freud and later psychoanalytic interpreters of religion.

Another difficulty of the *Theogonie* is that although Feuerbach intended to give an interpretation of religions generally, his discussion once more concentrates entirely on those religions in which anthropomorphic deities play a crucial role. He ignores those religions more characteristic of the Orient in which there are no personal deities and no doctrine of immortality. One thinks, for example, of those forms of Buddhism that emphasize the absoluteness of the phenomenal world, that reject any deity existing independently of the world, that stress the flow of all things and the acceptance of human natural dispositions, and that advocate benevolence towards all beings. Insofar as Feuerbach ignores this type of religious phenomena, one must ask not only whether he has proposed a theory of religion that is scientifically useful but whether the existence of these modes of religion call into question his central explanatory principle, namely, that religion is the projection of the attributes of human nature.

This omission is particularly puzzling. Since Feuerbach was aware these religions exist, we might have expected him to have valued them highly because they embody to some degree many of the values and beliefs he espouses. For despite his polemic against religion, he possessed a deep religious sensibility (Stirner called him a 'devout atheist'). Evidence of this sensibility is scattered throughout his scholarly writings as well as his letters, as these cryptic lines discovered in his *Nachlass* attest: 'There is only one true reasonable religion. It is the joy of life; the delight, which will not permit itself to be interrupted, in whatever is positive in life.'[69]

We may only speculate why Feuerbach did not seriously consider the significance these non-theistic types of religion might have had for his theory. One reason immediately suggests itself: Feuerbach, like so many atheistic critics of religion, believed that a non-religious interpretation of religion should provide an account of the historical origins of religion and he thought that the idea of objectification or projection best served that purpose. Another reason may have been that in his later work, especially, he wavered fatally between the view that religion is the wish to be free from the necessities of nature and the view that religion is the attempt of primitive peoples to control nature for the sake of happiness. The first view permits him to argue that the ultimate aim of religion is to be free from the laws of nature, that is, to become a god; the second allows him to claim that every scientific and technological advance means the diminution of religion. The first view is consistent with his notion that the religious sentiment is innate; the second with the proposition that religion is a product of ignorance and that people who have science have no need of religion. Feuerbach did not consider the view of the early Schleiermacher, later taken up by Ernst Cassirer, that religion is the apprehension of the universe under a different symbolic mode than science, resting as it does on a different emotional and valuational attitude. But even if Feuerbach had considered this possibility, his nominalism, which deepened in his later years, would have led him to reject it. He was committed to criticism of all metaphysical views that conceived of the universe (the class of all beings) as itself a unified being of some sort.

Although it is tempting to conclude that Feuerbach's explanatory scheme shatters on the rocks of the non-theistic religions, this conclusion would be premature until one has first explored more thoroughly the logical connexions between his theory of projection and more fundamental elements in his philosophical anthropology. It is possible, for instance, to see anthropomorphic religions as but only one type of projection of which non-anthropomorphic religions are another? In this regard, it might prove instructive to pursue briefly the suggestion made above that the later Feuerbach may be seen as a precursor of Freud and later psychoanalytic interpretations of religion. The structural similarity between them is most obvious in the work of Ernest Becker, who is endebted to both Freud and Otto Rank.[70]

Becker depicts the human situation in terms that are basically Feuerbachian. The human organism is an embodied consciousness driven by the urge to expand its powers but which is encased, as it were, in a decaying body. The individual ego can, in consciousness, transcend itself and the world and it achieves its distinctive identity by standing out and distinguishing itself from the patterns and vitalities of nature. As do animal organisms, the self decays and dies. The incongruity of this paradoxical situation is at the root of all cultural creativity (including religion) as well as the formation of character because the symbolically constructed world is an attempt by the self to conceal or deny the organism's grotesque physical fate, its helplessness and terror in the face of pitiless nature.

The vulnerability of the body and the omnipresence of death are mediated to the human organism through its own physical processes; through eating, sexuality and defecation. Becker believes that Freud more than any other thinker saw how this human vulnerability and fear were expressed in the psychological mechanisms that have come to be identified with his theory, namely, the Oedipal project, anality, the fear of castration, penis envy, the primal scene, fetishism, and the like. But whereas Freud, especially in his earlier work, argued that these expressions are to be explained primarily in terms of sexual repression, Becker argues that they may better be understood as screens through which the self discovers and deals with the vulnerability of the body. It is, in short, the fear of death rather than sexuality that is continually repressed; or more precisely, sexuality is at the heart of repression because sexuality is that bodily activity which is most intimately compounded with living and dying.

The self, confronted with the paradoxical situation where the fear of death actually leads to a fear of life, is dominated by what Becker labels 'twin ontological urges': to stand out as a distinctive individual, on the one hand, and to submerge itself in the rhythms and vitalities of the physical organism (nature), on the other. Becker holds that the phenomenon of transference, which Freud discovered and that became central to his theory, contains the key to understanding how both urges function because in all of its forms transference is the attempt to create an environment (world) that is less threatening to the self. It is a form of projection. In order to overcome the self's sense of its impotence, for example, it chooses an object or person upon whom it can project its human qualities and with which it can be identified. This form of transference may be analysed as fetishism. To understand the function fetishism serves is also to understand why the loss of the transference object strikes such fear in the human heart. It sums up all other natural dependences and emotions.

But transference may also take the form of construing the world so that it mirrors the rhythms and vitalities of the body. One falls back onto and merges with these rhythms and so overcomes the isolation of the individual ego. Significantly, both types of transference may be expressed in religious forms: in anthropomorphic religions, in which the entire symbol system is such that the ego or self is made to stand out; and in those participatory religions, which Mircia Eliade characteristically regards as paradigms of the religious consciousness, in which the organism surrenders itself to those rhythms and vitalities of nature in order to overcome the 'terror of history'. From the standpoint of some such psychoanalytic interpretation as this, one might say that Feuerbach explored only one of the basic modes of projection that his philosophical anthropology suggests.

It is, of course, impossible in this essay to explore further this line of inquiry. Perhaps it will suffice to note that the idea of religion as a symbolic projection continues to haunt the modern mind but as yet this idea has not yet found a theoretically impressive prosecutor who has explored its difficulties and ramifications for a theory of religion. It is difficult to believe that such a prosecutor will not soon appear. If and when one does, it is even more difficult to believe that he or she can or will want to ignore the extraordinary fund of insight to be found in the work of Ludwig Feuerbach.

Notes

1 Feuerbach writes, 'He was my second father . . . the only person who caused me to feel and experience what a teacher was.' Karl Grün, *Ludwig Feuerbach in seinem Briefwechsel und Nachlass sowie in seiner philosophischen Charakterentwicklung* (Leipzig and Heidelberg, 1874), vol. I, p. 387.

2 Karl Löwith, *From Hegel to Nietzsche*, transl. David E. Green (New York, 1967), p. 65.

3 Some scholars suspect that Marx had a hand in this anonymous work. See Lloyd D. Easton and Kurt H. Guddat (transl. and eds.), *Writings of the Young Marx on Philosophy and Society* (New York, 1967), p. 6.

4 Throughout this essay, I have cited the English titles of works of Feuerbach and Marx where translations exist; and, where possible, I have cited those translations readily available to the English-reading public. I have employed the editions of the original texts noted in the appended bibliography.

5 David F. Strauss, *Ausgewählte Briefe* (Bonn, 1874). Frederick Engels, *Ludwig Feuerbach* (London, 1835), p. 28.

6 Ludwig Feuerbach, *The Essence of Christianity*, transl. George Eliot (New York, 1957), pp. 91f.

7 Ludwig Feuerbach, *Principles of the Philosophy of the Future*, transl. with intro. by Manfred Vogel (Indianapolis, New York, and Kansas City, 1966), pp. 32f.

8 *Ibid.*, p. 34.

9 *Ibid.*, pp. 51–73.

10 *Ibid.*, p. 54.

11 *Ibid.*, p. 53.

12 Feuerbach, *Essence of Christianity*, p. 1.

13 *Ibid.*, p. 2.

14 *Ibid.*, p. 3.

15 *Ibid.*, p. 11.

16 *Ibid.*, p. 48.

17 *Ibid.*, chap. XIII. See also Feuerbach, *The Essence of Faith According to Luther*, transl. and with intro. by Melvin Cherno (New York, Evanston, and London, 1967); John Glasse, 'Why did Feuerbach concern himself with Luther', *Revue internationale de Philosophie*, 3 (1972), 364–85.

18 Feuerbach, *Essence of Christianity*, p. 26.

19 *Ibid.*, p. 31.

20 *Ibid.*, p. 53.

21 *Ibid.*, p. 89.

22 *Ibid.*, p. 73.

23 Sidney Hook, *From Hegel to Marx* (New York, 1950), p. 248.

24 Rodney Livingstone and Gregor Benton (transl.) with intro. by Lucio Colletti, *Karl Marx Early Writings* (New York, 1975), p. 281.

25 *Ibid.*, p. 381.

26 *Ibid.*, pp. 243.

27 Unfortunately, there is no agreement among translators of Marx as to the rendering of important terms like '*Entfremdung*' and '*Entäusserung*'. Most translators render '*Entfremdung*' as 'alienation' and '*Entäusserung*' as 'externalization'. Livingstone and Benton translate the former as 'estrangement' and the latter as 'alienation' whereas T. B. Bottmore renders them both as 'alienation' on the grounds that Marx makes no systematic distinction between them. Although I have used the Livingstone and Benton editions of Marx's early writings in my text, I have decided to translate '*Entfremdung*' as 'alienation' and '*Entäusserung*' as 'externalization'.

28 Livingstone and Benton, *Early Writings*, p. 329.

29 *Ibid.*, p. 386.

30 *Ibid.*, p. 384 ('alienated world' for '*entfremdeten Welt*').

31 *Ibid.*, p. 390.

32 Louis Dupré argues that Marx's criticism of Hegel is not altogether justified because '*Entfremdung*' in Hegel is a particular mode of '*Entausserung*' on the level of Spirit. Hegel, he argues, occasionally interchanged the two words but never confused them. See *Hegel-Studien*, 7 (Bonn, 1972), p. 218. Cf. his *The Philosophical Foundations of Marxism* (New York, 1966), p. 136.

33 Livingstone and Benton, *Early Writings*, p. 328.

34 Karl Marx and Frederick Engels, *The German Ideology, Part I*, ed. with intro. by C. J. Arthur (New York, 1976). See pp. 122f; 60ff; 121f.

35 *Ibid.*, p. 43.

36 *Ibid.*, p. 47.

37 *Ibid.*, p. 116.

38 Shlomo Avineri, *The Social and Political Thought of Karl Marx* (Cambridge, 1976), p. 73.

39 Robert K. Merton, *Social Theory and Social Structure* (Glencoe, Illinois, 1951), p. 219.

40 Marx and Engels, *The German Ideology*, p. 121.

41 István Mészáros, *Marx's Theory of Alienation* (New York, 1972).

42 Adam Schaff, *Marxism and the Human Individual*, intro. by Erich Fromm; ed. Robert S. Cohen; based on a transl. by Olgierd Wojtasiewicz (New York, 1970).

43 Erich Fromm (ed.), *Marx's Concept of Man* with a transl. from Marx's *Economic and Philosophical Manuscripts* by T. B. Bottomore (New York, 1966).

44 Mészáros, *Marx's Theory of Alienation*, p. 241.

45 *Ibid.*, p. 244.

46 *Ibid.*, p. 248.

47 This criticism of religion finds classic expression in Marx's early essay, 'On the Jewish Question'. See *Early Writings*, pp. 211–41.

48 Ludwig Feuerbach, *Lectures on the Essence of Religion*, transl. Ralph Mannheim (New York, 1967), p. 34.

49 *Ibid.*, p. 294.
50 *Ibid.*, p. 21.
51 *Ibid.*, p. 50.
52 *Ibid.*, p. 79.
53 *Ibid.*, chap. xx.
54 *Ibid.*, pp. 310ff.
55 *Ibid.*, chap. xx.
56 *Ibid.*, p. 311.
57 *Ibid.*, p. 312.
58 *Ibid.*, pp. 310f.
59 *Ibid.*, p. 322.
60 *Ibid.*, p. 111.
61 *Ibid.*, pp. 86f; cf. pp. 90f.
62 *Ibid.*, p. 86; cf. pp. 90f.
63 *Ibid.*, p. 231.
64 *Ibid.*, p. 302.
65 Ludwig Feuerbach, *Theogonie* (Berlin, 1969), p. 50.
66 *Ibid.*, p. 41.
67 *Ibid.*, chap. XXII.
68 *Ibid.*, chap. XXXII.
69 Karl Grün, *Ludwig Feuerbach in seinem Briefwechsel*, vol. I, p. 316.
70 See his *The Denial of Death* (New York and London, 1973).

Bibliographical essay

Before turning to books dealing solely with Feuerbach and Marx, it might prove useful to note three books that deal with the Young Hegelian movement as well as a work that places the Young Hegelians in the larger context of nineteenth-century German culture. The latter is Karl Löwith's provocative *From Hegel to Nietzsche: The Revolution in Nineteenth-Century Thought* (New York, 1967). Particularly useful are the sections in Part I that deal with the disputes among the post-Hegelians and those in Part II that consider the views of each of the important Young Hegelians on the fundamental themes Löwith believes were problematic for the German spirit: the nature of society, work, culture, humanity, and Christianity. The three books on the Young Hegelian movement are: William J. Brazill, *The Young Hegelians* (New Haven, 1970); Sidney Hook, *From Hegel to Marx: Studies in the Intellectual Development of Karl Marx* (New York, 1950); and David McLellan, *The Young Hegelians and Karl Marx* (New York, 1969). Of these, McLellan's book, in my opinion, is the most straightforward and judicious. It also contains a useful selected bibliography. Hook's work is both dated and somewhat tendencious although still profitable to read. His treatment of Feuerbach is too narrowly restricted to Feuerbach's relationship to Marx and he overemphasizes the importance Feuerbach attributed to Moleschott's materialism. Moreover, Hook's treatment of Moses Hess needs to be balanced by the excellent essay by Sir Isaiah Berlin in Philip Rieff (ed.), *On Intellectuals: Theoretical Studies, Case Studies* (New York, 1970).

Feuerbach

There are two editions of Feuerbach's collected works. The first is the Bolin–Jodl edition (*Sämtliche Werke*) published in ten volumes between 1903 and 1911 by the Frommann Verlag in Stuttgaart. These ten volumes were reprinted in facsimile between 1960 and 1964 under the editorship of Hans-Martin Sass. Two more volumes have been added, the twelfth being a double volume. The eleventh contains a photographic facsimile of Feuerbach's inaugural dissertation of 1828 (in Latin) and of his *Thoughts on Death and Immortality* (1830) as well as an extensive bibliography of all works on Feuerbach in German between 1833 and 1961. The double volume contains Sass's expanded version of Bolin's *Selected Correspondence from and to Ludwig Feuerbach* together with some of Bolin's memoirs.

The second edition of Feuerbach's work is a new critical edition prepared under the editorship of Werner Schuffenhauer (*Gesammelte Werke*), published by Akademie-Verlag in Berlin. When completed it will comprise sixteen volumes. It is indispensable for serious scholarly work since it presents the textual variations of all the editions of Feuerbach's major texts, and it restores the original text of the *Theogonie* that the Bolin–Jodl edition sought to make more comprehensible by radical editing.

Six of Feuerbach's major works have been translated into English although only five are probably available to most readers: (1) *The Essence of Christianity*, which is the famous translation of the second German edition by George Eliot (New York, 1957); (2) *The Essence of Faith According to Luther*, translated and with a brief but suggestive introduction by Melvin Cherno (New York, 1967); (3) *Principles of the Philosophy of the Future*, which contains a lengthy introduction by Manfred Vogel, the translator, that explores Feuerbach's philosophy of religion and his relationship to Hegel (Indianapolis, 1966); (4) *Lectures on the Essence of Religion*, a translation by Ralph Mannheim that seems based on the Bolin–Jodl version of 1908 and not the text Feuerbach himself published (New York, 1967); (5) *Thoughts on Death and Immortality* (Berkeley, Los Angeles, New York, 1981), a translation with a long introduction by James A. Massey of Feuerbach's first post-doctoral work which, though published anonymously in 1830, was responsible for Feuerbach's being barred from university teaching; (6) *The Essence of Religion* (New York, 1873), an abridged edition translated by Alexander Loos.

So far as bibliographies are concerned, there are at least three that enlarge and amend the definitive one prepared by Hans-Martin Sass in the eleventh volume of the *Sämtliche Werke* mentioned above. The first is by Sass himself and appears as an appendix to *Atheismus in der Diskussion, Kontroversen um Ludwig Feuerbach*, which is co-edited with Hermann Lübbe (Munich, 1975); the second is by Ewe Schott in *Die Jugendentwicklung Ludwig Feuerbachs bis zum Fakultätwechsel 1825* (Göttingen, 1973), which, though it is less extensive than Sass's enlargement, has a few items Sass seems to have missed; and the third is by Erich Schneider in his *Die Theologie und Feuerbachs Religionskritik: Die Reaktion der Theologie des 19. Jahrhunderts auf Ludwig Feuerbachs Religionskritik mit Ausblicken auf das 20. Jahrhundert und einem Anhang über Feuerbach* (Göttingen, 1972), which, as the title indicates, is an analysis of the reaction of nineteenth-century theologians to Feuerbach's work. A useful annotated bibliography may be found in Michael von Gagern, *Ludwig Feuerbach, Philosophie-und-Religionskritik Die 'Neue' Philosophy* (Munich and Salzburg, 1970). There are also selected bibliographies in the works by Kamenka and Wartofsky cited below.

There are many important scholarly studies of Feuerbach in the German language and it seems arbitrary to mention two or three. Still, of those dealing with Feuerbach's entire career one cannot omit S. Rawidowicz's still important *Ludwig Feuerbachs Philosophie-Ursprung und Schicksal* (Berlin, 1931 and 1964). Two recent works concentrate on Feuerbach's *Religionskritik*: Michael von Gagern's book mentioned above and H. J. Braun, *Die Religionsphilosophie Ludwig Feuerbachs, Kritik und Annahme des Religiösen* (Stuttgart–Bad Cannstatt, 1972). Braun tends to be more simply descriptive of Feuerbach's views than von Gagern, but he takes Feuerbach's later works, especially the *Theogonie* with greater seriousness. Because von Gagern argues that Feuerbach's *Religionskritik* stands or falls with the genetic-critical and historical-philosophic method, he treats Feuerbach's views monolithically and tends to minimize any development or tensions between the later and the earlier writings.

Until the recent publication of Marx W. Wartofsky's *Feuerbach* (Cambridge, 1977), there was no major full-length study of Feuerbach in English, with the possible exception of Eugene Kamenka's *The Philosophy of Ludwig Feuerbach* (New York, 1970), which is a straightforward and readable – Wartofsky calls it 'brief and breezy' – account of Feuerbach's thought organized around certain themes: anthropology, ethics, philosophy of religion, etc. There is also a short introductory book by William Chamberlain, quaintly entitled *Heaven Wasn't His Destination* (London, 1941), but it can hardly qualify as a scholarly work. Wartofsky's book is an attempt to correct the impression that Feuerbach is merely a transitional figure between Hegel and Marx. He regards Feuerbach as a serious philosopher whose importance lies in his practice of dialectic, the achieving of self-knowledge and self-transformation through criticism of the work of others. Wartofsky himself tries to emulate Feuerbach's example so that his book is not an 'objective' presentation of Feuerbach's work but a critical appropriation of it. This method, in my opinion, has both virtues and defects. The virtues are its exhaustive and probably definitive treatment of Feuerbach's development up to 1843. Especially useful are the discussions of certain ideas: the criticism of Hegel, feeling, imagination, religion, etc. The main defect is that everything Feuerbach wrote after 1843 is treated in a final chapter because Wartofsky regards this material as 'relatively uninteresting' for his purposes. As a result, Wartofsky does not even raise the question, much less explore it, whether Feuerbach's later interpretation of religion, in which nature moves to the fore, is compatible with, or in any sense substantially modifies, his earlier *Religionskritik*. We are left with the impression that Feuerbach's works on religion after *The Essence of Christianity* are unimportant.

Wartofsky's book is only one of many indications of revived interest of Feuerbach and of the necessity for a re-evaluation of his work. One expression of this new interest was the conference held in Bielefeld in 1973 in which philosophers, theologians, and sociologists gathered to discuss Feuerbach's work and the results of which were published in *Atheismus in der Diskussion*, which was noted above. In this connection, it is important to note also Erich Thies (ed.), *Ludwig Feuerbach* (Darmstadt, 1976) a collection of important essays by Ernst Bloch, Karl Lowith, Hans-Martin Sass, Nathan Rotenstreich, and John Glasse, among others. The emergence of the so-called 'secular theology' in the sixties has also fueled interest in Feuerbach, as can be seen by Marcel Xhaufflaire, *Feuerbach et la théologie de la sécularisation* (Paris, 1970), a German translation of which appeared in Munich in 1972.

Marx

Despite its limitations the standard German edition of the writings of Marx and Engels is *Werke* (Berlin, 1956–   ), which comprises some thirty-nine basic and two supplementary volumes, to which additional volumes are being added from time to time. The *Werke* supplants the *Gesamtausgabe* (Frankfurt, Berlin, Moscow, 1927) that was never completed. Until recently, there was no complete edition of these writings in English translation; but between 1975 and 1977 there appeared the first seven volumes of a projected fifty-one volume edition under the joint sponsorship of Lawrence and Wishart (London), International Publishers (New York), and the Institute for Marxism–Leninism in Moscow. This edition will contain all of the works, letters, extant preparatory materials (including marginal notes) and available letters written to and by Marx and Engels.

Scholars will find useful the bibliography of Marx's writings prepared by Maximilien Ruben: *Bibliographie des oeuvres de Karl Marx* (Paris, 1956). The lay reader can profit from the select, critical bibliography prepared by David McLellan for his book *Karl Marx, His Life and Thought* (New York, 1973). Especially useful for the lay reader is McLellan's *The Thought of Karl Marx, An Introduction* (New York, Evanston, San Francisco, London, 1971). In Part One, McLellan divides Marx's life into certain chronologically ordered periods and for each of them supplies a list of the writings produced, a brief biography, and a commentary. In the second part, there are texts and commentaries on various topics: alienation, historical materialism, labor, class, the state, revolution, etc.

There are many inexpensive editions of Marx's various works readily available to the public. *Selected Writings in Sociology and Social Philosophy* edited by T. Bottomore and

M. Ruben (London, 1956) is judged by McLellan to be the best anthology of Marx's work, drawing as it does on all of Marx's writings whether available in English or not. T. Bottomore's edition of Marx's *Early Writings* (London, 1963) is useful because it contains the complete text of the 'Paris Manuscripts' as well as the essays in the *Deutsch-Französische Jahrbücher*. Another fine anthology is *Writings of the Young Marx on Philosophy and Society* edited by Loyd D. Easton and Kurt H. Guddat (New York, 1967). It contains selections from the *Anekdota, Rheinische Zeitung*, the *Deutsch-Französische Jahrbücher* as well as important sections of the 'Paris Manuscripts', *The Holy Family*, and *The German Idealogy*. An anthology that covers most of the same materials is *Karl Marx, Early Writings* introduced by Lucio Colletti and translated by Rodney Livingstone and Gregor Benton (New York, 1975), except that it has the advantage of also containing the entire text of the *Economic and Philosophic Manuscripts*. Both of the latter two anthologies, incidentally, have very useful introductions dealing with the significance of the early writings for the interpretation of Marx's thought. Two anthologies that concentrate on Marx's writings on religion are: *Karl Marx on Religion*, edited by Saul K. Padover (New York, 1974) and *Karl Marx and Friedrich Engels on Religion*, edited by Reinhold Niebuhr (New York, 1964), which has a short but very interesting introduction.

The secondary literature on Marx is enormous, as the above bibliographies will indicate. So far as the themes in the above essay are concerned, the following seem relevant: (1) Shlomo Avineri, *The Social and Political Thought of Karl Marx* (Cambridge, 1968), which is especially good for the understanding of Marx's relationship to Hegel; (2) István Mészáros, *Marx's Theory of Alienation* (New York, 1972) which, despite my stated reservations about its argument, is a closely reasoned analysis of this concept in Marx; (3) Bertell Ollman, *Alienation: Marx's Conception of Man in Capitalist Society* (Cambridge, 1971), a fine and sympathetic study of Marx's anthropology that might profitably be balanced by (4) John Plamenatz, *Karl Marx's Philosophy of Man* (Oxford, 1975), which covers much of the same ground as Ollman does but more probingly and critically; (5) Nathan Rotenstreich, *Basic Problems of Marx's Philosophy* (New York, 1965), which approaches Marx's thought through an analysis of the *Theses on Feuerbach*; and (6) Adam Schaff, *Marxism and the Human Individual*, edited by Robert S. Cohen (New York, 1970), which remains one of the best introductions to the humanistic interpretation of Marx. Finally, mention should be made of Werner Post's *Kritik der Religion bei Karl Marx* (Munich, 1969), a good interpretation of Marx's criticism of religion which traces its development and places it in the context of contemporary European discussion of Marx.

INDEX

anthropology: of Feuerbach, 294, 296–8, 299, 313–21; influence on religious thought, 11

Aquinas, Thomas, 102, 124

Augustine, Saint, 102, 126, 167

Avineri, Shlomo, 307

Baader, Franz von, 51, 60, 66, 67, 70

Barth, Karl, 148, 149, 150, 151, 210, 245, 273

Bauer, Bruno, 292, 293

Bauer, Edgar, 292

Baur, Ferdinand Christian (1792–1860), 7, 215, 261–84; christology of, 266–8, 272, 274–84; and Church history, 264, 265–6, 268, 269–70, 281–2; concept of *Gegensatz*, 269–70, 271; consideration of incarnation and divine-human unity, 267–8, 274, 276, 277, 278–80; critique of Schleiermacher, 147, 249, 261–2, 272, 273, 274, 276; evaluation of historical judgements of, 269–71; and Gospel criticism, 243, 263, 267–9; and Hegelianism, 262, 264, 265, 272–81 *passim*; historical theology, historical critical method of, 261, 262, 263, 264–71, 273, 278, 282, 283–4; and idealist philosophy, 261, 269, 271, 272; and pauline theology, 269, 270, 271, 282, 283; and Strauss, 224, 235, 236, 263–5, 274, 276–7, 280, 281; view of resurrection, 267

Becker, Ernest, 210, 321–2

Bender, Wilhelm, 146

Bengel, E. G., 261

Benjamin, Walter, 57

Berdyaev, Nikolai, 51

Bible: appeal to authority of, 5, 217; change in apprehension of, during eighteenth century, 219; historical criticism of Gospels, 141, 222–4, 233–9, 242–3, 250–3, 263, 267–9, 275, 283; modern biblical scholarship, 271, 282; Old Testament theology, 47, 62–3, 273; Schleiermacher's attitude to, 126, 130

Biedermann, A. E., 125, 146

Boehme, Jacob, 59, 60, 65, 66–7, 262

Braun, H., 281

Bretschneider, K. G., 251

Brunner, Emil, 146, 148, 149, 150, 151

Buddhism, 112, 320; Hegel's treatment of, 96, 97; influence on Schopenhauer, 157, 161, 164, 170, 171, 174, 175, 176

Bultmann, Rudolf, 245, 280–1, 282

Caird, Edward, 14

Calvin, John, Calvinism, 124, 127, 132, 139, 149, 150, 151

Cassirer, Ernst, 321

Chateaubriand, F. R., 15

christology: difference between ancient and modern problems of, 254–5; *see also* incarnation; miracle; resurrection; *and under* Baur; Hegel; Kant; Schleiermacher; Strauss

Cieszkowzski, August von, 292

Cohen, Hermann, 5, 8

Coleridge, S. T., 6, 8, 12

comparative study of religion, 11, 12–14, 94–8, 112

Comte, Auguste, 9, 10

conscience, 7, 8, 44

329

Index

Lauer, Q., 108
Lauth, Reinhart, 55
Lessing, G. E., 12, 218–20, 221, 233, 263, 277
Lightfoot, J. B., 269
love, concept of: of Feuerbach, 296, 298, 299–300; of Fichte, 49; of Hegel, 100, 105; of Kant, 177; of Schleiermacher, 144; of Schopenhauer, 164, 171, 172, 173, 174, 177–8
Lovejoy, Arthur O., 59
Löwith, Karl, 292
Luther, Martin, Lutheranism, 107, 127, 149, 150, 264, 271, 298, 318

Maistre, J. de, 15
Marcuse, Herbert, 204, 210
Marheineke, P. K., 274, 277
Marquet, J.-F., 66
Marx, Karl (1818–1883), 6, 241, 291–2, 301–13; attitude to religion, 10, 291, 301–2, 308–10, 312–13; concept of 'species-being' (Gattungswesen), 302, 303, 304, 310; critique of Hegel, 110, 301–4, 309; Economic and Philosophic Manuscripts, 301, 302, 304; and Feuerbach, 291, 294, 301–2, 303, 305–6, 309; The German Ideology, 305; historicist interpretation of, 310–12; and human relationship to nature, 304–5, 306; and social and historical determinants of human nature, 292, 302, 304, 306–13; theory of alienation and objectification, 302–4, 309, 310–12; Theses on Feuerbach, 305, 308; view of dialectical relationship between consciousness and society, 306–8
Marxism, Marxists, 204, 210, 223, 310–12
Massey, Marilyn Chapin, 223
'mediating theology', 218, 219, 221, 230
Mendelssohn, Moses, 5
Merton, Robert K., 308
Mészáros, István, 310, 311
metaphysics, 6–7, 15, 130–1, 164–5, 272–3
miracle, 229, 244, 267, 298; Schleiermacher's notion of 'relative' and 'absolute', 247, 248, 249, 250, 251, 252, 253; Strauss's mythical interpretation of, 222–3, 234–6, 242
Möhler, J., 12, 271
monotheism, 96, 316
morality and religion, 7–8; see also under

Fichte; Kant
Moritz, K. P., 57
Mulert, Hermann, 149, 150
Müller, Friedrich Max, 13
mysticism, 31–2, 53, 61, 66, 148
myth, mythology: importance of, for Schelling, 52, 56–7, 61, 66, 67, 68; Strauss's mythical analysis of Gospels, 222–3, 234–6, 238, 242

natural theology, 5–6, 14, 90
Nauen, F. G., 52, 53
Neology, 140, 141, 218
Newman, John Henry, 6, 7, 8, 9
Nicolaus, Theophilus (Magnus Eiriksson), 197
Niebuhr, B. G., 51, 262
Niebuhr, Reinhold, 311
Niebuhr, Richard R., 151
Nietzsche, F. W., 7, 8, 111, 314

Oetinger, F. C., 66
Olsen, Regine, 184
Osborne, Kenan B., 71
Overbeck, F., 269

pantheism and panentheism, 71, 96, 97, 227, 277, 282, 295; Hegel and, 85, 102; Schelling and, 58, 59, 60, 70, 85
Pascal, B., 67
personal Deity, notion of, 227, 295, 320
philosophy and religion, relation between, see Glaube
pietism, 217, 221
Plato, Platonism, 92, 158, 161, 166, 167, 177, 264
polytheism, 94, 97, 314
'positive religion', 219
predestination, 60, 319
primitive religion, study of, 94, 95, 314–15, 317
Process Theology, 70, 71, 273, 295, 300
Protestantism, Protestant theology, 129–30, 149, 217, 220, 264, 271; neo-Protestantism, 280; Protestant Liberalism, 8, 145, 148; Schleiermacher and, 124, 126–7, 130, 131, 132, 139, 145, 149, 150–1
psychology, influence of, on study of religion, 11, 320, 321–3

Rank, Otto, 321

333